IPng and the
TCP/IP Protocols

Implementing the Next Generation Internet

Stephen A. Thomas

WILEY COMPUTER PUBLISHING

John Wiley & Sons, Inc.

New York • Chichester • Brisbane • Toronto • Singapore

Dedicated to C. P.

Illustrations in this text were created using *Visio*®, from Visio Corporation. Several of the figures include clip art images from various software packages. The copyright for those images belongs to the sources listed:

Clip art copyright © Corel Corporation.
DrawPerfect clip art copyright © 1990, Novell Inc. All rights reserved. Used with permission.
Images copyright © New Vision Technologies, Inc.
Visio® software by Visio Corporation, Seattle, Washington.

Publisher: Katherine Schowalter
Editor: Diane D. Cerra
Managing Editor: Frank Grazioli
Text Design & Composition: SunCliff Graphic Productions

Library of Congress Cataloging-in-Publication Data:

Thomas, Stephen A.
    IPng and the TCP/IP protocols: implementing the next generation internet/Stephen A. Thomas.
      p.   cm.
    Includes bibliographical references and index.
    ISBN 0-471-13088-5 (cloth: alk. paper)
    1. TCP/IP (Computer network protocol)   I. Title.
 'TK5105.585.T46   1996

95-46178
CIP

Printed in the United States of America

10 9 8 7 6 5 4 3 2 1

IPng and the TCP/IP Protocols

Contents

Preface

There are several characteristics of TCP/IP that have contributed to its immense success, perhaps none more important than its ruthless eradication of the impractical. The TCP/IP community discourages elaborate formal frameworks, unworkable schemes, and senseless strategies. Instead, TCP/IP's designers—a mix of academicians, engineers, network administrators, and users—concentrate on solving real problems with real applications. In this book I've tried to reflect that same practicality. Abstract theory receives less coverage than actual, working networks. The illustrations show real workstations and personal computers communicating over Ethernet, ISDN, and ATM networks. At the same time, the text describes not only the formats of various packets; it also explains how hosts and routers actually use those packets. I hope to give you as much of an understanding of real systems and real networks as of protocols and packets.

The catalyst of *IPng and the TCP/IP Protocols* is the newest version of the Internet Protocol, IP version 6. The book, however, considers much more than that single protocol. IPv6 forces the development of several new protocols, and it requires enhancements to many others. You'll read about all of these changes and their effects in the chapters that follow.

More significantly, the book's publication comes at a time when TCP/IP and computer networking are undergoing far-reaching changes above and beyond the introduction of IPv6. Simply updating the existing TCP/IP literature seems a great disservice to those of you who truly want to learn about the next generation networks. The text, therefore, covers many topics that lie outside the limited scope of IPv6. The chapter on TCP, for example, includes extensive discussion of the latest high-performance options and optimizations. Other chapters describe RTP and RSVP, key protocols for the support of real-time, multimedia applications. I also explain exciting new network technologies such as ATM LAN emulation. All of these developments, along with IPv6, constitute the next generation of TCP/IP networking.

A book on this subject would clearly not have been possible without the effort and enthusiasm of the IPng working group, especially Scott Bradner and Allison Mankin, co-directors of the IPng area of the Internet Engineering Task Force. My own modest contributions, as well as this text itself, reflect the considerable support of my colleagues at AT&T Tridom. Above all, though, I wish to acknowledge the immense patience and encouragement of my wife, Lisa. My gratitude to her far exceeds my ability to write of it.

Stephen A. Thomas (s.thomas@acm.org)

1

Introduction

TCP/IP's designers originally set out to create networks that could survive nuclear war. Thankfully, no one knows if they succeeded in that goal. There can be no doubt, however, that TCP/IP is a huge success. TCP/IP's Internet is now a part of popular culture throughout the world. Computers relying on TCP/IP can be found in more than 100 countries. The network created with them plays a key role in esoteric academic research, real commercial activity, and frivolous entertainment. It is the subject of (seemingly) daily stories on CNN, and an object of debate in the U.S. Congress.

The TCP/IP protocols—the languages that govern what computers say to each other and how they say it—define a framework for the Internet, as well as other computer networks. And that framework is about to undergo one of the most drastic changes in its history.

Growing Pains

TCP/IP protocols are changing because of the Internet. Technically, the Transmission Control Protocol (TCP) and the Internet Protocol (IP) can be used on virtually any network. It is the Internet, however, that drives their development. The engineers who design TCP/IP protocols are also responsible for the Internet, so when the Internet is in trouble, TCP/IP responds.

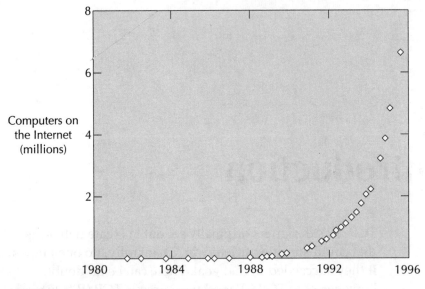

Computers on
the Internet
(millions)

Source: Network Wizards, available on the Internet at http://www.nw.com/

Figure 1.1 Growth of the Internet.

By the early 1990s, TCP/IP's engineers could see an approaching crisis. Every computer on the Internet must have a network address, and no two computers may share the same address. Unfortunately, the classic[1] IP protocols have a built-in limit on the number of network addresses that may exist. And the Internet was approaching that limit.

The reason for this crisis is simple. The Internet has become very popular. Figure 1.1 graphs the number of computers connected to the Internet. This figure's trend is unmistakable. With its projected rate of growth, the Internet will run out of network addresses sometime between 2005 and 2011.

This growth rate causes more problems than just exhausting the supply of network addresses. Another con-

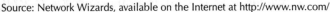

[1] Classic IP refers to the version of IP that made TCP/IP famous. The next generation IP represents the replacement for classic IP.

cern facing TCP/IP's designers is the explosion in the sizes of routing tables. Systems within the Internet use routing tables to track the location of computers connected to the network. As the number of connected computers grows, so does the size of these routing tables. Even in the mid-1990s, routing tables are stretching the limits of most systems. Unless steps are taken, many TCP/IP engineers feel that the routing table explosion will condemn the Internet even sooner than the exhaustion of network addresses.

The Next Generation

IP, IPng, and IPv6

The TCP/IP community does not usually spend a lot of time and effort with precise definitions of its terminology. The work on the next generation IP is no exception, and so the exact use of the various terms depends on the speaker. This text follows the strategy that appears most often within the community. It uses the term *IPng* to refer to all the aspects of the next generation Internet Protocol. As this book itself testifies, that work involves more than a single protocol. When the text refers specifically to the protocol, it uses *IPv6*, or, most often, just *IP*.

As awareness of these problems grew, the TCP/IP community mobilized for action. In late 1990, the Internet Engineering Task Force (IETF) began investigating options to replace classic IP with a new version, one that would solve the problems of address exhaustion and routing table explosion. By 1993, TCP/IP engineers had sketched out several possibilities. The IETF formed the Next Generation IP (IPng) Area to evaluate the various proposals and select a successor to classic IP.

In January 1995, the IPng Area published its recommendation for a new version of the Internet Protocol. This revision was assigned the version number 6^2, and the protocol is commonly known as *IPv6*. Unfortunately, revising the Internet Protocol takes more than simply changing a single protocol. Changes to IP affect many other TCP/IP protocols. In fact, at least 58 current TCP/IP standards must be revised to accommodate IPv6.

There is also the question of migration. It simply is not possible to "flip a switch" somewhere and magically convert all IPv4 systems to IPv6. There are literally millions of systems using IPv4. Most likely, some of those systems will never convert to IPv6, and it will take several years to

---

[2] Classic IP has the version number 4. An experimental protocol known as ST was assigned version number 5, but that protocol was never widely deployed.

upgrade those systems that do change. The IETF recognizes this concern. It has devoted considerable effort into making the migration to IPv6 as painless as possible. A lot of this effort is evident in the design of IPv6 itself. Even more has gone into documenting the steps and options of the transition.

Other Improvements

Internet Protocol upgrades aside, TCP/IP is not a static body of work. TCP/IP's engineers continually develop and introduce other improvements in the protocols. Sometimes, those improvements result in modifications to existing protocols. The Transmission Control Protocol, for example, has recently acquired several options that enhance its performance over very high-speed networks. Sometimes improvements result in entirely new protocols. To help support audio and video conferences, as well as other real time applications, TCP/IP is introducing the Real Time Protocol (RTP), the Real Time Control Protocol (RTCP), and the Resource Reservation Protocol (RSVP). Computer network technology also undergoes continuous improvements. Fast Ethernet and Asynchronous Transfer Mode are examples of important new network technologies.

Because this book strives to present a complete picture of the next generation Internet, it does not limit itself to IPv6 and its ramifications. The text examines many new developments in computer communications. Readers can find an explanation of the latest TCP options in the chapter on TCP, and they will note several chapters on the various protocols that support real time traffic. The book also introduces the latest network technologies, technologies that serve to build example networks throughout the text.

A Caution for Readers

Texts on the TCP/IP protocols always face a dilemma: the protocols themselves often change faster than the time it takes to write and publish the book. This problem is particularly acute for whole new areas like the next generation IP. At the time of this text's completion, only a few of the relevant specifications had reached the status of proposed standards; most were merely works in progress.

The author feels that the major concepts underlying the next generation IP are complete and stable. Any revisions to the standards are expected to be minor or cosmetic. One can never be sure, however, and readers are urged not to depend exclusively on this author's ability to predict the future. Appendix C describes the standardization process for TCP/IP protocols, a process open to all interested parties. Readers should feel free to join in this process. Not only will it keep them abreast of all the latest standardization efforts; it offers them the opportunity to contribute to the TCP/IP community. Ultimately, it is these scientists, engineers, programmers, network administrators, and users that are responsible for TCP/IP's success.

An Invitation to Readers

This book strives to present a complete and detailed picture of the next generation Internet. Its focus is making that presentation understandable, but there will be, undoubtedly, room for improvement. The author encourages corrections, comments, suggestions, and criticism. He can be reached through John Wiley & Sons, or via the Internet itself, where his address is `s.thomas@acm.org`.

2

The Architecture of Networks

Like all engineering disciplines, computer networking has rules and principles that guide its practitioners. These principles provide a framework for designing and using communication protocols like those of TCP/IP. This chapter examines that architecture.

The chapter begins with a discussion of the two fundamental ideas behind nearly all network architectures—layers and hierarchies. Both techniques can effectively divide complex problems into smaller, manageable pieces. They provide assurance that when those pieces are later assembled, the complete solution works as intended. Without both concepts, engineering TCP/IP and the Internet would have been a hopeless task. The chapter's second section demonstrates this dependency. It examines the role of both layers and hierarchies in the architecture of TCP/IP and the Internet.

The following section describes another important aspect of network architectures—the communication services they provide. Two alternatives are available; engineers call them *connectionless* and *connection-oriented*. Most architectures build on one or the other; in TCP/IP's case, fundamental services are connectionless. As TCP/IP demonstrates, though, architectures are not restricted to a single service type. To meet the needs of its users, a network can adapt either service to the other.

The chapter's final topic is network addressing. With this subject, the focus shifts away from abstract concepts. Network addresses identify real systems; they are as fundamental to networked computers as names are to people. This section explains the structure of TCP/IP's network addresses, how systems use them, and how they are assigned.

Organizing with Layers and Hierarchies

Computer networks are complex undertakings, and ambitious networks like the TCP/IP-based Internet are especially complicated. To help manage that complexity, protocol designers rely heavily on two time-tested principles—layers and hierarchies. Layers organize effort, and hierarchies organize information.

Layers

A great many things must happen to make a network successful. Electromagnetic fields have to travel across wires, fibers, or air; those fields must be translated to and from digital information, and something must ensure that the information arrives intact; somehow the information has to travel across the right media to reach its intended destination; communicating systems must cooperate to make sure that the sender does not transmit more than the receiver can manage.

Engineers who design networks must deal with all of these issues and more. To do so effectively, they use a variation of the old-fashioned "divide and conquer" approach. Layering works by dividing all the functions of a network into groups, and assigning those groups to *proto-*

col layers. Each protocol layer assumes responsibility for its own part of the entire network's functionality, and when all layers operate together, they create a complete, functioning network.

Layering may sound a bit abstract, but it is actually a very familiar concept. Take audio compact discs (CDs), for example. By most definitions, the important part of the CD is the silvery disc itself. That is the part that goes in a CD player to produce music. The product, as a whole, however, is more than a 130 mm disc. The other parts of the product act as layers around the disc, and each layer serves a particular function. For example, consumers want to store their discs conveniently, as well as protect them from damage. To solve those problems, the industry created the plastic *jewel box.* Jewel boxes provide easy storage, and they offer protection to CDs not in use.

Jewel boxes solve most of the problems facing CD consumers, but another level of problems exist at the retail music store. Especially when CDs first became available, most retail stores had display racks configured for long-playing (LP) albums. A compact disc in a jewel box did not fit in those racks very well. In addition, the small size of the jewel box made it a tempting target for shoplifters.

For these problems, the product has another layer. That layer is the display package. Early display packages were cardboard boxes about 300×150×15 mm in size. These boxes fit in an LP display rack without being swallowed completely, and they were large enough to discourage shoplifting. From the layering standpoint, though, a display package is a separate entity from what is actually inside a jewel box. The jewel box effectively isolates the display package from the disc. Figure 2.1 shows these layers and one more—the shipping carton that delivers groups of display packages to retailers.

What benefits does layering provide the music industry? It splits up many of the various functions that con-

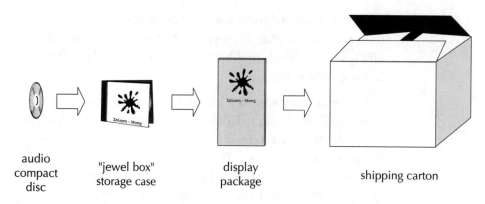

audio
compact
disc

"jewel box"
storage case

display
package

shipping carton

Figure 2.1 Layers of the audio compact disc product.

tribute to a successful product, and it isolates those functions from each other. The manufacturers of the disks themselves need not worry about how those disks are packaged for shipment; they can focus their efforts on producing discs efficiently. Similarly, the freight company that delivers cartons to retailers does not care about the contents of those cartons.

This isolation in turn creates substantial flexibility. As LPs became less popular, music retailers could afford to reconfigure their display racks just for compact discs. At the same time, electronic inventory control devices became available to reduce shoplifting. These changes allowed the industry to replace its bulky display case with more compact packaging. And, because of layering, the move to compact display cases could happen without changing disc manufacturing or the shipping methods. Imagine the problems if layers were not available. Any change to any function—shipping, display, storage, or disc manufacture—would require changes in every function. Such an environment would absolutely stifle progress.

So how does this relate to computer networks? Actually, the practice is very similar. Suppose a user needs to transfer a file from one machine to the other. The file itself is nothing but a series of digital bits, and computer networks

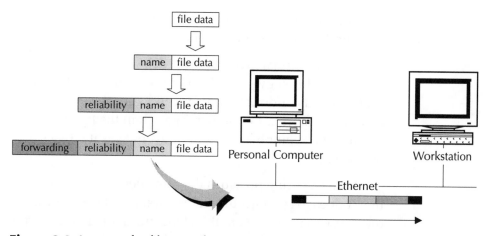

Figure 2.2 Layers of a file transfer.

transfer bits. It is not enough, however, to simply ship the bits across the cables; layering is essential. Figure 2.2 shows how a file transfer might be layered. Presumably, the file must be given a name on the remote computer. There may also be the question of a destination directory. This information can also be encoded as digital bits, and it can be added to the file's contents. In computer communications, layers are usually added to the front of digital data, so Figure 2.2 shows the file's name being prepended to its contents.

The next problem facing network designers is making the transfer reliable. It would not do for the file to acquire errors during its transfer. To provide this reliability, another layer of information may be added to the network, more bits on the front of the data (which already includes the file name). These bits may include error detecting codes, and they may contain information necessary to retransmit the file, should an error occur.

Once the network has taken care of errors, it must get the file to the right place. After all, most networks have many possible destinations, and somebody must ensure that the file gets to the right computer. This service requires functions known as *forwarding* and *routing*, and they add another layer of information to the front of the data.

The figure's final protocol layer belongs to the specific network technology—in this case, Ethernet. The Ethernet protocol adds information before and after the upper layer data. That information, shown in black in the figure, serves to mark the beginning and end of the data as it crosses the network.

All this layering provides the same benefits to networks that it does to compact disc sales. First it isolates the various services from one another. One group of engineers can go off and design a file transfer protocol without worrying about how the network forwards data. Another group can concentrate on reliable delivery, without concern for the type of data whose delivery they ensure.

The isolation gives TCP/IP flexibility. It makes it possible for protocol designers to upgrade the forwarding and routing services, without requiring massive changes to applications like file transfer. In fact, the next generation IP is just such an upgrade. There are no chapters on file transfer protocols in this book because no new protocols are necessary. Because layering provides isolation, the protocols designed for the classic IP work fine with the new IP.

Hierarchies

Like layers, hierarchies are another abstract concept that help organize computer networks. Hierarchies organize information and delegate responsibility. The effects of hierarchies are apparent in many aspects of everyday life. A common example is the global telephone system, which makes it possible to communicate between points anywhere in the world; it depends on a hierarchy. The hierarchy is that of telephone numbers themselves, and it makes sure that every telephone number is unique. Clearly this quality is important. Without it, there would be no way to guarantee whom callers would reach when they dialed the phone.

It is possible to distribute unique phone numbers without establishing a hierarchy. The world could set up a single master computer, for example, that assigned every phone number directly. When someone needed a phone number, he or she could apply to the master computer, which would search its massive database to find an available number.

Of course, the world does not assign phone numbers this way. The administrative burden would be too great. Instead, a simple hierarchy exists. The hierarchy is based on geography. To reach the United States from New Zealand, for example, a caller might dial 911-770-555-4261. As Figure 2.3 shows, each group of digits in this number indicates a successively more specific area of the world.

The benefits to this arrangement are no doubt obvious. If the local phone company in Marietta, Georgia, wishes to assign a new phone number, it only has to worry about the

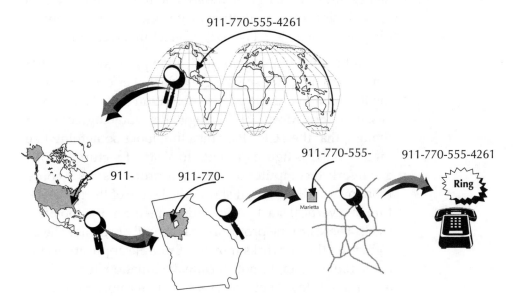

Figure 2.3 Phone number organized as a hierarchy.

last four digits. Everything else is preassigned and guaranteed to be unique, so there is no need for the local phone company to coordinate, for example, with its counterparts in New Zealand.

The TCP/IP Internet

The discussion of layering and hierarchies may seem a bit abstract, but without these concepts, the worldwide, TCP/IP-based Internet would not be possible. The communication protocols themselves rely heavily on layering to organize their tasks, and the Internet naturally organizes its components into hierarchies. This organization creates two distinct roles for systems that make up the global network. Those roles—that of a *host* and that of a *router*—apply to all TCP/IP-based networks.

TCP/IP Protocols

Readers who have experience with TCP/IP probably know that it is more than the two protocols it explicitly names. Indeed, TCP/IP standards define or reference over 1,000 distinct communication protocols. With this many different protocols, a layered architecture is essential.

Unlike some sets of communication protocols, TCP/IP's developers have not spent a great deal of effort formalizing its architecture. No precise definition of its layers exists, therefore. Most TCP/IP engineers would agree, though, that the TCP/IP architecture looks something like Figure 2.4. This figure presents an abstract picture of how a networked computer organizes its protocols. As is common in such diagrams, it shows the layers of the architecture in a vertical stack. Applications reside at the top of the stack. These are the protocols that actually organize the information the networks transfer. Example applications include file transfer, remote terminal emulation, mail, news, and time-of-day. They represent the innermost packaging of the architecture.

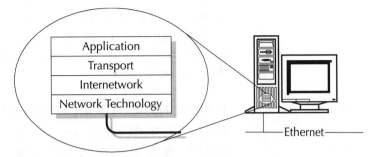

Figure 2.4 The TCP/IP architecture.

Immediately beneath the application is the transport layer. Transport layer protocols take the applications' information and deliver it to the destination. Transport protocols have the responsibility for distinguishing between multiple applications and for providing whatever reliability those applications require. The Transmission Control Protocol (TCP) is one transport protocol.

Transport protocols rely, in turn, on internetwork layer protocols. For TCP/IP, the primary internetwork protocol is the Internet Protocol, or IP. IP makes sure that information travels through networks appropriately and reaches its destination, a process known as forwarding. To do that successfully, the protocol has to understand the topology of the network; it needs to know who is connected to whom. Routing is the process of distributing that information. The TCP/IP protocol suite includes many different protocols that assist in routing.

The lowest level in TCP/IP's protocol stack is the network technology itself, where systems connect to each other and actually exchange information. TCP/IP supports a diverse set of network technologies, ranging from simple dialup modems to high-speed optical networks. Normally, the TCP/IP standards do not concern themselves with the details of these technologies. Other standards organizations, including the Institute of Electrical and Electronics Engineers (for local area networks) and the International

Telecommunications Union (for wide area networks), generally specify particular technologies. TCP/IP standards merely specify how the internetwork layer protocols use those technologies.

Links, Subnetworks, and Internets

Because TCP/IP builds upon other network technologies, its terminology may get confusing. A dialup phone connection can properly be called a *link*, but that term does not really suit a simple local area network such as Ethernet, much less a global frame relay infrastructure. The frame relay infrastructure is clearly a *network*, but how does one distinguish a single frame relay network from the TCP/IP network made up of several frame relay networks?

Some TCP/IP engineers make this distinction by defining two types of networks. A *subnetwork* consists of all systems that can directly communicate with each other using homogenous technologies. A single frame relay network forms a subnetwork. When TCP/IP joins several subnetworks together, the resulting collection is an *internetwork*, or *internet* for short. Figure 2.5 shows that internets consist of many subnets. A consistent use of these terms can become quite cumbersome, though, so this text, like much of the TCP/IP literature will often simply use the term *network*. Only if the distinction is important, and not otherwise clear from the context, does it resort to the more precise terminology.

Hosts and Routers

The TCP/IP protocols do more than just support various network technologies; they combine diverse technologies into a unified network. This unification highlights the distinction between the two roles that TCP/IP systems may play. TCP/IP systems may act as hosts, and they may act as routers. Systems that actually send or receive messages are hosts; systems that relay those messages across networks are routers.

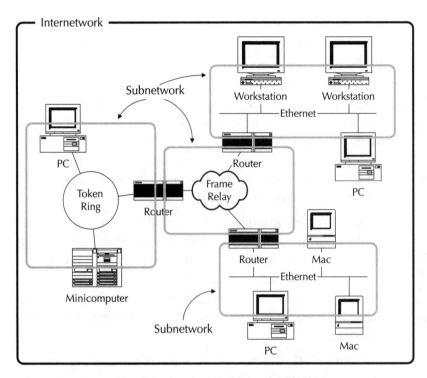

Figure 2.5 Internetworks contain many subnetworks.

Figure 2.6 shows a simple network with two hosts and two routers. The personal computer and the workstation are the systems that exchange information. They do not share a common subnetwork, however. The PC connects to the left Ethernet, while the workstation resides on the right Ethernet. Fortunately, routers are active on both Ethernets, and the two routers can connect to each other using a

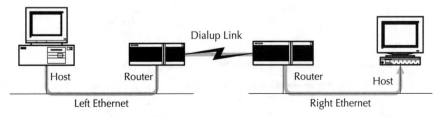

Figure 2.6 Hosts communicate through routers.

Routers in the Real World

Despite the nice clean definition, no pure routers actually exist. Commercial routers certainly focus on the internetwork layer and its routing and forwarding functions. Nonetheless, real routers do require some applications. They may support remote login sessions for administration, or file transfer to retrieve configuration data. Technically, therefore, these real products are both hosts and routers.

dialup link. These routers can accept messages from one host and relay them, through the other router, to the remote host.

Perhaps the easiest way to distinguish hosts from routers is to count the links to which they connect. If a system connects to a single link, then the system must be a host. With only one link, there is no opportunity for the system to relay messages. Routers, on the other hand, connect multiple links. They accept messages from one link and pass them to another.

Based on this discussion, it is possible to distinguish the protocol layers within hosts and routers. Hosts necessarily include all of TCP/IP's protocol layers. Routers, on the other hand, normally rely just on the internetwork layer. As long as a router is not originating or terminating traffic, it has no need for transport or application protocols. (See sidebar.)

Figure 2.7 shows an abstract view of the message exchange of Figure 2.6. Each router accepts messages from a particular network technology, processes them in the internetwork layer, and forwards the message to another network technology.

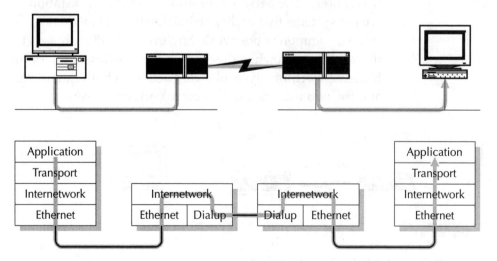

Figure 2.7 Routers relay messages at the internetwork layer.

The Internet

The TCP/IP specifications define a set of communication protocols. Anyone can build systems that implement those protocols, and anyone can connect such systems on a network. In TCP/IP's case, though, one particular network stands out. That network is, of course, the Internet.

The Internet (traditionally written with an uppercase I) began as a research network for the United States Department of Defense. Today, it has grown to a worldwide network connecting government agencies (from many countries), educational and research institutions, commercial enterprises, and private citizens. The Internet bases its organization on a hierarchy. At the center of this hierarchy lie providers. The Internet's various providers connect their networks to form the worldwide backbone for the Internet. Individual provider networks may be limited to small geographic regions or they may span entire continents.

At the outer edges of the Internet are sites. A site is a collection of networks, controlled by a single administrator. Sites include college campuses, government organizations, and corporations. Many sites contain multiple networks. Those networks may include local area networks (LANs) such as Ethernet or even larger-scale networks composed of frame relay links. In the simplest case, a site connects to a single provider. Figure 2.8 illustrates a simple case of this hierarchy.

Communication Services

Modern communication protocols give their users a great deal of flexibility. TCP/IP users who transfer files, for example, can choose from among at least five different protocols[1]. Furthermore, TCP/IP does not confine this

---

[1] File transfer protocols include FTP, TFTP, NFS, SFTP, and MIME/SMTP.

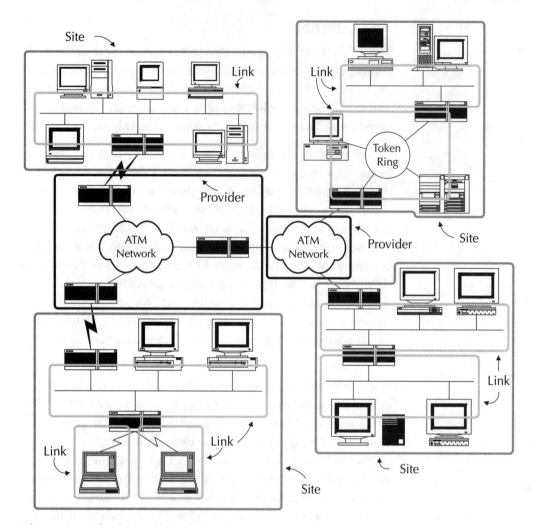

Figure 2.8 The hierarchy of the Internet.

flexibility to the application layer. Various communication services are available from the transport layer, as well as from many network technologies. And on a lesser scale, IP itself supports several optional extensions.

The most significant difference between communication services is how they deliver data. As mentioned in the beginning of this chapter, network engineers classify delivery services as connectionless or as connection-oriented.

Connectionless Delivery

Connectionless delivery is the simplest service to provide. When a protocol provides this service, it treats every message independently. The protocol itself requires no interaction before accepting a message, nor does it provide a context for different messages in a conversation.

It may suffer from overuse, but the simplest example of connectionless service is regular postal mail. Users enclose each message in an envelope and give it to the postal service to deliver. The postal service does not require any negotiations before accepting a letter. Figure 2.9 highlights the similarities between postal mail and connectionless communication. The postal service accepts letters, and the communication network accepts messages. Each must be explicitly labeled with its destination. Like the postal service, the network treats each message independently, delivering it to its destination.

Even though the network views each message independently, connectionless services do allow users to interact with each other. Users themselves must take responsibility for that interaction, though. If an author mails a book proposal to a publisher, the publisher may respond to that proposal. The postal service, however, does not force a response. The same principle applies to connectionless communication. A system that receives a message may respond with its own message. That re-

Letter (with destination address on envelope) given to postal service.

Message (marked with address of destination) transmitted on network.

Ethernet

Figure 2.9 Connectionless service from the postal service and computer networks.

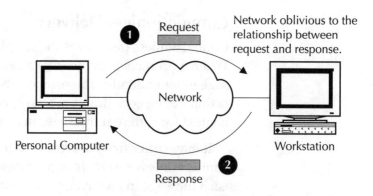

Figure 2.10 Interaction using a connectionless service.

sponse is a separate message, and the delivery service treats it as such. Figure 2.10 illustrates this scenario. As the figure notes, the network does not know that the response message is a reply to the request message.

Connection-Oriented Delivery

Connection-oriented services represent a different philosophy. A protocol that provides such a service does more than simply transfer independent messages. It also establishes a context for those messages. Frequently, that context includes a guarantee of delivery. To provide this extra service, the protocol must do extra work. The work typically involves interaction with the recipient before data is transferred and periodic interaction as long as the conversation continues.

A convenient example of connection-oriented communication is a facsimile transmission as shown in Figure 2.11. Think about how sending a fax differs from sending a letter. With a letter, there is no preliminary interaction with the destination. The sender just drops the letter in the mailbox. With a fax, however, more involved interaction is necessary. The sender first dials the recipient's phone number and waits for an answer. Then the two fax machines negotiate the options they will use for the document. These steps establish the connection.

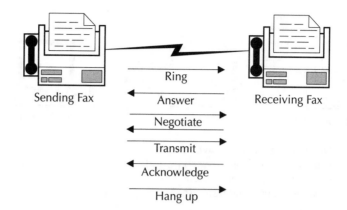

Figure 2.11 Fax transmissions are connection-oriented.

Once the connection is established, the sender begins its transmission. Even during the transmission, though, the two fax machines interact. Depending on the options they have negotiated, the receiver may update the sender on the quality of the reception. If necessary, the sender can even retransmit part of the document. Finally, when the transmission is complete, the sending machine hangs up the phone, terminating the connection.

Connection-oriented service works much the same way for data communications. Protocols that provide such service usually exchange their own messages before transmitting actual data. These preliminary messages establish the connection. During the life of the connection, the protocol continues to exchange its own messages in addition to any data it transfers, as Figure 2.12 illustrates. These extra messages report on the success (or failure) of previous receptions, and they may trigger the sender to retransmit some data. Once the users have finished their conversation, the protocol can exchange more of its own messages to terminate the connection.

Combining Services

It might sound as though connectionless and connection-oriented are totally incompatible services. They do, after

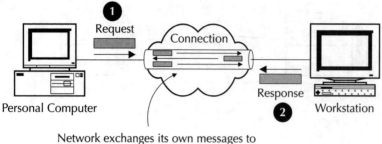

Network exchanges its own messages to
maintain connection between PC and
workstation; it recognizes relationship
between request and response.

Figure 2.12 Connection establishes a relationship between the systems.

all, represent a considerable difference in philosophy.
Despite that difference, however, many networks combine the services quite freely. One layer may offer one
type, while a different layer offers the other. To see this
process in action, consider the example network of Figure
2.13, which shows two systems connected by an Asynchronous Transfer Mode (ATM) network. For this example, the personal computer wants to transfer a file to the
workstation.

Communication begins when the PC's application program asks the transport layer protocol to establish communications with the workstation. This action is step 1 in
the figure. The application program uses TCP as a transport protocol, and TCP provides connection-oriented
services. TCP's first action, therefore, is to send its own
message to the workstation in order to begin establishing
the connection. At step 2, TCP builds this message and
hands it to the internetwork layer protocol (IP) to deliver.

IP provides a connectionless service, so it treats this TCP
message just like any other. It adds its own information to
the message and gives it to the ATM software to transmit
(step 3). Because IP is connectionless, it does not establish a
connection; it simply forwards TCP's message as soon as
that message arrives.

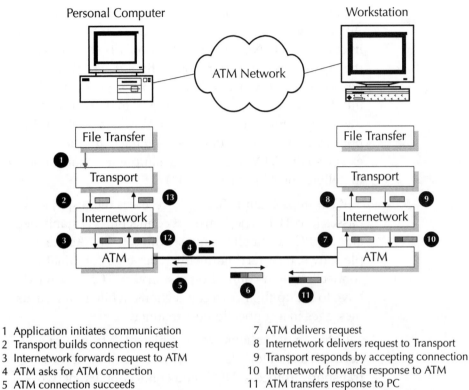

1 Application initiates communication
2 Transport builds connection request
3 Internetwork forwards request to ATM
4 ATM asks for ATM connection
5 ATM connection succeeds
6 ATM transfers request to workstation

7 ATM delivers request
8 Internetwork delivers request to Transport
9 Transport responds by accepting connection
10 Internetwork forwards response to ATM
11 ATM transfers response to PC
12 ATM delivers response to Internetwork
13 Internetwork delivers response to Transport

Figure 2.13 Combining connection oriented and connectionless service.

Like TCP, ATM provides a connection-oriented service. In order to deliver IP's message, the ATM software must establish its own connection to the destination. It builds an ATM-specific message and sends it to the network. This message (step 4) will establish the ATM connection. While the PC's ATM software waits for the connection, it holds the IP message.

At step 5, the ATM network responds by confirming the establishment of a connection with the workstation. Now the PC can send the IP message it has been storing. As step 6 shows, the ATM software adds its own information to the message and transmits it on the network.

After the message arrives at the workstation (step 7), the ATM software delivers it to the IP layer, which in turn delivers it to TCP. Now the workstation's TCP knows that the PC desires a transport connection. It accepts the connection request with another TCP message. In step 9, it builds this message and gives it to IP to deliver. IP adds its own information and hands it to ATM (step 10). At this point, an ATM connection between the computers already exists, so the ATM software can simply use that connection to deliver the response (step 11).

With steps 12 and 13, the PC receives the response and passes it to TCP. The transport connection is established, and the PC can finally begin sending its file. As the example shows, transferring the file relies on a combination of connections and connectionless service. TCP and ATM have to set up their own connections, while IP forwards messages in a connectionless manner.

Other combinations are possible at the transport and network technology layers. There are connectionless transport protocols (UDP) and connectionless network technologies (for example, Ethernet). TCP/IP's internetwork layer, however, is always connectionless.

Network Addressing

This chapter's final topic answers a crucial question for any network architecture: How do systems identify each other? The issue is clearly critical; communications—remote logins, file transfers, mail exchanges, video conferences, and any others—succeed only if the right parties communicate. In order to communicate with the right system, other systems must be able to unambiguously identify it. Network addresses provide that unambiguous identification.

The Role of Network Addresses

If a network address provides identification, then it must identify something. In TCP/IP's case, the something is a little different from other network architectures. Technically, TCP/IP addresses identify interfaces, not systems. The distinction rarely matters for hosts. In most cases, hosts have but a single interface. Effectively, the system and the interface are equivalent. Informally at least, network addresses are often thought to identify hosts rather than their interfaces.

Unlike hosts, routers usually support multiple interfaces. When they do, each of their interfaces may have a separate (and different) network address. Figure 2.14 shows a router attached to both an Ethernet and a Token Ring local area network (LAN). The router's Ethernet interface has the network address 1234, while the Token Ring interface has address 5678. Although both addresses belong to the same router, IP differentiates between the two when it delivers messages. Messages destined for address 1234 arrive at the router from the Ethernet, while messages for address 5678 arrive from the Token Ring.

In many cases, even this distinction remains unimportant. After all, both messages will reach the router. Particularly in an informal context, the router may be identified by the address of any of its interfaces.

Types of Addresses

TCP/IP supports three different types of network addresses; it names those types *unicast*, *multicast*, and *anycast*.

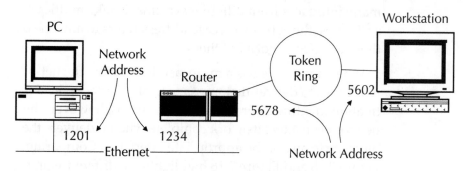

Figure 2.14 IP network addresses identify interfaces.

Unicast addresses are the most straightforward type of addresses. They refer to a single interface, and they do so unambiguously. When a system designates a unicast address as the destination of its message, it intends that the message reach that particular interface. The network takes responsibility for delivering the message to that interface.

Multicast addresses identify sets of interfaces. Most often, the set includes multiple interfaces that belong to different systems. When a message has a multicast destination address, the network strives to deliver it to all interfaces in the set. This function lets a system generate a message once and have that message delivered to many different recipients.

Broadcast Address

Unlike IPv4, IPv6 does not formally recognize a *broadcast address*, one that refers to *all* interfaces. To achieve the same effect, though, IPv6 can use a multicast address that happens to refer to the set of all interfaces.

Multicast addresses are obviously useful for multicast applications like video conferences. As Figure 2.15 shows, the messages that make up the conference are simultaneously delivered to all participants. TCP/IP protocols also rely on multicast services for some of their internal requirements. One router, for example, may need to quickly pass some information to all other routers. Instead of sending separate messages to each router one at a time, it can send the message once, but with a multicast destination that identifies all other routers.

Anycast addresses are a new feature with IPv6. They represent a compromise between unicast and multicast addresses. An anycast address refers to one of a set of interfaces. Like multicast addresses, this set usually includes many interfaces from different systems. Unlike multicast addresses, though, an anycast address refers to any one of those interfaces, not *all* of them.

When a message has a multicast destination, the network tries to deliver that message to all interfaces the destination identifies. For anycast destinations, however, the network considers its work complete when it delivers the message to any of the appropriate interfaces. Comparing Figure 2.15 and Figure 2.16 highlights the difference. In the second figure, the anycast message does not reach the

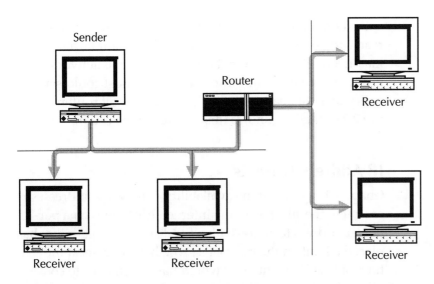

Figure 2.15 Sender's messages delivered to all receivers simultaneously via multicast.

workstations on the right Ethernet. In this case, the router recognizes that the message has already reached at least one appropriate interface (either of the workstations on the left network). Consequently, the router does not need to forward the message to the right Ethernet.

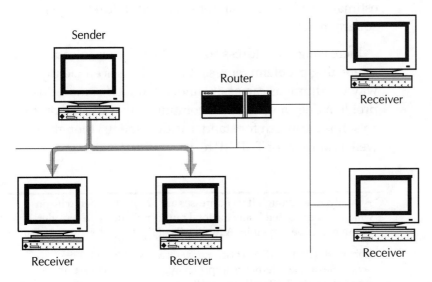

Figure 2.16 Anycast messages reach at least one destination, but not all.

Systems can use anycast addresses when they need to reach any one of a class of systems. For example, a host may need information that any router on the network can provide. To ask for this information, the host could send a query to an anycast address that identifies all routers. Figure 2.21 (page 37) shows this example application.

IP Address Formats

Chapter 1 noted that the availability of network addresses is crucial to the survival of the Internet. IPv4 relies on a particular address format—with a fixed size of 32 bits—that has placed a limit on the Internet's growth. Of course, at the time of IPv4's invention, it would have been hard to conceive of an Internet with more than 2^{32} computers[2].

IPv6 overcomes this limitation by increasing the size of network addresses. IPv6 addresses are 128 bits long. In theory, this size can accommodate over 6.65×10^{23} network addresses for every square meter of the surface of the planet Earth. Just as with IPv4, the hierarchies present in the address structure make the practical total somewhat less than the theoretical limit. Even the most pessimistic estimates still leave room for over 1,500 addresses per square meter[3].

Increasing the address size to 128 bits does introduce an interesting problem: representing addresses efficiently in a way that humans can easily understand. Of course, this problem does not affect the computers that use the protocols. It is a concern for standards documents, though, as well as authors of TCP/IP texts.

---

[2] Actually, even though IPv4 addresses are 32 bits, the hierarchy on which they are based limits the total number available to considerably less than 2^{32}. See Appendix A for details of IPv4.

[3] Robert M. Hinden. *IP Next Generation Overview*. May 14, 1995 (available on the Internet as http://playground.sun.com/pub/ipng/html/INET-IPng-Paper.html).

The IP standards present a preferred format for representing addresses in human-readable text. That format breaks the address into eight 16-bit pieces. Colons separate the pieces, which are themselves shown in hexadecimal notation. An example IPv6 address is:

```
FEDC:BA98:7654:3210:FEDC:BA98:7654:3210
```

If a 16-bit piece has a value less than 0x1000, the leading zeros are not necessary. At least one digit must be present, however. A sample IPv6 address that takes advantage of these shortcuts is

```
1080:0:0:0:8:800:200C:417A
```

For an even more compact representation, the preferred format permits a series of consecutive 16-bit pieces, all with a value of zero, to be abbreviated with two colons. (IPv6's designers expect that such series will be common). With this approach, the above address can also be written:

```
1080::8:800:200C:417A
```

Note that the "::" abbreviation may only appear once in an address.

The other major problem facing the Internet is routing table explosion. To solve this problem, IPv6 addresses rely heavily on a hierarchy. The hierarchy's top level begins with the address's most significant bit and continues down to the least significant bit. To see an example of an address hierarchy, consider Figure 2.17. The figure takes a sample address and breaks down its first 80 bits. The first three bits define the top level of the hierarchy. The next level uses five bits. The full process results in an address with five levels through the first 80 bits; the remaining 48 bits (which do not appear in the figure) define the particular system on the identified subnetwork.

The figure presents one example of how an address can embed a hierarchy. IPv6 has considerably more flexibility than this example indicates, though. Addresses can have

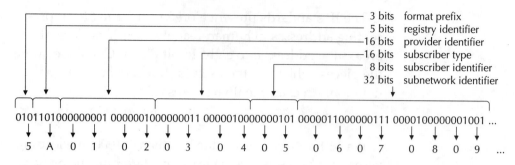

Figure 2.17 Hierarchy of an IP address.

an arbitrary number of hierarchy levels (up to 128, anyway), and each level may be represented by an arbitrary number of bits.

To represent this flexibility in text, IP uses address prefixes. An address prefix indicates both an address itself, and the number of significant bits in the address. The address is written normally, while the number of significant bits follows the address and is separated from it by a slash. For example, Table 2.1 shows the address prefixes that apply to Figure 2.17.

The address of the example illustrates one particular hierarchy. Even at this early stage, the IPv6 standards define several different hierarchies. The first few bits of any address determine the hierarchy to which it belongs. Table 2.2 lists the hierarchies available so far, along with the prefixes that distinguish them.

Table 2.1 Sample Address Prefixes

4000::/3	provider-based unicast addresses
5A00::/8	administered by InterNIC
5A01:0200::/24	provider 0x0102
5A01:0203:0400::/40	subscriber type 0x0304
5A01:0203:0405::/48	subscriber 0x05
5A01:0203:0405:0607:0809::/80	subnetwork 0x06070809

Special Addresses

In addition to the top-level hierarchy set out by Table 2.2, IP defines several particular addresses that have special significance. Most of these special addresses are allocated from the *reserved* hierarchy (0::/8).

The *unspecified address*, with all zeros for its value (0:0:0:0:0:0:0:0), is used when no true address is available. For example, a host may request its true IP address from the network. Until it gets an answer, though, it has nothing to use as the source address for its messages. The unspecified address can serve this role. The unspecified

Table 2.2 IPv6 Address Allocations

0::/8	0000 0000	reserved
100::/8	0000 0001	unassigned
200::/7	0000 001	ISO network addresses
400::/7	0000 010	Novell (IPX) network addresses
600::/7	0000 011	unassigned
800::/5	0000 1	unassigned
1000::/4	0001	unassigned
2000::/3	001	unassigned
4000::/3	010	provider-based unicast addresses
6000::/3	011	unassigned
8000::/3	100	geographic-based unicast addresses
A000::/3	101	unassigned
C000::/3	110	unassigned
E000::/4	1110	unassigned
F000::/5	1111 0	unassigned
F800::/6	1111 10	unassigned
FC00::/7	1111 110	unassigned
FE00::/9	1111 1110 0	unassigned
FE80::/10	1111 1110 10	link local addresses
FEC0::/10	1111 1110 11	site local address
FF00::/8	1111 1111	multicast addresses

address, however, may never appear as the destination of a message.

A second special address is the *loopback address*, 0:0:0:0:0:0:0:1. Any system can specify this address to send a message to itself. Such a message never actually leaves the system that generates it, but it is processed by at least some of the protocol software. Figure 2.18 shows how the IP protocol "turns around" any message with a loopback destination.

Loopback messages can assist in diagnosing problems, as they test the health of TCP/IP software without actually requiring a real network. In the figure, for example, the transport protocol must process a message for transmission and one for reception. It does not recognize that both are actually the same message. Since loopback addresses are limited to the originating system, messages with the loopback address as the destination (or the source) should never appear on an actual network.

Two types of special IPv6 addresses support the transition from IPv4. Those special addresses are *IPv4-compatible* addresses, and *IPv4-mapped* addresses. IPv4-compatible addresses can be converted to and from the older IPv4 network address format. They are used when IPv6 systems need to communicate with each other, yet find themselves separated by an IPv4 network. If the systems use IPv4-

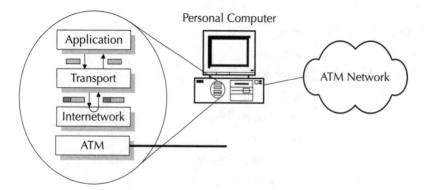

Figure 2.18 Loopback destination address restricts messages to a single system.

compatible addresses, routers at the boundary of the IPv4 network can convert those addresses to true IPv4 addresses, allowing messages to travel through the older network.

IPv6-compatible addresses are formed by prepending 96 bits of zero to a legitimate, 32-bit IPv4 address. For example, the IPv4 address of `1.2.3.4` can be converted to the IPv6 address `::0102:0304`. Appendix A details how these addresses assist in the migration from IPv4 to IPv6. Figure 2.19 hints at their use, though. In the figure, the left router uses an IPv4 address to transport an IPv6 message across an IPv4 network. Because the original IPv6 destination is compatible, the router can easily and automatically derive an IPv4 destination address for the message.

IPv4-mapped addresses may also be converted to legitimate IPv4 addresses, but they serve a different role. IPv4-mapped addresses indicate systems that do *not* support IPv6. They are instead limited to IPv4. As long as intervening routers perform the mapping, these addresses let IPv6 systems communicate with IPv4-only systems. Figure 2.20 shows how an IPv6 host can address an IPv4 host using an IPv4-mapped address. The right router translates the message into IPv4 format for its destination host. Appendix A contains further details of this process.

The form for IPv4-mapped addresses is 80 bits of zero, 16 bits of one, and 32 bits of an IPv4 address. The IPv4 ad-

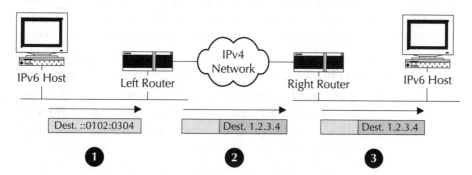

Figure 2.19 Routers translate IPv4-compatible addresses to traverse an IPv4 network.

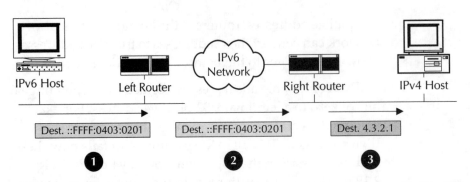

Figure 2.20 Host uses IPv4-mapped address to communicate with IPv4 host.

dress of `4.3.2.1`, when mapped to IPv6, becomes `::FFFF:0403:0201`.

The structure of both IPv4-compatible and IPv4-mapped addresses is not arbitrary. Both formats were chosen because of the particular checksum algorithm that many TCP/IP protocols use (see page 445). Either address format contributes the same values to the checksum, whether it is specified as an IPv6 address (all 128 bits) or as an IPv4 address (32 bits only). This property means that routers can convert from an IPv6-formatted message to an IPv4-formatted message *without* recomputing the message's checksum; the change to IPv4 addresses does not alter the checksum value. Without this property, the translation between the two formats become much less efficient, and network performance would suffer.

The final special address is an anycast address. It is the *subnet-router address*, which can be part of any IPv6 hierarchy. It is formed by a (nonzero) subnet prefix that distinguishes a particular link or subnetwork, followed by trailing bits of zero. For example, the specific subnetwork in Figure 2.21 has the prefix `5A01:203:405:607:809::/80`. On that subnetwork, the subnet-router anycast address is `5A01:203:405:607:809::`. Systems on the network may use this address when they need to send a message to any single router, and it does not matter which router they reach.

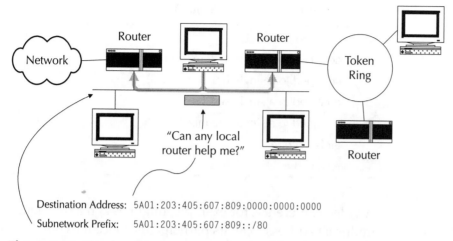

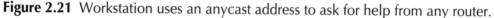

Destination Address: 5A01:203:405:607:809:0000:0000:0000

Subnetwork Prefix: 5A01:203:405:607:809::/80

Figure 2.21 Workstation uses an anycast address to ask for help from any router.

Multicast Addresses

IPv6 multicast addresses have their own special format. As Table 2.2 indicates, all multicast addresses begin with eight bits of 1. The next eight bits give more information about the address. Figure 2.22 shows the breakdown.

The first four bits are flags. So far, only the fourth bit has a defined meaning. If it is zero, then a global authority has permanently assigned the address to a particular group. For example, the address FF02::1 identifies the group of all systems on a link. This address is permanently assigned, and its meaning is known to all IP hosts and routers.

If the fourth bit of the flags field is one, then the address is transient. Transient addresses are used only temporarily.

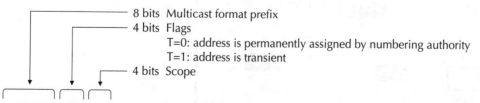

8 bits Multicast format prefix
4 bits Flags
        T=0: address is permanently assigned by numbering authority
        T=1: address is transient
4 bits Scope

1111 1111 000T xxxx ... (remaining 112 bits provide a group identifier)

Figure 2.22 Structure of multicast addresses.

Table 2.3 Multicast Address Scope Values

0	reserved
1	confined to a single system (node-local)
2	confined to a single link (link-local)
5	confined to a single site
8	confined to a single organization
E	global scope
F	reserved

A video conference, for example, might assign a transient multicast address to all its participants. Once the conference concludes, the address is available for reassignment elsewhere.

The next four bits of the address define its scope. The scope determines the extent of the address, and it is based on the hierarchical organization of the networks themselves. Table 2.3 lists the assigned scope values.

Figure 2.23 shows how the scope affects the distribution of multicast messages. The PC's message has, as its destination, a link-local scope. Since the scope confines the message to a single link, routers on the Ethernet do not propagate the message beyond that local network. The figure shows that the messages travel no farther than the left router.

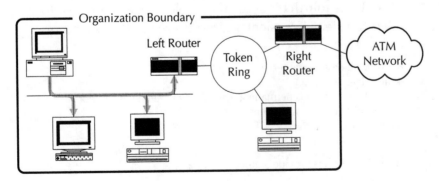

Figure 2.23 Link-local scope limits multicast to a single Ethernet.

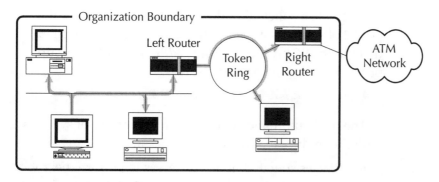

Figure 2.24 Organization-local scope limits multicast to organization boundary.

The workstation, on the other hand, sends a message with an organization-local scope in Figure 2.24. Routers on the Ethernet do relay this message to their connected networks. The right router, however, does not allow the message to reach the ATM network. That network does not belong to the organization.

As IPv6 gains popularity, many multicast addresses are likely to be assigned. Already, though, the standards have identified five permanently assigned addresses. Table 2.4 lists all five.

The standards also define a special type of multicast address called a *solicited node address*. These addresses are formed from unicast and anycast addresses. Every unicast (or anycast) address maps to exactly one solicited node address. Different unicast addresses, however, may form the same solicited node address.

Table 2.4 Assigned Multicast Addresses

FF01::1	all systems	node-local scope
FF02::1	all systems	link-local scope
FF01::2	all routers	node-local scope
FF02::2	all routers	link-local scope
FF02::1:0	all DHCP servers and relay agents	link-local scope

To create a solicited node address, a system takes the last 32 bits of its unicast or anycast address and appends them to the 96-bit prefix FF02::1/96. For example, suppose a host has the unicast address:

```
FEDC:BA98:7654:3210:FEDC:BA98:7654:3210
```

The host automatically belongs to the group of systems with the multicast address FF01::1:7654:3210.

ICMP uses solicited node addresses to perform neighbor discovery and duplicate address detection. Chapter 5 describes both functions.

Assigning Addresses

To clarify the various aspects of IPv6 network addresses, it is helpful to consider which addresses must be assigned to IPv6 hosts and routers. Table 2.5 gives a complete list of the addresses that each host must recognize.

Routers are special devices. They must support a few special addresses in addition to the standard host addresses. Table 2.6 gives a complete list of router addresses. The additions (beyond the hosts' requirements) include the subnet-router anycast address, and the all-routers multicast address.

Table 2.5 Addresses Each Host Must Support

- a link-local unicast address for each interface
- any other assigned unicast or anycast addresses
- the loopback address
- the all-systems multicast address (node-local and link-local)
- solicited node multicast addresses for all unicast and anycast addresses
- multicast addresses for any other groups to which the host belongs

Table 2.6 Addresses Each Router Must Support

- a link-local address for each interface
- the subnet-router anycast address for each interface
- any other assigned unicast or anycast addresses
- the all-systems multicast address (node-local and link-local)
- the all-routers multicast address (node-local and link-local)
- solicited node multicast addresses for all unicast and anycast addresses
- multicast addresses for any other groups to which the router belongs

Summary

This chapter introduced several concepts that underlie computer communications. The most pervasive of those concepts are layers and hierarchies. Networks use layers to divide their job into smaller, manageable pieces, and they use hierarchies to organize information. Both ideas appear throughout this text. The book's very organization, in fact, is layered. Each chapter presents a separate protocol; different protocols at the same layer follow each other in order. (Of course, the book is also organized in a hierarchy, with chapters, sections, and subsections.)

Hierarchies reappear frequently in subsequent chapters, as they reappear in many aspects of TCP/IP. IP's network addresses form one important hierarchy, as do its routing protocols and its name service. As later chapters show, these hierarchies help protocols and users manage (possibly) tremendous amounts of information.

This chapter also described the format of IPv6 network addresses. IPv6 defines three distinct types of network addresses—unicast, multicast, and anycast. The address formats also leave room for IPv4's network addresses. By providing a way to convert the older addresses to and from the new format, IPv6 can operate across an IPv4 network, and IPv6 hosts can communicate directly with IPv4 hosts. Both qualities are essential for an orderly transition to IPng.

3

Network Technologies

It may be difficult to single out the most important factor in the success of TCP/IP. Clearly, though, a major strength is its ability to adapt to a wide variety of network technologies. TCP/IP supports everything from dialup phone lines and amateur radio links to high-speed optical networks and satellite transmission channels.

Describing such a wide variety of networks would require an entire book. This chapter does not attempt that. Instead, it highlights several key network technologies. The organization is roughly geographic. The first section discusses the most popular network for connecting systems within buildings, the Ethernet local area network. The chapter extends its coverage to remote offices. Increasingly, a popular approach for connecting remote offices is the Integrated Services Digital Network, or ISDN. The final section moves on to wide area networks (WANs). The future of wide area networks depends on two high-speed technologies that the chapter introduces, frame relay and asynchronous transfer mode.

Ethernet Local Area Networks

If an office has connected its computers to form a network, chances are the technology behind that network is Ethernet. Originally, one of many technologies for local area networks (LANs), Ethernet is increasingly the LAN technology of choice. Ethernet reached this position because it has evolved into a simple, flexible, inexpensive, and high-performance way to connect systems.

Local Area Networks

Local area networks resist precise definition, but they share important characteristics that distinguish them from other computer networks. Their most obvious characteristic is geography. LANs serve a limited area. Usually, they are confined to a single building or even a single department within a building.

In exchange for this limitation, LANs offer speed. When compared to most network technologies that span countries, LANs can transfer more information in the same amount of time, and with less delay. Data rates for LAN range from 4 Mbit/s to 100 Mbit/s; and the delay between sending and receiving is often measured in microseconds.

Sharing the Wire

Like other local area networks, Ethernet begins with a simple premise: it is not economical to connect every computer directly to every other computer. Even a small network of half a dozen systems, like that of Figure 3.1, requires 15 different connections. A large building with 100 computers would have to manage nearly 5,000 connections. The burden facing such a network administrator would be immense.

Instead of this excess of connections, Ethernet asks its systems to share. The heart of a typical Ethernet network is single, coaxial cable. That cable winds it way through the area, and each computer has a single connection to the cable. When two computers need to communicate, they do so over the shared Ethernet cable. (Actually, as the upcoming section, "The Evolution of Ethernet Technology" discusses, most modern Ethernets do not use this exact

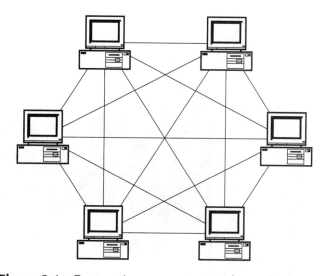

Figure 3.1   Connecting computers without sharing media.

topology; this description applies to the original Ethernet design. It serves to introduce the principles behind all Ethernet variations, however.) Figure 3.2 shows how six computers can share a cable. The network reduces the number of required connections from 15 to 6.

In order to share the main Ethernet cable efficiently, Ethernet specifies a protocol. That protocol tells the computers how to behave. At a general level, the Ethernet protocol resembles the protocol that people use in an in-

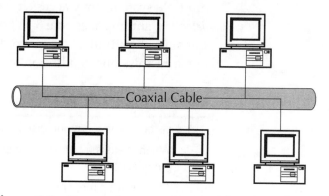

Figure 3.2   Connecting computers with a shared cable.

Figure 3.3 Protocol in use during a meeting.

formal meeting. Consider the woman in Figure 3.3. Suppose she wishes to mention something to the man on the far right. What steps would she be likely to take? Table 3.1 lists some possibilities.

These simple rules capture the same principles as Ethernet's protocol. In Ethernet's case, that protocol goes by the name of Carrier Sense Multiple Access, with Collision Detection (CSMA/CD). *Carrier sense* is the technical term for rule 1. It means that computers on a Ethernet listen to the network before attempting to transmit. If another computer is already transmitting, they wait for it to finish. Multiple access simply means that the network is shared; multiple systems may access it. The final phrase, *collision detection*, summarizes rule 3. When a system begins to transmit, it continues to monitor the network. If it encounters transmissions in addition to its own, the network has

Table 3.1 Protocol for Speaking in a Meeting

1. Listen to see if anyone else is speaking.

2. When there is a pause in the conversation, begin phrasing the question.

3. At the same time, continue listening just to make sure no one else also used the opportunity to begin speaking.

experienced a *collision*. Each system immediately halts its transmission.

The only part of the Ethernet protocol that is even slightly tricky is its response to a collision. After each computer aborts its own transmission, it waits a brief period of time for the network to settle. The length of that time period is random. Without a random delay, both colliding systems would wait the same amount of time and, almost certainly, collide again on their next attempt. The Ethernet protocol further specifies the nature of that random delay. The first time a computer experiences a collision, its random delay may range up to a specified value. If, on the second attempt, the computer again encounters a collision, the delay ranges up to an even larger value. The delay continues to increase with each successive collision. Once the computer finally transmits successfully, it restarts the process.

Ethernet Frame Structure

The basic unit of information that Ethernet transfers is called a *frame*. The Ethernet protocol provides a specific structure for the format of those frames. Figure 3.4 shows what that format looks like. The first 64 bits of the frame form the preamble, which is a particular, well-defined pattern that all senders must use. It allows receivers on the network to synchronize with the sender. Since the preamble is the same for all frames, most illustrations (including subsequent figures in this text) omit it.

An Alternate Frame Format

The Institute of Electrical and Electronics Engineers (IEEE) has tried to unify all LAN protocols through the work of its 802 committee. The IEEE specification for Ethernet-like technology is standard 802.3, and it specifies a frame structure slightly differently than Figure 3.4. Some protocols, such as the ISO protocol suite, have chosen to use the IEEE format, while others, including TCP/IP have stuck with the original Ethernet framing of Figure 3.4.

First byte transmitted

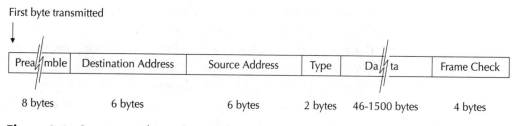

Figure 3.4 Structure of an Ethernet frame.

The next 48 bits of a frame are the destination address. Every system on an Ethernet has its own unique address. The destination address identifies the system that the sender is trying to reach with its message.

Destination addresses are important because the Ethernet cable is a broadcast medium. When any system sends a frame, every other station can hear the transmission. Normally, however, a sender only wants a particular recipient to hear its message. It specifies the destination address in its frames to identify that recipient. Other systems, as soon as they recognize that the destination address is not their own, can quit listening to the frame.

Sometimes, a sender does not want to limit its information to a single recipient. It may need to tell every computer on the network something. Ethernet allows this kind of operation as well. It sets aside certain destination addresses for such communication. A destination address composed entirely of *ones* forms the special broadcast address. Every system on the LAN listens to this address.

Ethernet also supports multicast communications. Frames with multicast destination addresses can reach more than one recipient, but not necessarily every system on the network. The main difference between multicast and broadcast is choice. Computers can choose whether or not they wish to receive multicast frames addressed to particular destinations; they have no such choice with broadcast.

Ethernet addresses are usually written as a series of six 8-bit bytes. The leftmost byte is the first transmitted, and within each byte, the least significant bit is transmitted first. Multicast destination addresses are distinguished by their first bit; it is always one. Therefore, when a multicast address is written, its first byte is odd. Figure 3.5 shows all the formats that a multicast address may take. The hex value is the one normally used in text. As the figure shows, the odd value 63 marks the address as multicast.

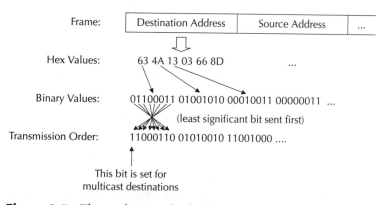

Figure 3.5 The order in which Ethernet transmits bits.

It is important that no two computers on an Ethernet have the same address. Otherwise, the LAN could not distinguish them from each other, and chaos would almost certainly result. To ensure this uniqueness, manufacturers of Ethernet hardware assign each piece of equipment its own address prior to shipping. In this way, the Ethernet address acts much like a serial number. To make sure that two different manufacturers do not assign the same address, each manufacturer has its own organization identifier. This organization ID forms the first three bytes of all Ethernet addresses assigned by the manufacturer. The Institute of Electrical and Electronic Engineers, headquartered in New York, assigns organization IDs.

Following the destination address, the Ethernet frame contains the address of the sender. Broadcast and multicast addresses are not permitted in this field.

The next two bytes of the Ethernet frame specify the frame type. The Ethernet protocol itself does not actually specify the contents of this field. To Ethernet, the value of these bytes does not matter; instead, Ethernet merely sets them aside as a convenience to its users. To senders and receivers, however, the frame type is significant. The frame type identifies which protocol is using the data portion of the frame.

The frame type field allows many different protocols to use a LAN simultaneously. Each frame identifies its upper-level protocol, so no confusion results. IPv4, in fact, relies on multiple protocols to operate over Ethernet. With IPv6, however, TCP/IP has consolidated all those protocols into one. All IPv6 traffic uses the frame type of 0x86DD (hexadecimal).

After the frame type comes the data portion itself. This field is where Ethernet carries actual information from sender to receiver. Notice in Figure 3.4 that there is both a minimum and maximum size for this field. All Ethernet frames are required to carry between 368 and 12,000 bits of data. Furthermore, that data must consist of an integer number of 8-bit bytes.

The minimum data size makes sure that every frame is at least large enough to be heard by all stations. Otherwise, collisions may go undetected. The maximum data size places a limit on how long any one station can tie up the network with a transmission. It ensures that all stations have an opportunity to transmit.

The last part of each Ethernet frame is a 32-bit frame check sequence (FCS). The FCS serves as an error-detecting code for the frame. When the sender prepares to transmit a frame, it performs a special mathematical operation on the information that comprises the frame. That operation results in the FCS, which the sender appends to the frame during transmission.

When the recipient receives the frame, it performs the same operation on the frame's information. Since the network does not intentionally alter any bit in the frame, the recipient's result should match the sender's. If they do not match, then some part of the frame was accidentally altered as it traversed the network. Because there is no way to determine which part, the recipient immediately discards the frame without further processing. If, on the other hand, the FCS matches, it is likely that the frame arrived without errors.

The Evolution of Ethernet Technology

Ethernet was invented in the early 1970s. The fact that it remains so popular is a testament to its original designers. Ethernet technology has not become stagnant in the last 20 years, however. Quite the contrary; Ethernet has evolved many times to meet the needs of new LAN users. None of these changes has altered the frame structure just described, but they have revised the way Ethernet LANs are deployed and managed. The more recent changes have also significantly improved Ethernet's performance.

One of the first problems Ethernet administrators encountered was the difficulty of installing and maintaining the hardware. The main Ethernet coaxial cable was bulky and expensive. Most buildings had it installed in ceilings, making it difficult to access for inspection and troubleshooting. Attaching computers to this cable was also time-consuming and error prone. It was literally necessary to drill into the cable, attach special boxes called transceivers, and run an additional cable from the transceiver to the computer. Figure 3.6 shows how a computer might be connected to the network.

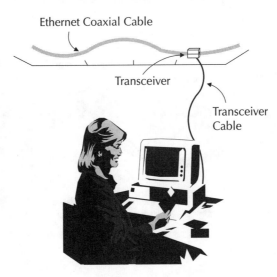

Figure 3.6 Early Ethernet technology.

To ease the burdens of installation and maintenance, engineers modified the LAN to work with standard laboratory cabling. As an advertisement of the benefits of this new cable, the technology quickly gained the nicknames ThinNet and CheaperNet. More precisely, the technology goes by the name 10BASE2. The final 2 is significant, as the original Ethernet technology is known as 10BASE5. In both cases, the final digit represents the maximum size of a single LAN, in hundreds of meters. ThinNet LANs are limited to 200 meters in total length.

10BASE2 also changed the method of connecting computers to the LAN. It relies on standard coaxial connectors like those Figure 3.7 illustrates. They can be engaged or disengaged in a few seconds. With 10BASE2, there are no transceivers and no transceiver cables.

Perhaps the most important evolution of Ethernet was the introduction of 10BASE-T technology. 10BASE2, even though it is less expensive than the original Ethernet, still requires snaking a special coaxial cable to all computers on the LAN. 10BASE-T changes that requirement drastically. It lets Ethernet use the same twisted pair cables as telephone systems. These cables are readily available in most

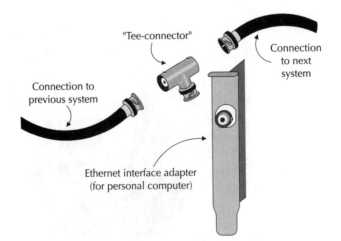

Figure 3.7   Connecting to a 10BASE2 Ethernet.

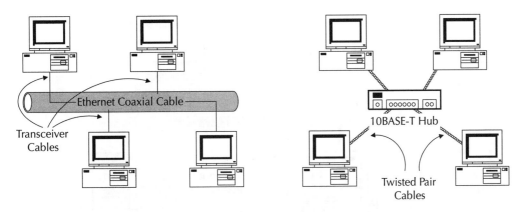

Figure 3.8 Comparing original Ethernet to twisted pair Ethernet.

offices, and make the installation of an Ethernet LAN much easier.

In 10BASE-T technology, the twisted pair cables do not replace the main Ethernet coaxial cable. Instead, they act more like original Ethernet's transceiver cables. As Figure 3.8 shows, 10BASE-T collapses the shared coaxial cable into a small box called the hub. Twisted pair cables connect each computer to this hub[1].

The next step in Ethernet's evolution tackled some of the technology's performance limitations. The fact that Ethernet relies on a shared medium introduces some restrictions. For an example, consider Figure 3.9. As long as the Macintosh transmits to the workstation, the PC and the minicomputer cannot communicate. The Mac has exclusive use of the share cable. This same restriction applies to traditional 10BASE-T hubs as well. In effect, the shared medium places a bandwidth limitation on the aggregate traffic from all systems on the LAN. For traditional Ethernet, the total bandwidth available to all systems is limited

---

[1] Despite the popularity of 10BASE-T and Ethernet hubs, this text, like most others, usually illustrates Ethernet LANs using the original topology.

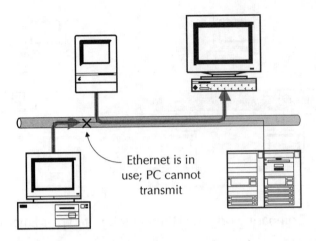

Ethernet is in use; PC cannot transmit

Figure 3.9   All Ethernet systems share the same cable.

to 10 Mbit/s. A system can achieve only 10 Mbit/s of throughput if no other systems on the LAN are transmitting at the same time.

To eliminate this bottleneck, hub vendors introduced a technology that has come to be called *switched Ethernet*. Switched Ethernet has the same topology as 10BASE-T. In fact, to the computers using the LAN, things appear exactly the same. The difference is the hub itself. Switched Ethernet hubs have an internal matrix switch that allows them to directly connect each computer to every other computer. Most important, the switch supports multiple connections at the same time. With switched Ethernet, the Mac and workstation can communicate at the same time as the PC and minicomputer. Figure 3.10 shows that one conversation does not impede another.

The latest enhancements to Ethernet also improve performance, but as a direct result of increasing the speed at which the network operates. Most previous Ethernet technologies operated at 10 Mbit/s. (This is the source of the 10 in 10BASEx.) New signaling technologies have allowed engineers to increase that speed to 100 Mbit/s.

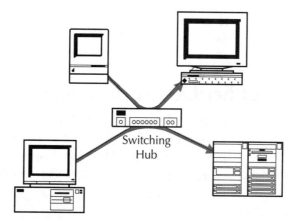

Figure 3.10 Switching technology allows simultaneous use of the LAN.

The most straightforward speed upgrade is the 100BASE-T technology. Also known as *fast Ethernet*, 100BASE-T LANs operate much the same as 10BASE-T. The obvious difference is a speed increase. Fast Ethernet operates at 100 Mbit/s. Otherwise, fast Ethernet operates just like 10BASE-T. Like the lower-speed technology, fast Ethernet hubs can use switching technology to further improve network performance.

An alternative approach to higher speeds is the 100VG-AnyLAN technology, which is also known by its IEEE standard number of 802.12. Like fast Ethernet, 100VG boosts the speed of the network to 100 Mbit/s. 100VG, however, relies on an entirely new access scheme called *demand priority*. With demand priority, there are no collisions. Instead, the hub polls each computer in turn. If the system has a frame to transmit, it does so only when the hub grants it access. This new access scheme lets 100VG hubs support a simple priority scheme, allowing some frames to have priority over others. 100VG hubs can also support frame formats other than Ethernet. In particular, they can transfer Token Ring frames. This flexibility positions 100VG as a viable upgrade to both Ethernet and Token Ring networks.

Other LAN Technologies

Despite the popularity of Ethernet, other important LAN technologies do exist. Two in particular, Token Ring and Fiber Distributed Data Interconnect (FDDI), commonly carry TCP/IP traffic. This section takes a brief look at both technologies.

Token Ring

In some applications, Ethernet's collisions and the random delay they introduce cause concern. This aspect of Ethernet's design makes it impossible to predict exactly how long it will take a system to transmit a frame. Furthermore, it is not even possible to determine an upper bound on this time. Technically, Ethernet is a *nondeterministic* protocol.

Token Ring removes that uncertainty by using a different scheme for sharing the network. Systems on Token Rings take turns, and a system only transmits when its turn arrives. Furthermore, a system may only transmit one frame during its turn.

To handoff from one system to the next, Token Ring uses a special frame called the *token*. As Figure 3.11 shows, this token represents permission to transmit, and systems pass the token to each other in the order that they are connected to the ring.

This order is also how actual data frames travel across the LAN. Figure 3.12 shows how the personal computer sends a frame to the minicomputer. Notice that the intervening Macintosh passes the frame along to its destination. Although the figure does not show it, the minicomputer also returns an indication of whether the frame arrived successfully. This indication passes back via the workstation.

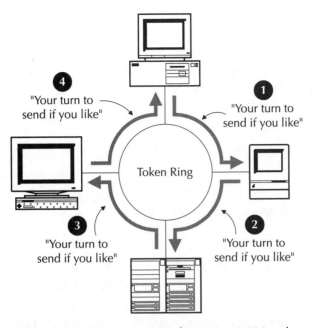

Figure 3.11   Systems on Token Ring LANs take turns.

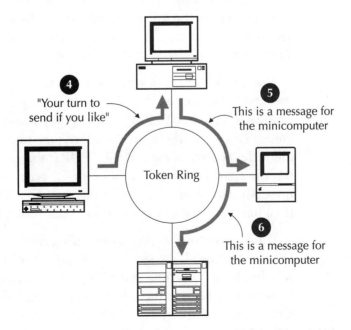

Figure 3.12   Sending data across a Token Ring LAN.

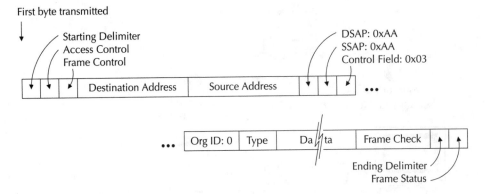

Figure 3.13 Token Ring frame format for TCP/IP.

Token Ring, which operates at speeds of 4 Mbit/s or 16 Mbit/s, supports several different frame formats. (Technically, Ethernet can support all of these frame formats; in practice, though, it rarely does.) For TCP/IP traffic, however, only one frame format is important. Figure 3.13 shows that format's structure. The fields at the beginning and end of the frame control the token. They allow stations to pass the token to each other. These fields may also indicate priority, and they can return an indication of successful (or unsuccessful) reception.

The destination and source service access points (DSAP and SSAP), as well as the control field, play a role in other frame formats. For TCP/IP frames, they always take the values shown in the figure. Similarly, the organization identifier is always zero. For TCP/IP frames, the *type* field has the same function as it does for Ethernet frames. It distinguishes different protocol types. Just as with Ethernet, IPv6 has the Token Ring type value of 0x86DD.

The amount of data in a Token Ring frame is not rigidly specified. Instead, the standards specify a minimum token rotation time. This time is the limit on how long a system must wait to receive the token. In practice, Token Rings limit frames to about 2,000 bytes on 4 Mbit/s LANs, and about 8,000 bytes on 16 Mbit/s rings.

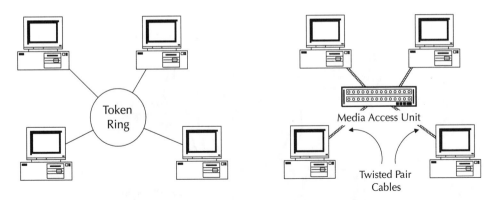

Figure 3.14 Token Ring acts like a ring but is physically configured as a star.

Token Ring shares one interesting characteristic with Ethernet: the way it looks in illustrations often differs from its real life appearance (Figure 3.14). Token Rings are not built by stringing cable from one computer to another, chaining those computers together in a ring. Instead, the ring itself is concentrated in a small system known as a Media Attachment Unit (MAU). Today, cables connecting computers to the MAU are usually twisted pair.

Fiber Distributed Data Interface

The Fiber Distributed Data Interface (FDDI) is one of the earliest examples of a high-speed local area network. From its inception, FDDI has operated at 100 Mbit/s. To achieve this speed, FDDI relies on fiber optics instead of electrical cables. In the years since FDDI was first released, engineers have devised ways to support those speeds on twisted pair cabling. Recognizing the convenience such cables offer users, FDDI has evolved a variation known as CDDI (the C is for copper). CDDI uses the same protocol as FDDI.

The FDDI protocol closely resembles Token Ring. FDDI networks are constructed from logical rings, and the systems on those rings pass a token to each other. A computer may transmit a frame only when it has the token.

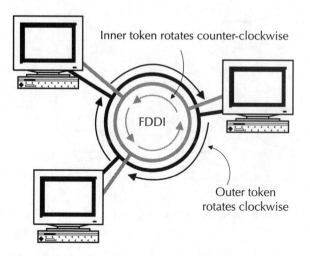

Inner token rotates counter-clockwise

FDDI

Outer token
rotates clockwise

Figure 3.15   FDDI uses two separate rings.

FDDI rings have the interesting property of being *self-healing*. This property allows the LAN to detect failures and reconfigure the ring to avoid them. FDDI can support this function because, in normal operation, the LAN actually consists of two separate rings. As Figure 3.15 illustrates, this topology requires two separate fibers between all systems. Tokens rotate in opposite directions on these rings. Normally, only one ring is used for traffic.

If one of the fibers fails, however, the second ring can save the day. Figure 3.16 shows a ring in which one connection has been severed. When this break occurs, the systems on either side of the damaged cable detect the failure and join the two separate rings. With those splices, the LAN creates a single ring that encompasses all of the systems. Traffic flow can continue around this new ring, and the LAN continues to function despite a major fault.

FDDI frames look much the same as Token Ring frames, though the terminology differs slightly. FDDI supports frames up to 4,500 bytes in length. The exact size that remains for TCP/IP varies, but there are always considerably more than 4,000 bytes available for an IP message.

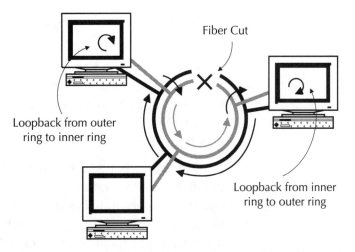

Figure 3.16 Automatically repairing an FDDI fiber cut.

Integrated Services Digital Networks

In recent years, a new technology has become an increasingly popular addition to regular telephone service. That technology is the Integrated Services Digital Network, or ISDN. ISDN replaces analog phone connections with high-speed, reliable, and flexible digital connections. Those digital connections make the telephone network much friendlier to data, including TCP/IP traffic. This section takes a quick look at the ISDN technology, and then considers the protocol that can control that technology—the point-to-point protocol, or PPP. PPP makes it possible for TCP/IP to exchange messages across an ISDN link.

Narrowband ISDN

ISDN means different things in different contexts. In some settings, it includes the revolutionary technologies that are proposed for the next generation of telephone networks, in particular Asynchronous Transfer Mode (ATM). This text uses a more restrictive meaning, in which ISDN is thought of as providing digital services on the existing telephone network. In some environments this technology is given the name *narrowband ISDN,* to distinguish it from the *broadband ISDN* of ATM.

The distinction is important, because narrowband ISDN involves no significant changes within today's network. For the most part, that network is already digital. Narrowband ISDN simply extends support for digital data all the way to the user's premises.

With narrowband ISDN, two different interfaces are possible. They are known as the Basic Rate Interface (BRI) and the Primary Rate Interface (PRI). BRI typically serves home users or small businesses, while the Primary Rate Interface supports the higher traffic volumes of larger organizations. Both types of interfaces consist of a number of logical links, known as channels. The BRI contains two B channels and one D channel, while the PRI contains 23 B channels (in the United States) or 30 B channels (Europe or Japan) plus one D channel. Figure 3.17 shows a common illustration of ISDN's interfaces. If each interface is viewed as a pipe with a specific capacity, the individual channels act like smaller pipes with smaller capacities.

For the most part, only B channels carry TCP/IP traffic, and each one provides 64 Kbit/s of bandwidth. A basic rate interface, therefore, can carry as much as 128 Kbit/s of data, and a PRI supports 1.472 Mbit/s or 1.92 Mbit/s.

Although the D channel can theoretically carry some data as well, in practical installations it is limited to control and management of the B channels. It is through the D channel that ISDN devices perform the equivalent of dialing the destination's phone number.

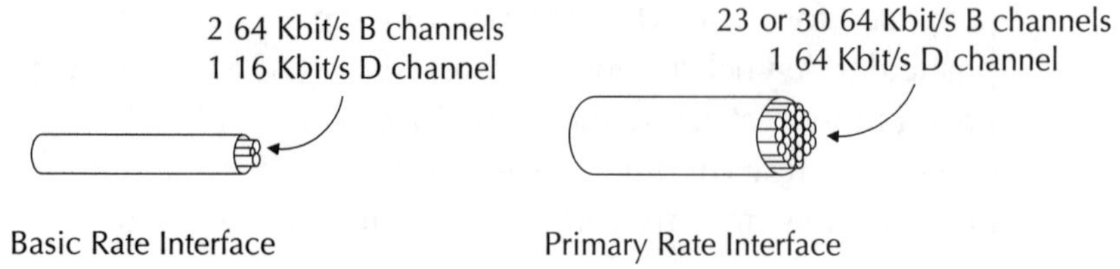

2 64 Kbit/s B channels
1 16 Kbit/s D channel

23 or 30 64 Kbit/s B channels
1 64 Kbit/s D channel

Basic Rate Interface

Primary Rate Interface

Figure 3.17 ISDN basic and primary rate interfaces.

The user's interface to ISDN depends on where that user is located. U.S. laws force local phone companies to allow maximum competition for telephone services, while most other countries grant phone companies tighter control of what connects to their networks.

In the United States, the typical ISDN BRI is a single twisted pair cable, like that in Figure 3.18. In ISDN terminology, this point is the U interface. The device that connects to the U interface acts somewhat like an old-fashioned modem. It provides signal conditioning, echo cancellation, and, possibly, time compression. ISDN labels such a device an NT1 (for network termination 1).

In many countries, the NT1 is provided by the phone company. In those installations, the customer's equipment attaches to the NT1 at the T interface.

The U and T interfaces are logically equivalent; the significant difference is that for BRI, the T interface consists of two twisted pairs of cable, one for each direction of data transfer. The U interface combines both directions on a single pair.

At either interface, the actual bytes that travel across the wires are complex shufflings of bytes from the B and D

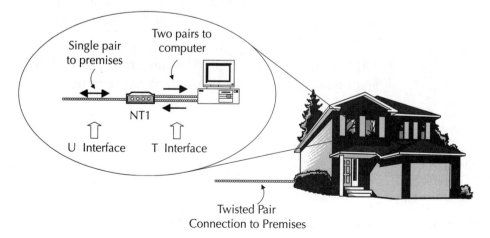

Figure 3.18   Interfacing to ISDN.

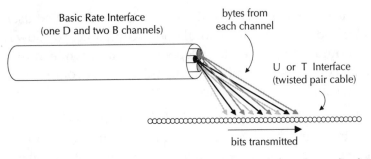

Figure 3.19 U and T interfaces interleave bytes from the logical channels.

channels, much like Figure 3.19 illustrates. ISDN interleaves the channels in this way to keep any one channel from significantly delaying the others. Looking at the link before this shuffling takes place, both B channels transfer data in well-defined frames. Figure 3.20 shows that such frames begin and end with flags. A flag has the binary value 01111110, and it serves to mark the beginning and end of the frame. The ISDN protocol takes special steps to prevent this pattern from appearing anywhere else in the frame, but those steps are transparent to the protocol's users.

The 16-bit address field, sometimes called a data link control identifier (DLCI) specifies the particular piece of equipment (at the other end of the link) to which the frame is destined. In many installations, there will only be one piece of equipment at each end of the link, so this field is not important.

The control field distinguishes from among several different types of frames. In the simplest configurations,

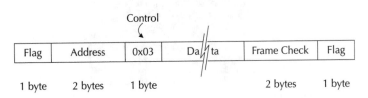

Figure 3.20 ISDN frame structure for connectionless transfer.

TCP/IP traffic travels in Unnumbered Information (UI) frames, in which the control field has a value of 3. The frame's information follows the control field. This is the data that ISDN transfers for its user protocols.

Preceding the closing flag is a 16-bit frame check sequence (FCS). Like the Ethernet field of the same name, these 16 bits provide an error-detecting capability. The sender, before transmitting a frame, calculates the FCS using the frame's contents. The receiver can perform the same calculation before it accepts a frame, rejecting the frame as an error if the results do not match.

Like IP datagrams, UI frames are connectionless messages. ISDN protocols do not guarantee that they reach their destination without error. If a UI frame encounters an error crossing the link, the ISDN protocols take no steps to retransmit it. In most cases, this is not a significant problem, as the TCP/IP protocols themselves can recover from the error. Sometimes, however, this behavior is not acceptable. If the link employs data compression, for example, it is crucial that frames not be lost. In such an environment, the two systems can use a reliable delivery service across the ISDN link.

When they use a reliable service, the two systems number each frame they transmit. As a numbered frame arrives, the receiver acknowledges its reception. Figure 3.21 illustrates this behavior. If the sender fails to get an acknowledgment soon enough, it assumes that the frame was lost or corrupted in transit. In that case, the sender transmits the frame again. It repeats this process as often as needed to successfully transfer the frame across the link.

To provide this reliable service, the ISDN protocol (known by its acronym LAPD) establishes a connection between the two stations. Establishing and maintaining connections requires several different frame types, and Figure 3.22 shows how the control field varies among those frames. Note that the control field can be either one

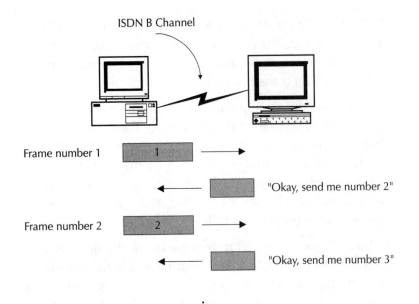

Figure 3.21 ISDN connection-oriented transfer numbers each frame.

or two bytes in size. The two least significant bits of the first byte (which are the first two bits to be transmitted) determine the specific format of the control field for a particular frame.

Table 3.2 lists the different frame types. It shows how the first byte of the control field identifies among them. The table shows the least significant bit of that byte first, just as in Figure 3.22.

To initiate a connection, the systems exchange SABME and UA frames. (SABME stands for Set Asynchronous Balanced Mode Extended, and UA is short for Unnumbered Acknowledgment.) After this exchange, the data itself travels in Information or I frames. As Figure 3.22 shows, I frames include two sequence numbers. The seven bits labeled N(S) number the current frame, while the N(R) value acknowledges frames that the system has successfully received. As Figure 3.21 hints, the N(R) value speci-

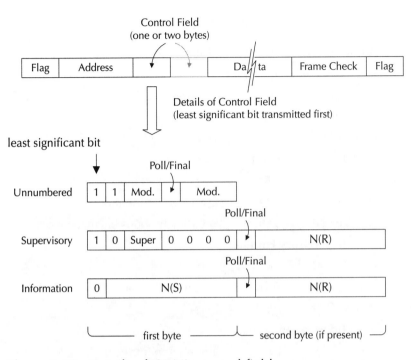

Figure 3.22 Details of ISDN's control field.

fies the number of the next frame the sender expects rather than the number of the last frame it received. It implicitly acknowledges all frames with lesser numbers.

There is an obvious problem with the N(S) and N(R) values. They are only seven bits each, but ISDN links can certainly transfer more than 128 separate information frames. To accommodate this behavior, both of these numbers "wrap around" to zero once they reach 127. Frames number 128 and 129, for example, are given N(S) values of 0 and 1, respectively. Figure 3.23 illustrates this behavior.

By wrapping the sequence numbers around, the ISDN protocols introduce another problem. How does a system determine whether an N(S) value of zero represents frame number 0, 128, 256, 384, or any other multiple of 128? There is an intuitive answer to that question, though. The system can tell from the context. If the previous frame was

Table 3.2 ISDN Control Field Values

Control Field	Frame	Usage
Unnumbered Format		
1100P000	UI	Unnumbered information
1100P010	DISC	Disconnect
1100F110	UA	Unnumbered acknowledgment
1110F001	FRMR	Frame reject
1111F000	DM	Disconnected mode
1111x101	XID	Exchange information
1111P110	SABME	Set asynchronous balanced mode
Supervisory Format		
10000000	RR	Receiver ready
10100000	RNR	Receiver not ready
10010000	REJ	Reject
Information Format		
0xxxxxxxx	I	Information transfer

frame number 127, then the zero almost certainly represents frame number 128. Similarly, if a recent frame was definitely number 257, then zero most likely is frame number 256. To make sure that this context always pro-

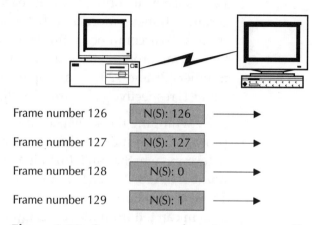

Frame number 126	N(S): 126
Frame number 127	N(S): 127
Frame number 128	N(S): 0
Frame number 129	N(S): 1

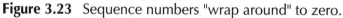

Figure 3.23 Sequence numbers "wrap around" to zero.

vides the correct interpretation, systems follow a simple rule. They never allow more than 64 frames to be outstanding without an acknowledgment.

Two other ISDN frame types are Receiver Ready (RR) and Receiver Not Ready (RNR) frames. These two frames serve a couple of purposes. First, they let a system acknowledge received frames without actually transmitting information frames themselves. Since they are supervisory frames, each of these frames includes an N(R) value in its control field. They carry no information, though, so they do not have N(S) values.

The second purpose of RR and RNR frames is flow control. When a system sends an RNR frame, it is telling its peer that it cannot accept any more I frames. It asks the peer to cease sending such frames, at least temporarily. When the system is once again able to accept information, it indicates that with an RR frame.

Another important frame type is the Disconnect, or DISC, frame. This frame terminates the connection. Like a SABME, it is acknowledged with a UA response.

The Point-to-Point Protocol

When an ISDN link is part of a TCP/IP network, the link will be governed by the Point-to-Point Protocol (PPP). PPP actually supports many other types of links, including asynchronous connections using standard dialup modems, as well as high-speed leased lines. This section focuses on PPP's operation over ISDN, though its operation remains much the same for other link types.

In addition to supporting just about any type of point-to-point link, PPP also works with many protocol suites, not just TCP/IP. To achieve this flexibility, PPP actually includes several different "mini-protocols." Those protocols provide three major functions, listed in Table 3.3. In the case of ISDN links, most of the first function is already provided. ISDN's LAPD protocol defines the beginning

Table 3.3 Major Functions of PPP

- frame encapsulation and protocol identification
- coordination of overall link operation
- coordination of the various protocols that use the link

and ending of each frame and, if necessary, a protocol to transfer those frames reliably. The only thing missing from LAPD is protocol identification. Unlike Ethernet, LAPD provides no intrinsic way to distinguish TCP/IP messages from, for example, IPX traffic.

PPP also uses several of its own protocols on the link. To distinguish all of these different protocols, PPP defines a 16-bit protocol field. This field is the first two data bytes of any frame. On ISDN links, it follows the address and control fields. Figure 3.24 shows a PPP frame carried within an ISDN LAPD frame. The LAPD fields are shown in gray.

The protocol field has a particular format. All values must have an even most significant byte and an odd least significant byte. Although the standards do not yet allow it, this structure permits the field to expand once there are too many protocols for 16 bits. If more bits are needed in the future, they will continue the same pattern. All bytes except the least significant will be even, and the least significant will be odd. Receivers will identify the end of the protocol field by looking for an odd byte.

The protocol field has many defined values; Table 3.4 lists some of the most common, though many more have been standardized. These values fall into four groups. The first group, with values ranging from 0x0001 to 0x3EFF,

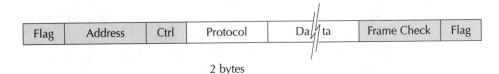

2 bytes

Figure 3.24 Format of a PPP frame within an ISDN LAPD frame.

Table 3.4 PPP Protocol Numbers

0x0021	IPv4
0x0023	ISO Network Protocol
0x0027	DECnet Phase IV
0x0029	AppleTalk
0x002B	Novell IPX
0x4003	Cellular Data Network Registration
0x8021	IPv4 Network Control Protocol
0x8023	ISO Network Layer Control Protocol
0x8027	DECnet Phase IV Network Control Protocol
0x902B	IPX Network Control Protocol
0xC021	Link Control Protocol
0xC023	Password Authentication Protocol
0xC025	Link Quality Report
0xC223	Challenge Handshake Authentication Protocol

Protocol Field Compression

The particular format of the protocol field (even most significant byte and odd least significant byte) has inherent support for single byte values. They simply need to have an odd value. This abbreviation is not standard for PPP, but the two stations can negotiate to use it. Of course, this option only applies to protocols with protocol field values less than 256.

identify network protocols such as IP. The second group, 0x4001 to 0x7EFF are set aside for protocols with low volume traffic. The range from 0x8001 to 0xBEFF is reserved for special PPP protocols that control network protocols. These are the network control protocols, or NCPs. There is usually a one-to-one correspondence between a network protocol and network control protocol. The final range of protocol fields are for link-level control protocols. Like the NCPs, these protocols are usually specific to PPP. Instead of coordinating a network protocol, however, LCPs coordinate the link.

Multilink Protocol

So far, the PPP discussion has focused on a single link. ISDN, however, has the potential to support multiple links. Even the basic rate interface includes two separate B channels. PPP's multilink protocol allows two stations to connect using both of these channels simultaneously. It treats the combined links as a single logical link. The logical link, known as a *bundle*, provides a bandwidth equal to the sum of all bandwidth available from the individual physical links. In the case of BRI, the bundle makes 128 Kbit/s of bandwidth available.

The Multilink Protocol (MP) acts as a separate protocol for each of the physical links. The value for its protocol field is 0x003D. Each physical link can negotiate protocol field compression to reduce this to a single byte. MP has its own protocol header, which can take two forms. Figure 3.25 shows both formats.

The first form in the figure is for long sequence numbers; it has 24-bit sequence numbers. The second form employs 12-bit sequence numbers. These numbers define the relative order of frames among the multiple links. They tell the receiver how to reconstruct the original order in which the various frames belong. The size of the sequence number places a limit on how skewed the multiple links can become. If the systems choose 12-bit sequence numbers, they must be confident that the skew between the links will not approach 2048 (2^{11}) frames.

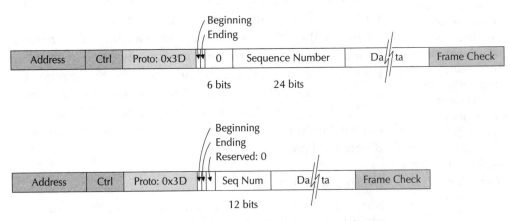

Figure 3.25 Alternate forms for PPP multilink protocol frames.

Both formats include a beginning and ending fragment indication. These flags allow a sender to split a large frame into several smaller pieces. Senders may do this because of frame size restrictions on individual links. A more likely use, though, is to transmit pieces of a large frame simultaneously, one piece for each link in the bundle. This technique can reduce the delay of transferring the large frame to the recipient.

The first fragment of the original frame has the beginning bit set, while the last fragment has the ending bit set. If the original frame is not fragmented at all, the sender sets both bits.

Link Control Protocol

PPP's link control protocol (LCP) establishes and maintains each point-to-point link. It has three major tasks. First, it sets up the link in an orderly manner. As part of that process, it performs its second function; it negotiates configuration for the link's operation. Finally, once the conversation is complete, PPP ensures that the termination of the link is graceful.

Authentication Protocols

Since PPP frequently operates over dialup links (either ISDN or analog lines with modems), it is important that systems verify each other's identity. PPP defines two separate protocols to provide this authentication.

The simplest authentication protocol is the password authentication protocol, or PAP. Using PAP, one system can send identification (often a username) and a password to the other. The peer validates the password and either accepts or rejects the connection. For those sites with stringent security requirements, this approach is usually too weak. In particular, any third party that monitors the link can discover passwords. Despite this weakness, PAP may offer sufficient security for some installations.

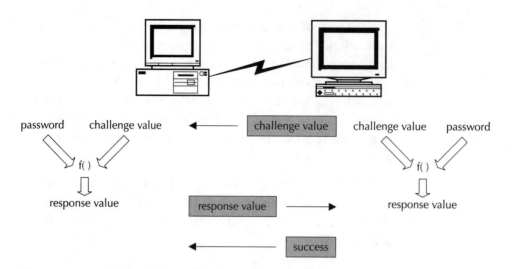

Figure 3.26 Challenge handshake authentication protocol.

The challenge handshake authentication protocol (CHAP) provides stronger security than PAP. A quick look at how CHAP is used shows why. Figure 3.26 illustrates a CHAP exchange between a personal computer and a workstation. The exchange begins when the workstation sends a challenge to the PC. This message includes a challenge value, typically an arbitrary sequence of bytes. The PC receives the challenge and combines the challenge value with a secret password. It then performs a series of mathematical operations on the combined data. (The most common algorithm is MD5, discussed further on page 121.) Finally, the PC returns the result of this calculation to the workstation. Since the workstation also knows the secret password, it can determine whether the result is correct.

Note that CHAP does not transmit the password itself across the link, which means that an eavesdropper cannot learn the password. An eavesdropper could learn the correct response to a particular challenge value but, presumably, the challenger is careful to use different challenge values each time it issues a challenge.

Network Control Protocols

Just as LCP coordinates the operation of a link, PPP has several network control protocols (NCPs) to coordinate the operation of various network protocols over that link. As of this writing, no NCP for IPv6 has been proposed. When one is defined, it will likely resemble that for IPv4. IPv4's network control protocol allows the two systems to negotiate particular compression protocols, and it lets a system ask its peer for an IPv4 address.

Putting Everything Together

To summarize the operation of PPP across an ISDN link, it is worthwhile to look at how all the pieces fit together. To see the big picture, consider the simple state diagram of Figure 3.27. It shows the major phases though which a PPP link can pass.

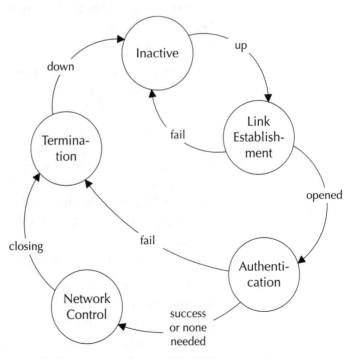

Figure 3.27 Major phases of a PPP connection.

A point-to-point link starts out in the inactive phase. In that phase, the link just waits for something to happen. For ISDN links, one system is waiting for the phone to ring, while the other is waiting for its user to initiate the call. Whichever event occurs, the link moves to the establishment state.

Link establishment is the domain of the link control protocol. LCP exchanges its frames to set up and configure the link. Once the link is configured, it moves to the next phase. If, as part of configuration, the systems require authentication, then the next phase is the authentication phase. Otherwise, the link skips right to the network control phase. Should the two systems fail to agree on a configuration, the link returns to the inactive phase.

The authentication phase allows the systems on the link to verify each other's identity. LCP negotiation determines the particular authentication algorithm. If authentication fails, the link moves to the termination phase. Otherwise, the link proceeds to the network control phase.

The network control phase belongs to network layer control protocols (NCPs). For each network protocol that the two systems wish to use, they must invoke the appropriate NCP to prepare the link for that protocol. Each NCP negotiates and configures independently of the others. Once the configuration is complete, the link is ready to transfer network level packets. This phase continues until one or both parties wishes to close the link, the network administrator takes action, the link remains idle for a specified time, or the link fails. When any such event takes place, PPP moves to the termination phase.

The termination phase concludes any activity on a link. The two systems perform any necessary last-minute negotiations and command the link to take an appropriate action (such as hanging up the phone). Once the termination phase is complete, the link returns to the inactive phase.

High-Speed Wide Area Networks

So far, this chapter has discussed two important network technologies. Ethernet and other local area networks form high-speed connections within a small geographic area, and ISDN can provide moderate speed links across greater distances. High-speed wide area networks (WANs) offer more ambitious services than any of the previously discussed technologies. They provide high-speed services across great distances.

Two important network technologies currently support high-speed wide area networks. They are frame relay and asynchronous transfer mode (ATM). Frame relay is the more mature technology; it is available now in most advanced regions of the world. ATM, on the other hand, is still somewhat experimental, but because it provides much more capacity than frame relay, it is expected to be the primary WAN technology of the future.

Both frame relay and ATM have a great deal in common. Like most WAN technologies, they provide a service that, at least superficially, looks much like that of a local area network. Just like a LAN, many systems can connect to the WAN, and they can all communicate with each other. There is a difference, though, between appearance and reality. On a LAN, computers really do communicate directly with each other. WANs, however, do not directly connect every system to each other. Instead, each system connects directly to a network switch. The network switches are, in turn, connected directly and indirectly to other switches. Computers send frames directly to their network switch, which passes it to another switch, and so on, until the frame reaches its destination.

This description of network switches makes them sound a lot like IP routers. (See page 18.) Indeed, switches and routers perform a similar role. In theory, there is a difference between the two. By operating at the link level,

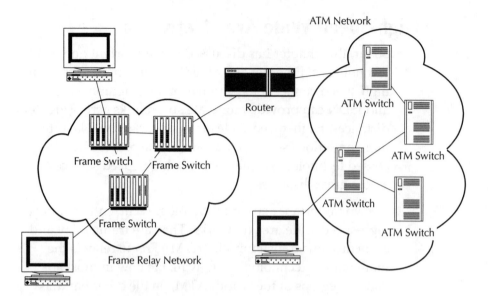

Figure 3.28   Wide area networks built from switches.

switches are normally dedicated to a specific network technology. Figure 3.28 highlights this distinction by distinguishing frame relay switches from ATM switches. Routers, on the other hand, can connect virtually any network technology to any other. They operate at the internetwork layer. As the figure shows, routers can, in turn, rely on switches to transfer their messages.

The distinction between switches and routers makes a nice theory, and it is a distinction that this text uses. In reality, though, some vendors are rapidly moving toward incorporating both functions in the same product. Many of today's high-end routers, for example, can also function as ATM switches.

Frame Relay

Frame relay was originally conceived as a simple upgrade to an earlier WAN technology—X.25 packet switching. Frame relay's main goal was to streamline X.25, making it efficient enough to support higher speeds. Frame relay's designers wanted a protocol so simple that they could implement it almost entirely in hardware. To achieve this result, they eliminated nearly all the processing required in network switches, including error recovery and sophisticated flow control. (As Chapter 7 details, those functions are normally provided by a transport layer protocol anyway, so there is no great loss in eliminating them from the WAN.) Networks built from frame relay are usually limited only by the bandwidth of the links connecting the switches.

At the interface between a host or router and a frame relay switch, the protocol is quite simple. In fact, it is the same protocol already described for ISDN, LAPD. Frame relay, however, does not normally support LAPD's reliable service. The only frame types it typically exchanges are unnumbered information (UI) frames. Figure 3.29 shows an example UI frame.

The only real difference between LAPD for frame relay and LAPD for ISDN is the address field. For ISDN links, this field had little meaning. ISDN links are point-to-point links; when one system sends a frame, it always goes to the single system at the other end of the link. Frame relay, on the other hand, is truly a network. One system can ultimately send to many other systems through the single link to the network switch. In this environment, there must be some way to indicate the destination for a frame. The address field serves this purpose.

Frame relay uses only 10 bits of the address field to indicate destinations. These 10 bits form the data link control identifier (DLCI). Specific DLCI identifiers are a local matter between the host or router and its initial network

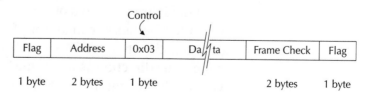

Figure 3.29 Frame relay's LAPD frame format.

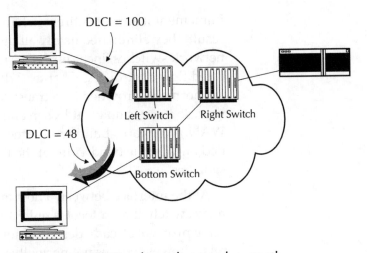

Figure 3.30 DLCI values change along path.

switch. As Figure 3.30 shows, a path between two systems may use different DLCI values at all intermediate links.

The frame enters the network from the top workstation with a DLCI value of 100. That DLCI value is used by the workstation and the left switch to identify the path. When the left switch forwards the frame to the bottom switch, however, it may replace the DLCI field with a new value. The bottom switch can do the same thing; in the figure, it sets the DLCI value to 48. All of these different DLCI values refer to the same path between the two workstations. Each of the two systems along the path agree on its own independent DLCI value to identify that path.

Frame relay appropriates the remaining six bits of the address field for other purposes. Two of the extra bits are available to extend the size of the address field beyond two bytes. For now, they are always set to the values indicated in Figure 3.31. Two other bits can indicate when the network experiences congestion. The forward explicit congestion notification (FECN) is set when there is congestion in the same direction as the frame itself, while the backward explicit congestion notification (BECN) indicates that congestion exists in the reverse direction of the frame.

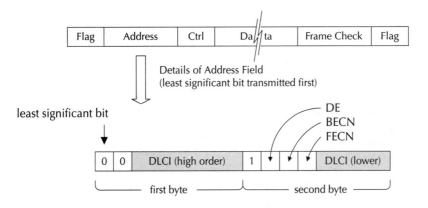

Figure 3.31 Details of frame relay address field.

Systems are asked to take that congestion into account if they reply to the frame.

One additional bit of the frame relay address field is the discard eligibility (DE) bit. Systems may set this bit on frames that have lower priority than others. Should a frame relay switch need to discard frames (perhaps because of congestion), it will first seek frames with DE set. Not only can users set discard eligibility to indicate lower priority traffic, they can also use the field as part of their contract with a frame relay provider. Most frame relay services are sold on the basis of a committed information rate (CIR). The CIR specifies the amount of bandwidth that the provider is willing to ensure will be available to the user. Naturally, it cannot be any greater than the link speed between the user and the network switch.

In most cases, the CIR is actually less than the link speed. This approach minimizes the cost of the service. It does result in excess capability on that link, though. If, for example, a user purchases 64 Kbit/s of CIR and connects to the network with a 256 Kbit/s link, there are 192 Kbit/s of excess bandwidth available from the link. Most providers allow their customers to use this extra capacity, as long as it does not interfere with the rest of the network.

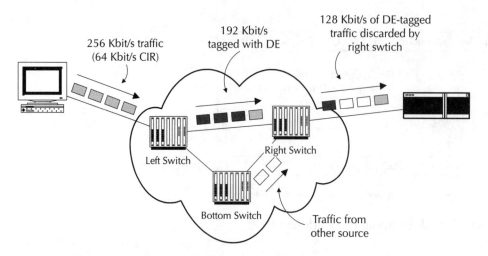

Figure 3.32 Using discard eligibility to eliminate excess traffic.

In Figure 3.32, the workstation sends 256 Kbit/s worth of traffic across a link for which it only has a CIR of 64 Kbit/s. The left switch can accept the extra traffic, so it does. The switch sets the discard eligibility bit on the excess, however. When this traffic reaches the right switch, it runs into a problem. That switch is also processing traffic from another source, and it cannot keep up with both traffic demands. Something has to go, and the prime candidates are those frames with DE set. The right switch discards as many as it needs. As a result, only 128 Kbit/s of the workstation's 256 Kbit/s make it through the frame relay network to the router.

Even though frame relay relies on the same LAPD protocol as ISDN, frame relay networks are not normally used in a point-to-point mode. Frame relay systems do not usually employ PPP to encapsulate their messages inside of frames[2]. PPP's support for multiple protocol suites is very valuable, though, and frame relay supports an equivalent functionality.

---

[2] Such encapsulation is possible, however. There are standards that specify how to use PPP on frame relay links. So far, though, this method has not proven very popular.

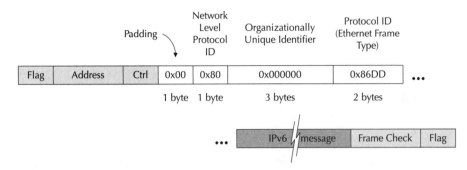

Figure 3.33 Carrying IPv6 messages within frame relay frames.

Instead of the PPP protocol, frame relay relies on its own method of identifying and encapsulating upper layer protocols. Figure 3.33 shows how frame relay encapsulates an IPv6 message. The extra fields at the front of the message indicate the particular network protocol. Notice that the two bytes that immediately precede the IPv6 message have the same value as IPv6's Ethernet's *frame type*. This choice is not an accident. Whenever any network protocol receives an Ethernet frame type value, it automatically gets a frame relay protocol identifier.

Asynchronous Transfer Mode

Frame relay and asynchronous transfer mode (ATM) have very different origins. Frame relay is an effort to get the highest performance possible from 1980s technology. Its designers focused on existing technology (X.25 packet switching), simplifying it by eliminating all nonessential functionality.

In contrast, ATM is a complete redesign of the world's telecommunications infrastructure. The most revolutionary aspect of that redesign is integrated support for all kinds of traffic: voice, video, and data.

Relaying Cells

To integrate these diverse services in a single technology, ATM relies on a new approach to transferring information.

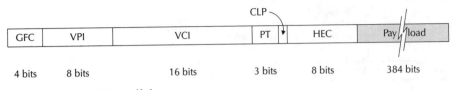

GFC	VPI	VCI	PT		HEC	Pay//load
4 bits	8 bits	16 bits	3 bits		8 bits	384 bits

Figure 3.34 ATM cell format.

That approach is *cell relaying*. It gets its name from the basic unit of transfer—the *cell*. Despite the emphasis, cells are not really all that different from frames. Cells are small—in ATM's case, 53 bytes, and they are always that exact size. Otherwise, cells are just a unit of information that networks transfer.

Figure 3.34 shows the format of an ATM cell. It consists of a 5-byte header and 48 bytes of payload. Though it takes a few protocol layers to get there, this payload field eventually carries TCP/IP messages.

The important fields in the ATM header are the virtual path and virtual channel identifiers. Together, these two fields identify a particular connection. ATM divides the connection identifier into two parts to aid routing. The virtual path identifier (VPI) defines a destination system, while the virtual channel identifier (VCI) distinguishes specific circuits to that system. The VPI/VCI value has only local significance, just like frame relay's DLCI. Figure 3.35 shows how switches can modify the cell's VPI/VCI value as it travels through the ATM network.

Another interesting field in the ATM header is the *header error control* (HEC). This field provides error detection for the header only; it does not protect the payload. HEC does offer something unusual, though. Not only can it detect header errors, it can also correct any single-bit error in the header.

A final field that is important to TCP/IP is the *payload type* field. ATM gives its users control over this field. To support IP traffic, it marks the end of an IP message spanning multiple cells. (See page 87.)

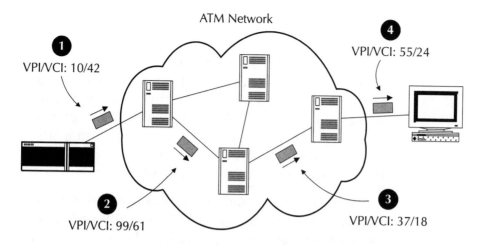

ATM Network

VPI/VCI: 10/42

VPI/VCI: 55/24

VPI/VCI: 99/61

VPI/VCI: 37/18

Figure 3.35 A cell's VPI/VCI value changes as it travels through the network.

Connection-Oriented Communications

As the VPI/VCI pair implies, ATM is a connection-oriented service. Before two systems can communicate, they must establish a connection. When a system wants to initiate communication, it asks its switch to establish the connection. If successful, the switch will return a VPI/VCI value for the system to use for that connection's traffic.

While setting up connections, systems refer to each other with a 20-byte address called a network service access point (NSAP). Once the connection is established, though, the VPI/VCI values are sufficient to identify the destination.

ATM also supports permanent connections, which a network administrator sets up in advance. There is no need for systems to go through the connection setup procedure; they can simply begin using the assigned VPI/VCI values.

In addition to standard point-to-point connections, ATM supports point-to-multipoint connections. When a sender transmits a cells for those connections, the network delivers a copy of that cell to all of the connection's destinations.

Adaptation Layers

Cells are efficient units of data for ATM switches, but they are not particularly convenient for the protocols that use ATM networks. These protocols rarely have messages that fit exactly in the cells' 48-byte payload. To accommodate upper-level protocols, ATM relies on an ATM adaptation layer (AAL). Several different AALs exist; each supports particular services that an ATM network may provide. In TCP/IP's case, the AAL of choice is AAL5.

AAL5 starts with a frame of any size and breaks it into pieces small enough to fit into ATM cells. Since cells must contain exactly 48 bytes of payload, AAL5 may also pad a frame so that its size is an exact multiple of 48 bytes. The complete AAL5 frame looks like Figure 3.36. Notice that it differs from most other protocols; it places its own information at the end of the frame, rather than the beginning. As this position implies, the AAL5 information is called a *trailer* rather than a header.

The AAL5 trailer contains a *user-to-user* (UU) field, which TCP/IP ignores, and a *common part indicator* (CPI)

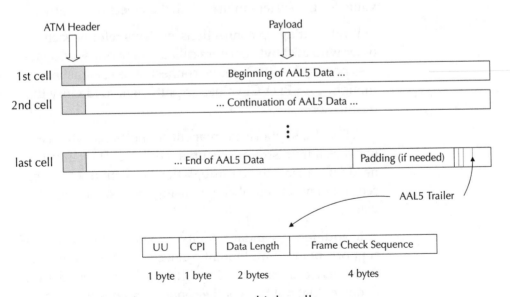

Figure 3.36 AAL5 frames may span multiple cells.

that aligns the trailer to 64 bits. Presently, the CPI is always set to zero. The first useful field is the length field, which contains the length of the frame in bytes. This length does not include the AAL5 trailer or any added padding. The final four bytes contain a frame check sequence for detecting transmission errors.

The AAL5 frame format does not, by itself, solve the problem of fitting messages into the payload area of ATM cells. Here is where the payload type field of the ATM header plays a role. AAL5 starts with a whole frame and breaks it into 48-byte pieces. Each piece goes into its own cell, and, except for the final one, each has the last bit of this field clear. The final cell sets this bit. The payload type value thus indicates the end of a frame.

Encapsulating Protocols

The ATM adaptation layer provides a way to fit frames into ATM's cells, but it does not automatically identify which protocol suite has generated the frames. A frame could be carrying a TCP/IP message, but it could also contain an IPX or ISO message.

Identifying different protocol suites requires another protocol layer. Figure 3.37 shows what the additional layer does to each frame. This format, known as LLC/SNAP encapsulation[3], is identical to that used on Token Ring and FDDI LANs. As in that case, the last two bytes of the 8-byte header distinguish different protocols.

ATM as a Local Area Network

Even though ATM began as a wide area network technology, it has promise as a local area network as well. For many users, ATM's 155 Mbit/s bandwidth is an attractive improvement over Ethernet or Token Ring. Furthermore,

---

[3] The first three bytes are controlled by the IEEE's logical link control (LLC) protocol, and the remaining five specify a subnetwork access protocol (SNAP).

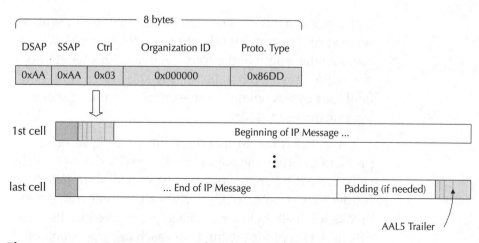

Figure 3.37 LLC/SNAP encapsulation for ATM.

ATM is not limited to 155 Mbit/s. The ATM standards also define a data rate of 622 Mbit/s. (Indeed, lower-speed interfaces of 51 Mbit/s and 25 Mbit/s are also available, primarily to operate over lower-quality twisted pair cables. As yet, neither of these lower rates has received much vendor support.)

Operating ATM as a local area network does not seem too unusual when ATM switches are compared to Ethernet switches. Figure 3.38 makes the comparison explicit. Both provide similar services in similar configurations; only their low-level interfaces differ. In addition to the similar services, ATM also has a well-defined protocol for connecting switches to a wide area network. This facility makes it easy for users to extend a LAN to distant sites.

LAN Emulation

ATM may be attractive as a local area network, but it does suffer some shortcomings when compared to traditional LANs like Ethernet and Token Ring. The first shortcoming is its communication service. ATM is connection-oriented, while (at least for TCP/IP) traditional LANs are connectionless. Connections are not necessarily bad, but most TCP/IP software implementations are designed for con-

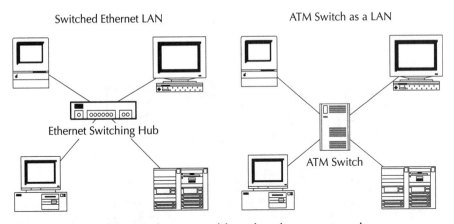

Figure 3.38 ATM switch can act like a local area network.

nectionless LANs. Changing those implementations to use a connection-oriented service is a major logistical problem.

Another shortcoming facing ATM is its lack of support for true broadcasts and multicasts. ATM does have point-to-multipoint connections, but those are not nearly as convenient as broadcast services on a traditional LAN. In particular, users must explicitly specify all destinations for a multipoint connection during its setup. Destinations cannot easily be added or subtracted from the connection during its lifetime.

To overcome these shortcomings, ATM's designers have developed a service known as LAN emulation (LANE). LANE defines a way for ATM networks to provide the same services as traditional LANs, including connectionless and broadcast delivery. LAN emulation also relies on normal LAN addresses to identify stations rather than 20-byte ATM NSAPs. In theory, network layer protocols like IP use emulated LANs exactly as they do traditional LANs.

To support broadcast delivery, LANE relies on a broadcast server. When any system on the network (such as the Mac in Figure 3.39) needs to transmit a broadcast frame, that system sends the frame to the broadcast server (step 1). The server can then distribute the frame to all other stations on

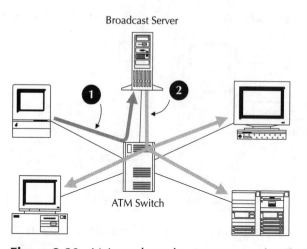

Figure 3.39   Using a broadcast server to distribute broadcast frames.

the emulated LAN (step 2). If point-to-multipoint connections are available, the server can use them; otherwise, it sends a separate copy to each station using traditional, point-to-point connections.

If the ATM LAN supports point-to-multipoint connections, it might seem like the broadcast server is unnecessary. The original sender should be able to broadcast the frame itself. While this approach might seem reasonable in theory, it turns out to be impractical. Point-to-multipoint ATM connections are expensive. If source systems used them for broadcast delivery, then every system on the LAN would need a point-to-multipoint connection to every other system. The broadcast server approach, on the other hand, requires only a single point-to-multipoint connection. In real world ATM LANs, the cost savings justify the inefficiencies of using the server.

Connectionless delivery is the second function of LAN emulation. Since network protocols "believe" that they are using a LAN, they will not be prepared to set up ATM connections. Instead, LANE does that for them. When the network protocol must transmit a frame, it hands it to the

LANE software. This software, which the standards call a LAN emulation client (LEC), examines the destination LAN address. If a connection to that destination already exists, the frame is transmitted on that connection.

If a LEC does not have a connection on which to deliver a frame, it takes two steps in parallel. First, it sends a request to the LAN emulation server (LES). This request identifies the destination LAN address and asks for an ATM NSAP that corresponds to it. In most cases, the LES actually forwards the request to the destination system, which replies back to the LES. The LES then forwards the reply to the station that made the original request. Knowing the destination NSAP, the original LEC can establish an ATM connection. Figure 3.40 shows these steps on a sample ATM LAN.

Of course, all these message exchanges can take some time, and it is not desirable to delay the original frame while these exchanges take place. To avoid this delay, the LEC can take an additional step in parallel to this address resolution and connection setup. It can send the frame to the broadcast server for distribution to all stations.

As Figure 3.41 illustrates, this system is the same machine that forwards broadcasts. Because of its dual role,

1. PC requests NSAP of workstation.
2. LES forwards request to workstation.
3. Workstation replies to LES.
4. LES forwards reply to PC.
5. PC requests connection to workstation.
6. Switch acknowledges connection establishment.

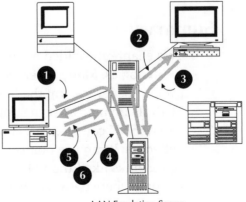

LAN Emulation Server

Figure 3.40   Setting up a LAN emulation connection.

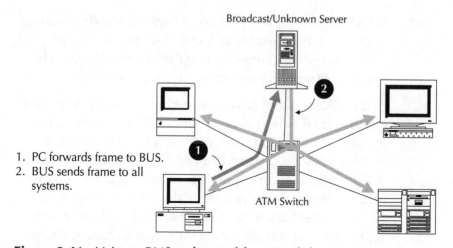

1. PC forwards frame to BUS.
2. BUS sends frame to all systems.

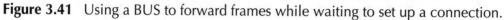

Figure 3.41 Using a BUS to forward frames while waiting to set up a connection.

the system's full name is the broadcast/unknown server (BUS). As the figure also hints, the BUS need not be the same system as the LAN emulation server.

This approach—sending frames with unknown destinations as if they were broadcast—works even though the frame is not a broadcast frame. Stations that receive traffic from the broadcast server must check the destination LAN address in each frame; if the destination is not a broadcast or multicast, and if it is not their own address, they simply discard the frame.

Summary

This chapter provided a quick look at a few key network technologies. Many other technologies are available, but even these few hint at the flexibility of TCP/IP. The TCP/IP architecture can support fast LANs, moderate-speed ISDN connections, and very high-speed wide area networks. It can use point-to-point links like ISDN, multi-access links like Ethernet, and switch-based networks that lie somewhere between these two. By accommodating new network technologies as they develop, TCP/IP ensures that it will not become obsolete.

4

Internet Protocol Version 6

Computer networks are built from a great variety of network technologies. The Internet itself includes everything from dialup phone connections to high-speed asynchronous transfer mode circuits. Such diversity naturally presents many challenges to network engineers, but ultimately it is the key to any network's success. Networks exist for communications; the more they communicate, the more value they provide.

To its credit, the TCP/IP architecture supports and encourages connection of nearly every network technology available. For TCP/IP networks, the Internet Protocol (IP) provides a common thread. IP unites disparate network technologies in a unified, global internetwork.

The Role of IP

The best indication of IP's importance is its name. IP is *the* Internet Protocol. It is the protocol that makes possible interconnected networks such as the Internet. Such networks require some independence from specific network technologies. The whole world cannot migrate to asynchronous transfer mode (for example) overnight. To provide that independence, IP isolates the transport and

For IPv4 Veterans: Changes in IPv6

The rest of this chapter does not assume that its readers have any knowledge of IP version 4, the classic IP. Those readers who have worked with IPv4 might find the following list helpful. It highlights the differences between IPv4 and IPv6. Readers unfamiliar with IPv4 should feel free to skip this box.

Streamlined Header Format

The IPv6 header is optimized for efficient processing. Superfluous fields have been eliminated, and all multi-byte fields align on their natural boundaries. (Page 97)

Flow Label

The header now includes a flow label. Flow values may be assigned to particular streams of traffic with special quality-of-service requirements. (Page 99)

128-bit Network Addresses

As expected, IPv6 now supports 128-bit network addresses. (Page 106)

Elimination of Header Checksum

IPv6 no longer includes a checksum of its own header.

Fragmentation Only by Source Host

Intermediate routers can no longer fragment a datagram. Only the sending host can create fragments. (Page 117)

Extension Headers

IPv6 is much more flexible in its support of options. Options appear in extension headers that follow the IP header in the datagram. (Page 107)

Built-in Security

IPv6 requires support for both authentication and confidentiality. (Page 120)

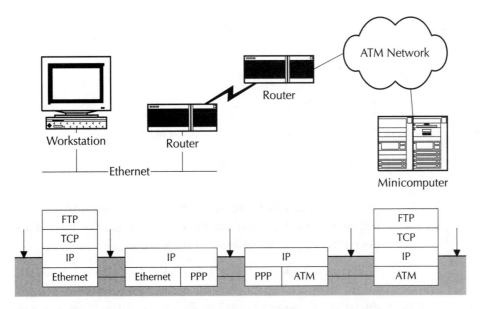

Figure 4.1 IP isolates upper layers from specific network technologies.

application protocols from the messy details of each network. Those protocols simply hand data to IP, and IP takes care of transferring the data across real networks.

Figure 4.1 illustrates this operation by showing the protocol layers involved in a communication exchange. IP resides above each particular network, whether that network is Ethernet, ATM, or a point-to-point link. IP isolates the specifics of each network so that the transport (TCP in the figure) and application (FTP) protocols can ignore them.

Figure 4.1 highlights another major role for the Internetwork Protocol. Notice how every system in the figure relies on IP. All the systems shown—the workstation, minicomputer, and the routers—have a role in forwarding packets between the workstation and the minicomputer. IP is the protocol charged with packet forwarding.

In general, a packet's destination may be many networks away from its source. (In the figure, three different networks separate the workstation from the minicom-

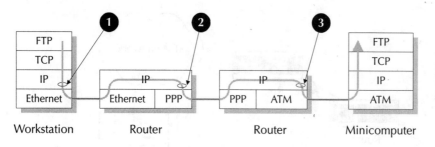

Figure 4.2 IP makes forwarding decisions for data traffic.

puter.) As packets travel from one to the other, the IP protocol in each system decides where to send it next. This decision is the very essence of forwarding.

Figure 4.2 shows the path from the workstation to the minicomputer. It indicates the three different forwarding decisions along the way. The first forwarding decision occurs in the workstation that originates the data. That workstation must decide to send its traffic to the first router. (Chapter 5 discusses how the workstation learns where to send messages.) Although the figure does not show it explicitly, this truly is a decision for the workstation. Presumably, there are other systems on the Ethernet LAN, and the workstation could just as easily send its messages to them. Instead, it sends them correctly to the first router.

As each message arrives at the first router, that router's IP must make a second forwarding decision. The router could send the message to a system on the Ethernet (even, in theory, back to the workstation), or the router could forward traffic across the point-to-point link. Clearly, the latter choice is the right decision, and, as the figure shows, the first router correctly makes it. (Knowing the correct choice is even more difficult for routers than for other systems; Chapters 8, 9, and 10 describe how routers learn to route.)

The final forwarding decision takes place in the second router. It eschews sending the data back across the point-

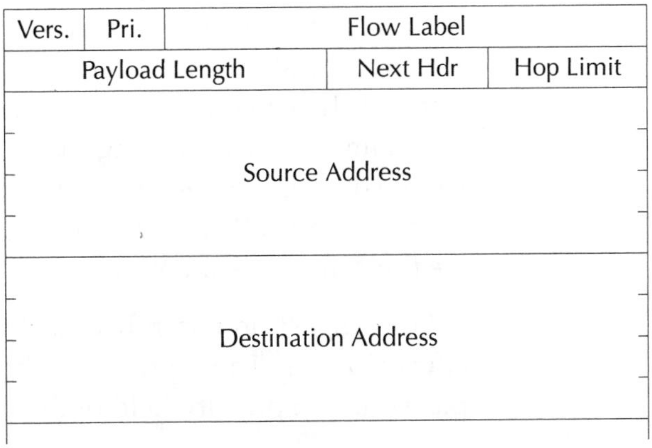

Vers.	Pri.	Flow Label		
Payload Length			Next Hdr	Hop Limit
Source Address				
Destination Address				

Figure 4.3 IP version 6 basic header.

to-point link or to an inappropriate system on the ATM network. Instead, the second router delivers the data to its correct destination, the minicomputer.

The IP Datagram

The Internet Protocol is a connectionless protocol. It treats each message independently, forwarding it through the network to its final destination. By convention, the packets that IP transfers are called *datagrams*. Each IP datagram begins with a common format, as shown in Figure 4.3.

Version

The first four bits of each IP datagram contain the version number of IP. Of course, since this chapter's subject is IPv6, all datagrams in this chapter have a value of 6 in this field.

Priority

The next four bits of the datagram indicate its priority. This value defines the priority of each datagram, relative to other datagrams traveling across the network. The priority field first distinguishes among two broad types of traffic, and then it further refines the relative priorities

Byte Order

Figure 4.3, like most figures in this text, organizes the packet into groups of 32 bits. As far as the underlying networks are concerned, however, an IP datagram is nothing but a series of bytes. Networks should order the bytes so that the top left byte is transmitted first. For IP datagrams, for example, the first byte should be the combined version and priority.

within each traffic type. The broadest distinction is between congestion-controlled and noncongestion-controlled traffic. When a system sends congestion-controlled traffic, it remains sensitive to congestion in the network. If the source detects congestion, it slows down, reducing traffic to the network. By slowing down, the system helps alleviate the congested situation.

For congestion-controlled traffic, IP defines seven specific priorities. These priority values, listed in Table 4.1, are placed in the priority field of the traffic's IP datagrams.

The second traffic type, noncongestion-controlled, does not adjust to congestion in the network. Such traffic sources include real time audio, which cannot be delayed. IP reserves the priority values 8 through 15 for such traffic. For now, however, the IP standards offer no guidelines for specific assignments of these priorities. The source marks each datagram based on how willing it is for the network to discard that datagram. Lower priority values indicate a greater willingness to have a datagram discarded.

Real time audio offers an excellent example of how an application may use noncongestion-controlled priority. Many algorithms that digitize audio can tolerate the loss of some packets. In most cases, though, the algorithms have

Table 4.1 IP Priorities for Congestion-Controlled Traffic

0	no specific priority
1	background traffic (e.g., news)
2	unattended data transfer (e.g., email)
3	reserved for future definition
4	attended bulk transfer (e.g., file transfer)
5	reserved for future definition
6	interactive traffic (e.g., remote login and windowing systems)
7	control traffic (e.g., routing protocols and network management)

more difficulty reconstructing the audio when successive packets are lost. To reduce the probability of this happening, an audio application may vary the priority of its datagrams. It might choose to alternate the priority between 8 and 9 with each datagram. Should the network have to discard two of the application's datagrams, it will try to discard two of priority 8, before any of priority 9.

Note that there is no relative ordering between congestion-controlled and noncongestion-controlled traffic. A datagram of priority 8 (noncongestion-controlled), for example, has neither a lower nor higher priority than a datagram with priority 7 (congestion-controlled).

Flow Label

The 24-bit flow label remains somewhat experimental for IP. At the same time, many consider it the key to TCP/IP's future. The flow label, together with a source address, identifies a particular traffic flow in the network.

Figure 4.4 shows two traffic flows across a simple network. One flow distinguishes traffic from the Mac to the minicomputer. The second flow consists of traffic from the PC to the workstation. All traffic for any particular flow should require the same handling by the network. All datagrams must have the same destination, and they must all contain the same options for routers along the path. (As later sections detail, such options comprise the hop-by-hop options and routing extension headers.)

Figure 4.4 illustrates a simple, yet effective use of flow labels. They can serve as keys into a route cache. Normally, when a datagram arrives in the router, the router must perform a significant amount of processing to determine where the datagram goes next. If the datagram contains a flow label, however, the router may choose to remember the results of that processing. That way, the next time it sees a datagram from the Mac with a flow label of 1, the router merely has to consult a simple table in memory. There it finds that the next hop is the minicomputer, and

Choosing a Flow Label

Since the combination of flow label and source address uniquely defines a flow, the source system must choose the label to achieve this uniqueness. To help routers optimize any route caches, the IPv6 standard further requires the choice to be random, ranging from 1 to $2^{24}-1$.

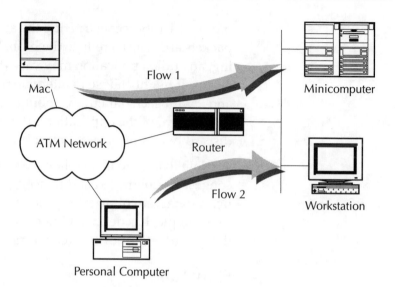

Figure 4.4 Flows across a small network.

the router can forward the packet there immediately, avoiding extensive calculations.

When routers choose to use flow labels in this manner, they cannot keep information for any flow label longer than six seconds. After six seconds, the router must forget a cached entry, perhaps relearning it when the next packet for the flow appears. This time limit is needed in case a host resets and begins reusing its flow label values. For example, suppose the Mac resets and forgets that it was using flow label 1 for a conversation with the minicomputer. Then suppose that it starts a new conversation, this time with the workstation. If the Mac happens to assign flow label 1 to this conversation, the router could get confused. Fortunately, the time limit prevents any such confusion. The router must forget about flow label 1 after six seconds, and the Mac must delay at least six seconds before using any flow label values. (Most resets take longer than six seconds, but if the Mac can reset in, for example, four seconds, it must wait an additional two seconds before reusing any flow labels.)

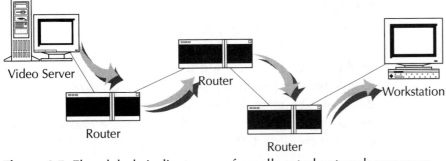

Figure 4.5 Flow labels indicate use of preallocated network resources.

A more ambitious use of flow labels supports advanced TCP/IP applications. Video transmission in Figure 4.5 serves as an example application. Digital video can require a substantial amount of resources from a network—bandwidth, buffers, and processing power. To make sure that its video transmission succeeds, an application can reserve those resources in advance. Then, throughout the video transmission, the application's datagrams can use a particular flow label to indicate that they are allowed to use the reserved resources.

If a system uses flow labels in this manner, to indicate a special service, then the six-second time limit may not be appropriate. Establishing the labels and their lifetime is the responsibility of protocols other than IP. RSVP (Chapter 12) is one such protocol. If a flow's time limit exceeds six seconds, a host must refrain from using flow labels for more than six seconds after a reset. The waiting time is determined by the lifetime of flow labels previously in use. Alternately, a host may have some way of determining which flow labels were previously in use, and it can simply avoid reusing those particular values.

In either case—route caching or special services—flow labels are still a new concept. If an application does not support true flow labels, it should set the flow label field in its datagrams to zero.

Payload Length

The *payload length* field indicates the total length of the IP datagram in bytes, less the IP basic header itself. Since this field is 16 bits in size, it normally limits IP datagrams to 65,535 bytes or less. It is possible, however, to send larger datagrams by using the jumbo payload option in the hop-by-hop options extension header. (See page 112) When this option is employed, the payload length is set to zero.

Next Header

The *next header* field identifies which header follows the basic IP header in the datagram. It can indicate an optional IP header or an upper layer protocol. Table 4.2 lists the major next header values. Some values identify extension headers, and the following section describes those more fully. The remaining entries are complete protocols; each merits an entire chapter in this text.

The list of next header values is not complete. As new options are required and new protocols developed, more next header values will be assigned.

Table 4.2 IP Next Header Values

0	Hop-by-Hop Options Header
4	Internet Protocol
6	Transmission Control Protocol
17	User Datagram Protocol
43	Routing Header
44	Fragment Header
45	Interdomain Routing Protocol
46	Resource Reservation Protocol
50	Encapsulating Security Payload
51	Authentication Header
58	Internet Control Message Protocol
59	No Next Header
60	Destination Options Header

Hop Limit

The *hop limit* field determines how far a datagram will travel. When a host creates a datagram, it sets the hop limit to some initial value. Then, as the datagram travels through routers on the network, each router decrements this field by one. If the datagram's hop limit becomes zero before it reaches it destination, the datagram is discarded.

The hop limit serves two purposes. First, it breaks routing loops. Routing loops should not occur in a healthy network, but, unfortunately, networks are not always healthy. When a loop appears, routers in the network base their routing decisions on incorrect information, and, as a result, datagrams circulate endlessly in the network without reaching their destination.

Figure 4.6 shows a simple routing loop. The workstation sends to the laptop, and the first stop is router A. Unfortunately, router A thinks (incorrectly) that the laptop is connected to router B, so it sends the datagram to router B.

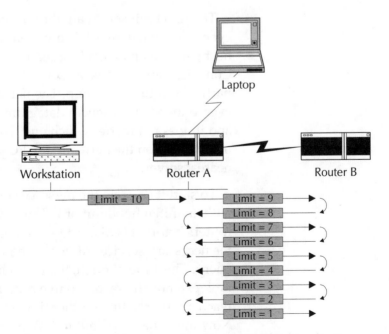

Figure 4.6 Breaking a routing loop with the hop limit.

That router knows the true location of the laptop. The only way to get the datagram to its destination is through router A, so router B sends it right back. Router A still has incorrect information, though, so the datagram goes back to router B. A loop exists between the two routers, and datagrams for the laptop continue to circulate in this loop, never reaching their destination.

IP cannot correct the wrong information in router A, so it cannot get the datagram to its destination. With the hop limit, IP can prevent datagrams from circulating (and using network resources) forever. The workstation in Figure 4.6 sets the initial hop limit of the datagram to 10. When router A forwards the datagram to router B, it decrements the hop limit to 9. Router B decrements the hop limit as well, until the limit eventually reaches zero. When it does, router B, rather than return the datagram to router A, simply discards it. The datagram never makes it to the laptop, but at least it eventually exits from the network.

The hop limit serves another purpose, one that is useful even when the network is functioning perfectly. It lets a host perform an expanding search across the network. Consider Figure 4.7 as an example. All servers belong to a particular multicast group. The personal computer, however, only needs to send a datagram to one of the servers, and it does not matter which one. To avoid placing too much stress on the network, the PC prefers to find the nearest server.

To start its search, the personal computer sends a query with an initial hop limit of 1. That first query reaches two routers before it is discarded, but neither router provides the necessary service. After a timeout, the PC resends its query. This time, though, the initial hop limit is 2. This limit extends the search to five routers, but it still fails to reach a server. After another timeout, the PC tries again. Now the initial hop limit is 3. With this attempt, the query does reach the topmost server in the figure. This server answers the request, and the PC terminates its search. The other servers in the network, those 4 and 5 hops away, are not bothered by this search.

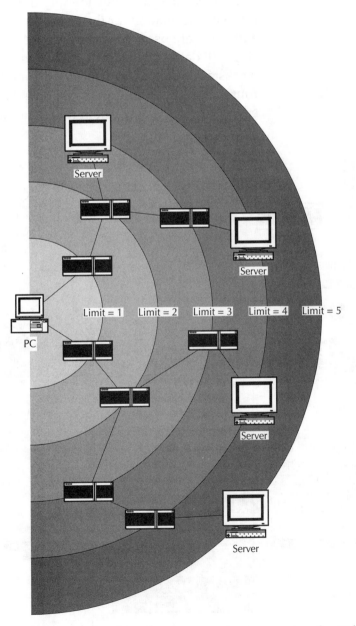

Figure 4.7 Searching for the nearest server using the IP hop limit.

Source and Destination Addresses

The final fields in the basic IP header are the source and destination addresses. Each one is a 128-bit network address. (See page 30.) They identify the original source and ultimate destination for the datagram. To clarify how IP addresses are used, consider Figure 4.8, which shows a single IP datagram as its travels across a network. The workstation originates the datagram and forwards it to router A over the Ethernet LAN. The datagram then crosses the ATM network in two separate cells. Finally, it

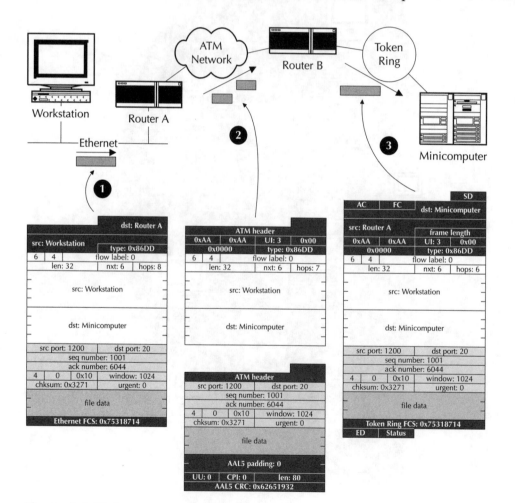

Figure 4.8 IP datagram traversing a network.

reaches its destination when router B sends it across the Token Ring to the minicomputer.

Pay particular attention to the IP header, shown in white in the figure. Note that the source and destination addresses are always the workstation and minicomputer, respectively. This is true even though it passes through two intermediate systems along its route. To get it to or from the appropriate intermediate system, IP relies on the addressing of the underlying network.

The contrast is clearly seen at step 1, when the datagram travels from the workstation to router A. Note that the Ethernet header, shaded in the figure, specifies a destination address of router A. The IP header, however, lists the ultimate destination as the workstation.

IP Extension Headers

All IP datagrams start with the basic header. In most cases, this header can get the datagram to its destination appropriately. For the exceptions, IP provides a simple mechanism to add to its functionality. To convey extra information to the destination or to intermediate systems along the path, IP uses extension headers.

Extension headers follow the basic header in the IP datagram. The IP standard defines several different extension headers; each one is identified by a particular value for the next header field. Table 4.3 lists the initial extension headers. Every extension header (except 59) has its own next

Table 4.3 IP Extension Headers

0	Hop-by-Hop Options Header
43	Routing Header
44	Fragment Header
51	Authentication Header
59	No Next Header
60	Destination Options Header

header field. This structure allows IP to string multiple extension headers together, one after the other. The final extension header uses its next header field to identify the upper-level protocol.

Figure 4.9 shows an IP datagram with several extension headers. Notice how each header identifies the next header all the way to the authentication header. At that point, the next header field identifies the upper-level protocol; in this case, TCP.

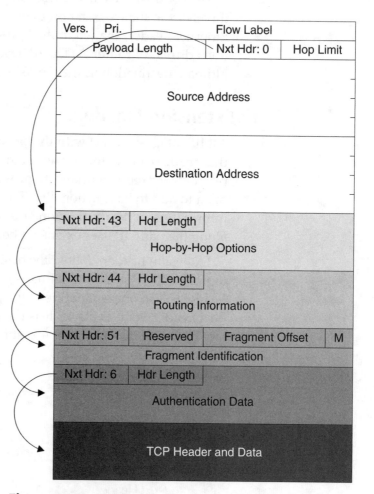

Figure 4.9 Extension headers in an IP datagram.

Header Order

Both Table 4.3 and Figure 4.9 show the headers in the recommended order. This order is important because it makes it easy for intermediate routers to process the datagrams efficiently. In most cases, routers only care about hop-by-hop options and the routing header. Once a router reaches a header other than one of these, it need look no further in the datagram.

The only exception to this order is the destination options header. In many cases, destination options are truly for the final destination only. Those options should appear in the datagram's final extension header, just before the upper-level header.

Destination options may also be intended for some intermediate routers along the way, though not necessarily all of them. In these cases, those options are used in conjunction with a routing header, and the destination options header should immediately precede the routing header in the datagram. A single datagram may include destination options in both places. In that case, some options are for intermediate routers, while others are solely for the host destination.

Hop-by-Hop Options

The hop-by-hop header contains IP options for every system on the datagram's route. Every router in the path must examine and process the hop-by-hop options header. In general, each option in this header consists of a type, a length, and a value. The type and length are each a byte in size. The type identifies the specific option, while the length indicates the number of bytes in the option value. The single exception to this rule is the Pad1 option, which consists of a single byte with a value of zero. It has no length or value field.

Table 4.4 lists the hop-by-hop options defined so far. Note that the size column in this table indicates the total

Table 4.4 Hop-by-Hop Options

Type	Option	Size	Alignment
0	Pad1	1 byte	none
1	PadN	2+n bytes	none
194	Jumbo Payload Length	2+4 bytes	4·n+2

size of the option, including the type and length fields. This number differs from the value of the option's length field, which does not include those two bytes. The fourth column of the table specifies the alignment requirements for each option. These requirements ensure that the option is positioned for most efficient processing.

The notation $x·n+y$ specifies alignment. It states that the option type (not the value) must begin at an integer number of x bytes from the start of the header, plus y bytes. The Pad1 option discussion (page 111) explains the importance of proper alignment.

The value of the option type does more than simply identify the particular type of an option. It also tells routers how to handle the option when they encounter it. In particular, the two most significant bits tell a router what to do with an option type that it does not recognize. Table 4.5 shows the possible values of those two bits, along with the required response.

Table 4.5 Responding to Unrecognized Option Types

Type (binary)	Action if Type is Unrecognized
00xxxxxx	Ignore the option and continue processing the datagram.
01xxxxxx	Discard the datagram and take no further action.
10xxxxxx	Discard the datagram and return an ICMP error message to datagram's source.
11xxxxxx	Discard the datagram and return an ICMP error message to its source only if the destination is not a multicast address.

Table 4.6 Option Value in Transit

Type (binary)	Behavior In Transit
xx0xxxxx	Option value does not change in transit.
xx1xxxxx	Option value may change in transit.

The third most significant bit identifies those options that may change their value as the datagram traverses the network. Table 4.6 lists these options.

Pad1 Option

The simplest option is Pad1. It consists of a single byte with a value of zero. It has no explicit length byte, and its value is implicit in its first and only byte. This option serves to shift other options' positions in the header. Most frequently, it places those other options so that they satisfy their alignment requirements.

Proper alignment is important for the most efficient processing of IP datagrams. Modern microprocessors, with natural word sizes of 32 and 64 bits, can access multi-byte quantities much more efficiently if those quantities reside on their natural boundaries in memory. Digital's Alpha processor, for example, is a 64-bit processor, and 64-bit values can either align naturally with the processor's memory or they may be out of alignment. A value whose first byte was at an odd address, for example, would be unaligned. Figure 4.10 depicts each case.

In both cases, the processor is able to access the value, but when the value is aligned, the Alpha can read or write it 30 times faster than when it is not[1]. Other modern processors realize similar efficiency gains for aligned memory access.

To help achieve this alignment, IP defines its header fields so that, as long as the first byte in the datagram is

---

[1] *Alpha Architecture Handbook.* Digital Equipment Corporation, 1992, p. A-6.

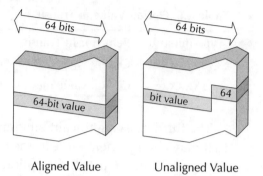

Aligned Value   Unaligned Value

Figure 4.10 Alignment with processor memory.

suitably aligned, other fields in the headers will also be aligned. The Pad1 option (as well as the PadN option discussed next) helps to create the proper alignment. If a field fails to fall in the right place, one or more Pad1 options can be inserted ahead of it to shift the field to the correct position.

PadN Option

The PadN option serves the same purpose as the Pad1 option. It shifts the position of subsequent options so that they may be properly aligned. Where the Pad1 option always shifts values a single byte, however, the PadN option adds an arbitrary shift. The smallest shift possible is two bytes, corresponding to an option length of zero. Figure 4.11 shows a PadN option that adds five bytes of padding to the extension header.

Jumbo Payload Length Option

The jumbo payload length option overcomes a limit of the payload length field in IP's basic header. That field, de-

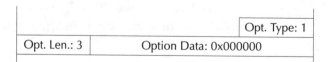

Figure 4.11 PadN option.

fined as 16 bits, cannot indicate a payload size greater than 65,535 bytes. For datagrams larger than this, the jumbo payload option is used. In such datagrams, the basic header's payload length field is set to zero, while this option carries the total size of the IP datagram, less the 40-byte basic header. Note that this option does include the size of the hop-by-hop extension header that contains it.

Of course, this option has a predefined length (4 bytes). This means that it too places a limit on the size of the IP datagram. But with 32 bits, that limit is 4,294,967,295 bytes of payload. IP's designers consider this sufficient for the foreseeable future. Should it prove inadequate, they can simply define another option.

The jumbo payload length option has an alignment requirement of 4·n+2. As Figure 4.12 shows, this requirement places the 4-byte option value squarely on a 4-byte word. In this position, modern microprocessors can read and write it most efficiently.

Routing Header

Normally, the source of an IP datagram leaves it to the network to deliver that datagram to its destination. Sometimes, though, the source desires more control over the datagram's route. The source may wish to give the network hints as to the best path for the datagram, or it may wish to control the path to make sure the datagram does not travel through inappropriate routers. The routing header gives the source this control. This extension header, combined with the destination address in the IP basic header, defines a path through the network for the datagram.

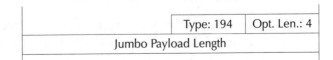

Figure 4.12 Jumbo payload length option.

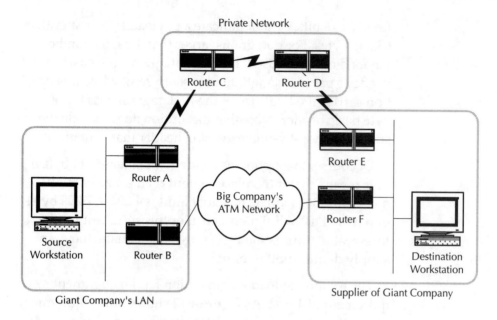

Figure 4.13 Communication using routing headers.

Imagine the situation in Figure 4.13. Giant Company needs to communicate with one of its suppliers. The natural communication path relies on an ATM network from Big Company, one of Giant's major competitors. For most traffic, this presents no problems; however, Giant is paranoid about particularly sensitive data. It wants to make sure that the sensitive traffic does not travel across its rival's network. Fortunately, an alternate path exists through the private network at the top of the figure. But that path relies on a relatively slow, point-to-point link. The trick is to make sure that sensitive traffic takes that alternate path, and not the more efficient route through the high-speed ATM network. If the source workstation knows about this alternate path, it can force its use with a routing extension header.

So far, only one type of routing header has been defined. Known as type 0, that header looks like Figure 4.14. As the figure shows, it consists mostly of a list of network addresses. When the datagram first leaves the source

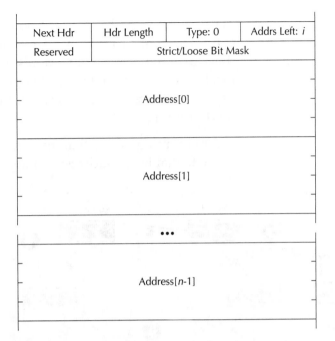

Figure 4.14 Routing extension header.

workstation, the basic IP header's destination address indicates the first hop on the desired path. The list in the routing header identifies subsequent hops along that path. As the datagram arrives at each hop, that system takes the next hop from the list and swaps it with the destination address. The datagram then continues on its journey.

The Addrs Left field keeps track of the current position in the list. When the source first generates the datagram, this field has the value n, where n is the total number of addresses in the list. At each stop on the list, the router decrements this field by one. When it reaches zero, the header requires no further processing and the datagram makes its way to its final destination.

Figure 4.15 traces the results of this processing on a datagram from Giant Company. The datagram uses a routing header to avoid traversing Big Company's network. The figure shows the relevant fields of the datagram at three places along its path. The strict/loose bit mask adds an extra twist to the routing header. It determines how tightly the source controls the datagram's route. Each bit in the mask, beginning with the most significant, designates a listed address as requiring strict (if the bit is 1) or loose (if it is 0) routing.

Strict routing means that the datagram must proceed directly to that listed address; no intervening hops are al-

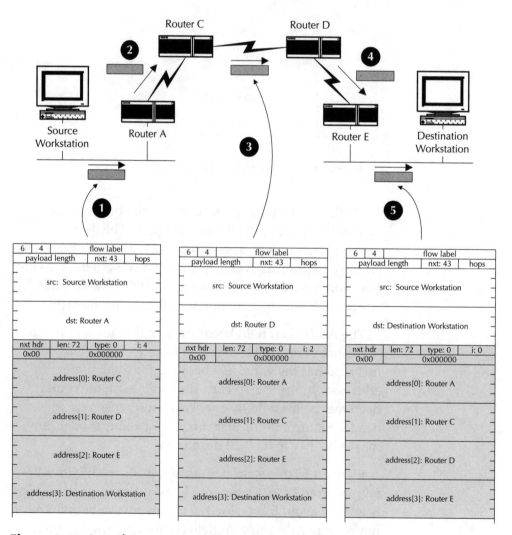

Figure 4.15 Specifying a route with a routing extension header.

lowed. Loose routing allows the datagram to pass through intermediate routers on its way to the next listed address. If a router finds it cannot satisfy a strict route, it returns an ICMP error message to the datagram's source. (See page 154.)

Fragment Header

The fragment header solves another problem for IP: What if a datagram is too big for a particular network technology? Ethernet LANs, for example, can transfer frames no larger than 1,514 bytes. A single IP datagram, on the other hand, may be much larger than that. The fragment header lets a host divide a large datagram into several smaller pieces and send those pieces through the network. The receiving host puts them back together.

Figure 4.16 shows the format of a fragment header. The *fragment offset* specifies how far within the original datagram the first byte of the current piece belongs. Its value is in units of 8 bytes. With such a unit, IP must break all fragments (except the last) into pieces whose size is an integer multiple of 8 bytes. The *M* bit—short for more—is set on all fragments except the final one. The final field, the *fragment identification*, unambiguously indicates the original datagram to which this fragment belongs. The sender picks this field, and it must be sure to pick a different value for every datagram it sends to a particular destination. The receiver uses this value to distinguish fragments from different datagrams, so it can reassemble them properly.

Figure 4.17 illustrates how fragment headers help divide a datagram. The original datagram, with 2,902 bytes of

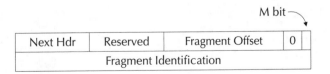

M bit

Next Hdr	Reserved	Fragment Offset	0
Fragment Identification			

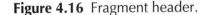

Figure 4.16 Fragment header.

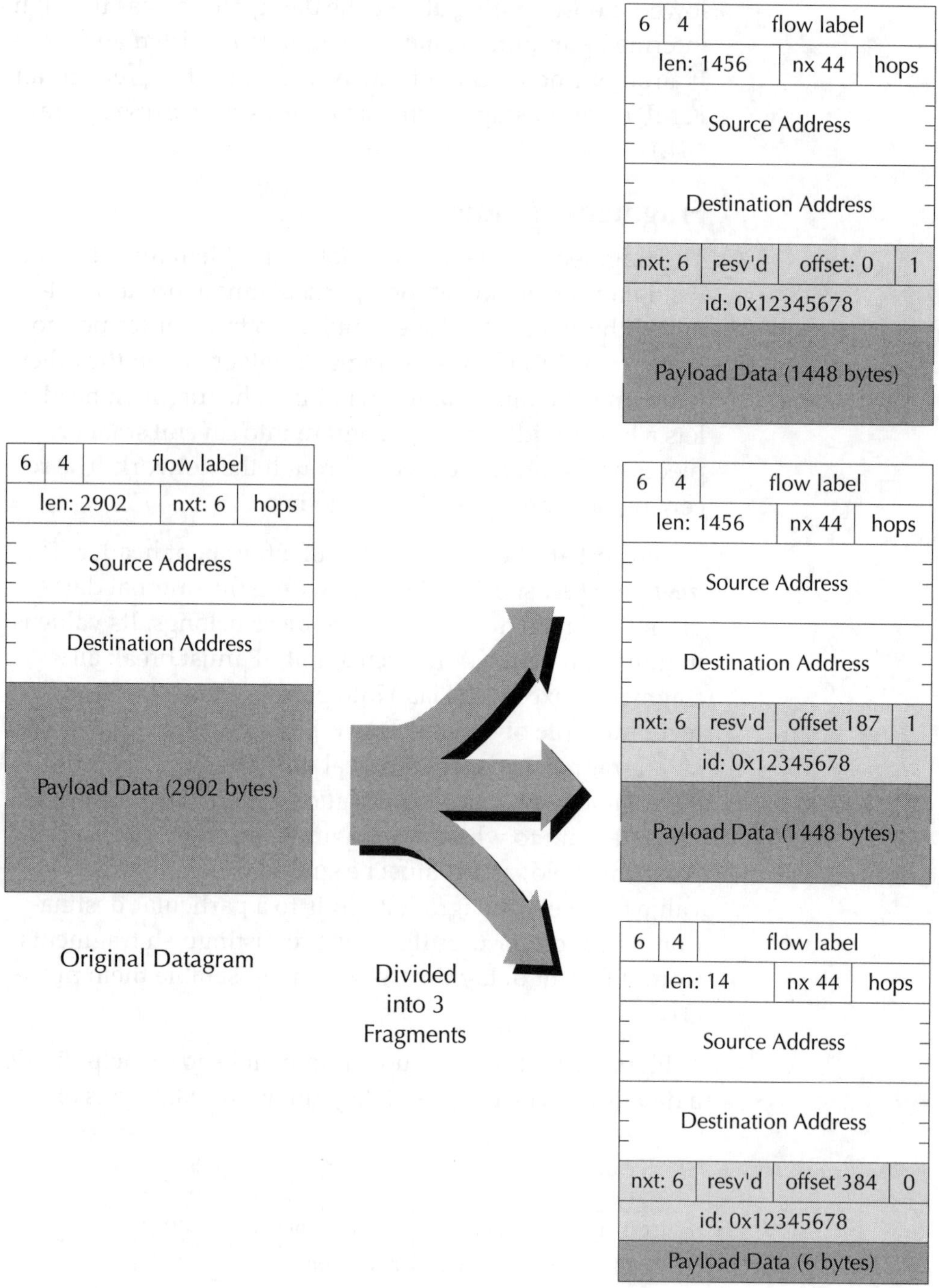

Figure 4.17 Fragmenting an IP datagram.

Future Options

With its flexibility, IP gives engineers at least two ways to define future options for the protocol. They can be placed in the destination options header, or they can be given their own extension header. The biggest difference between the two is error handling. With the two most significant bits of the option type, destination options allow a variety of different responses to unrecognized options. (See Table 4.5.) Datagrams with unrecognized extension headers, on the other hand, must be discarded and an ICMP error message returned.

payload data, is to be transmitted across an Ethernet LAN. Since Ethernet frames can only carry 1,500 bytes of data (including the IP basic header), fragmentation is necessary. Note in the figure that three separate fragments are needed, even though 2,902 bytes is less than twice the 1,500-byte limit. The third fragment is not even required because of the overhead of IP's basic and extension headers. Together, they total 48 bytes, so two sets plus the 2,902 payload bytes still does not exceed twice 1,500.

The reason for the third fragment is IP's restriction on fragment sizes. Since the first fragment must contain a multiple of eight bytes, it cannot completely fill a 1,500-byte Ethernet frame. Instead, IP must settle for 1,496 bytes. That leaves room for only 1,448 bytes of payload data. The same restriction applies to the second fragment, so again 1,448 payload bytes are included. The final fragment includes the remaining 6 bytes of payload. Since there is no fragment offset for a following fragment (indeed, there is no following fragment), the 8-byte restriction does not apply.

Authentication Header

The authentication header ensures that a received datagram is authentic—that it was not altered in transit and that it truly came from the claimed sender. Authentication is part of the enhanced security features of IP version 6. The following section, "IP Security," discusses authentication and other aspects of security in detail. Figure 4.18 in that section shows an authentication header.

Destination Options

The destination options header contains IP options for the datagram's destination. If the datagram includes a routing header, this header can also precede that header. In that case, its options will be processed by each intermediate hop included in the routing header's list.

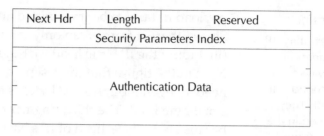

Figure 4.18 Authentication extension header.

So far, only two options have been defined for the destination options header, Pad1 and PadN. Of course, padding options such as these are not particularly useful by themselves. At this time, these options are in place only to support other destination options that may be defined in the future.

IP Security

The TCP/IP protocols began as research for the U.S. Department of Defense. In spite of its background, TCP/IP has reached its current level of popularity without providing meaningful security for the data it transfers. With IP version 6, TCP/IP offers several important security features. All IP version 6 hosts are required to support authentication. In addition, IP has a well-defined framework for exchanging confidential messages. Both features were initially designed just for IP version 6. As a testament to their power and usefulness, though, both have been adapted for use with IPv4 as well.

Security Association

Both authentication and confidentiality rely on security associations. A security association establishes the context for the communication, and it usually defines several security aspects of that communication. Table 4.7 lists the important characteristics of a security association.

Table 4.7 Characteristics of a Security Association

- specific encryption or authentication algorithm in use
- specific key or keys to the communication
- other parameters of the algorithm (e.g. synchronization data or initialization vectors)
- time limits on the keys or the entire association
- sensitivity of the protected data (e.g. secret, top secret, and so on)

Keys and Key Management

Nearly all authentication and encryption algorithms rely on a *key*. The key is a secret value that only the sender and receiver know. It is, in effect, how the sender locks a message and how the receiver unlocks it. If a key falls into the wrong hands, then the security of any communication using that key is compromised. Distributing keys, as well as other aspects of key management, are an active research area. In many cases, the network itself is the most convenient way to distribute them. But, of course, if the network is not secure (and why else would security be needed?) then it may not be safe to distribute keys using it.

Authentication

The Internet Protocol has defined a special extension header for authentication, and all IPv6 hosts must support this header. IPv6 further specifies the Message Digest 5 (MD5) algorithm as the default authentication algorithm, and all hosts must support this algorithm. If both parties agree, they may optionally use a different authentication algorithm. Note that all hosts are required to support authentication, but they are not required to use it. In particular, if two hosts do not feel authentication is needed for a communication, they are free to omit it from their datagrams.

Figure 4.18 shows the standard authentication header. The authentication information itself begins with the *security parameters index*, or SPI. When combined with the destination address, the SPI defines the security association for the communication. Actual authentication data follows the SPI. It must consist of an integer number of 32-bit words. The security association determines which authentication algorithm is in use. If the default MD5 algorithm is employed, then the authentication data consists of 16 bytes.

To compute the authentication data using MD5, the sender starts with a secret authentication key. If that key is shorter than 128 bits, enough zero bits are added to make it 128 bits long. Immediately after these 128 bits, the sender appends the complete IP datagram itself. That datagram

Implementing MD5

The MD5 algorithm performs a set of convoluted calculations on its input and derives a 128-bit digest. The algorithm itself is moderately complicated, and it is certainly filled with various random and other magic numbers. Fortunately, RFC 1321 includes a complete implementation of MD5 in the C language.

should have an authentication header in place, but the authentication data within that header is set to zero. In addition, all fields in the datagram that can change in transit (the hop limit field, for example) are temporarily set equal to zero. After the datagram, the sender adds the authentication key once more. It is this block of data that the sender passes through the MD5 algorithm. The algorithm generates a 128-bit digest, which is used as the authentication data within the authentication header.

The receiver performs the same steps. It starts with the padded authentication key, adds the datagram (temporarily zeroing the authentication data and other fields that may have changed in transit), and appends the key once more. The MD5 digest for this block of data should match the authentication data. If it does not, the datagram is not authentic, and the receiver takes appropriate steps.

The whole process works because only the sender and receiver know the secret authentication key. Since no other system knows this key, no other system can generate a datagram that will have the correct digest when the receiver checks it.

Confidentiality

Authentication is important for the security of IP datagrams, but it does not guard against the most basic security threat—eavesdropping. As IP datagrams traverse a network, they may travel through many different systems and networks. These intermediate links offer opportunities for someone other than at the destination to examine datagrams and discover their contents. As Figure 4.19 implies, it takes only a protocol analyzer looking at one of the path's links.

Protecting against this threat requires confidentiality, and IP provides that with its encapsulating security payload (ESP). ESP is the standard way to send encrypted in-

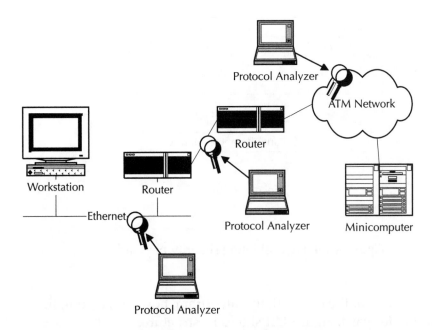

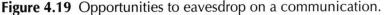

Figure 4.19 Opportunities to eavesdrop on a communication.

formation within IP datagrams. The general format of ESP is deliberately as unrevealing as possible. Figure 4.20 shows the payload following a basic IP header. As the figure reveals, the payload contains only a single defined field, the security parameters index. Encrypted data comprises the rest of the payload.

All systems that support ESP must support the default encryption algorithm. That algorithm is the cipher block chaining (CBC) mode of the data encryption standard (DES). The algorithm itself, specified by the United States government[2,3,4,5], is beyond the scope of this text. The for-

---

[2] U.S. National Bureau of Standards. *Data Encryption Standard* [FIPS 46]. January 1977.

[3] U.S. National Bureau of Standards. *Data Encryption Standard* [FIPS 46-1]. January 1988.

[4] U.S. National Bureau of Standards. *Guidelines for Implementing and Using the Data Encryption Standard* [FIPS 74]. April 1981.

[5] U.S. National Bureau of Standards. *DES Modes of Operation* [FIPS 81]. December 1980.

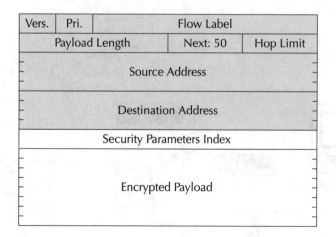

Figure 4.20 Encapsulating security payload.

mat of the ESP with this algorithm, however, is straight-forward. Figure 4.21 shows its structure.

An initialization vector follows the security parameters index; its contents are used by the DES-CBC algorithm. After this vector comes the encrypted data itself. The ESP ends with a payload type byte, and, immediately before that, a padding length field. Padding is added to force the entire ESP size to be an integer multiple of 32 bits. The payload type field contains the same values as IP's next header field. It indicates which protocol has been encrypted.

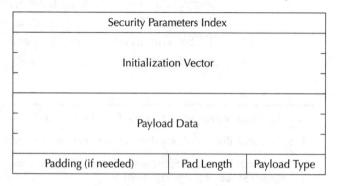

Figure 4.21 ESP for DES-CBC encryption.

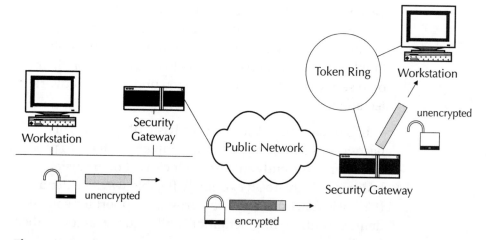

Figure 4.22 Security gateways supporting tunnel mode operation.

Like all ESP encryption algorithms, DES-CBC can be used in two ways. If the encrypted data is a standard transport level packet (a UDP datagram or TCP segment, for example), then the payload type indicates the appropriate transport protocol. The security standards call this operation *transport mode*, and they suggest its use when both the source and destination directly support ESP.

In some environments, as in Figure 4.22, the hosts themselves may not implement ESP. Instead, they may rely on external devices known as *security gateways* to provide encryption and decryption. In this environment, hosts send unencrypted datagrams to the security gateway. That device then encrypts the entire datagram, including any IP headers. It encapsulates the resulting payload in a new datagram, and sends that datagram to the destination (or its security gateway). With this operation, known as *tunnel mode*, the payload type indicates IP itself.

Summary

The Internet Protocol acts as the glue that binds diverse network technologies. It is responsible for forwarding packets from source to destination across these diverse networks. In this role, IP also isolates the particular characteristics of each network from the transport and application layers. It allows these layers to concentrate on their own services, without regard to the underlying network technology.

IP's datagrams all start with a basic IP header. This header is as simple as possible, allowing systems to process it very efficiently. IP also defines a set of extension headers, which are an extremely flexible way to extend IP's basic functionality. They provide support for source-defined routing, fragmentation, and security, among other functions.

Unlike classic IP, IP version 6 emphasizes the importance of security by making it a mandatory feature of the protocol. All IPv6 systems must support both authentication and encryption, and the IP standards provide default algorithms for each.

5

Using ICMP to Coordinate Systems

The Internet Protocol focuses on one major task—moving data from its source to its destination. Internetwork layer protocols, though, must do more than simply move data. Systems rely on the internetwork layer to coordinate many aspects of their operation. This coordination includes discovering neighbors, controlling address assignments, and managing group membership. Internetwork layer protocols also assist in reporting errors and providing diagnostic support.

These functions complete the minimal responsibilities of the internetwork layer, and TCP/IP assigns them all to a separate protocol. That protocol is ICMP, the Internet Control Message Protocol. This chapter examines ICMP in depth. Since ICMP plays such a variety of roles in TCP/IP networks, the text follows an organization different from most other chapters. It begins with a discussion of the common ICMP message format. This format applies to all ICMP messages, and the first section provides a framework for those that follow. The following sections describe ICMP's various functions. Each section includes the details of the ICMP messages for the services it describes.

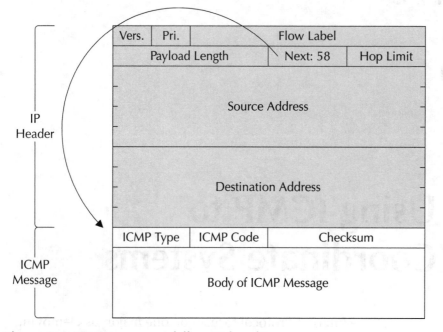

Figure 5.1 ICMP messages follow IP headers.

ICMP Message Format

Even though ICMP is a network layer protocol, it sends its messages inside IP datagrams. As Figure 5.1 shows, the next header value of 58 indicates ICMP messages. The figure also shows the common, four-byte header that begins every ICMP message. That header consists of a type byte, a code byte, and a 2-byte checksum.

The type and code bytes distinguish different kinds of ICMP messages. The type field provides the coarsest distinction. There are currently 14 different ICMP message types. Table 5.1 lists them, along with their type field values. From these values, it is clear that ICMP divides its messages into two classes. The first class, with type values ranging from 1 to (in principle) 127, are error messages. "Error Reporting" (page 151) discusses the special treatment they receive. Type values of 128 and higher are informational messages.

Table 5.1 ICMP Message Types

1	Destination Unreachable error message
2	Packet Too Big error message
3	Time Exceeded error message
4	Parameter Problem error message
128	Echo Request message
129	Echo Reply message
130	Group Membership query
131	Group Membership report
132	Group Membership termination
133	Router solicitation
134	Router advertisement
135	Neighbor solicitation
136	Neighbor advertisement
137	Redirect message

Checksum

The 16-bit checksum protects against corruption that may appear in an ICMP message. Because it is such a visible feature of transport level protocols like TCP, it is easy to overlook the fact that other protocols can take advantage of a checksum's error-detecting properties.

Before sending an ICMP message, a system calculates the checksum to place in this field. The system starts with the complete ICMP message. It temporarily sets the checksum value to zero. If the message contains an odd number of bytes, then the system adds an imaginary trailing byte equal to zero. The extra byte is used in the checksum calculation, but it is not transmitted with the message.

The system then prepends a *pseudo header* to the message. This pseudo header consists of the source and destination IP addresses, the payload length, and the next header byte for ICMP (58). Figure 5.2 shows a pseudo header preceding an ICMP message. Like the extra trailing

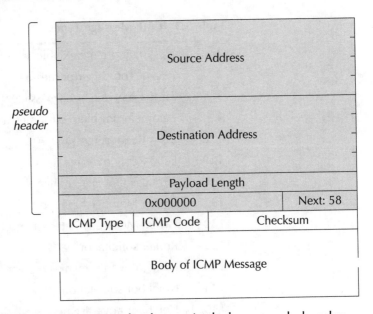

Figure 5.2 ICMP checksums include a pseudo header.

The Purpose of the Pseudo Header

By including the pseudo header in its checksum, ICMP protects against more than simple data corruption in transit. It also ensures that the systems' protocol implementations interface correctly. Suppose IP mistakenly delivers a UDP message to ICMP. Since UDP and ICMP rely on the same checksum algorithm, checking the message itself would not protect against this misdelivery. The pseudo header also checks the IP next header value, and this value differs for ICMP and UDP, letting the checksum ensure that IP delivers the message to the correct upper level protocol.

zero, this pseudo header is not actually transmitted with the message. It is simply used as part of the checksum calculation and then discarded.

When creating a pseudo header, the sender must be sure to use the destination address that the message will contain when it reaches the recipient. If the sender plans on using a routing header (page 113), this value will differ from the message's initial destination address.

With the ICMP message, the pseudo header, and (if needed) the trailing zero byte, ICMP has an integer number of 16-bit words. To calculate the checksum, ICMP performs a 16-bit, ones complement addition of this data. It ignores any carries and places the 16-bit sum in the checksum field of the ICMP header.

When a system receives an ICMP datagram, it verifies the checksum in much the same way. It prepends a pseudo header, adds a trailing zero if necessary, and calculates the 16-bit, ones complement sum. If the result is 0xFFFF, then the checksum is correct, and ICMP can accept the message.

If the result differs from 0xFFFF, however, the checksum is invalid. ICMP immediately discards such a message without any further processing.

Selecting a Source IP Address

An important decision that faces every system is selecting a source IP address for ICMP messages. Sometimes (if the system has a single interface with a single address), this decision is easy. In many cases, however, systems will have a choice, and it is important that they choose appropriately. The ICMP standard provides four specific rules for selecting the source address.

The first two rules consider ICMP replies. The source address of the reply should be the same as the destination address of the original message. If the original message was sent to a multicast or anycast group, then the response should use as its source an IP address of the interface on which the request arrived.

The third rule applies to ICMP error messages. Error messages are often generated by systems that are not the ultimate destination of the datagram in error. Error messages, therefore, cannot use the original destination as the error's source. Instead, they should use a source address that provides the most information about the error being reported. For example, if the ICMP message is a Packet Too Big error, then its source should be an IP address of the interface over which the original datagram would not fit.

Unsolicited ICMP messages, as well as those not covered previously, follow the fourth rule. The source address for such messages should be an IP address of the link on which the message is transmitted.

Neighbor discovery also constrains the destination address of its ICMP messages. That destination must be a link-local address. (If the destination is multicast, then the multicast address must be of link-local scope.) This restriction confines neighbor discovery to the local link, protecting against an accidental (or deliberate) "leaking" of neighbor discovery beyond its intended scope.

Neighbor Discovery

A Special Caution

As of this writing, the final details of ICMP's neighbor discovery process were still under debate. The principles underlying neighbor discovery are not in doubt, but minor changes to the message formats are possible. Readers are urged to consult the latest TCP/IP standards to verify the details of this protocol.

One of ICMP's most important functions is neighbor discovery. Neighbor discovery lets a system identify other hosts and routers on its links. Systems learn about hosts on their links so that they can forward datagrams addressed to those hosts. Hosts learn of at least one router so they can forward datagrams to systems not on their links. Neighbor discovery also lets routers direct a host to the most appropriate router, in case the host chooses a router inefficiently.

Neighbor discovery takes place on all networks, but it is most interesting on multicast networks like Ethernet LANs. Figure 5.3 shows a sample Ethernet network with four hosts. Because each host has an interface to the network, it has its own IP address. In addition, by virtue of connecting to an Ethernet LAN, each system also must have an Ethernet physical address. Table 5.2 assigns values for each of those addresses to the systems on this sample network.

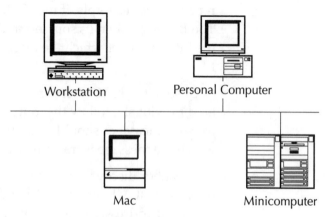

Workstation   Personal Computer

Mac   Minicomputer

Figure 5.3 Ethernet LAN with four hosts.

Table 5.2 Addresses for Hosts in Figure 5.3

Host	IP Address	Ethernet Address
Workstation	FE80::0800:2001:C782	080020-01C782
Personal Computer	FE80::0000:C033:6382	020701-33D692
Mac	FE80::0800:0704:0388	080007-040388
Minicomputer	FE80::0800:5A00:B2C4	08005A-00B2C4

Address Resolution

Whatever Happened to ARP?

IPv4 relies on a separate protocol for address resolution. That protocol is called (no surprise) the address resolution protocol (ARP). With IPv6, ARP's functions are part of the responsibility of ICMP.

Neighbor discovery comes into play with the first IP datagram sent across the network. Suppose that the workstation must send a datagram to the personal computer. The workstation knows the IP address of the PC; that is, the destination address of the IP datagram. The workstation does not yet know the PC's Ethernet address, however. Without that information, it cannot transfer the datagram across the LAN. Mapping IP addresses to network addresses is the job of *address resolution*, and it is one of ICMP's key responsibilities.

ICMP relies on a rather simple strategy to find the appropriate Ethernet address: it asks. As Figure 5.4 indicates, the workstation multicasts a request to all hosts on the

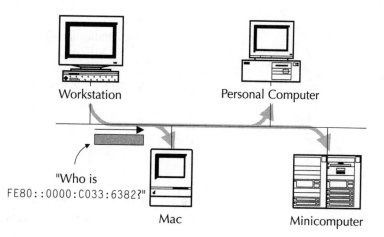

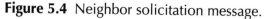

Figure 5.4 Neighbor solicitation message.

Confining Address Resolution to the Local Link

IPng takes extra steps to ensure that address resolution exchanges remain confined to a single link. These precautions provide extra security, as they prevent a remote system from masquerading as a local system and intercepting that local system's messages.

network. That request asks for the Ethernet address corresponding to the desired IP address. This request is a *neighbor solicitation* message. Figure 5.5 shows its exact format. Before considering the ICMP message itself, note the IP header the message employs. Two fields in that header are particularly important. The first is the hop limit field, which has a value of 255. This value is the maximum possible for the field, and all systems that receive a solicitation must verify the value before responding. If a solicitation arrives with a hop limit less than 255, it could only have come through a router. Since address resolution is confined strictly to a single link, messages arriving from off the local link must be ignored. (See sidebar.)

The second unusual IP field is the destination address. As Figure 5.5 shows, that address is FF02::1:C033:6382. This is a special multicast address just for the neighbor so-

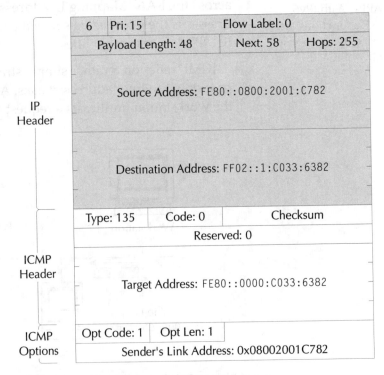

Figure 5.5 Neighbor solicitation message.

licitation query. It maps to a specific, well-known multicast Ethernet address, so the workstation does not have to find an Ethernet address for the solicitation.

The particular multicast address is defined by the IP address the workstation seeks. To construct the multicast destination, the workstation appends the last 32 bits of the address it is seeking (C033:6382) to the 96-bit prefix FF02::1:0:0. The resulting destination IP address is FF02::1:C033:6382.

ICMP uses this special multicast destination to reduce the load on other systems on the network. The PC must be listening to FF02::1:C033:6382 since it owns the corresponding IP address of FE80::0000:C033:6382. Other hosts on the network however—the Mac and the mini-computer, for example—do not have to listen to that address. They will not hear the neighbor solicitation, and they will not have to waste CPU resources by processing and then discarding the request.

The ICMP message itself contains few surprises. The ICMP type is 135, indicating a neighbor solicitation. The code value of 0 identifies the sender as a host. Routers use a code of 1. The target address is the IP address the sender is soliciting. In Figure 5.5 its value is the IP address of the personal computer, as expected.

A series of options can follow the target address in the message. The example query, like all neighbor solicitations, contains exactly one option, each of which begins with a code that identifies its type, followed by its length in 8-byte words.

The neighbor solicitation always includes the sender's link address option, which has an option code of 1. The length of the option depends on the particular network. For Ethernet LANs, it is one 8-byte word, which is just enough to hold the 6-byte Ethernet address. Notice that the workstation correctly inserts its own Ethernet address in this field.

Sender's Link Address

It may seem odd that the sender of a solicitation includes its own link address in the query. The reason is rather simple. If the workstation has to send a datagram to the PC, then most likely the PC will want to send datagrams back to the workstation. To do that, the PC will need to know the workstation's Ethernet address. The workstation includes that address in its own query so the PC can remember it when it responds. In the future, when the PC has datagrams to send to the workstation, no solicitation from the PC is needed.

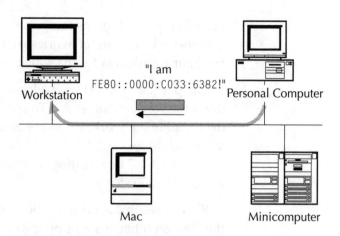

Figure 5.6 Responding to a neighbor solicitation.

If the workstation fails to get a response to its solicitation, it may repeat the request as many as nine additional times. To avoid straining the network, though, successive requests must be at least one second apart.

To continue this example, assume the PC receives the solicitation and replies. Figure 5.6 illustrates this reply, and Figure 5.7 details the resulting Neighbor Advertisement message. The neighbor advertisement has much the same format as the solicitation. It includes the target address and, through an option, the link address of that target. The target's link address option has the same format as the sender's link address option in the solicitation. The only difference is the option code. For the target's address the code has a value of 2. The two extra flags, labeled R and S in Figure 5.7, indicate whether the system sending the message is a router (if R is 1) and whether it is responding to a solicitation (if S is 1).

Note that the PC sends its neighbor advertisement directly to the workstation. There is no need to multicast the message; doing so would unnecessarily burden the other hosts on the LAN (which are presumably not interested in the PC's Ethernet address). Once the workstation receives this reply, it knows the Ethernet address of the personal

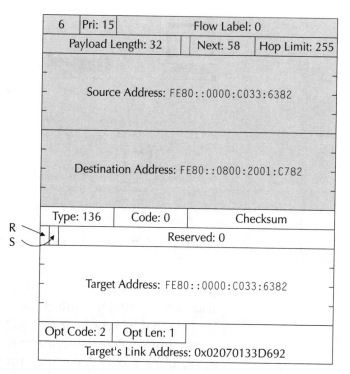

Figure 5.7 Neighbor advertisement message.

computer. It can then send the datagram that it originally wanted to forward to the PC.

The workstation should not simply forget the addressing information as soon as it sends the first datagram to the PC. Most TCP/IP conversations require several datagrams, so the first datagram to the PC is not likely to be the last. The workstation should store the PC's Ethernet address in memory. It will then be available for subsequent datagrams without the need for another solicitation exchange.

Router Discovery

The neighbor discovery functions discussed so far allow hosts to find other hosts on the same network. Frequently, a host also needs to communicate with a system on a distant network. In such cases, address resolution does no

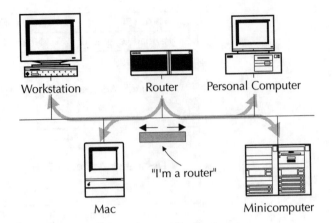

Figure 5.8 A router advertises its presence.

good. The host needs to find a router. As part of neighbor discovery, ICMP lets routers identify themselves to hosts. They do that by sending *router advertisements* on the network. Figure 5.8 introduces a router to the sample network, and it shows that router advertising itself to the network's hosts.

The router advertisement message follows the basic ICMP format, but it includes many options. Figure 5.9 shows a router advertisement with options. Much of the additional information suggests how hosts on the network should operate.

The *max hops* field recommends a maximum hop limit for any datagram a host transmits. This value gives hosts an idea of what a reasonable hop limit might be. The *reachability timeout* suggests a time limit to place on neighbor information that a host learns. If a host fails to hear from a neighbor within this time period, it can suspect that the neighbor is no longer reachable. The next parameter, the *reachability retransmission interval*, limits the frequency of neighbor solicitations for a destination. When a host has to retransmit neighbor solicitations because it receives no response, it should not do so more often than this interval specifies. Both of these time values are measured in milli-

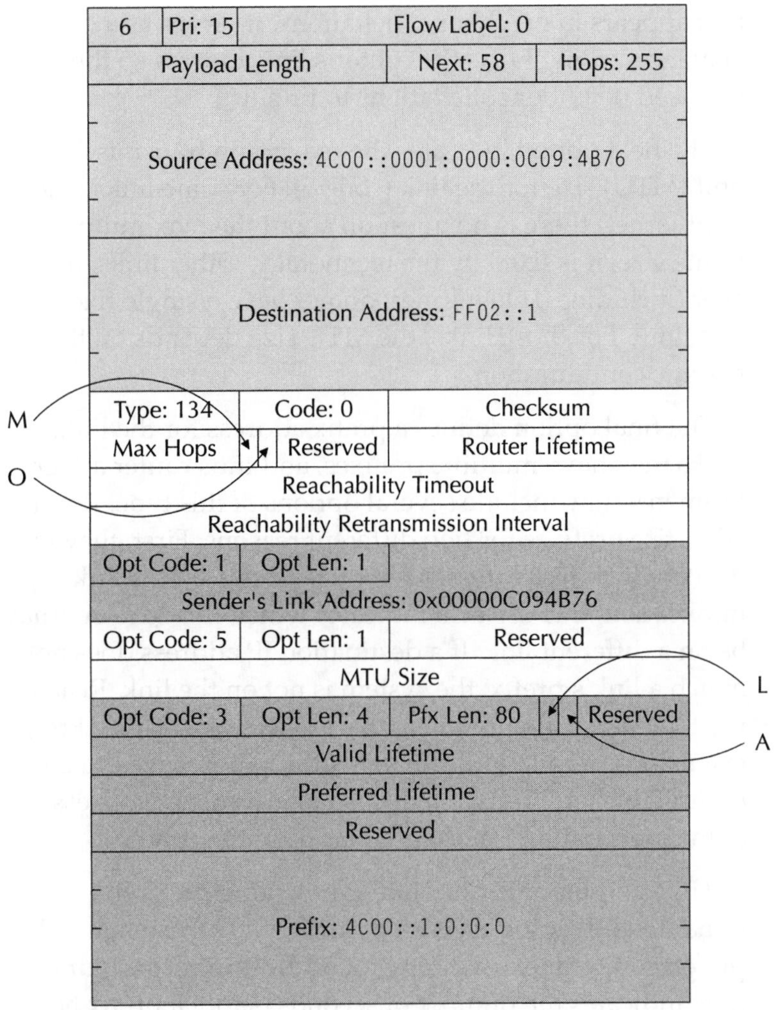

6	Pri: 15	Flow Label: 0	
Payload Length		Next: 58	Hops: 255

Source Address: 4C00::0001:0000:0C09:4B76

Destination Address: FF02::1

Type: 134	Code: 0	Checksum
Max Hops	Reserved	Router Lifetime
Reachability Timeout		
Reachability Retransmission Interval		
Opt Code: 1	Opt Len: 1	
Sender's Link Address: 0x00000C094B76		
Opt Code: 5	Opt Len: 1	Reserved
MTU Size		
Opt Code: 3	Opt Len: 4	Pfx Len: 80	Reserved
Valid Lifetime		
Preferred Lifetime		
Reserved		

Prefix: 4C00::1:0:0:0

M

O

L

A

Figure 5.9 Router advertisement format.

seconds. The *router lifetime* field determines how long hosts should consider the source of this message available. If this time interval passes without another router advertisement, hosts view the router as unavailable.

The two 1-bit fields in the basic ICMP message, shown as M and O in Figure 5.9, are used for address autoconfiguration. (See page 146.) The first option (code 1) includes the sender's link address. This is the same option that appears in neighbor solicitations. It serves as a convenience, telling hosts the router's link address so they do not need neighbor solicitations to find it.

The next option indicates the maximum transmission unit (MTU) size for the link (code 5). For some links (such as Ethernet) there is no question about the maximum frame size; it is fixed by the technology. Other links, however (including Token Ring), do not have a single fixed size limit. For those links, the MTU size depends on their specific configuration.

The final option defines a prefix address for the link. Links may have multiple prefixes, and thus router advertisements may include several options of this type. Routers advertise prefixes for two different reasons. First, they indicate which IP addresses refer to systems on the link. By implication, this use also indicates which IP addresses may be on a different link. If a destination IP address does not match a link's prefix, the system is not on the link. Reaching this destination requires the services of a router. Prefix extensions used to indicate this information have the L (for on-link) bit set. Prefixes may also play a role in address autoconfiguration. Those prefixes have the A bit set.

The valid lifetime determines how long the prefix will remain valid, in the absence of further advertisements. The preferred lifetime, used only for address autoconfiguration, indicates the number of seconds before a prefix becomes obsolete. An obsolete prefix may still be used so long as its valid lifetime has not expired. When the preferred lifetime expires, however, hosts are urged to begin phasing out its use. If an advertisement uses 0xFFFFFFFF for either of these fields, then the associated lifetime is considered infinite.

In addition to the router advertisement message, ICMP also defines a router solicitation message. This message lets hosts ask if any router is present on the network. Figure 5.10 shows a laptop added to the sample network. This

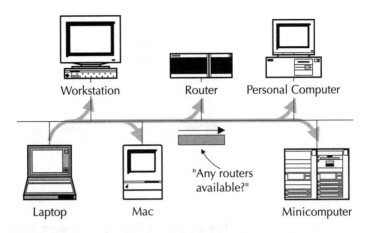

Figure 5.10 New hosts asks for a router.

host may issue a router solicitation as soon as it connects to the network, which allows it to find routers without having to wait for the next router advertisement.

The format of a router solicitation, shown in Figure 5.11, should be familiar by now. The option, indicating the sender's link address, is present as a convenience to any

6	Pri: 15	Flow Label: 0	
Payload Length: 16		Next: 58	Hops: 255
Source Address: FE80::0260:8C14:9252			
Destination Address: FF02::2			
Type: 133	Code: 0	Checksum	
Reserved: 0			
Opt Code: 1	Opt Len: 1		
Sender's Link Address: 0v02608C149252			

Figure 5.11 Router solicitation message.

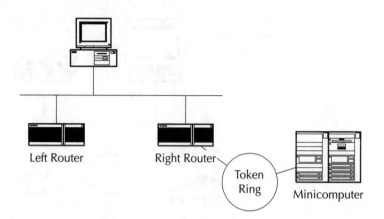

Figure 5.12 Choosing between two routers.

router that responds. That router does not have to go through the neighbor solicitation process to return its response. When a router responds to a solicitation, it does so by sending a router advertisement directly to the system making the request. This advertisement is not sent to a multicast address.

Redirection

Router solicitations and advertisements let a host find a router, but they do not guarantee that the host finds the best router for a particular destination. Consider the network of Figure 5.12, where the personal computer has a choice of two routers. Suppose that the PC had heard router advertisements from the routers, and knows that the address prefix for its local Ethernet is 4C00::0001:0:0:0/80. The PC needs to send traffic to the minicomputer, and that host's IP address is 4C00::0002:0800:5A01:3982. By comparing the destination prefix with the prefix of its local LAN (as in Table 5.3), the PC knows that the destination is not on the Ethernet. Reaching it requires the help of a router.

Table 5.3 Destination Does Not Match Link Prefix

Link Prefix	4C00:0000:0000:0000:0001:xxxx:xxxx:xxxx
Destination	4C00:0000:0000:0000:0002:0800:5A01:3982

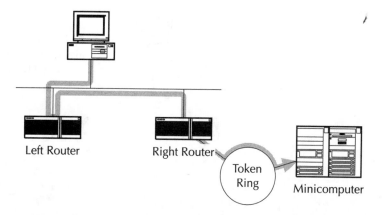

Figure 5.13 Inefficiently forwarding a datagram through the network.

At this point, the personal computer has a choice. It has heard advertisements from both routers. With nothing to guide its selection, the PC chooses to forward the datagram to the left router. Figure 5.13 shows the datagram's path through the network. Of course, the PC has not made the most efficient choice. It could have forwarded the datagram directly to the right router. Still, there is nothing illegal in its choice, and the packet does reach its destination.

Of all the systems involved, the left router can most easily detect the problem. It received a datagram from the Ethernet interface, and then turned around and sent it right back out that same interface. This situation calls for an ICMP *redirect* message, which tells the host system of a more efficient path to a particular destination.

After forwarding the PC's original datagram, the left router sends it a redirect message. Figure 5.14 shows this message. The redirect lets the original sender know about the better path. Figure 5.15 shows the format of a redirect. Its ICMP type value is 137, and the code is either 0 (if the destination is a host) or 1 (if it is a router). Following the basic ICMP header is the target address. This address identifies the router to which the traffic is being redirected.

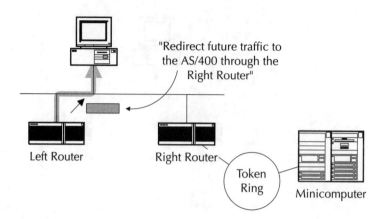

Figure 5.14 Redirecting a host.

The destination address that follows the target is the destination being redirected. As the figure shows, this example has the right router as the target and the minicomputer as the destination.

The redirect message, like other neighbor discovery messages, can have options added to it. Figure 5.15 shows two options. The first is the familiar link address of the target; in this case, the right router. The left router provides this as a courtesy to the PC. Including this address in the redirect saves the PC from having to perform a neighbor solicitation to find the target. The final option (code 4) holds a copy of the original datagram that triggered the redirect. The personal computer may find this information useful in processing the redirect.

Detecting the Loss of a Neighbor

All aspects of neighbor discovery—address resolution, router discovery, and redirection—let a system meet its neighbors. But even on healthy networks, neighbors do not remain present indefinitely. Hardware can fail, a system may change its interface card (and thus its link address), or a mobile system can move to a new link. When these changes occur, systems must recognize the new topology and react appropriately. The process by which

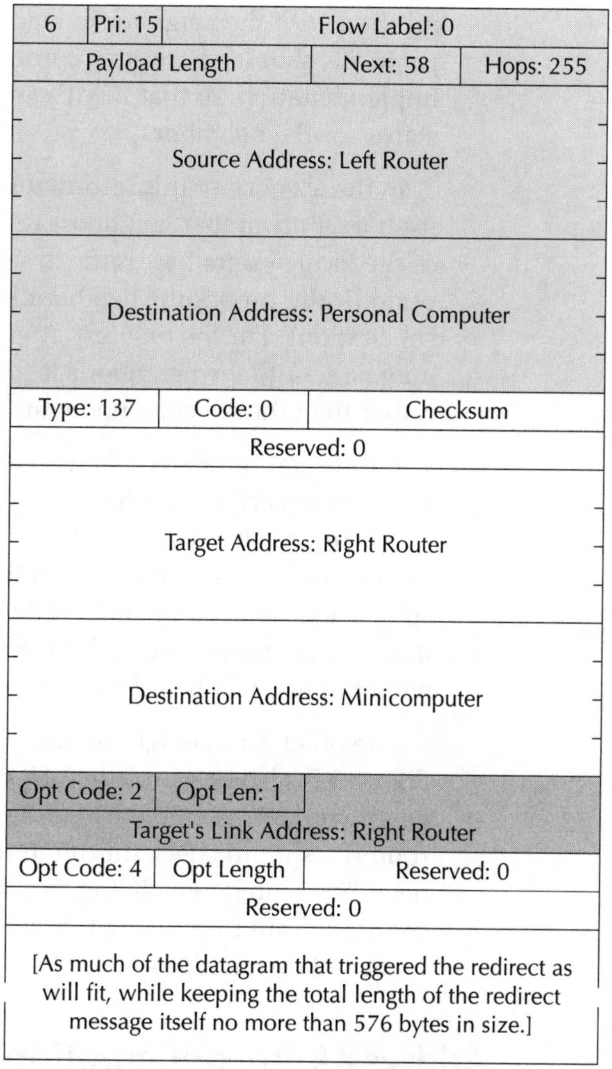

6	Pri: 15	Flow Label: 0	
Payload Length		Next: 58	Hops: 255

Source Address: Left Router

Destination Address: Personal Computer

Type: 137	Code: 0	Checksum
Reserved: 0		

Target Address: Right Router

Destination Address: Minicomputer

Opt Code: 2	Opt Len: 1	
Target's Link Address: Right Router		
Opt Code: 4	Opt Length	Reserved: 0
Reserved: 0		

[As much of the datagram that triggered the redirect as will fit, while keeping the total length of the redirect message itself no more than 576 bytes in size.]

Figure 5.15 Redirect message format.

systems learn of these changes is *neighbor unreachability detection* (NUD).

As part of NUD, systems continually monitor the status of neighbors that they know about. In most cases, upper-level layer protocols can help with this monitoring. If an upper layer receives a response to its query, then communication with the neighbor remains healthy. Upper layer protocols should share such confirmation with their ICMP implementation, so that ICMP can maintain an up-to-date status for the neighbor.

In the absence of this information, ICMP takes it upon itself to confirm that neighbors remain reachable. As long as the local system has traffic to send to a neighbor, ICMP periodically probes the neighbor by sending it neighbor solicitations. For the first few attempts, these solicitations may be sent to the neighbor's last known link address, rather than the solicited node multicast address.

If the neighbor responds with a neighbor advertisement, and that advertisement has the S bit set, the neighbor remains reachable. The S bit, shown initially in Figure 5.7, is important because it means that the advertisement is in response to a solicitation. If the bit is clear, then the advertisement is unsolicited, and there is no guarantee that the neighbor actually heard the solicitation.

The other bit in neighbor advertisements, the R bit of Figure 5.7, also has a role in NUD. When a host hears a neighbor advertisement from a system it believes to be a router, it should check this bit. If the bit is clear, then the neighbor is no longer acting as a router. The local system should refrain from using this neighbor to forward traffic to distant destinations.

Address Autoconfiguration

TCP/IP networks rely heavily on IP addresses. All of TCP/IP's protocols specify the source and destination of their communications with IP addresses. That makes it particularly important that a system know its own IP addresses, but this task is not always easy. Indeed, network administrators complain more often about the complexities of configuring IP addresses than any other aspect of IPv4. Fortunately, IPv6 simplifies matters considerably.

IPng provides two ways to ease the administration of IP addresses. The standards name them *stateless address auto-configuration* and *stateful address configuration*. The stateful approach relies on the Dynamic Host Configuration Protocol, discussed in Chapter 14. Stateless configuration is ICMP's responsibility.

ICMP's approach to address autoconfiguration combines information from two sources. First, many network technologies have their own addressing structure for local links. Often, the network requires that these link addresses be unique on the particular network. Some link addresses may be globally unique (Ethernet addresses, for example), but address configuration does not require it. Address configuration does, however, require that a system's link address be available to ICMP. As Figure 5.16 shows, that information may be installed in the hardware that interfaces to the network.

As a second source of information, ICMP can look for router advertisements on the network. These advertisements may contain a prefix IP address for the network. If they do, ICMP can combine the prefix address with a link address, yielding a full IP address. Why does this work? Because the prefix identifies the link on an internet, and

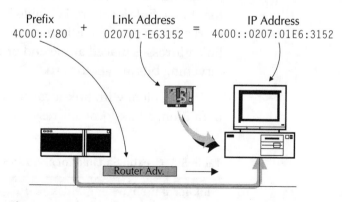

Figure 5.16 Combining router advertisements and link addresses.

Table 5.4 Flags in Router Advertisements

M	If set, hosts should not use address autoconfiguration, instead, they should rely on DHCP to determine their IP address.
O	If set, hosts can use address autoconfiguration, but should use DHCP for other configuration information.

the link address identifies the interface on the link. Together, they identify the interface on the internet, the very definition of a valid IP address.

Router advertisements provide more information than a simple address prefix. Each advertisement includes two flags, designated M and O, that regulate how hosts should behave. Figure 5.9 shows their position in the ICMP message, while Table 5.4 indicates their meaning.

Link-Local Addresses

This general approach can even work when there are no router advertisements. IP addresses include a set defined as link-local. (See page 33.) These addresses are intended for use only within a single network; they do not have to be unique across an entire internetwork. Any host that has a link address can form a valid IP address by appending that to the link-local prefix. Table 5.5 shows how this works for an example Ethernet address. Notice that the link address is placed at the end of the IP address, and intervening bits are set to zero.

The problem with link-local addresses is their scope. By definition, a link-local address is only valid on the particu-

Table 5.5 Creating a Link-Local Address

Link-local prefix:	FE80::/10
Ethernet address:	080020-1FC889
IP address:	FE80::0800:201F:C889

lar link. It has no meaning to systems beyond that local network.

Detecting Duplicate Addresses

Before a system uses its IP address, it can make sure that the address is truly unique. If by some mistake the system has obtained the same address as another system, communication to either system will almost certainly fail. Furthermore, such problems are often very difficult to diagnose and correct. By detecting duplicate addresses automatically, a system can make life a lot easier for network administrators.

Since address autoconfiguration always bases its IP addresses on link addresses, duplicate detection can focus on the link address only. All systems form link-local IP addresses, so the most reliable way to detect duplicate link addresses is to check link-local IP addresses. If a system's link-local address is unique, then its link address must also be unique, as must any other IP address formed from router advertisements.

To check for duplicates, a system simply sends a neighbor a solicitation message for its own link-local IP address. If no other system answers this solicitation, then no duplicate address exists. To distinguish these solicitations from normal neighbor solicitations, they should have a source IP address of zero, and they should not contain the sender's link address extension.

If a duplicate address does exist, a system will hear a neighbor advertisement in response to its solicitation. At that point, the system should immediately cease operation on that interface. Naturally, it should also indicate an error to its operator.

Systems should employ duplicate address detection as part of their startup procedure. When doing so, they should delay a random amount of time before beginning the process. Such a delay will prevent hosts from flooding the link with solicitations should they all restart at the same time (after a power failure, for example).

Group Membership

**Whatever
Happened to
IGMP?**

IPv4 uses a separate
protocol to manage
group membership.
That protocol is the
Internet Group Mul-
ticast Protocol
(IGMP). In the IPv6
environment, ICMP
assumes responsibility
for services that IPv4
left to IGMP.

In addition to administering unicast IP addresses, ICMP also manages group addresses. It provides a way for systems to announce (and later renounce) their membership in groups. Routers listen to these messages to track group membership on the link. They can then know whether to forward datagrams addressed to specific groups.

All group membership messages have the same format, shown in Figure 5.17, but each message has its own ICMP type. The query messages ask if a system belongs to a particular group. The report and termination messages allow systems to join or leave a group. Report messages also serve as the response to queries. Table 5.6 lists the ICMP types for these messages.

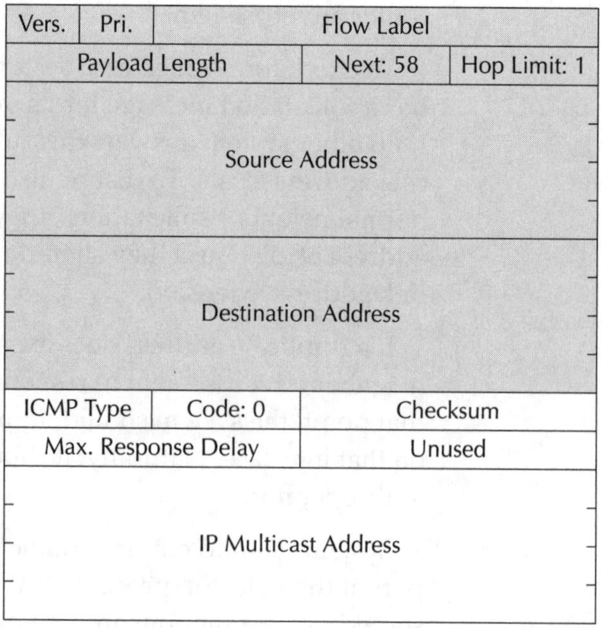

Vers.	Pri.	Flow Label		
Payload Length			Next: 58	Hop Limit: 1
Source Address				
Destination Address				
ICMP Type	Code: 0		Checksum	
Max. Response Delay			Unused	
IP Multicast Address				

Figure 5.17 ICMP group membership message format.

Table 5.6 ICMP Group Membership Messages

Type	Message
130	Group Membership Query
131	Group Membership Report
132	Group Membership Termination

In most cases, the messages are sent to the group address in question. The destination IP address will then be the same as the multicast IP address in the message body. It is also possible to query for membership in all groups. In such cases, the destination address is the All Nodes address, and the IP multicast address is set to zero.

The *maximum response delay* field is only used in queries. It defines the maximum amount of time, in milliseconds, that a system may delay before responding to the query. To prevent every group member from responding simultaneously, each should delay a random amount of time before transmitting a response. That delay should range from zero to the maximum response delay value.

Error Reporting

It is an unfortunate fact that networks do not always perform flawlessly, and some errors are truly unavoidable. For many common errors, ICMP takes the first step in correcting them; it reports their occurrence. ICMP reports errors that arise as part of IP's processing of datagrams. Those errors can include invalid IP headers, datagrams that are too big for intervening links, datagrams that do not reach their destination before the hop limit runs out, and destinations that simply cannot be reached. In all such cases, ICMP reports an error back to the source of the datagram.

Consider what happens when IP's hop limit expires, for example. Figure 5.18 shows the situation. The personal computer intends to send a datagram to the minicomputer. It starts its datagram with a hop limit of 3, but the destina-

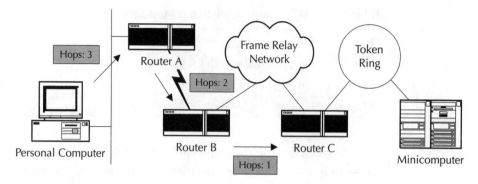

Figure 5.18 Exceeding an IP hop limit.

tion is 4 hops away; therefore, when the datagram reaches router C, its hop limit expires. Router C cannot forward the datagram any further. (The fact that the datagram almost reaches its destination is irrelevant.)

Router C responds to this condition by sending an ICMP error message back to the datagram's source, in this case, the personal computer. Figure 5.19 shows router C sending the PC an error report. Note that the error report is itself an ICMP message, and it is contained in an IP datagram. To avoid choking a network with error messages, ICMP has specific rules that define when error messages are permissible, which are listed in Table 5.7.

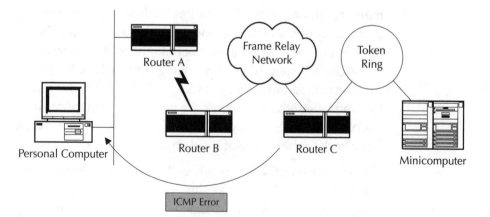

Figure 5.19 Returning an ICMP error message.

Table 5.7 Prohibitions Against ICMP Error Messages

- Do not send an error message in response to an ICMP error message.
- Do not send an error message in response to a datagram destined for a group address.
- Do not send an error message in response to any datagram that arrives via a multicast or broadcast link address.

Destination Unreachable

One of the most important error messages indicates that a destination cannot be reached. Figure 5.20 shows the format of this ICMP message. The ICMP Code field explains why the destination is unreachable. The unreachable codes are given in Table 5.8.

Packet Too Big

The second type of error occurs when a datagram is too big to cross an intervening link. Figure 5.21 shows how this problem might arise on a simple network. The two

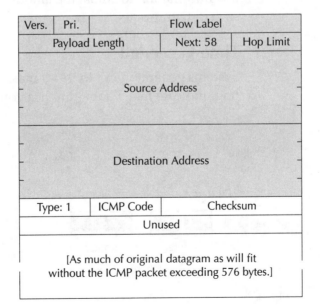

Vers.	Pri.	Flow Label		
Payload Length			Next: 58	Hop Limit
Source Address				
Destination Address				
Type: 1	ICMP Code		Checksum	
Unused				
[As much of original datagram as will fit without the ICMP packet exceeding 576 bytes.]				

Figure 5.20 Destination unreachable message.

Table 5.8 Destination Unreachable Codes

0	No path to the destination.
1	Communication with destination prohibited by administrative control.
2	Routing header (page 113) requests strict forwarding to a system that is not a neighbor.
3	Destination address is unreachable.
4	Requested port (pages 163 and 179) is not available.

host systems, each on Token Rings, are separated by an Ethernet LAN. Token Rings can transfer packets of 8,000 bytes and more, but Ethernet has a fixed limit of 1,500 bytes. If the personal computer sends an 8,000-byte packet, that packet will make it to the first router, but it cannot cross the intervening Ethernet link. The first router must return an ICMP error message. Figure 5.22 shows the format of this message. Note that it includes the actual MTU of the link that caused the problem. In the preceding example, this field will have a value of 1,500. The PC can use this information to adjust the amount of data it puts in each datagram.

Time Exceeded

Systems generate *Time Exceeded* messages for two reasons. Both indicate that a datagram has gone too long without

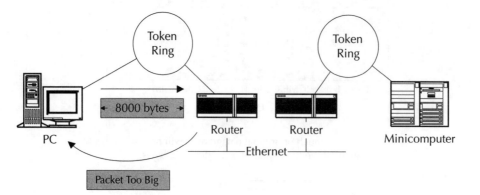

Figure 5.21 Reporting a Packet Too Big error.

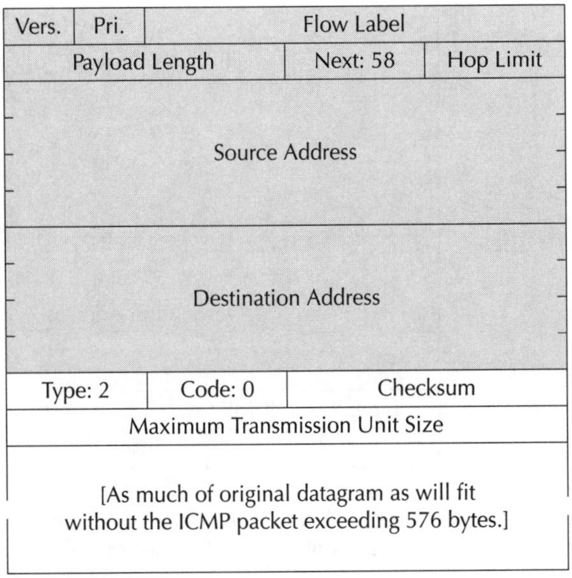

Vers.	Pri.	Flow Label		
Payload Length			Next: 58	Hop Limit
Source Address				
Destination Address				
Type: 2	Code: 0		Checksum	
Maximum Transmission Unit Size				
[As much of original datagram as will fit without the ICMP packet exceeding 576 bytes.]				

Figure 5.22 Packet Too Big message format.

reaching its destination. The most direct cause of this error is the exhaustion of a datagram's hop limit. This is the situation in Figure 5.18, discussed earlier in this chapter. The last router that handles the datagram returns an ICMP error to the source.

A Time Exceeded error also occurs if a system fails to complete reassembly of datagram fragments in a reasonable amount of time. This time limit should range between 60 and 120 seconds. To avoid generating a lot of error messages for the same datagram, systems should only generate this error if the fragments they have received include the fragment at offset zero. Once a system returns this Time Exceeded error, it should discard the fragments that it has been retaining.

The format of Time Exceeded messages resembles other ICMP errors, as Figure 5.23 shows. The ICMP Code field distinguishes the different reasons for the error. As given in Table 5.9, a code of 0 indicates a hop limit has been exceeded, while reassembly timeouts use a code of 1.

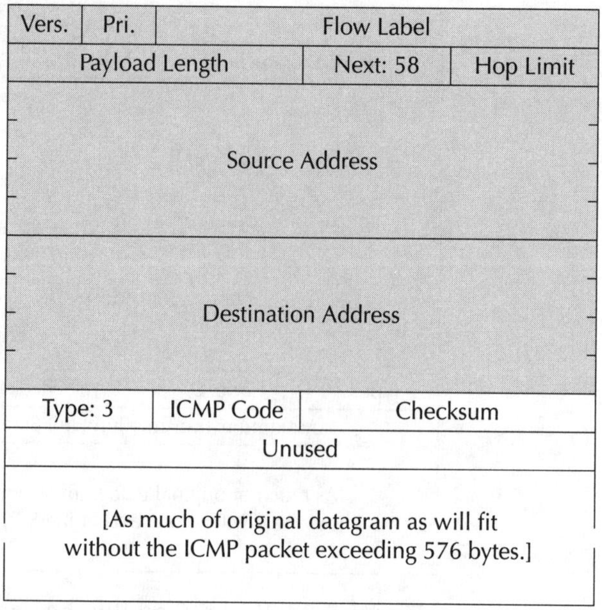

Vers.	Pri.	Flow Label		
Payload Length			Next: 58	Hop Limit
Source Address				
Destination Address				
Type: 3	ICMP Code		Checksum	
Unused				
[As much of original datagram as will fit without the ICMP packet exceeding 576 bytes.]				

Figure 5.23 ICMP Time Exceeded error message.

Parameter Problem

The final ICMP error message is particularly onerous. The *Parameter Problem* message indicates that something was wrong with the IP header in the original datagram. Such problems include errors in the base IP header, as well as extension headers or options in the datagram. The code value indicates the specific problem encountered (detailed in Table 5.10).

To help pinpoint the error, the message includes a *pointer* field as well as the code field. This field indicates the offset within the original datagram of the first byte in error. A pointer of zero, for example, indicates that the version or priority field in the original IP header is invalid.

Table 5.9 ICMP Time Exceeded Codes

0	hop limit exhausted
1	reassembly time expired

Table 5.10 ICMP Parameter Problem Codes

0	invalid header field
1	unrecognized Next Header value
2	unrecognized option

Figure 5.24 shows a complete parameter problem message. Note that the error message may not include all of the offending datagram. If necessary, the original datagram is truncated to make sure that the resulting ICMP message does not exceed 576 bytes. Even if only part of the original datagram fits, though, the pointer still indicates the actual byte in error. The pointer, in other words, may indicate an erroneous byte that is not itself contained in the ICMP message.

Network Diagnostics

One of ICMP's simplest functions is network diagnostics. As users and administrators alike can attest, this is also

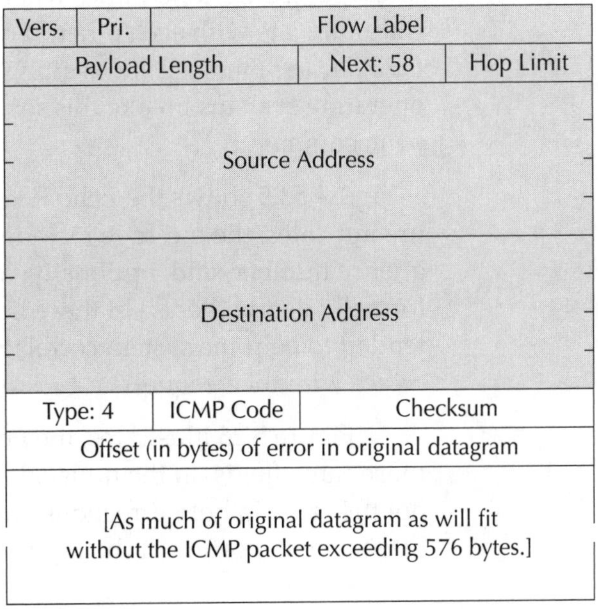

Vers.	Pri.	Flow Label		
Payload Length			Next: 58	Hop Limit
Source Address				
Destination Address				
Type: 4		ICMP Code	Checksum	
Offset (in bytes) of error in original datagram				
[As much of original datagram as will fit without the ICMP packet exceeding 576 bytes.]				

Figure 5.24 ICMP Parameter Problem error message.

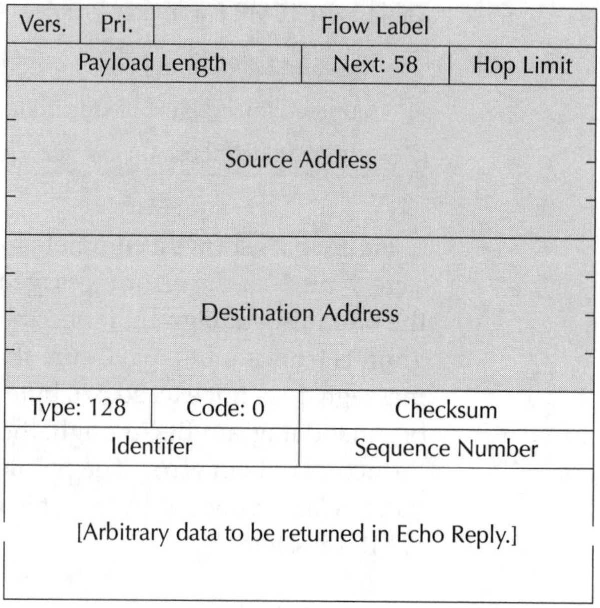

Vers.	Pri.	Flow Label		
Payload Length			Next: 58	Hop Limit
Source Address				
Destination Address				
Type: 128	Code: 0		Checksum	
Identifer		Sequence Number		
[Arbitrary data to be returned in Echo Reply.]				

Figure 5.25 ICMP Echo Request message format.

one of its most appreciated functions. With its diagnostic messages, ICMP determines whether two systems can communicate with each other. It does this by sending an *Echo Request* message and waiting for an *Echo Reply*. Most operating systems invoke this service with the familiar `ping` command.

Figure 5.25 shows the Echo Request format. As the figure indicates, the message includes an identifier, a sequence number, and, optionally, extra data. ICMP does not formally define the use of these fields, but they are intended to help the system correlate any responses it receives with their requests.

As Figure 5.26 illustrates, the Echo Reply simply repeats those same fields. In the unusual event that path MTUs are not the same in both directions, the responder may truncate the data portion of the reply.

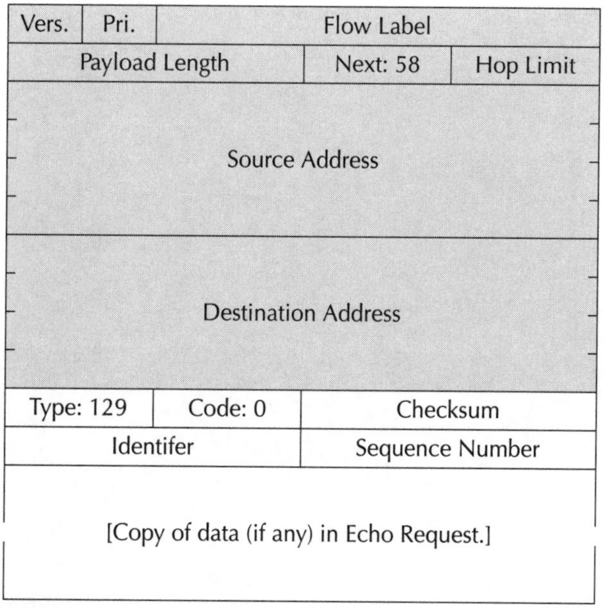

Vers.	Pri.	Flow Label		
Payload Length			Next: 58	Hop Limit
Source Address				
Destination Address				
Type: 129	Code: 0		Checksum	
Identifer		Sequence Number		
[Copy of data (if any) in Echo Request.]				

Figure 5.26 ICMP Echo Reply message format.

Summary

Even though ICMP is classified as a separate protocol from IP, it is truly essential to IP's operation. ICMP coordinates the interaction among systems through neighbor discovery and with group membership messages. It provides a simple way for systems to automatically determine their own IP addresses.

ICMP also coordinates a network's response to potential problems. When IP detects a problem with a datagram, ICMP reports that error to the datagram's source. Finally, ICMP provides an essential diagnostic tool to users and administrators with its echo request and reply.

6

Datagram Delivery via UDP

The protocols of the previous chapters move packets across networks. This chapter, the first to consider a transport layer protocol, shifts the focus to the systems on those networks. Just as the Internet Protocol uses the services of subnetworks, transport protocols build upon the services of IP. They rely on IP to deliver packets to the right place, and then they take over.

Transport protocols have two major responsibilities. First, they must distinguish the traffic of different applications within a system. The TCP/IP protocol suite contains a wide variety of applications. Frequently, several applications will be active in a system at the same time. Transport protocols sort out the various traffic streams, making sure to deliver exactly the right data to the right application. This chapter's first section describes how TCP/IP protocols differentiate applications.

The second obligation facing a transport protocol is reliability. Recall that IP cannot guarantee delivery of packets. Nor does it typically ensure that the data within those packets arrives free from corruption. Transport protocols compensate for these problems, although different transport protocols compensate in different ways, and to different degrees. Each provides a particular level of service to its applications. This chapter considers the simplest level of service—datagram delivery. Datagram delivery is not a guaranteed service, but it does protect against corruption. The second section in this chapter outlines the important characteristics of datagram delivery.

The specific transport protocol that provides TCP/IP's datagram delivery service is the User Datagram Protocol, or UDP. This chapter concludes with a detailed discussion of the UDP standard.

Distinguishing Applications

One of the strengths of the TCP/IP protocol suite is the diversity of its applications. TCP/IP's layered architecture makes it easy to develop and deploy application protocols for almost any purpose. As a consequence, TCP/IP-based systems often support many applications at the same time. Each application may simultaneously take part in conversations with peers across the network.

Consider the workstation at the top of Figure 6.1. It is carrying on three conversations—network management,

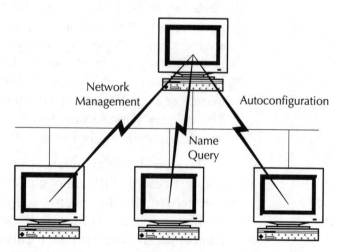

Figure 6.1 Many applications at once.

autoconfiguration, and a name query—at the same time. UDP distinguishes the traffic for each application and, within the workstation's software, distributes that traffic to the right place. Figure 6.2 looks inside the workstation to illustrate this process.

Ports

To identify different applications, TCP/IP protocols tag each packet with a number known as a port. Different applications use different values for port fields, and a transport protocol can use the port value to decide which application should receive a packet's data. In this way, the port value acts like the IP next header field. The next header value distinguishes different transport protocols for IP, and the port value distinguishes different application protocols for a transport protocol.

Applications select a port in one of two ways. The two approaches correspond to the two roles that an application can play in a conversation. These roles correspond to a *client* and a *server*. Clients initiate most conversations by actively requesting information, while servers simply respond to such requests.

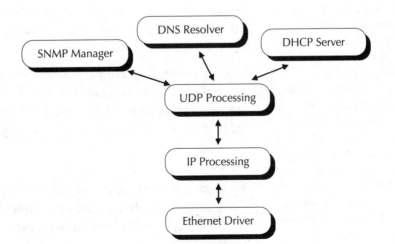

Figure 6.2 UDP distinguishing application traffic.

When a client application needs to make a request, it must know how to get that request to a server; it must know, in advance, which port value to use for the particular application. A server, on the other hand, doesn't have to know the port value to use for its response. It can have the client designate a port as part of the initial request.

This contrast occurs outside of communication protocols. In the United States, for example, local phone systems provide directory assistance to translate names into phone numbers. In most cases, the caller (acting as a client) accesses this service by dialing 411. The client has to know this number in advance. The server, on the other hand, does not need to know the client's phone number. The operator simply responds on whatever line the call arrives.

The same principles apply to computer communications. Suppose that a client application needs SNMP network management information from a remote system. The client builds an SNMP request and sends it to the remote system. In order to ensure that the request reaches the SNMP application in that system, the client must specify a port value that it knows belongs to the SNMP protocol. The SNMP server, on the other hand, does not have to know the client's port in advance. When the server gets the request, it can examine the request to see which port the client has chosen to use. The server can then return its response to that same port.

Port values that are predefined for specific applications are *well-known ports*. Table 6.1 lists the port values for important applications that use UDP. Many other experimental and informational protocols also rely on UDP.

Sockets

By themselves, ports merely define application protocols. They do not identify actual application programs running in real machines. By combining a port value with a network address, however, just such a distinction is possible. The combination is known as a socket.

Privileged Ports

Many computer systems restrict access to particular port values. Programs without adequate privileges (such as user programs) are allowed only a certain range of port values. This range does not include values typically assigned to server applications, and so the restriction prevents any user from running programs that act as servers. Using a server port requires special privileges from the operating system, and so the server port values are often known as *privileged ports*.

Table 6.1 Well-Known Port Values for Important UDP Applications

7	Echo Server
9	Discard Server
53	Domain Name Server
67	Configuration (DHCP) Server
68	Configuration (DHCP) Client
69	Trivial File Transfer Protocol

Figure 6.3 shows two different conversations on a computer network. The workstation at the top exchanges management information with the two other workstations. As the figure shows, these two conversations use a total of four sockets. Sockets 1 and 2 define the conversation between the left and top workstations, while sockets 3 and 4 form the conversation between the top and right workstations. As this example shows, different sockets can have the same values for both their port and network address. Sockets 2 and 3, for example, may have both the same network address (the top workstation's) and the same port value (management traffic).

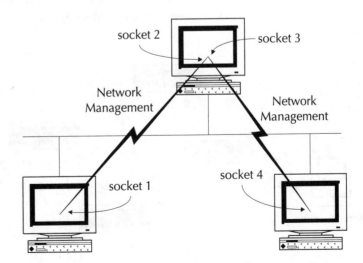

Figure 6.3 Sockets define endpoints of conversations.

Datagram Delivery

Ports allow the User Datagram Protocol to identify different applications. Of course, UDP needs to distinguish applications so it can transfer data for them. UDP provides a particular type of service to those applications called datagram delivery. Datagram delivery is a connectionless service, which means that each unit of data (a datagram) exists entirely independently of all other datagrams, even datagrams between the same two sockets. There is no reference to tie multiple datagrams together, and there is no reference that allows a receiver to acknowledge reception of a datagram. Finally, there is no reference that can establish a relative ordering of different datagrams.

In practice, this means that UDP provides a best effort delivery; that is, it does its best to transfer datagrams for its applications, but UDP makes no guarantees. Datagrams may get reordered, even lost, in transit, and the applications must be prepared for such events.

Figure 6.4 illustrates how datagrams may get lost in transit. A personal computer sends four different datagrams to a workstation. While traversing the link between routers A and C, one of those datagrams (number 2) is damaged and discarded. Since router D never correctly re-

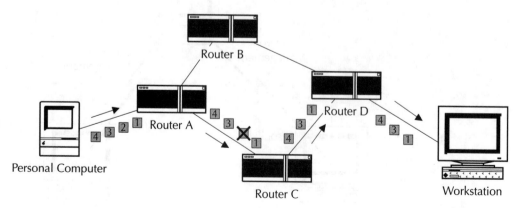

Figure 6.4 Datagram loss in transit.

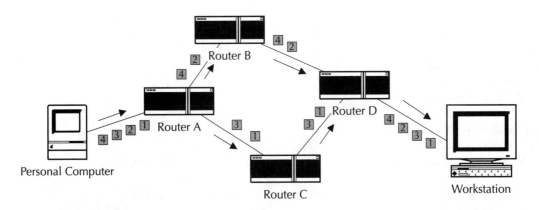

Figure 6.5 Datagrams arriving out of order.

ceives datagram 2, it cannot forward it to the destination workstation. UDP provides no mechanisms to recognize or recover from this loss. If the applications need either, they must provide it themselves.

Figure 6.5 shows how datagrams may arrive out of order. In this example, router A sends every other datagram to router B. Router B, however, is slower than router C, and the datagrams it forwards experience a delay. Router D, therefore, receives datagrams 1 and 3 before datagrams 2 and 4. That is the same order that router D delivers datagrams to the workstation, and so the workstation receives the datagrams out of order.

UDP does provide one enhancement to the network service available from IP. It includes simple error-checking that can detect corrupted datagrams. When UDP receives a datagram that it determines to be corrupt, it discards the datagram instead of delivering it to an application.

User Datagram Protocol

Because datagram delivery is such a simple service, the User Datagram Protocol is a very simple protocol. Every UDP packet contains a fixed, 8-byte header followed by the application's data. Figure 6.6 shows a UDP datagram.

Why UDP?

The shortcomings of datagram delivery– loss and misordering– are not present in TCP, the connection-oriented transport protocol. And since TCP is widely available, it is reasonable to wonder why an application would use UDP instead of TCP. The answer lies in UDP's simplicity. Since UDP has no connections, applications do not have to establish or clear them. When an application has data to send, it just sends it. This approach makes things simpler for the application, and it can eliminate a substantial delay in the communication. UDP is also ideal for those systems that are so limited that they cannot afford to implement TCP. Regular computer systems do not usually suffer this limitation, but special purpose systems (like uninterruptable power supplies) might.

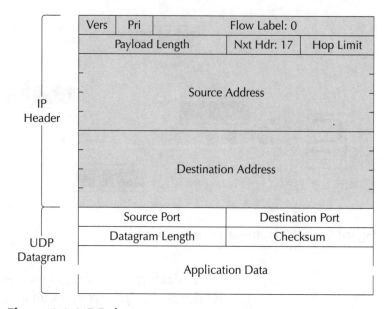

Figure 6.6 UDP datagram.

The port values identify the ports of the source and destination of the data. If the datagram carries a request for a server, then the destination port usually contains a well-known value. (See Table 6.1.) In such cases, the source port is often arbitrary. It normally indicates the port to which the server should address its reply. When the datagram carries a server's reply, the source port is typically well known, and the destination port identifies the requester.

The datagram length is the total length of the datagram, including both the UDP header and the application data. Length is measured in bytes.

The final part of the UDP header is the checksum. This field provides a simple mechanism to detect many errors in the datagram. The data that the checksum protects includes more than the UDP datagram. It also includes the source and destination network addresses and the IPv6 next header value. By including these fields, the checksum protects against datagrams that are not themselves corrupt, but have been delivered to the wrong place. Figure

Omitting the Checksum

The current IP standards require that all UDP datagrams include a checksum. With IPv4, however, a sender could effectively omit the checksum by setting its value to zero. Receivers disregarded the checksum of any datagram with a checksum value of zero. Even though this omission is no longer legal with IPv6, IPv6 implementations must still be prepared to receive UDP datagrams from systems using IPv4.

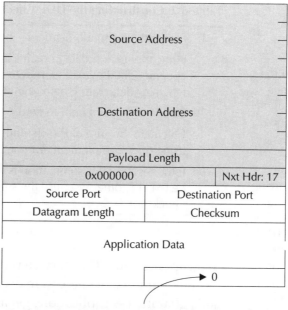

Last byte of zero added only if application data consists of an odd number of bytes; note that neither the payload length nor the datagram length fields is adjusted to include it.

Figure 6.7 Data covered by UDP checksum.

6.7 shows how this additional data is added to the UDP datagram. The added fields, shown in gray in the figure, are called a pseudo header.

Table 6.2 summarizes the rules that a sender follows to construct the checksum. Note that the sum requires ones complement arithmetic. This operation is not the same as twos complement addition, which is the standard addition provided by most modern microprocessors.

A receiver takes much the same approach. Table 6.3 lists its steps. If a receiver finds a checksum invalid, it discards the datagram without delivering it to an application.

Summary

This chapter introduced the User Datagram Protocol, or UDP. UDP provides the simplest possible transport service

Calculating Checksums Efficiently

A major factor in the performance of network implementations is their performance in calculating checksums. Several RFCs are devoted to the subject of maximizing this performance; the most thorough RFC on the topic is RFC 1071, which includes several suggestions for improving checksum algorithms, as well as sample code in C, Motorola 68020 Assembly, Cray Assembly, and IBM 370 Assembly language.

Table 6.2 Constructing the UDP Checksum

1. Prepend the pseudo header to the UDP datagram.
2. If the application data contains an odd number of bytes, append a final byte of zero. (Do not increase the payload length or datagram length to include this byte.)
3. Set the checksum field to zero.
4. Calculate the sum of the resulting series of 16-bit values, using ones complement arithmetic.
5. If the result of this summation is zero, set the checksum to be 0xFFFF; otherwise, use the summation result as the checksum.

to its applications. That service is datagram delivery, and it has no guarantee of success. In exchange for giving up such guarantees, applications get a much simpler service to use, and they get more of the computer system's memory and CPU resources for themselves.

Table 6.3 Validating the UDP Checksum

1. If the checksum value is zero, assume that it is correct and skip the remaining steps. (See sidebar on page 169.)
2. Prepend the pseudo header to the UDP datagram.
3. If the application data contains an odd number of bytes, append a final byte of zero. (Do not increase the payload length or datagram length to count this byte.)
4. Calculate the sum of the resulting series of 16-bit values, using ones complement arithmetic.
5. If the result of this summation is 0xFFFF, the checksum is valid; otherwise, the checksum is invalid.

7

Reliable Delivery with TCP

The User Datagram Protocol (Chapter 6) represents the simplest transport protocol, but it is also the most limited. In particular, UDP adds little reliability to IP's connectionless service. UDP also makes no attempt to preserve the sequence of messages it delivers. Many applications cannot tolerate these limitations. They need assurance that their data actually makes it to the destination. In addition, their messages must often arrive in a particular order. These applications need reliable data delivery, and the Transmission Control Protocol (TCP) provides it for them.

This chapter examines reliable delivery and TCP in three stages. First, it introduces the concepts behind reliable delivery. To achieve reliability, TCP provides a connection-oriented service. The chapter next details the TCP specification. It documents how a system must behave when using TCP. The chapter concludes with a section on implementing TCP. This section presents several important guidelines for TCP implementation. The TCP standard does not require that systems adhere to these guidelines, but they can make a substantial difference in how systems perform on TCP/IP networks.

The Principles behind Reliable Delivery

As stated, although some applications can make do with the delivery service UDP provides, many cannot. Most TCP/IP applications expect the transport protocol to provide reliable data delivery. Of course, these applications must have a clear understanding of what reliability means. This section describes how TCP defines reliability. In then explains why a separate protocol like TCP is needed to provide that reliability. It concludes with a discussion of the important principles behind TCP's operation. After this background, the chapter moves to a detailed examination of TCP itself.

The Meaning of Reliability

By providing reliable delivery, TCP offers a robust service to its applications. For TCP, reliability includes four major properties, summarized in Table 7.1.

TCP Eliminates Errors

Perhaps the most basic quality of reliable delivery is that it be free from errors. Data that TCP delivers to the recipient should be exactly the same data that the sender gave TCP originally. In a rigorous sense, this quality is impossible to attain. Even if TCP took the drastic step of sending a thousand copies of each message and comparing all of those copies in the destination system, undetected errors could still occur. Theoretically, after all, the same error could appear in all thousand copies. TCP compromises, therefore, by providing a nearly error-free service. TCP cannot abso-

Table 7.1 Qualities of TCP's Reliable Delivery Service

- Error-Free
- Assured Delivery
- In Sequence
- No Duplication

TCP Cannot Provide Absolute Reliability

With the extensive service that TCP provides, it is sometimes easy to forget that TCP, by itself, cannot provide absolute reliability. When data reaches its destination, TCP can reliably deliver that data to an application protocol. TCP cannot, however, guarantee that the application protocol successfully processes the data. Consider a file transfer, for example. TCP can deliver data to the file transfer application. If the disk crashes, however, and the application is unable to write the data, then there is nothing that TCP can do. If an application needs absolute reliability, then it must provide that itself.

lutely prevent all undetected errors, but it can make them extremely rare.

TCP Assures Delivery

When TCP accepts a message from an application, it also accepts responsibility for delivering that message. TCP guarantees that data reaches its destination. Of course, successful delivery is not always possible. The recipient, for example, may lose power before the data arrives. When TCP cannot deliver data, it will tell the sending application of the failure.

TCP Provides In-Sequence Delivery

From TCP's perspective, reliable delivery means more than simply delivering data without errors. TCP also endeavors to deliver data in sequence. This service ensures that the recipient receives the data in the same order that the sender sends it.

Sometimes, it is easy to overlook the importance of in-sequence delivery. Does order really matter as long as the data actually arrives? The answer is definitely yes, as Figure 7.1 shows. In the figure, the PC sends simple commands in its messages. If those commands arrive out of order, the server would delete the old file before it could be copied to a new file. That is clearly not what the user wants.

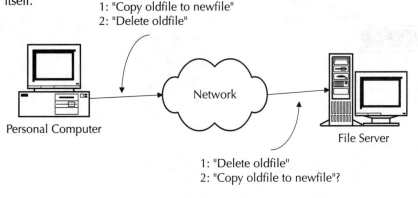

Figure 7.1 The consequences of out-of-sequence delivery.

TCP Eliminates Duplication

Almost as a corollary to in-sequence delivery, TCP makes sure that data messages are only delivered once. Sometimes receiving many copies of a message is just as bad as (or even worse than) not receiving the message at all. Again, the clearest examples arise when the message contains commands as well as data. Imagine the consequences if a single request for a wire funds transfer arrives at a bank several times.

TCP Operates End-to-End

All of the qualities of reliable delivery that this section discusses are part of a transport layer service. Transport protocols are end-to-end protocols. TCP, like other transport protocols, operates only at the original source and ultimate destination of the data. As Figure 7.2 shows, TCP does not participate at intermediate routers along the data path. Only by operating at the communication endpoints can TCP provide a true delivery service to its users. After all, a user probably cares little if its message reaches the first router along the way to the destination; users want their messages to complete the journey to the destination.

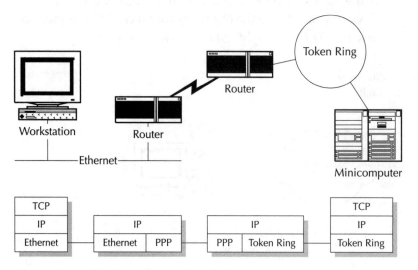

Figure 7.2 TCP provides end-to-end service.

The Need for Transport Protocols

The characteristics of TCP's reliable delivery—error-free, assured, in sequence, without duplication—are often characteristics of subnetwork technologies. Many of the subnetworks that Chapter 3 discusses provide this level of service for data that they transfer. Given this fact, why are transport protocols even needed? If a packet travels across several subnetworks, each of which is reliable by itself, how could the overall path not be reliable?

Perhaps the most surprising failure of interconnected, reliable subnetworks is correctness. Even though the subnetworks themselves all provide error-free delivery, it may still be the case that a packet traveling through them does not arrive error-free. Of course, like TCP itself, subnetwork error-detection methods are not perfect; they cannot detect every possible error. Most of them, however, are far better than TCP's approach.

A more likely source of errors is not the subnetworks, but the routers that connect subnetworks. Consider Figure 7.3, which looks inside a router. In the figure, a packet ar-

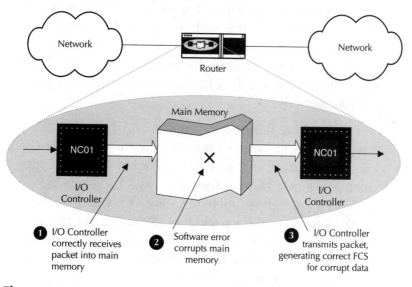

Figure 7.3 Data corruption within a router.

rives from the left network. The packet carries with it a frame check sequence (FCS) appended by the previous hop. The receiving router recalculates the FCS from the packet's data, and compares the result with the actual FCS in the packet. If they match, the packet is accepted as error-free by the router. At this point, the left subnetwork has done its job and reliably delivered the packet through the subnetwork.

The important point is that (in most cases anyway) FCS checking is a job for the hardware that actually interfaces to the subnetwork (the I/O controller in the figure). The router's software is not involved because software is generally not fast enough to perform the complex mathematical calculations required to check an FCS. For the same reason, the router's software cannot compute the FCS on packets that it forwards. That job, too, is left to the hardware that interfaces to the subnetwork. To see the consequences, follow the packet as it travels through the router.

Once the router receives the packet (successfully) from the left subnetwork, the router's software takes over. Suppose, however, that the software has a bug, which causes the router to corrupt part of the packet while it sits in the router's memory. At this point (step 2 in the figure), the packet is no longer free from errors. Unaware of this problem, the router moves the packet to the right subnetwork. It asks the interface hardware to transmit the packet on that subnetwork.

This is where things really go wrong. The interface hardware has no way of knowing that the packet now contains an error, and so the interface hardware happily calculates a new FCS for the packet as it transmits the packet on the right subnetwork. This FCS will be correct for the data now in the packet, even though the data is wrong! The packet continues through the interconnected subnetworks, each of which is blissfully unaware that an error has now been introduced.

Detecting these types of errors requires work at the endpoints of the connection. Transport protocols can detect such errors because they rely on error-detection codes inserted by the original sender. These codes are not recomputed by hardware interfaces along the way, and they will thus detect errors that the subnetworks can miss.

It is fairly simple to construct similar examples for the other aspects of reliable delivery. In each case, a collection of reliable subnetworks does not ensure that the entire path remains reliable. Transport level protocols like TCP provide that reliability.

Connection-Oriented Operation

For TCP, the basis for reliable delivery is a connection. Like transport protocols from other protocol suites, TCP relies on connection-oriented operation. Chapter 2 introduced the concepts of connectionless and connection-oriented communication. For reliable delivery, there is one key difference between the two: connections establish a context for communications. This context allows TCP to relate different packets with each other, and with such a relationship, TCP can identify the sequence of individual packets. The context also gives TCP a way to recognize duplicate packets, and it can determine when particular packets are missing. Together with a simple checksum, a connection's context gives TCP the tools it needs to deliver data reliably.

This section looks more closely at TCP connections. It explains the principles behind connection establishment and clearing, and examines normal data transfer, urgent data transfer, acknowledgments, and flow control.

Identifying Connections

Before discussing the mechanics of a connection, it is important to understand how TCP identifies individual connections. Most TCP implementations can simultaneously support many connections to many different systems. Fig-

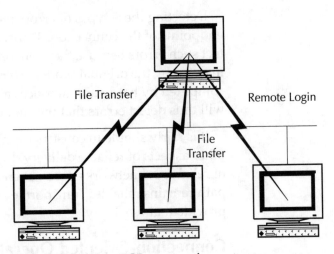

Figure 7.4 Many TCP connections at once.

ure 7.4 shows an example of such support. The top work-station is supporting a remote login and two file transfer sessions, all at the same time.

Within that top workstation, TCP must differentiate three distinct connections. Conceptually, TCP acts as in Figure 7.5. It distinguishes packets for each connection,

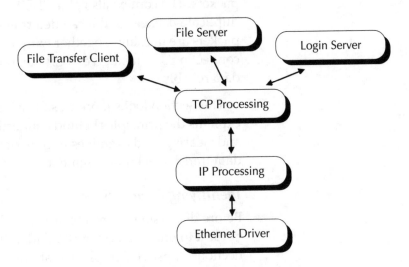

Figure 7.5 TCP support for multiple connections.

manages each connection appropriately, and, of course, delivers data to the appropriate application.

TCP relies on socket pairs to identify individual connections. The description of UDP in Chapter 6 introduced the concept of a socket. Sockets consist of an IP address and a port value. The IP address identifies a particular system, and the port distinguishes different applications within that system. TCP uses sockets to identify endpoints of a connection, and, since every connection has two endpoints, a pair of sockets can uniquely identify a connection.

Many applications that use TCP depend on well-known ports. Well-known ports are predefined port values that, by prior agreement, belong to particular application protocols. Table 7.2 lists some of the most important well-known ports.

In most cases, an application protocol operates either as a server or a client. Servers typically just listen for connections. When they do, they listen only for connections to their well-known port. A client contacting a server initiates a connection to that port. Since the client takes the initiative to contact the server, it must know both the IP address and the port for that server. The server, on the other hand, does not need to know the identity of the client in advance. The server simply waits for any client to initiate the con-

Table 7.2 Well-Known Port Values for Important TCP Applications

20	File Transfer Protocol Data
21	File Transfer Protocol Control
23	Telnet Remote Login
53	Domain Name Service
80	Hypertext Transfer Protocol
110	Post Office Protocol (version 3)
111	Remote Procedure Call
119	Network News Transfer Protocol

nection, and it responds to whichever IP address and port value that the client has chosen for itself.

Establishing Connections

A TCP connection begins its life when two systems complete the connection establishment process. This process identifies the connection to both systems and prepares the connection for data transfer.

TCP establishes connections with a procedure known as a *three-way handshake*. Despite its name, the three-way handshake usually consists of four distinct events. Normally it proceeds as Figure 7.6 shows. First, an application protocol in one system tells its local TCP that it is willing to accept a connection. This event is often called either a *listen*, or a *passive connection request*. In the figure, the workstation performs this first step. In this case, the workstation is acting as a server.

Next, an application in the second system (the figure's personal computer) asks TCP to actively establish a connection to the first application. This stage is the *call*, or the *active connection request*. To carry out its application's wishes, the PC's TCP constructs a request packet and sends it to the workstation.

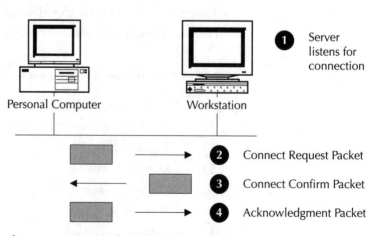

Figure 7.6 Normal connection establishment.

The third event in the handshake takes place when the workstation's TCP receives this packet. Since an application has previously issued a listen request, TCP responds with a positive confirmation. This confirmation is carried in the second packet of the establishment exchange.

At this point, the PC's TCP knows that the connection establishment is complete. It has sent the request on behalf of its application, and it has received a positive response from the workstation. The workstation's TCP, however, is not quite as certain. Yes, it has responded to the request, but it does not have any assurance that the response has successfully reached the personal computer. To provide that assurance, the PC's TCP generates a third packet (and the fourth event of the establishment process). This third packet explicitly acknowledges receipt of the positive response. When it reaches the workstation, both systems know that connection establishment is complete. The term three-way handshake comes from the three distinct packets that the peer TCPs exchange.

Although connection establishment is part of TCP's responsibility, this example shows that application protocols must initiate it. An application in the workstation must indicate its willingness to accept connections, and an application in the PC must actively seek such a connection. Without two agreeable applications, TCP cannot establish a connection.

This example shows the typical way that TCP establishes a connection. In it, one application makes a passive request and another application makes an active request. It is also possible for both applications to make active requests, in which case, the connection establishment still succeeds. Figure 7.7 shows such an establishment. Both systems try to initiate a connection by sending connection request packets. Instead of sending positive connection responses, each system merely acknowledges each other's connection request.

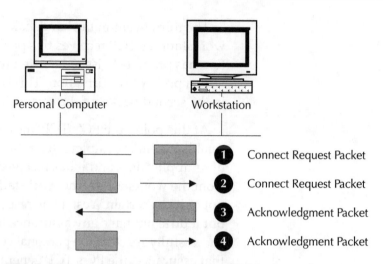

Figure 7.7 Two active requests establishing a connection.

Transferring Data

Once TCP establishes a connection, it can begin to use it, which means transferring data across it. Of course, the whole point of connections is to make this data transfer reliable. The key to this reliability is sequence numbers.

TCP transfers application data by packaging that data within a TCP packet. Most commonly, TCP packets are called *segments*. In addition to the data itself, segments contain sequence numbers. As Figure 7.8 shows, sequence numbers give every byte of application data its own number. When packets arrive at their destination, the receiving TCP can use these numbers to reconstruct the correct order for the data. If TCP receives data with the same sequence number, it recognizes that the data is duplicated, and it discards the extra copies. Similarly, if TCP finds gaps in the sequence numbers, it realizes that it is missing some data. It can then take appropriate steps to recover that missing data.

Note that sequence numbers are independent for each direction in a connection. If, for example, a client is communicating with a server, the client uses its own sequence

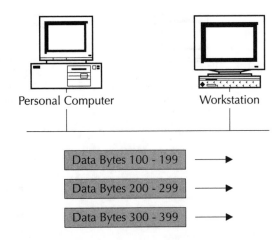

Figure 7.8 Numbering each data byte.

numbers for its requests, while the server uses a separate set of sequence numbers for its responses. These two sets of sequence numbers have no relation to each other.

Acknowledgment

Sequence numbers alone let TCP recognize missing data. But TCP must do more than simply recognize when data is missing; it must recover that missing data. To recover missing data, the peer TCPs must communicate directly with each other. After all, the receiver knows that data is missing, but it is the transmitter that has the data and needs to send a new copy. TCP exchanges the necessary information through acknowledgments. When one TCP sends a packet to the other, it may include an acknowledgment number. By including an acknowledgment number, TCP says "I have successfully received all data up to (but not including) the data with this sequence number." To see this in action, consider Figure 7.9.

In the figure, the personal computer sends data in three different packets. The first packet contains bytes 100 to 199; the second packet has bytes 200 to 299, and the third packet has 300 through 399. After receiving the third packet, the workstation generates a packet with an ac-

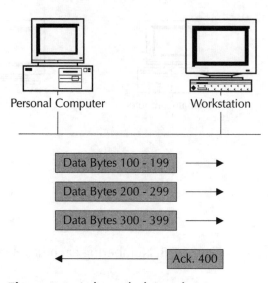

Figure 7.9 Acknowledging data.

knowledgment number. Since the workstation next expects to receive byte number 400, the acknowledgment number in the packet is 400. When the PC receives this acknowledgment, it knows that all of its data has successfully made it to the destination.

If data fails to reach the destination, clearly the destination system cannot acknowledge its arrival. Instead, the remote system can only acknowledge data prior to the missing bytes. Figure 7.10 shows this situation. The second packet containing bytes 200 to 299 never makes it to the workstation. Consequently, the workstation's acknowledgment contains the sequence number 200.

Note that the third packet (300 to 399) makes it safely across the network, but there is no way for the workstation to acknowledge it. Eventually, the personal computer realizes that its second packet did not arrive. It then retransmits the packet. With this second chance, the packet does make it, and the workstation promptly acknowledges data up to byte 400. As the example shows, there is no need for the PC to retransmit the third packet (with bytes 300 to 399).

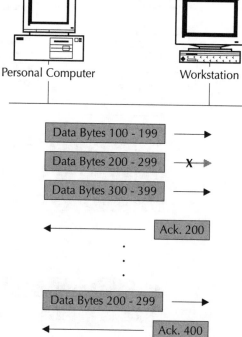

Figure 7.10 Acknowledging retransmitted data.

Flow Control

Sequence numbers also play a role in another important function—flow control. Flow control allows a receiver to limit the amount of data that the sender transmits. Such limits might be needed, for example, if the receiver has only a limited amount of memory in which to hold received data. Without flow control, the sender could transmit data without limit, overrunning the receiver's capacity.

Flow control is an ongoing part of every connection. As soon as TCP establishes a connection, and throughout the connection's life, each system tells the other how much data it can accept. It does so by specifying a window size. Figure 7.11 shows how window size limits the sender. In the figure, the workstation initially grants a window of 200

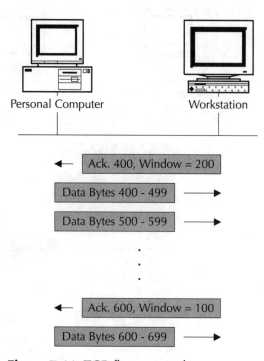

Figure 7.11 TCP flow control.

bytes. It does so with an acknowledgment packet. This packets says that the workstation next expects byte number 400, and that it can accept an additional 200 bytes of data. The personal computer then sends two packets, each with 100 bytes of data. At that point, however, the PC must cease transmission. Since it has filled the allowable window, it has to wait before it can send any more data.

Urgent Data

In addition to regular data, TCP understands the concept of urgent data. Sometimes an application has data that it must treat more urgently than regular data. If the application has already sent regular data on the connection, this urgent data will inevitably take its place behind less urgent data on the connection. TCP delivers data in sequence, so it cannot do anything to give the urgent data any special treatment. Instead, it lets the application tell its peer that urgent data follows. Presumably, when the receiver gets this indication, it will process the regular data as fast as possible in order to get to the urgent information.

Closing Connections

Of course, if TCP establishes connections for its applications, it will also close those connections once the applications are finished. As with connection establishment, TCP generally closes connections only when an application requests it.

Figure 7.12 shows the sequence of packets that the two systems exchange. When an application requests termination, its TCP sends a close indication packet. The peer acknowledges that packet, and data flow in one direction ceases. In the figure, this exchange corresponds to steps 1 and 2. After the exchange, the PC no longer transmits data to the workstation.

To completely close the connection, TCP waits for the workstation's application to make its close request. When it does so, TCP repeats the exchange, but in the opposite direction. The workstation sends a close indication and the PC responds with an acknowledgment. After steps 3 and 4

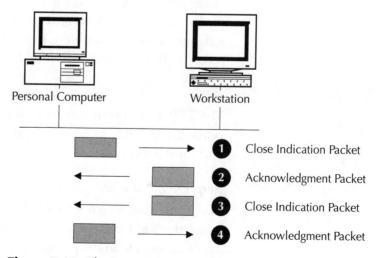

Figure 7.12 Closing a TCP connection.

of the figure, no data may flow in either direction, and the TCP connection ceases to exist.

Transmission Control Protocol Specifications

The previous section introduced many of the principles behind TCP's operation. This section examines TCP in depth. It begins by describing the format of TCP packets, and then presents the TCP state machine, which formally specifies how TCP behaves. Following the state machine are detailed examinations of each important aspect of TCP's operation. These subsections mirror the previous general subsections, but they describe the function in greater detail. Note that this section only considers the requirements that the TCP specification places on TCP programs. The next section looks at the different ways that TCP implementations can adhere to the standard. Many times, implementation details can have a major effect on system and network performance.

TCP Packet Format

All TCP packets have the same basic format. The details of that format appear in Figure 7.13. The header that precedes application data is the same for every type of TCP packet, from connection requests to user data. To distinguish packets with different functions, TCP employs different settings of the control field.

Ports

The TCP header starts off with source and destination ports. These fields indicate the port values for the sender and for the receiver.

Sequence Number

The 32-bit sequence number follows the ports. In most cases, this field is the sequence number for the first byte of application data in the packet. The exception occurs in

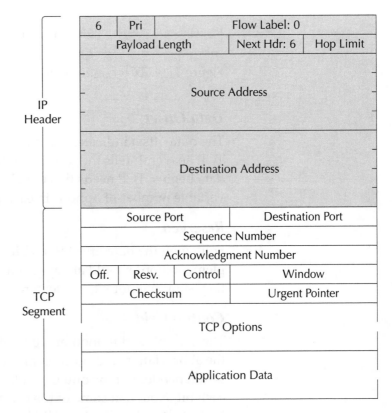

Figure 7.13 TCP packet format.

packets with the SYN bit set. (See "Control Field," upcoming.) In those packets, the sequence number field defines where the sender will start numbering its data. The data itself has the sequence number one greater than this field.

Acknowledgment Number

The next field is the 32-bit acknowledgment number. This field only has meaning if the ACK bit in the control field is set. When it is set, this value indicates the next sequence number the sender expects. It acknowledges receipt of all data up to (but not including) this value. Once TCP establishes a connection, it must include this field in every packet. (In other words, it should always set the ACK bit.)

URG	ACK	PSH	RST	SYN	FIN

Figure 7.14 TCP control field.

Data Offset

The data offset indicates the number of 32-bit words in the TCP header. It tells the recipient where the application data begins. TCP needs this field because it can include a variable number of options in each packet.

Reserved

Following the data offset is a 6-bit reserved field. TCP implementations should always set this field to zero, and they should ignore its value in received packets.

Control Field

The control field is another 6-bit field. Figure 7.14 shows the abbreviation and position of each bit in the field. Each is independent of the others. Table 7.3 lists the meaning of each bit. Note that some of the control field bits simply indicate whether another field in the header is significant. If the control field bit is clear, then the corresponding header field has no meaning. The header field is, however, still present in the packet.

Window

Following the control field is the 16-bit window. This number indicates how many bytes of data the system can

Table 7.3 Bits in TCP Control Field

URG	Urgent field is significant.
ACK	Acknowledgment field is significant.
PSH	Push function invoked.
RST	Reset the connection.
SYN	Synchronize sequence numbers.
FIN	Sender is finished with connection.

accept. The first byte the system can accept is the one numbered by the acknowledgment field. Since the window value only has significance when combined with an acknowledgment number, this field is meaningful only when the acknowledgment field is valid. That is true when the ACK bit in the control field is set.

Checksum

The next field in TCP's header is the checksum. It detects errors in the packet, and allows TCP to provide error-free delivery. In fact, the TCP checksum covers more than just the TCP packet. It also includes source and destination network addresses, as well as the IPv6 next header.

By including these fields, the checksum protects against packets that are not themselves corrupt, but have been delivered to the wrong place. Figure 7.15 shows how the additional data is added to the TCP packet. The added fields, shown in gray in the figure, are called a pseudo header.

Calculating Checksums Efficiently

As is the case for UDP, a major factor in the performance of network implementations is their performance in calculating checksums. Several RFCs are devoted to the subject of maximizing this performance; the most thorough RFC on the topic is RFC 1071.

The rules for constructing a checksum are identical to those for UDP. But since TCP has never permitted the sender to omit checksums (see page 169), there is no need to handle a checksum value of zero in any special manner. Table 7.4 summarizes the rules TCP uses to construct the checksum value. Note that the summation uses ones complement arithmetic. This calculation differs from the twos complement arithmetic commonly available with modern microprocessors. Most TCP implementations, therefore, have to rely on a special software to perform the addition. (See sidebar.) Clearly this is less efficient that simply performing the sum in hardware (using twos complement). In exchange for the loss of efficiency, TCP improves its ability to detect common errors.

A receiver takes much the same approach. Table 7.5 lists its steps. When a receiver finds an invalid checksum, it discards the packet without further processing.

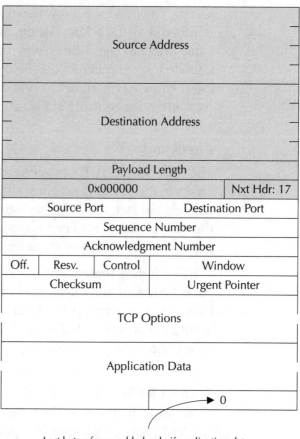

Last byte of zero added only if application data
consists of an odd number of bytes; note that
the payload length is not adjusted to include it.

Figure 7.15 Data covered by TCP checksum.

Table 7.4 Constructing the TCP Checksum

1. Prepend the pseudo header to the TCP packet.

2. If the application data contains an odd number of bytes,
   append a final byte of zero. (Do not increase the payload
   length to count this byte.)

3. Set the checksum field to zero.

4. Calculate the sum of the resulting series of 16-bit values,
   using ones complement arithmetic.

5. Use the resulting sum as the TCP checksum.

Table 7.5 Validating the TCP Checksum

1. Prepend the pseudo header to the TCP packet.

2. If the application data contains an odd number of bytes, append a final byte of zero. (Do not increase the payload length to count this byte.)

3. Calculate the sum of the resulting series of 16-bit values, using ones complement arithmetic.

4. If the result of this summation is 0xFFFF, the checksum is valid; otherwise, the checksum is invalid.

Urgent Pointer

The final required field for TCP headers is the urgent pointer. Unless the URG bit in the control field is set, this pointer has no meaning. When the field is valid, the packet indicates two things. First, the sender wants to send data that it considers urgent. Second, the pointer value itself identifies the end of that urgent data. If the receiver processes all data up to and including the urgent pointer, then it will have processed the urgent data.

To see an example, look at Figure 7.16. There the TCP packet has a sequence number of 1,000 and an urgent pointer of 200. With these values, the application data in the packet begins at byte number 1,000. Urgent data extends up to and including byte number 1,200, and normal data resumes at byte 1,201.

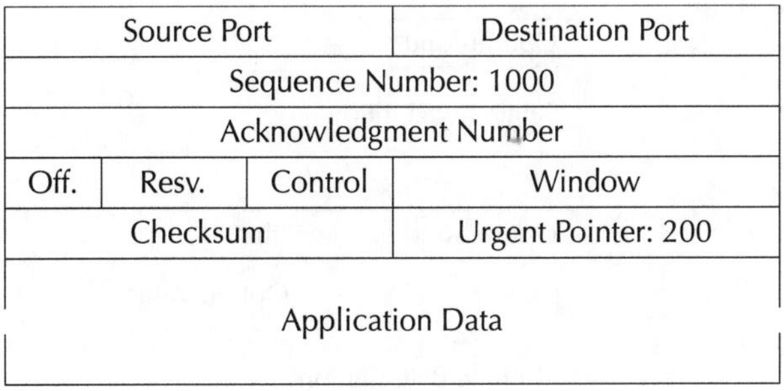

Source Port			Destination Port	
Sequence Number: 1000				
Acknowledgment Number				
Off.	Resv.	Control	Window	
Checksum			Urgent Pointer: 200	
Application Data				

Figure 7.16 Urgent pointer example.

Two things are significant about the urgent pointer. First, it gives no indication of where the urgent data actually begins. If it is important, applications must determine this on their own. Second, the urgent data may not be included in the packet with an urgent pointer. If, in the example, the data packet contained only 100 bytes of data, then the urgent data could conceivably be waiting for another packet. The urgent pointer's intent is simply to urge the receiver to process data as fast as possible.

Options

For minimal TCP headers, the urgent pointer is the last TCP header field. Everything that follows is application data. If the data offset has a value greater than 5, however, then the packet includes TCP options, which precede application data. To determine the size of the options, TCP implementations subtract the minimum header size (five 32-bit words) from the data offset value.

The options area of the header may contain several individual TCP options. Those options take one of two forms, depicted in Figure 7.17. The simplest type of option is a single byte option. It consists of a single byte that indicates its type and, implicitly, its value.

Options larger than a single byte take the second format in the figure. The first byte indicates the type of the option; the second byte counts the option's length (including the kind and length bytes), and the remaining bytes of the op-

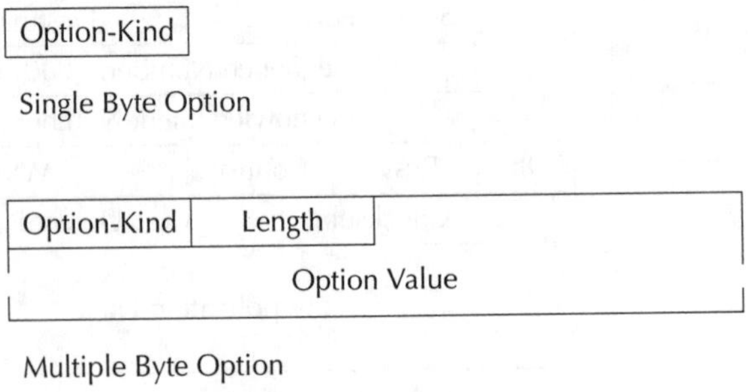

Option-Kind

Single Byte Option

Option-Kind	Length	
	Option Value	

Multiple Byte Option

Figure 7.17 TCP option formats.

Table 7.6 TCP Options

Option-Kind	Length	Value
0	1	End of valid options in header
1	1	No operation (ignore this byte)
2	4	Maximum segment size
3	3	Window scale factor
8	10	Timestamp

tion contain the option value. TCP must know in advance which kinds of options are single byte and which are multiple byte. Otherwise, it cannot correctly interpret the options field. Table 7.6 lists the defined TCP options, and indicates which are single byte options and which have multiple bytes.

End of Options

An option-kind of 0 indicates the end of options in the TCP packet. It instructs the recipient to stop looking for additional options in the remaining TCP header. TCP needs this option because of the format of its data offset field. That field defines the size of the TCP header in 32-bit words, so all TCP headers must be a multiple of four bytes in size.

If the sender does not have enough legitimate options to fill out a 4-byte word, it can use this option. TCP places it after the legitimate options, and then adds extra bytes with arbitrary values. Since this option indicates the end of valid options, the recipient knows to ignore the extraneous bytes. Note that TCP does not have to use an end of options in all packets. If the actual options naturally end on a 4-byte boundary, then TCP can simply conclude its header with those options.

No Operation

An option-kind of 1 identifies a no operation option. It tells the recipient to ignore this particular byte, but continue processing the options field. The noop option (as it is frequently called) lets TCP align following options on appropriate word boundaries. For an example of its use, see the upcoming "Timestamp" discussion.

Maximum Segment Size

TCP uses this option only during connection setup. If present, it indicates the largest packet size (in bytes) the sender is prepared to receive. Its peer TCP must not send packets larger than this value. The maximum segment size does not include the TCP header; rather, it refers only to application data. Both endpoints in a TCP connection are free to specify their own maximum segment size. Figure 7.18 shows the format of the MSS option.

Window Scale Factor

The window scale factor supplies a multiplier for the window field. Without a scale factor, the window field simply specifies bytes. Because the field has only 16 bits, TCP cannot specify a window greater than 65,535 bytes without this option. At first glance, 65,535 bytes might seem like an extraordinarily large window. On high speed or long delay networks, however, this window size can artificially and severely limit performance. For a practical example of this effect, consider a connection across a fiber optic link from Tokyo to New York.

Without the window scale option, the largest window that such a connection can employ is 65,535 bytes. Figure 7.19 illustrates how this limits throughput. Given the distance between Tokyo and New York, and the speed of light in glass, it takes at least 50 milliseconds for packets to travel from one site to the other. From the moment the Tokyo workstation transmits a packet, at least 100 millisec-

Kind: 2	Length: 4	Maximum Segment Size

Figure 7.18 TCP maximum segment size option.

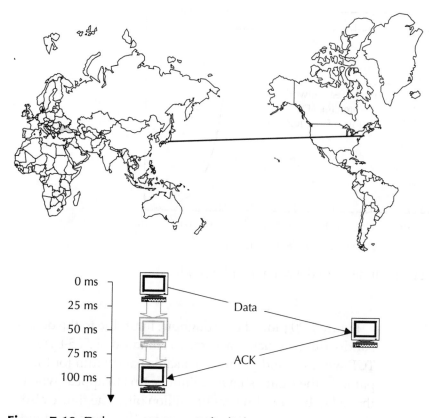

Figure 7.19 Delay on a transpacific link.

onds must pass before it can receive an acknowledgment from New York.

With a window size of 65,535 bytes, the greatest throughput possible over the connection is 65,535 bytes per 100 milliseconds. That number is only a little more than 5 Mbit/s. Even if the fiber optic link is a high-speed OC-24 link with 1.24 Gbit/s of bandwidth, the TCP connection is limited to 5.2 Mbit/s of throughput.

The culprit in this case is not simply the delay. Rather it is the product of the delay and bandwidth of the path. If, for example, the Tokyo-to-New York link relied on a T1 line with a 1.54 Mbit/s bit rate, TCP throughput would be limited by the bit rate, not the window size.

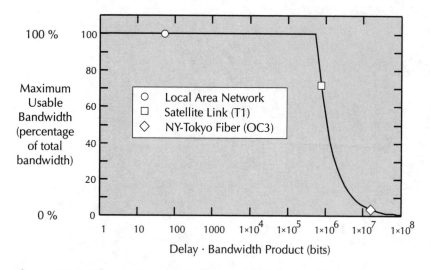

Figure 7.20 Throughput limit from delay-bandwidth product.

Figure 7.20 plots the throughput limit due to the delay-bandwidth product. It assumes a standard 65,535-byte TCP window, and graphs the usable bandwidth for the path. As the figure shows, a limit begins to appear when the delay-bandwidth nears 1 million bits. The figure also shows three representative values for the delay-bandwidth product. Those values correspond to a small (500 meter) Ethernet LAN, a T1 (1.54 Mbit/s) satellite link, and an OC-3 (155 Mbit/s) fiber link across the Pacific. The graph clearly demonstrates that in high-speed, large-scale networks common today, a window size of 65,535 bytes can severely limit throughput.

The window scale option, shown in Figure 7.21, provides a way to overcome this limit. The scale option only appears in connection requests and responses, and both systems must agree to use it. When the option is in use on a connection, any window size fields that appear in pack-

Kind: 3	Length: 3	Shift Count

Figure 7.21 TCP window scale option format.

A Limit to Window Scaling

Even though the window scale option could conceivably hold a value as large as 255, TCP limits the valid values to between 0 and 14 (inclusive). The upper limit ensures that the maximum difference between the sender and receiver can be no greater than 2^{31}. Without such a limit, TCP might not be able to tell when the 32-bit sequence number had rolled over from $2^{31}-1$ back to 0. If TCP receives a window scale option greater than 14, it treats it as if it were 14.

ets are multiplied by a power of two. The specific power of two is the *shift count*. (Shifting a binary value n bits to the left is the same as multiplying that value by 2^n.)

When, for example, a system agrees to use the window scale option with a shift count of three, any window size it advertises is multiplied by 2^3. If the system sets the window size to 100, then the receiver should interpret the window size as being 800 bytes.

The window scale option allows TCP to use windows as large as 16 million bytes. That window does not artificially limit a transpacific fiber unless its bandwidth exceeds 1.3 Gbit/s.

Timestamp

The timestamp option is the only option that has meaning in regular data packets. All of the other TCP options are only significant in connection requests and responses. This option provides a way for TCP implementations to continuously monitor the round-trip time for a connection.

Figure 7.22 shows the structure of a timestamp option. Its total length is 10 bytes, and it consists of two 4-byte values. Both of those values represent time. The first value is the primary timestamp value. When a system builds a packet for transmission, this value represents the local time within that system.

The TCP specification places few requirements on this timestamp value. It does not have to represent seconds, minutes, or some other standard time reference. It is sufficient when the sender merely uses a value that it guarantees will not decrease at any point in the future. (Of course,

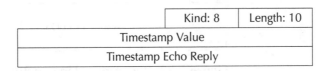

Figure 7.22 TCP timestamp option format.

once the value reaches its maximum 32-bit quantity, it will have to roll over to zero.)

The second timestamp value is valid only when it appears in acknowledgment packets, where it is a copy of the timestamp that was contained in the data packet being acknowledged. Suppose, for example, that TCP receives a data packet with a timestamp value of 500. When the system accepts that packet, it will return an acknowledgment packet to the original sender. Within that acknowledgment packet, it can use its own time reference for the primary timestamp value. The timestamp echo value, however, should be 500. (There are exceptions to this principle; see the "Acknowledgment and Retransmission" section late in this chapter.)

Since the timestamp option appears in regular data packets, TCP implementations should take steps to make processing the option as efficient as possible. One way to improve efficiency with some processors is to make sure that the 32-bit timestamp values align with 32-bit addresses in the processor's memory. To provide that alignment, the TCP specification recommends the format of Figure 7.23 for timestamp options. Note that the recom-

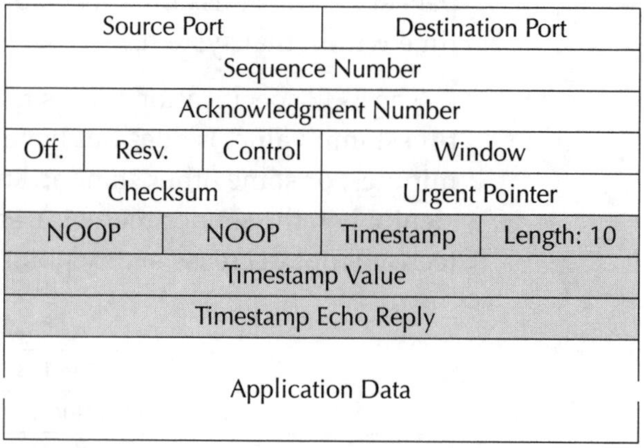

Source Port			Destination Port	
Sequence Number				
Acknowledgment Number				
Off.	Resv.	Control	Window	
Checksum			Urgent Pointer	
NOOP		NOOP	Timestamp	Length: 10
Timestamp Value				
Timestamp Echo Reply				
Application Data				

Figure 7.23 Recommended structure for TCP timestamp option.

Table 7.7 States in TCP Connection State Transition Diagram

Closed	An imaginary state that represents a connection that does not exist.
Listen	Application has issued passive connect request.
SYN Sent	Application has issued active connect request.
SYN Rcvd	Connection has responded to a connect request.
Estab	Connection is established.
Close Wait	Peer has closed the connection.
Last ACK	Waiting for acknowledgment of close.
FIN Wait-1	Application has requested closing the connection.
FIN Wait-2	Waiting for peer to close connection.
Closing	Waiting for peer to acknowledge closing connection.
Time Wait	Waiting to ensure that no packets from connection remain in network.

mended structure inserts two no operation (noop) options in front of the timestamp option. These two extra bytes force the 32-bit timestamp values to align on 32-bit words.

The TCP State Machine

TCP uses its packets to establish, maintain, and close connections. Its operation is guided by a well-defined series of states, listed in Table 7.7. TCP changes states in response to application requests, received packets, and timer expirations. Figure 7.24 summarizes this behavior in a state transition diagram. The diagram uses arrows to indicate transitions between states. Each transition has a label that indicates which event initiates the transition and any actions TCP takes that coincide with the transition. The events appear above the horizontal bar, and actions appear below it. Some transitions do not require that TCP take any action, and those transitions have nothing below their horizontal bar.

Table 7.8 lists the events that cause state transitions. As the table shows, there are three different types of actions.

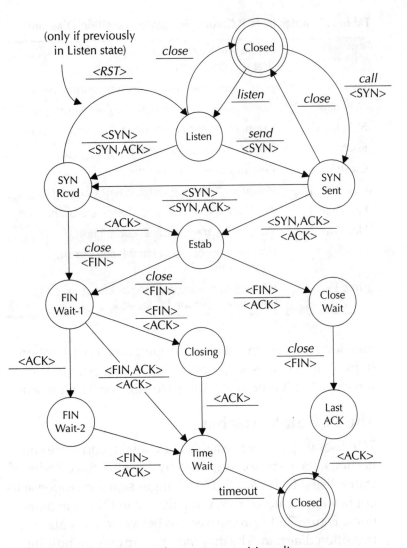

Figure 7.24 TCP connection state transition diagram.

They include requests from the application, packets received from the peer TCP, and timer expirations.

The actions that the state transition diagram includes are packets that TCP sends to its peer. As Table 7.9 shows, the state transition diagram only considers four possible packets. Pure data packets that do not have acknowledgments are not the result of state transitions.

Table 7.8 Events in TCP Connection State Transition Diagram

listen	Application issues passive connect request.
call	Application issues active connect request.
send	Application provides data to transfer.
close	Application requests closing the connection.
<SYN>	Connection request packet from peer TCP.
<SYN,ACK>	Connection response packet from peer TCP.
<RST>	Reset packet from peer TCP.
<ACK>	Acknowledgment packet from peer TCP.
<FIN>	Finish packet from peer TCP.
timeout	Timer expiration.

Establishing Connections

As the state transition diagram reveals, TCP establishes connections in a straightforward manner. In most cases, one application starts with a passive connection request, or listen. This action causes no packets to pass between any systems, but it does place one system's TCP in the Listen state.

Network activity begins when the peer application issues an active connection request. The TCP supporting that application transmits a connection request packet to the listening peer. Figure 7.25 shows a sample connection request packet. The packet begins with the source and destination port. These values identify the application. (In the example, the destination port is the well-known port for the file transfer protocol.) The sequence number follows. Even though this packet contains no application

Table 7.9 Actions in TCP Connection State Transition Diagram

<SYN>	Connection request packet
<SYN,ACK>	Connection response packet
<ACK>	Acknowledgment packet
<FIN>	Finish packet

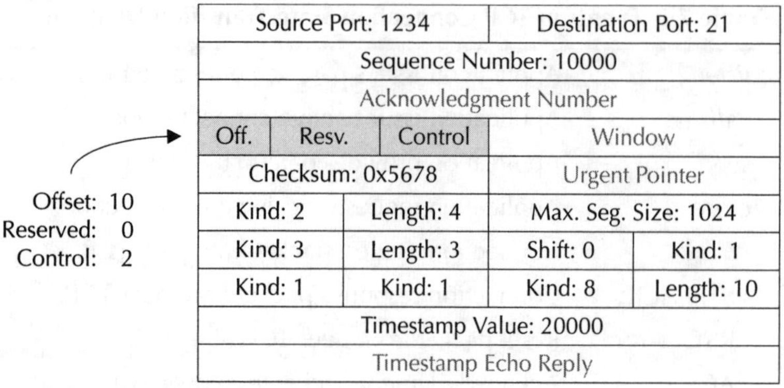

Source Port: 1234			Destination Port: 21	
Sequence Number: 10000				
Acknowledgment Number				
Off.	Resv.	Control	Window	
Checksum: 0x5678			Urgent Pointer	
Kind: 2		Length: 4	Max. Seg. Size: 1024	
Kind: 3		Length: 3	Shift: 0	Kind: 1
Kind: 1		Kind: 1	Kind: 8	Length: 10
Timestamp Value: 20000				
Timestamp Echo Reply				

Offset: 10
Reserved: 0
Control: 2

Figure 7.25 Example active connection request packet.

Initial Sequence Numbers

Since packets can survive on a network after their connection closes, TCP must take care in choosing an initial sequence number. It must be sure to select a number that can no longer exist (from a previous connection) on the network. The TCP standard recommends basing initial sequence numbers on a clock that increments about every 4 µs. If a system loses the value of this clock (perhaps because of a crash), it should avoid sending any TCP packets for several minutes after it restarts. This delay is called *quiet time*.

data, the sequence number remains important. For connection request packets, TCP assigns a sequence number to the packet itself. In this case, the packet has a sequence number of 10,000. Should the sender need to retransmit this particular connection request, it must use the same sequence number.

This sequence number also indicates where TCP will begin numbering its data. Application data begins with a sequence number one greater than the connection request, so data on this connection will be numbered starting at 10,001.

The acknowledgment number has no meaning in the connection request, so its value is arbitrary. The offset field, however, is significant, even though there is no application data at any offset in the packet. In this case, the offset value indicates the length of the TCP header. Its value is 10, so the packet contains 10 32-bit words, or 40 bytes, of TCP header.

The control field has a single bit set. That bit is the SYN field, and it identifies the packet as a connection request. Since the window field is relative to the acknowledgment number, and since the connection request has no acknowledgment number, the window field is also arbitrary. It has no significance in the packet.

The checksum and urgent pointers round out the standard TCP header. The checksum contains the appropriate value for the packet, while the urgent pointer is irrelevant. Following these two fields are TCP options. The first option is the maximum segment size. With it, the sender claims that it can accept TCP packets as large as 1,024 bytes. The sender asks its peer to break its data into packets that size or smaller.

Compatibility with Older TCPs

Both the window scale and timestamp options were absent from the original TCP standard. Many older TCP implementations, therefore, may not understand them. To interoperate with old implementations, a system only uses these options if its peer indicates it can understand them. TCPs indicate their support for options by including them in connection packets. If a system includes an option in its connect request, but the peer does not include the same option in the connect response, the system cannot use the option on the connection.

The packet then includes a window scale option. This option suggests a value that TCP wants to use for its window scale. The connection request packet does not have the final say in this option, though. TCP can only use a window scale (other than zero, of course) when both the connection request and connection response contain the option. The same rule applies to the peer TCP. For this reason, TCP includes an explicit window scale option of zero, even though zero has no effect on the window scale. A value of zero says that this TCP does not want to scale its window, but the peer TCP may do so if it wishes (see sidebar).

After three noops (to force alignment) the packet contains a timestamp option. Even though the option contains a valid value, it actually serves no direct purpose in a connect request. A system uses it strictly to indicate that it understands the option and that it wants to use the option in data packets for the connection (see sidebar). Timestamp options do not help detect duplicate packets from previous connections, even though they would seem to be useful for that purpose. Unfortunately, to use them that way would require precise behavior on the part of TCP implementations, and TCP's designers thought such behavior too burdensome for all systems. Instead, TCP relies on the initial sequence number selection and quiet time (see sidebar on page 204) to detect such duplicate packets.

When this packet reaches its destination, the peer TCP responds. Assuming that an application is listening for the connection, the response could take the form of Figure

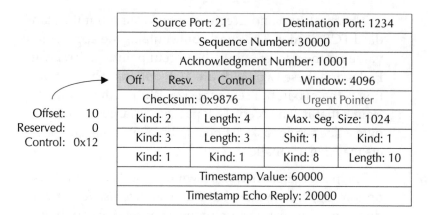

Source Port: 21			Destination Port: 1234	
Sequence Number: 30000				
Acknowledgment Number: 10001				
Off.	Resv.	Control	Window: 4096	
Checksum: 0x9876			Urgent Pointer	
Kind: 2	Length: 4		Max. Seg. Size: 1024	
Kind: 3	Length: 3		Shift: 1	Kind: 1
Kind: 1	Kind: 1		Kind: 8	Length: 10
Timestamp Value: 60000				
Timestamp Echo Reply: 20000				

Offset: 10
Reserved: 0
Control: 0x12

Figure 7.26 Example connection response packet.

Refusing a Connection

This example assumes that the system receiving the connect request will accept that request. If, instead, the recipient does not accept the connection, it refuses the connection by generating a reset packet. See the next section, "Resetting a Connection."

7.26, where the connection response packet corresponds to the request packet of Figure 7.25. As expected, the connection response reverses the source and destination ports. The source is the file transfer protocol server, and the destination is the source of the original request.

The sequence number serves the same function as it does in the request. It implicitly numbers the connect response itself, and it indicates where the sender wishes to start numbering its data. In this case, the response is given sequence number 30,000, and the data will begin with byte 30,001.

The acknowledgment number indicates acceptance of sequence number 10,000, which was the sequence number of the original connect request. The acknowledgment number also indicates that the sender is expecting byte number 10,001 next.

The offset of the response, like that of the request, defines the TCP header size as 10 32-bit words. As the figure confirms, the response's TCP header is 40 bytes in size.

The control field sets two bits—the ACK and the SYN bits. Together, these two control bits define the packet type as a connect response.

Since this packet includes an acknowledgment number, it also includes a window. In this case, the window value is 4,096. When combined with the window scale option (whose shift count is 1), this window gives the peer TCP permission to send 8,192 bytes of data. Those bytes will be numbered 10,001 to 18,192.

The last half of the header contains TCP options. First, the sender specifies a maximum segment size of 1,024 bytes. This value, coincidentally, is the same as its peer's.The second option specifies a window scale factor of 1. As described, this option multiplies by 2^1 all windows that the sender advertises.

The packet then includes a timestamp option. As with the connect request, this option has no real significance in the connect response. It does confirm to the peer, however, that timestamps are acceptable on the connection. The timestamp echo reply value reflects the timestamp in the original connect request. Although this value provides no help in detecting duplicate packets from old connections, the peer may use it to estimate the round-trip time for the connection.

The final step in the three-way handshake is an acknowledgment of the connect response. Figure 7.27 shows a sample acknowledgment packet. The acknowledgment packet travels in the same direction as the connect request,

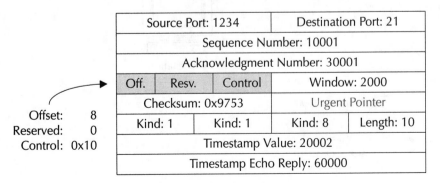

Figure 7.27 Example acknowledgment packet.

a direction it reflects with its source and destination port values. For a sequence number, the packet includes the number of the first byte of data (even though the packet itself contains no application data. The acknowledgment number acknowledges the peer's connect response. Its value is one more than the sequence number of that response. The offset gives the TCP header size as 32 bytes, and the control field sets the ACK bit to indicate that the packet is an acknowledgment. The window field advertises the sender's window. Its value is 2,000, and, since the window scale factor is zero for this sender, that value is in bytes. Finally, the header concludes with a timestamp option. The two noop options that precede it allow the timestamp values to align on 32-bit words (see page 199).

When the acknowledgment packet makes it to its destination TCP, the three-way handshake is complete. At this point, the connection is established. Figure 7.28 summarizes this example. It shows only those TCP header fields that are significant.

When both systems actively ask for a connection, the procedure is very similar. Instead of showing the packets in great detail, Figure 7.29 outlines the exchange. The TCP header fields omitted from the figure are the same as for the normal case.

Application Data During Connection Establishment

Though the examples do not show it, the acknowledgment, as well as the connect request and response packets, can carry application data. TCP cannot deliver that data to the application, however, until connection establishment is complete. In most cases, only the final acknowledgment actually carries data.

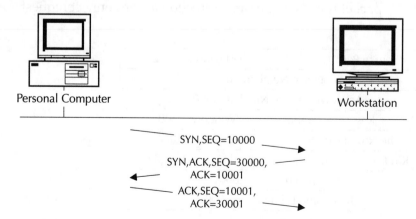

Figure 7.28 Normal connection establishment.

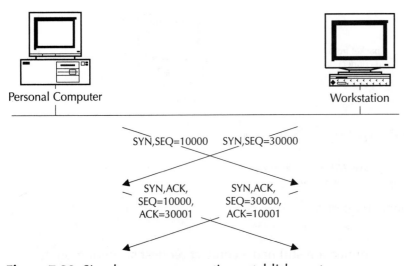

Figure 7.29 Simultaneous connection establishment.

Resetting a Connection

From the previous subsection, connection establishment appears to be quite straightforward. The peer systems simply exchange the requisite TCP packets. Real networks, of course, introduce complications in this process. In particular, networks can sometimes preserve an old packet for far longer than they should and then deliver that packet to its destination.

Without extra precautions, this characteristic could wreak havoc with a connection establishment. Consider the example of Figure 7.30. There, the personal computer wants to connect to the workstation. As expected, it transmits an active connect request. But before that request arrives, an old request from an earlier connection arrives at the workstation. Of course, the workstation doesn't know that the request is out-of-date, so it accepts the connection.

When the PC receives the <SYN,ACK> packet, it recognizes the problem. The packet's acknowledgment number is 9,001, but it should be 10,001. The workstation has accepted the wrong connect request. The PC cannot just start using this inappropriate connection. After all, if the old

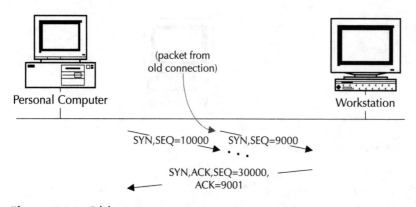

Figure 7.30 Old connect request.

connection still had a connect request surviving on the network, it is quite possible that data packets from the connection are also out there somewhere too.

To correct the problem, the personal computer sends a special reset packet. This packet has the RST bit set in the TCP control field. When the workstation receives the reset, it reverts back to the Listen state. Then, when the real connect request finally does arrive, the workstation can respond appropriately. Figure 7.31 shows the full recovery sequence.

Note that the figure shows the PC's reset overtaking its original connect request. This makes the picture simpler, but it is not very realistic. In most cases, the workstation receives the real connect request just after accepting the old connection. The workstation then responds with its own reset, and both systems start the connection establishment over again.

The reset packet serves additional functions beyond protecting against connect requests. As the sidebar on page 206 indicates, resets also provide a way for TCP to refuse a connect request. In general, TCP responds with a reset whenever it receives a packet that does not apparently belong to the current connection. Table 7.10 lists the rules TCP follows when considering whether to send a reset.

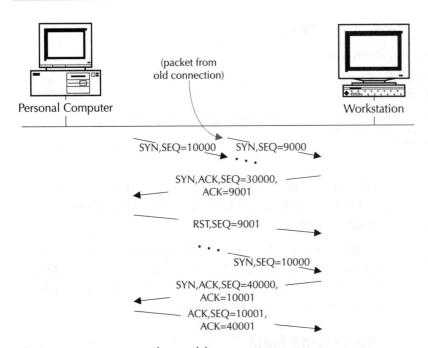

Figure 7.31 Recovery from old connect request.

Whenever TCP responds to a packet with a reset, it follows precise rules for formulating the reset. If the packet has an acknowledgment number, TCP uses it as the sequence number of the reset. Otherwise, TCP gives the reset a sequence number of zero and an acknowledgment number equal to the sum of the packet's sequence number and segment length.

Table 7.10 Sending Reset Packets

Current State	Factors in Sending Reset Packets
Closed	Send a reset in response to any packet except another reset.
Listen, SYN Sent, or SYN Rcvd	Send a reset if the incoming packet acknowledges something not yet sent. The connection does not change state.
Otherwise	Do not send a reset, but an acknowledgment packet with the latest window information and no application data. The connection does not change state.

Table 7.11 Validating a Received Reset Packet

Current State	Reset Validity Test
SYN Sent	Does the reset's acknowledgment number acknowledge the sequence number of the connect request?
Otherwise	Is the reset's sequence number within the window that the peer is currently granted?

When TCP receives a reset packet, it first decides if the reset is valid. Table 7.11 lists the rules that determine when a reset is valid.

If the reset is valid, then TCP responds to it in one of several ways. As Table 7.12 shows, these responses depend not only on the connection's current state, but also on how the connection reached that state.

Transferring Data

Once TCP establishes a connection, the connection is available for transferring application data. Indeed, that is the reason for the connection's existence. To make the transfer reliable and in order, TCP numbers every byte of data that it transfers. When a system establishes a connection, it tells its peer the sequence number it will use for the first byte of data.

Ordering Data

Since the TCP header dedicates a specific field for sequence numbers, the size of a sequence number is limited by whatever numbers fit in that field. The field is 32 bits,

Table 7.12 Responding to a Received Reset Packet

Current State	Actions on Valid Reset
Listen	Ignore the reset.
SYN Rcvd	If previous state was Listen, return to the Listen state. Otherwise, abort the connection.
Otherwise	Abort the connection.

so sequence numbers can range from 0 to $2^{32}-1$. The natural question that arises, then, is what about byte number 4,294,967,296 (2^{32})? TCP's answer is to start over again. Byte number 0 follows byte 4,294,967,295. Sequence numbers wrap around in this way as many times as necessary over the life of a connection.

Of course, wraparound brings up another question. How does TCP tell an "old" byte number 0 from a "newer" one? This question is important when TCP must distinguish the order of two sequence numbers. Which one is "less than" the other? Because of wraparound, the calculation is slightly more complicated than normal mathematics. TCP uses a special rule to determine the order of two sequence numbers, A and B. A is considered "less than" B if the following condition is true.

$$0 < (B - A) < 2^{31}$$

For low- and moderate-speed networks, this special test does not create a problem. On such networks, it takes a long time to reach the wraparound point. And, since all packets have some reasonable lifetime, there is generally no question about whether a packet that is demonstrably still alive is old or new. The key measurement is how long it takes the network to reach halfway to the wraparound point. In other words, how fast can a network transfer 2^{31} bytes of data? Table 7.13 lists that time for several popular networks.

As the table shows, it is not likely that a packet can survive on an ISDN or Ethernet network long enough to

Table 7.13 Wraparound Time Limits for Various Networks

Network	Bit Rate	Half Wraparound Time
ISDN	128 Kbit/s	36.4 hours
Ethernet	10 Mbit/s	28.6 minutes
Fast Ethernet	100 Mbit/s	2.9 minutes
ATM (STM-16)	2.5 Gbit/s	6.9 seconds

cause confusion. Practically speaking, packets do not persist in a network for much more than a couple of minutes. With the higher-speed networks, however, particularly asynchronous transfer mode (ATM), the wraparound time becomes a major cause for concern. It is quite possible for an occasional packet to get "stuck" somewhere for six or seven seconds. When that packet arrives later at its destination, the receiver will not be able to determine that the packet is old just by looking at the sequence number.

To operate effectively in high-speed networks, TCP uses the timestamp option. This option adds a 32-bit timestamp to each packet. The value must increase monotonically, and it must increment at a rate between once a millisecond and once a second. As long as the network speed is less than 17 Gbit/s, it is not possible for the sequence number to wrap around before the timestamp increments at least once. Furthermore, the timestamp value itself cannot wrap around in less than 24 days.

Given these limits, TCP can safely use the timestamp as a 32-bit extension of the sequence number. Together, the timestamp and sequence number can act as a single 64-bit quantity. Of course, this combination is only appropriate for deciding the relative order of two packets. It is not valid for sizing windows or building acknowledgments.

For examples of combining timestamps and sequence numbers, consider Table 7.14. The first example is straightforward. Both timestamps are the same, so only the se-

Table 7.14 Timestamps and Sequence Numbers

A		B		
Timestamp	**Seq. Num.**	**Timestamp**	**Seq. Num.**	**Order**
0x00000004	0x00000001	0x00000004	0x00000002	A < B
0x00000004	0x00000001	0x00000004	0xFFFF9876	A > B
0x00000004	0x00000002	0x00000005	0x00000001	A < B
0x00000004	0x00000001	0xFFFF1234	0x00000002	A > B

quence numbers matter. Even when considering wraparound, 1 is less than 2 and so A is less than B.

The second example illustrates wraparound. As before, the timestamps are identical, so only the sequence numbers are relevant. Note that in normal arithmetic, 4,294,940,790 (which is the decimal equivalent of 0xFFFF9876) is greater than 1. However, B − A is greater than 2^{31}, so A is greater than B.

The third example introduces different timestamp values, but its comparison is just as simple as the first. Since B has a larger timestamp than A, B is greater than A, no matter the sequence numbers.

The final row shows that timestamps wrap around just like sequence numbers. The same comparison rules apply. In this case, the difference between A's timestamp and B's timestamp is greater than 2^{31}. Therefore, A is greater than B. Again, because the timestamps differ, the sequence numbers are irrelevant.

Flow Control

TCP uses sequence numbers for more than just ordering data. They are a key element in TCP's flow control. With flow control, a system regulates the amount of data that its peer transmits. Such regulation can prevent the peer from sending more data than the local system can comfortably accept.

TCP flow control is based on a sliding transmission window. With every packet that contains an acknowledgment number, TCP also includes a window size. Those two numbers define the limits of what the system is prepared to receive. For example, consider the TCP packet of Figure 7.32. This packet advertises a window from 1,000 to 2,023 (1,024 bytes). The system that receives this acknowledgment uses those values to calculate how much data it can send on the connection. Note that the sender in the following discussion is the host that wants to send data. It

Source Port	Destination Port
Sequence Number	
Acknowledgment Number: 1000	

Off.	Resv.	Control	Window: 1024
Checksum			Urgent Pointer

Application Data

Figure 7.32 Example flow control window.

is not the host that transmitted the acknowledgment packet of Figure 7.32.

The sender knows that transmitting any data prior to byte number 1,000 is unnecessary. The receiver has already accepted all such data. Furthermore, the peer knows it cannot send data beyond byte number 2,023. Such data is outside the window, and will be ignored by the receiver.

To work with the flow control window, TCP maintains three values for each connection. These values regulate how much data TCP can send. The three values are the last data sent but not yet acknowledged (SndUna), the next new data byte to send (SndNxt), and the window's limit (SndUna+SndWnd). The intermediate value SndWnd is the sender's view of the window, as determined by the latest acknowledgment it has received. In the example SndWnd is 1,024.

As Figure 7.33 illustrates, these values divide the sender's sequence number space into four regions. The figure shows the sender's state just after it accepts the acknowledgment of Figure 7.32. At that point, the latest acknowledgment received is 1,000, and the window's upper limit is 2,023. The gray regions are out of bounds. They represent data that has either already been accepted or is beyond the current flow control window.

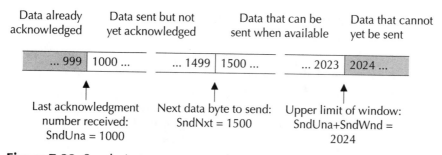

Figure 7.33 Sender's sequence numbers.

Acknowledgment and Retransmission

The last two subsections explain how sequence numbers preserve the order of data and regulate its flow. Sequence numbers are also key to making TCP's data delivery reliable. TCP expects acknowledgments of data from its peer, and, if necessary, it retransmits the data until an acknowledgment arrives.

When TCP receives a packet with application data, it must decide how much of the data, if any, is valid. Valid data is data that fits within the system's flow control window. To make that determination, the TCP relies on two values that it maintains for each connection. Those values—the next byte expected (RcvNxt) and the flow control limit (RcvNxt+RcvWnd)—divide the receiver's sequence number space into three regions. (RcvWnd is the receiver's analog of the sender's SndWnd; it is the last window that the receiver advertised.)

Figure 7.34 illustrates the perspective of the system that transmits the example packet of Figure 7.32. With that packet, the acknowledgment number is 1,000 and the flow control limit is 2,024. As before, the gray areas represent invalid data. Data to the left has already been accepted, while data to the right is outside the flow control window.

When the system receives a packet, it subjects that packet to tests that determine the packet's validity. Table 7.15

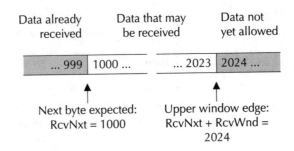

Figure 7.34 Receiver's sequence numbers.

summarizes those tests. (In the table, SegSeq is the sequence number of the first data byte in the packet, and SegLen is the amount of data in the packet.) The most interesting (and most common) case in the table is the last one. There, the local system has advertised a nonzero window, and it has received a packet that contains application data. As the table shows, TCP must apply two tests to the received data. The first test checks to determine if the beginning of the data lies in the window, while the second test checks the same thing for the end of the application data. If either test passes, then at least some of the packet's data is valid. TCP must accept and process at least that much of the data.

When TCP receives valid data that is contiguous with the last byte it acknowledged, it updates the acknowledgment number in subsequent packets to its peer. If there is a gap between the new data and last acknowledgment, then

Table 7.15 Testing the Validity of Received Data

Data Length	Window Size	Test
zero	zero	$RcvNxt = SegSeq$
zero	nonzero	$RcvNxt \leq SegSeq < RcvNxt + RcvWnd$
nonzero	zero	The segment is not valid
nonzero	nonzero	$RcvNxt \leq SegSeq < RcvNxt + RcvWnd$ or $RcvNxt \leq SegSeq + SegLen - 1 < RcvNxt + RcvWnd$

the acknowledgment number cannot advance. In fact, in this case, TCP cannot even deliver the data to its application.

When TCP returns an acknowledgment to its peer, it is normally expected to include a timestamp option in that packet. (Timestamps are not included if the systems did not negotiate their use during connection establishment.) That option includes an echo of the timestamp in the received packet. In most cases, deciding which value to echo is straightforward. TCP simply copies the timestamp value from the latest received packet. Some situations introduce complications, however.

Why Complicate Timestamp Echoes?

Tracking LastAck and TSRecent values may seem unnecessarily complicated for timestamp echoes. Such behavior does, however, provide the maximum benefit in three unusual situations. Those cases include delayed acknowledgments, missing data, and recovered data. TCP's timestamp echo strategy ensures that even in those situations, the peer gets an accurate (and conservative) estimate of the connection's round-trip time.

To make the timestamp option as useful as possible, TCP has detailed rules about which value to echo in a timestamp option. Those rules require TCP to maintain two additional values for each connection. The first value is normally the most recent timestamp value received; it is abbreviated TSRecent. This value is what TCP echoes in timestamp options that it sends. The second value is the last acknowledgment number sent, or LastAck. Often, this value is the same as the next byte expected (RcvNxt), but some TCPs may choose not to acknowledge every packet immediately. In such cases, RcvNxt may temporarily advance ahead of LastAck.

When a system receives a packet, it performs the following test. SegSeq is the sequence number of the packet, and SegLen is its length.

SegSeq ≤ LastAck < SegSeq + SegLen

If LastAck does fall within this range, then TCP saves the packet's timestamp value in TSRecent. This value is what it echoes in the next packet it sends.

Just as TCP checks incoming data for validity, it also validates incoming acknowledgment numbers. These numbers identify the data that its peer has accepted. To be valid and useful, a newly received acknowledgment number must be greater than the last number received from the peer. (If the acknowledgment number is the same as before, the packet itself may still be valid, but the acknowledgment number in the packet conveys no useful information.) In addition, the acknowledgment number cannot be greater than the next byte the sender plans to send. If that were the case, it would be acknowledging data not yet sent, clearly an impossibility.

Implicit behind the use of acknowledgment numbers is retransmission. The whole point of keeping track of the data that has been acknowledged is to identify data that has not. Since TCP provides reliable delivery, it must retransmit that lost data.

There are several factors that influence a retransmission strategy. How long does the system wait before retransmitting? How much of the lost data should the system retransmit at once? How many times should the system try retransmitting? The answers to such questions may have a profound effect on system and network performance. As a consequence, they are an active area of network research. The TCP standard, however, does not require a specific retransmission strategy. (It does offer several guidelines, some of which are now considered obsolete.) Since the standard leaves retransmission details to local implementations, this section does not cover them. Instead, they are deferred to the following section on implementation issues.

Urgent Data

If, during the course of a conversation, an application needs to send particularly urgent data to its peer, TCP provides a mechanism to do so. As the application gives TCP the data, it indicates that the data is urgent. TCP remembers where the urgent data ends, and it conveys that location to its peer with the urgent pointer in the TCP header. The peer TCP, in turn, indicates the urgency to its application.

Other than noting its urgency, TCP does not give special treatment to urgent data. It still delivers the data, in order, to the recipient. TCP does notify the application, however, whenever there is urgent data waiting. Presumably, the application will expedite processing all data ahead of the urgent data.

Closing Connections

When applications no longer have the need to exchange data, they may ask TCP to close their connection. In some ways, connection termination resembles connection establishment. Both peers must agree to it, and it requires an exchange of TCP packets. Furthermore, there is both a normal close, where one system initiates the activity, and a simultaneous close, where both systems do so.

Where connection establishment relies on the SYN bit in the TCP control field, connection termination uses the FIN (short for finish) bit. When a system has sent all the data it wishes, that system sends a TCP packet with the FIN bit set. Figure 7.35 illustrates the normal close sequence beginning with this packet. Like the SYN bit, the FIN bit is given an imaginary sequence number one greater than the

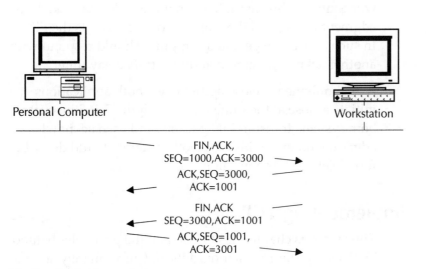

Figure 7.35 Normal close sequence.

last data byte. So, when the personal computer generates the FIN packet, the FIN bit itself effectively has a sequence number of 1,001. (As always, the sequence number field explicitly refers to application data. The figure assumes that none of its packets carry any application data.)

The peer responds by acknowledging the FIN packet. As the figure shows, the workstation advances its acknowledgment number to account for the FIN bit. At the same time, the workstation's TCP informs the application of its action, and then it waits for that application to confirm that it is also finished with the connection. With that confirmation, the workstation sends its own FIN packet, which must also be acknowledged. Again, the FIN bit has an implicit sequence number, and the PC includes that number in its final acknowledgment.

When the packet exchange is complete, the two systems take different approaches to deleting the connection. The workstation does so as soon as it receives the PC's final acknowledgment. The PC defers the actual deletion for a short period of time, in case there are any stray packets from the connection still surviving on the network. In particular, the PC may receive another FIN packet from the workstation. This might happen if the PC's final acknowledgment is lost, and the workstation retransmits the FIN. In such a case, the personal computer should respond with another acknowledgment and restart its delay timer.

A simultaneous close occurs when both applications initiate a close at the same time. As Figure 7.36 illustrates, both systems transmit FIN packets, and each acknowledges the other. In this case, both systems should delay before deleting the connection.

Implementing TCP

Thus far, this chapter has focused on the principles behind TCP and on the TCP standard itself. Unfortunately, as many developers have discovered, it takes more informa-

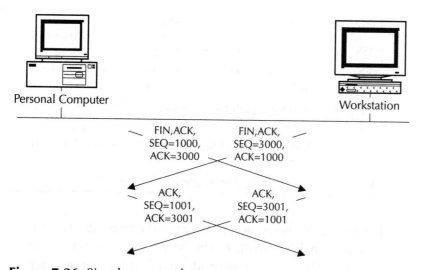

Figure 7.36 Simultaneous close sequence.

tion than the standard alone to produce a solid TCP implementation. This section examines those issues that are beyond the scope of the basic TCP standard. Its techniques can maximize both an individual host's and the whole network's performance.

Path MTU Discovery

In the IPv4 architecture, routers as well as hosts could fragment datagrams. This approach reduced the burden on the source of a packet, as the sender did not have to worry about the maximum transmission unit (MTU) size along the path. If the packet was too big to cross a link, the routers took care of the necessary fragmentation. Unfortunately, fragmentation placed a far greater burden on the intermediate routers and the ultimate destination.

The delay introduced by fragmentation in routers is substantial, and reassembly requires complex software in the destination host. These characteristics are not appropriate for the next generation networks and protocols. IPv6, therefore, does not provide hop-by-hop fragmentation. Indeed, even the destination option that it does offer

Table 7.16 Variables in MSS Calculation

MSS	Effective maximum segment size.
MSS$_{rcv}$	MSS option received from peer. If peer did not specify a MSS, a default value of 516 is assumed.
MSG$_{max}$	Maximum path message size, as indicated by local IP.
TCP$_{hdr}$	TCP header size in use. With no options, this value is 20 bytes. If the timestamp option is in use, this value is 32 bytes.
IP$_{opts}$	Size of IP options in use on the connection.

is a reluctant concession to backward compatibility and ease of transition. Instead, IPv6 expects its users to learn the MTU size for the path and, once it is known, restrict their data packets so that they fit within that limit.

To meet this expectation, TCP must do more than simply honor the maximum segment size option it receives from its peer. It must determine the true segment size for the connection. Table 7.16 lists the variables that determine the usable maximum segment size. To calculate the value for the effective MSS, a host uses the following equation.

$$MSS = \min(MSS_{rcvd}+20, MSG_{max}) - TCP_{hdr} - IP_{opts}$$

Out-of-Order Buffering

Some early TCP implementations took too much advantage of TCP's reliability. They did so by ignoring data received out of order. If such an implementation were expecting byte 100, for example, and it actually received bytes 200 to 300 in the next packet, it would simply discard the unexpected packet. This approach works (after a fashion) because the sending TCP must eventually retransmit the discarded packet. The implementation gains by avoiding the complication of saving the extra packet until the missing bytes arrive.

Unfortunately, this approach also carries a high penalty. All of the retransmissions it triggers waste network bandwidth and drastically reduce the connection's performance. Because of this performance penalty, TCP implementations should always strive to save out-of-order data. Once the missing packets arrive, TCP can deliver the out-of-order data to its application straight from local memory. It does not have to wait for its peer to retransmit.

Zero Window Probes

As this chapter has explained, TCP provides a reliable delivery service. It ensures that data packets make it to their destination, retransmitting them if necessary. TCP does not, however, guarantee the reliability of acknowledgments; it does not retransmit packets that contain only acknowledgment numbers.

Normally, this behavior does not pose a serious problem. If an acknowledgment is lost, the peer will eventually retransmit the data that the lost packet acknowledged. As Figure 7.37 shows, the workstation correctly receives bytes 100 to 199, but its acknowledgment does not make it to the personal computer. Without an acknowledgment, the PC eventually assumes that its data was lost in transit. It re-

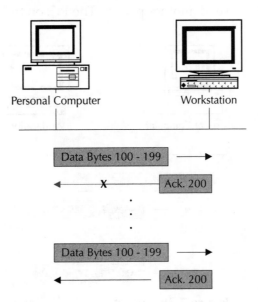

Figure 7.37 Recovering from a lost acknowledgment.

transmits the data packet. By responding to the second data packet, the workstation, in effect, gets a second chance to send its acknowledgment. This time it makes it to the PC, and the connection continues normally. The recovery forces an unnecessary retransmission of data, but it works effectively without the complications of retransmitting acknowledgments.

There is a danger to not explicitly retransmitting acknowledgments, and Figure 7.38 illustrates it. As shown, the initial acknowledgment makes it back to the personal computer without problems. Notice that in this acknowledgment the workstation has reduced the window to zero. For the moment at least, it is too congested to accept even a single byte of data from the connection.

When the congestion clears, the workstation sends a new acknowledgment, reopening the window. This packet, however, *is* lost. The PC never receives it, nor does it learn that the window is open again.

At this point, the connection could be in trouble. If the workstation has no data to send, it will have no reason to send another packet. The PC, on the other hand, believes

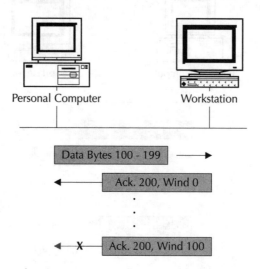

Figure 7.38 Losing a critical acknowledgment.

that the window is closed, and, therefore, it is not allowed to send another packet.

To break this deadlock, the personal computer's TCP must take special actions. Whenever the window closes completely, TCP periodically sends a data packet. Of course, it expects its peer to reject the data packet, since the packet is (apparently) outside of the window. This rejection, which will come in the form of an acknowledgment packet, will either confirm that the zero window still exists, or effectively retransmit the lost acknowledgment that should have opened the window.

The extra packets that the PC sends are known as *zero window probes*. Figure 7.39 illustrates their effectiveness. Once the PC receives the first acknowledgment that closes the window, it starts a timer. When this timer expires and the window remains closed, the PC sends a single byte of data, byte number 200. At this point the window is still closed, and the workstation confirms that with its response.

Later, when the workstation can accept more data, it transmits an acknowledgment that opens the window. In the figure, that packet is lost. Fortunately, the PC will probe the zero window again. When it does, the workstation accepts byte 200. When the PC receives that acknowledgment, it sees that the window is now open. Data flow can resume on the connection.

Because zero probes rarely succeed in transferring data, TCP must be careful to limit their use. The TCP specifications recommend sending the first zero probe packet when the window has been closed for the same amount of time as set on the connection's current retransmission timer. Subsequent probes should be sent at exponentially increasing intervals, up to some maximum value.

Silly Window Syndrome

The silly window syndrome is a classic example of the pitfalls of ignoring implementation issues. Two TCP peers,

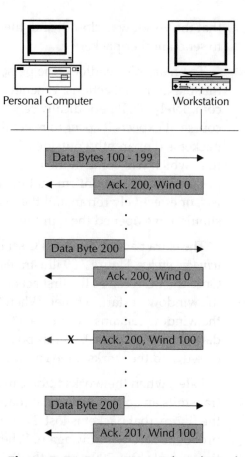

Figure 7.39 Reopening a closed window with zero probes.

both conforming to the TCP specification, can rely on reasonable implementation decisions and still artificially and severely limit their performance. As David Clark[1] notes from observations of early TCP behavior, the silly window syndrome can reduce the effective throughput of a connection by a factor of 10 or more.

Silly window syndrome is best understood by following an example. Figure 7.40 illustrates a simple case. It shows part of the communication between a personal computer

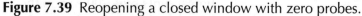

[1] David D. Clark. *Window and Acknowledgment Strategy in TCP* [RFC 813]. July 1992.

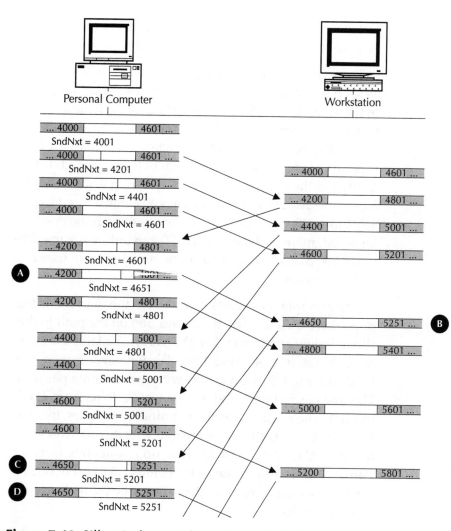

Figure 7.40 Silly window syndrome in action.

and a workstation. At the start of the example, the connection is idle and stable. Both systems understand the PC's send window to range from 4,000 to 4,600, and the PC has no data unacknowledged.

The activity starts when the PC has data to send to the workstation. With its initial window of 600 bytes, it sends three packets, each with 200 bytes of data. These three packets advance the PC's SndUna (see page 216) variable to 4,201, 4,401, and finally to 4,601. At that point, the PC has exhausted its window, and transmission ceases.

The workstation, for its part, acknowledges everything as soon as it arrives. It always advertises a window of 600 bytes, so both the left and right edges of the window advance with each packet. The first acknowledgment advances the PC's window by 200 bytes. The first byte of unacknowledged data moves from byte number 4,001 to 4,201, and the window limit increases from 4,601 to 4,801. Note, however, that the PC has already transmitted bytes 4,201 to 4,600. So, even though the window in the acknowledgment is 600 bytes, the PC can only send an additional 200 bytes. The first 400 bytes are already in transit on the network.

The example now reaches point A in the figure. It is this step where the PC starts the connection on the path to the silly window syndrome. The PC has an available window of 200 bytes, from 4,601 to 4,801. For whatever reason, the PC decides to fill that window with two separate packets. The first has 50 bytes, and it advances SndUna from 4,601 to 4,651. The second uses the remaining 150 bytes, increasing SndUna to 4,801. There are many legitimate reasons that the PC might choose to break up its data this way. Perhaps, for example, the 50 bytes fell at the end of one record in the data. Whatever the reason, the PC is clearly in its rights to do so.

The next interesting step occurs when the 50-byte packet reaches the workstation. That point is marked by a B in the figure. As always, the workstation immediately acknowledges the 50 bytes while maintaining a window of 600 bytes. This acknowledgment advances the window limit from 5,201 to 5,251.

Now consider what happens when that acknowledgment reaches the personal computer; step C in the figure. As expected, the PC's window moves to 5,251. The window size is still 600 bytes, but now the PC has already used 550 of those bytes. Its usable window has only grown by 50.

At point D, the PC may be in some trouble. Its usable window is 50 bytes, but, presumably, it has many more bytes to send. Despite the inefficiency, the PC chooses to send what it can, so it takes 50 bytes of its waiting data and transmits them in a packet. Of course, this behavior perpetuates the problem. Sometime later the PC will receive an acknowledgment for this packet, which will advance the window a mere 50 bytes, which will force the PC to send yet another 50-byte packet.

At this point, the effects of the silly window syndrome are clear. Because at one point (A in the figure) the PC naturally sent a small packet, it will be forced in the future to break its data into more packets of this size. During a sustained file transfer of several million bytes, this effect can gradually and insidiously reduce throughput. First, the sender naturally breaks off its data in a 50-byte packet, and from then on it is forced to continue to send 50-byte packets periodically. Then, a natural boundary occurs with a 20-byte packet, and the sender forces itself into sending more 20-byte packets. Next, a 10-byte packet defines a natural break, and so on. Soon the connection is trying to transfer millions of bytes 10 or 20 at a time.

To avoid the silly window syndrome, TCP requires specific behavior in both the sender and receiver. Either behavior alone will prevent most occurrences of the problem. Together, they eliminate all practical opportunities for the silly window syndrome to appear.

The receiver's behavior is easiest to describe. TCP simply avoids advertising an updated window until the update is larger than some reasonable value. Formally, that reasonable value is defined to be the minimum of two quantities—the effective maximum segment size (MSS) for the path and a fraction (typically half) of the actual buffer space available. Since the receive buffer space is nearly always much greater than the effective MSS, this policy usually results in window updates of the effective MSS or greater. The receiver determines the effective MSS of the path through the path MTU discovery mechanism (see page 223).

To see how this behavior prevents the silly window syndrome, Figure 7.41 focuses on the same connection as Figure 7.40, but this time the workstation avoids the problem. It does so at point B. In the previous figure, the workstation immediately acknowledges the 50-byte packet and advertises an updated, 600-byte window.

In Figure 7.41, the workstation still acknowledges the small packet, but now it withholds the window update due to that small packet. Instead of advertising a 600-byte window, the workstation offers only 550 bytes. Later, when the 150-byte packet arrives, the window grows by 150 more bytes from 5,251 to 5,401. Since the total growth is now 200 bytes, and since 200 bytes is presumably the effective MSS for the connection, the workstation does update its advertised window.

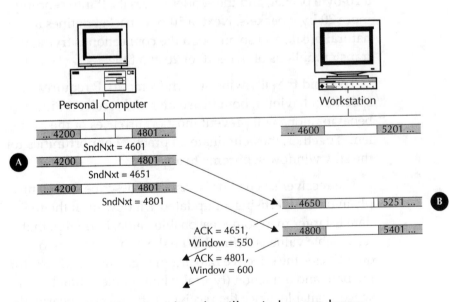

Figure 7.41 Receiver avoiding the silly window syndrome.

Pushing Data

TCP has no obligation to transmit data packets as soon as it gets data from the application. It may choose to delay transmission until a more favorable time. Sometimes, however, the application cannot afford that delay. The data is not urgent, but it is important enough to send soon. To indicate this requirement, the application gives TCP a special signal called a *push*. In early TCP implementations, the push signal was actually carried in the TCP header (via the push bit in the control field). Even modern implementations are likely to do so. As TCP has developed more sophisticated delivery algorithms, the push bit can no longer be assumed to have that meaning.

If the workstation does not adopt this behavior, the silly window syndrome can still be avoided. The personal computer, by sending data only at judicious moments, can break the cycle that leads to the syndrome. The sender's behavior depends on three auxiliary values. The first value is the usable window, or U. This value is the amount of new data that the sender can transmit without overrunning the window. In the standard notation (see page 216):

$$U = SndUna + SndWnd - SndNxt$$

The second extra value is the amount of data available to send, denoted by D. The third value, Max(SndWnd), represents the maximum window seen on the connection so far. TCP uses this value as an estimate of the receive buffer space in its peer. This value can only be an estimate, so the sender must be careful in employing it. To avoid deadlocks when the estimate is wrong, the sender must time how long it delays sending available data. If the delay exceeds a defined timeout value, then data should be sent regardless of the window state. The timeout value should be in the range of 0.1 to 1.0 seconds. The rules for sending data packets are summarized in Table 7.17. If any one of the four cases applies, the sender should transmit a packet. The fraction in the third case, shown as ½, may be adjusted up or down in some special circumstances.

Slow Start and Congestion Avoidance

TCP connections rely on a shared resource—the computer network. Unfortunately, that resource always has a limited capacity, and sometimes a connection cannot use as much as it would like. In particular, networks become congested

Table 7.17 When to Send a Packet

(a) $min(D,U) \geq MSS$
(b) (SndNxt = SndUna) and (pushed) and (D ≤ U)
(c) (SndNxt = SndUna) and $(min(D,U) \geq \frac{1}{2} \cdot Max(SndWnd))$
(d) (pushed) and (timeout)

as their users try to transfer more data than the network can carry. TCP's policies have a major effect on network performance in the face of congestion. To help relieve network congestion, TCP implementations employ policies known as *slow start* and *congestion avoidance*. Together, they improve performance for TCP connections and the network in general.

To see why slow start and congestion avoidance are crucial, consider the network of Figure 7.42. Several traffic streams are converging in a single router, and that router cannot process the inrush of packets fast enough. As the data flows continue, packets start backing up in the central router. Figure 7.43 shows the situation as this occurs.

Many of these packets are TCP packets, including those from the personal computer to the workstation. Of course, if the packets are stuck in the central router, they can't make it to their destination. The personal computer is not aware of this, though. It is waiting patiently for an acknowledgment from the workstation.

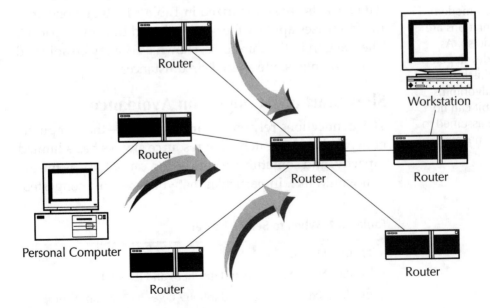

Figure 7.42 Traffic converging on a router.

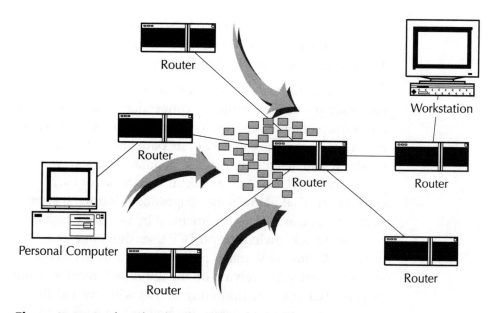

Figure 7.43 Packets backing up in a router.

At this point, the problem can explode. The PC may give up on hearing an acknowledgment, assume its packets are lost, and retransmit them. To make matters worse, many other traffic sources could reach the same conclusion and retransmit their data. Of course, these retransmissions are more packets, and more packets are just what the network does not need. These additional packets further clog the network, delaying packets even more, and triggering still more retransmissions. The network is said to be in *congestion collapse*.

Congestion collapse is not just an abstract theory. It has been observed in actual networks. Van Jacobson[2] reported the first incident on the Internet in October 1986. During congestion collapse, throughput between two sites dropped from 32 Kbit/s to 40 bit/s. Fortunately, in the

---

[2] Van Jacobson. "Congestion Avoidance and Control." *Proceedings of the ACM Special Interest Group on Communications [SIGCOMM].* August 1988.

same paper, Jacobson proposed a solution to the problem. His solution, a combination of slow start and congestion avoidance, is now required in TCP implementations.

Slow start addresses one of the most common sources of increased traffic (and resulting congestion) in a network—the startup of a new connection. It forces a new connection to gradually test the capacity of its path and not overwhelm it with a sudden increase in data. Slow start requires that TCP maintain an additional value for each connection. That value is the congestion window. It starts at one packet, and TCP increments it by one each time it receives an acknowledgment. TCP uses the congestion window to limit how many packets it permits to be outstanding, instead of relying on the window it receives from its peer. TCP uses the minimum of that window and the congestion window to determine how many packets to transmit.

When a TCP connection begins, the congestion window is one. TCP, therefore, sends a single packet to its peer. When that packet is acknowledged, TCP increments the congestion window to two, and sends two packets. As the peer acknowledges each of these two packets, the congestion window increases to three and then four.

Slow start continues in this fashion until TCP gets an indication that it has pushed matters too far. That indication is a retransmission timeout for a packet. TCP assumes that such a timeout means that the network has become congested. There are other reasons that an acknowledgment may fail to arrive for a packet. The packet (or the acknowledgment) may have been lost or damaged in transit, for example. Such events are far less likely than congestion, however. By treating all retransmission timeouts as indications of congestion, TCP plays it as safe as possible.

Once congestion appears, TCP takes three actions. First, it doubles the value it is using for retransmission timeout on the connection. Second, it remembers the value of the congestion window when congestion appeared. Finally, TCP begins the slow start process again by lowering its congestion window to one.

As slow start naturally increases the congestion window again, TCP modifies its behavior when the window reaches half of the value at which congestion appeared. At that point, instead of incrementing the window with each acknowledgment, it increments the window with each window full of acknowledgments.

Figure 7.44 shows a full slow start and congestion avoidance sequence. The top half is pure slow start. As each acknowledgment arrives from the workstation, the personal computer increments its congestion window by one. The congestion window reaches eight in a very short time. At that point, however, the connection places too much additional stress on the network, and congestion occurs. When the retransmission timer expires in the PC, the PC begins slow start again. It remembers the value of its congestion window—eight, in this case.

Slow start continues as before until the window reaches four, half of the remembered value. There, slow start gives way to congestion avoidance. When the connection enters the congestion avoidance phase, the congestion window does not increment with each individual acknowledgment. Instead, the congestion window only increments with a window's worth of acknowledgment.

In the example of Figure 7.44, the window at the start of congestion avoidance is four. It does not increment until the PC receives four acknowledgments. At that point, the window is five. Now it takes five acknowledgments to move it to six. As the figure shows, the PC treats the network much more gently once it closes in on the congestion point.

A key element of successful congestion avoidance is a finely tuned retransmission timer. Its timeout value must accurately reflect the uncongested round-trip time for the

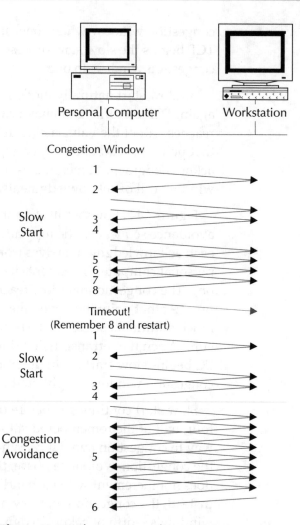

Figure 7.44 Slow start and congestion avoidance.

connection. If the timeout is too short, it will expire need-lessly. On the other hand, if it is too long, it may fail to de-tect the onset of congestion, and prevent TCP from taking appropriate steps to reduce its load.

The algorithm currently deemed the best at setting timeouts relies on sampling the actual round-trip time for packets on the connection. The most reliable samples are from timestamp options in the acknowledgments. If timestamp options are not in use on the connection, TCP can locally time the transmission and acknowledgment of each packet. As Karn and Partridge[3] explain, TCP implementations should only sample those packets that are acknowledged without a retransmission. From those samples, TCP estimates both a mean and standard deviation of the round-trip time. It then computes a retransmission timeout from those estimates. In these equations, RTT represents a sample round-trip time; m_{RTT} is the estimated mean, and s_{RTT} is the estimated standard deviation.

Efficient Calculation of Retransmission Timeouts

The equations to the right that calculate retransmission timeouts have several factors that are engineering choices. Note that all factors are a power (or inverse power) of 2. These choices make calculation particularly easy, as multiplication and division by two can be achieved with logical shifts.

$$\Delta = RTT - m_{RTT}$$

$$m_{RTT} = m_{RTT} + \frac{\Delta}{8}$$

$$s_{RTT} = s_{RTT} + \frac{|\Delta| \cdot s_{RTT}}{4}$$

$$\text{timeout} = m_{RTT} + 4 \cdot s_{RTT}$$

Delayed Acknowledgment

Even when a system has no data to send on a connection, it must still acknowledge data that it receives from its peer. The acknowledgment packets that it uses carry no application data themselves, and so, in some way, they waste network bandwidth. To minimize this wasted bandwidth, a TCP implementation need not acknowledge every packet as soon as that packet arrives. Instead, the system can delay the acknowledgment for a brief period. Perhaps, during that delay, the local application will have something to send. (Many times, the application will wish to respond to its peer.) If that happens, that return data can carry the latest acknowledgment number, avoiding the wasted bandwidth altogether. And even if the local application remains

---

[3] Phil Karn and Craig Partridge. "Improving Round-Trip Time Estimates in Reliable Transport Protocols." *Proceedings of the ACM Special Interest Group on Communications [SIGCOMM].* August 1987.

silent, more data might arrive from the peer. In that case, the local TCP can acknowledge all the data at once, at least reducing the number of acknowledgment-only packets. In either case, TCP reduces its utilization of network bandwidth.

If an implementation uses delayed acknowledgments, the delay should be small. Various TCP/IP standards recommend a delay of no longer than 0.5 seconds. In addition, TCP should not withhold an acknowledgment for too many packets. When it is receiving full-size packets, TCP should explicitly acknowledge at least every other packet from its peer.

Header Prediction

Many software implementations, particularly protocol implementations, spend a great deal of effort checking for invalid operations, errors, and other unusual events. But the goal, of course, is that such events do not occur. Typical implementations spend most of their time checking for things that rarely happen. To maximize performance, TCP software should be optimized for the common cases.

TCP header prediction, first proposed by Jacobson[4], represents, perhaps, the ultimate example of this optimization. With header prediction, when TCP receives a packet, it predicts, in advance, the next packet's likely header. Then, when the next packet arrives, TCP merely has to check it against the earlier prediction. If the prediction was correct, TCP immediately accepts the packet as valid, avoiding the lengthy checks it might otherwise make.

To see this in action, consider the example packet in Figure 7.45. Assuming that the packet is valid, what can TCP expect to see in the next packet it processes? The following discussion considers each header field in turn.

---

[4] Van Jacobson. "4BSD Header Prediction." *ACM Computer Communication Review*, April 1990.

Source Port: 1234		Destination Port: 21	
Sequence Number: 10000			
Acknowledgment Number: 500			
Off: 8	Ctrl: 0x10	Window: 1024	
Checksum: 0x2468		Urgent Pointer: 0	
NOOP	NOOP	TStamp	Length: 10
Timestamp Value: 40000			
Timestamp Echo Reply: 60			
Application Data (1024 bytes)			

Figure 7.45 Sample packet for header prediction.

The first field is the source port. Though it will clearly err sometimes, TCP can predict that the next packet it receives will have the same source port, or 1234. Research has shown that packets from the same connection tend to travel in groups across a network. Even if the average size of such groups is only two packets, this prediction will be correct half of the time. Just as for the source port, TCP can expect the destination port of the next packet to be the same. It should predict the destination port to be 21.

Assuming that packets do not arrive out of order, TCP can predict that the next sequence number will be the current number, plus the size of the application data. In this case, that prediction yields a sequence number of 11,024.

If the connection is primarily a one-way conversation (at least for the moment), TCP can expect no change in the acknowledgment number of the next packet. It predicts, therefore, a value of 500. Presumably, this is also the value of the local TCP's SndUna value. Since all data packets for a connection use the same options, the offset should not change in the next packet.

The ACK bit is the only bit normally set for normal data transfer. As with this packet, therefore, TCP can predict a control field value of 0x10 for the next segment. The peer

TCP is not likely to change its advertised window, especially if the local TCP has not sent it any data. The predicted value for the window field of the next packet is the same as this one, 1,024.

With the checksum, TCP finally comes to a field that it cannot predict. Implementations have no choice but to validate the checksum of all incoming packets. Based on the prediction of the next packet's control field, the urgent pointer should not be meaningful in that packet. There is no need to validate a meaningless field.

Finally, the header concludes with the options. The next packet should have the same options present, though its timestamp values may have increased. This field, like the checksum, cannot be reliably predicted in advance.

As this discussion shows, TCP is capable of predicting nearly all of the TCP header of the next packet. In most cases, the CPU resources required to make that prediction, and then to verify it, are far fewer than the CPU resources required to exhaustively validate an incoming packet. And yet, by definition, if the packet matches the prediction, it will be valid.

The resulting optimization should be fairly clear. On receipt of a packet, TCP checks it against the predicted header. If there is a match, TCP simply accepts the packet as valid, avoiding the tedious validation checks. Only if the prediction fails does TCP have to carry out those checks.

Summary

As the length of this chapter indicates, TCP is a complex and powerful protocol. It has an important job making sure that data reaches its destination reliably. To meet this responsibility, TCP relies on connections. Connections establish a context for communications, allowing the protocol to recognize and correct missing, out-of-order, or duplicate data.

To accommodate the high-speed networks of the future, TCP now includes several options that maximize its performance. Those options include timestamps and window scale factors. In addition, there is large body of research that presents ways to optimize TCP implementations. This research includes sophisticated techniques like slow start and congestion avoidance that significantly improve network performance. In addition, the TCP literature includes many approaches that improve local implementations. Those techniques include efficient checksum algorithms and header prediction.

8

Routing with OSPF

Networks exist to deliver data. The data may take many forms, and it may serve many different transport and application protocols. For any network to be useful, however, data must reach its intended destination. Chapter 4 showed how the Internet Protocol accepts data packets and moves them one step closer to their destination. Until now, this text has neglected to answer two important questions: How does IP know which step is the next step? How does IP know where to route?

This chapter looks at the protocol that answers those questions. The Open Shortest Path First, or OSPF, protocol is TCP/IP's primary routing protocol. Routers rely on OSPF to exchange information among themselves. That information gives each router a map of the network. By checking their maps, routers know how to move packets through the network to their destinations.

OSPF is an example of a particular type of routing protocol—a *link state* protocol. All link state protocols share the same basic principles, and this chapter begins by examining those principles. It then discusses the ways that OSPF organizes networks, and how OSPF deals with unusual network technologies. It concludes with a detailed look at OSPF messages and their use in all aspects of the protocol.

Link State Routing

Link state routing has a reputation for complexity. Certainly the size of the OSPF specification—currently 226 pages—does little to allay such concerns. Actually, link state routing is based on a few simple principles. It may take several words to describe those principles with the precision required by a protocol specification, but the principles themselves are easy to understand.

Routing protocols are the primary tool of routers, and routers have a simple goal. They want to understand how the network is put together so that they can tell how to get from one point to another. In a real sense, routers just want a map of the network, and routing protocols help them create such a map.

Link state protocols create the map in three distinct phases. First, each router meets its neighbors. In that phase, the routers learn about their local neighborhood. In the second phase, routers share that information with all other routers on the network. During this phase, routers learn about every other neighborhood. In the final phase, routers combine the information about individual neighborhoods. This combination describes the entire network, and from it routers calculate routes.

With apologies to those readers outside the United States, the U.S. interstate highway system provides a convenient example for discussing link state routing. Cities take the place of routers, and the roads between them act as links. Figure 8.1 shows the part of that system the following text considers. (Note that the figure sometimes combines several real highways into one, and it distorts a few distances. Do not plan a family vacation using this map.)

Meet Your Neighbors

Systems that participate in link state routing begin learning routes by meeting their neighbors. This phase could

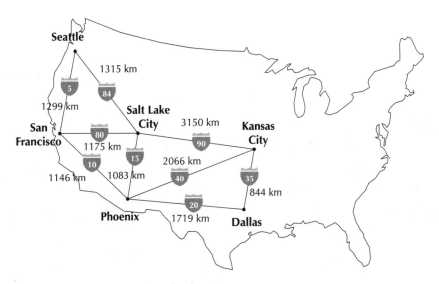

Figure 8.1 U.S. interstate highway system.

hardly be any easier. Each system simply sends a packet on all its links. That packet, called a *hello packet*, introduces the sender.

Referring to the example, Kansas City starts the process by sending a courier on all of its roads. The courier carries a message that says "Hello, I'm Kansas City." All the other systems take the same action, so Kansas City also receives couriers from its neighbors with their introductions. Figure 8.2 shows Kansas City introducing itself, and its neighbors introducing themselves to Kansas City.

Once Kansas City receives hello packets from Dallas, Phoenix, and Salt Lake City, it knows the identity of its neighbors. Kansas City also knows the distance, or cost, to each neighbor[1]. Kansas City could summarize the information it has learned in a list like Table 8.1. Of course, all the other cities take the same actions as Kansas City. Each,

---

[1] The highway analogy breaks down here. Highway distances are real physical values. Short of building new roads, they do not change. Network costs, on the other hand, are arbitrary, and set by network administrators. For this discussion, the distinction is not important.

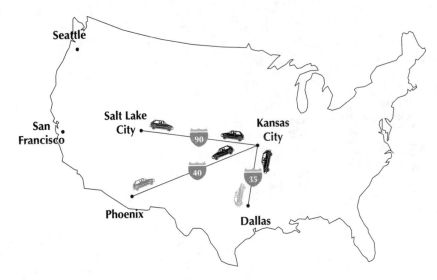

Figure 8.2 Kansas City neighbor greeting.

therefore, quickly meets its neighbors, and each is able to construct a similar table.

Share the Information

Once each city learns the identity of its neighbors, the second phase of link state routing takes over. In this phase, the cities share the information they have learned. Each city constructs a packet containing its neighbor list, and it sends that packet to all other cities. These packets are *link state advertisements*, or LSAs. An LSA from Kansas City, for example, contains exactly the information in Table 8.1.

Most link state protocols, including OSPF, share neighbor information by *flooding* LSAs. Systems flood a packet

Table 8.1 Kansas City Neighbors

Neighbor	Highway	Distance
Salt Lake City	I-90	3150 km
Phoenix	I-40	2066 km
Dallas	I-20	1719 km

by resending a copy of that packet to nearly every link. More precisely, when a system participates in flooding, it considers every LSA it receives a candidate to be flooded. First, the system makes sure that the candidate packet is new. If it is an old packet that the system has already seen, then it has already been flooded. The system can simply discard it.

If the candidate packet is a new one, the system remembers the information it contains (if, for no other reason, to ensure it can recognize future, duplicate copies). The system then transmits a copy of the packet on all links except the one from which it arrived.

Figure 8.3 shows how flooding distributes Kansas City's link state advertisement across the network. The vans, representing LSA packets, have numbers that correspond to the steps in Table 8.2. That table outlines the complete flooding procedure.

The example illustrates the most important feature of flooding. It ensures that all systems receive a copy of the LSA packet. Of course, in the sample network, Kansas City

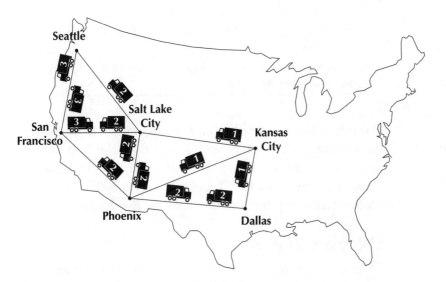

Figure 8.3 Flooding Kansas City's link state advertisement.

The Efficiency of Flooding

As this example clearly shows, flooding does waste some network bandwidth. Systems receive multiple copies of the same LSA, and they end up discarding all but the first. In exchange for this extra bandwidth, however, flooding makes life a lot easier on the routers. Furthermore, any other approach is fraught with peril. Reducing the duplicate copies would require some knowledge of the network's topology. Routers would have to know who is connected to whom so they could avoid the extra copies. But, of course, flooding LSAs is one step in determining that connectivity. Routers cannot share information more efficiently without knowing the topology, and they cannot easily learn that topology without flooding.

Table 8.2 Flooding Kansas City's Link State Advertisement

1. Kansas City transmits LSA on all links: to Dallas, Phoenix, and Salt Lake City.

2a. Dallas receives the LSA from Kansas City and copies it to all other links, in this case to Phoenix.

2b. Phoenix receives the LSA from Kansas City and copies it to all other links: Dallas, San Francisco, Salt Lake City.

2c. Salt Lake City receives the LSA from Kansas City and copies it to Seattle, San Francisco, and Phoenix.

3a. Dallas receives the LSA from Phoenix. Having already received it, Dallas discards this copy of the LSA.

3b. Phoenix receives the LSA from Dallas and from Salt Lake City. Already having seen the LSA, Phoenix discards it.

3c. Salt Lake City receives another copy from Phoenix and discards it.

3d. San Francisco receives the LSA from Phoenix and copies it to Seattle and Salt Lake City.

3e. San Francisco receives another copy of the LSA from Salt Lake City and discards it.

3f. Seattle receives the LSA from Salt Lake City and copies it to San Francisco.

4a. Salt Lake City receives yet another copy of the LSA, this time from San Francisco. Salt Lake City discards it.

4b. Seattle receives another copy from San Francisco and discards it.

4c. San Francisco receives a duplicate copy of the LSA from Seattle and discards it.

is not alone in flooding LSAs. All other cities do the same. As a result, every system soon learns the neighbors of every other system as well as its own. Each system has the view of the network that Table 8.3 describes. That information makes up the *link state database* for the network.

Calculate Routes

Once all systems have an up-to-date link state database, they can begin the final phase of link state routing—

Table 8.3 Example Link State Database

Kansas City	Dallas	Phoenix	Salt Lake	San Francisco	Seattle
Dallas 844	Kansas City 844	Kansas City 2066	Kansas City 3150	Phoenix 1146	Salt Lake 1315
Phoenix 2066	Phoenix 1719	Dallas 1719	Phoenix 1083	Salt Lake 1175	San Francisco 1299
Salt Lake 3150		Salt Lake 1083	San Francisco 1175	Seattle 1299	
		San Francisco 1146	Seattle 1315		

actually calculating routes. The technical details of this calculation are not a formal part of most link state protocol specifications. The protocols take care of distributing the information; systems use that information however they like, as long as they reach appropriate and consistent conclusions.

One particular algorithm is so much more efficient at determining routes, though, that nearly all link state implementations rely on it. The particular algorithm, originally proposed by Dijkstra[2], is so prevalent that most routing protocols assume its implementation and are optimized accordingly.

Shortest Path First

Dijkstra's algorithm is often called the *shortest path first* algorithm. Indeed, that is how the OSPF protocol gets its own name. This name comes from step three of the algorithm in Table 8.4, which locates the shortest (closest) system and treats it next.

Dijkstra's algorithm constructs a directed graph, or tree, of the network. The tree's root is the system conducting the calculation, and its branches are links to other systems. Table 8.4 describes the steps in the algorithm. To see Dijkstra's algorithm in action, consider how Kansas City would employ it. Figure 8.4 shows the computation; it is based on the link state database of Table 8.3.

Once the Dijkstra calculation is complete, the system has a complete picture of routing in the network. To find the best path to any particular destination, the system need

---

[2] E.W. Dijkstra. "A Note on Two Problems in Connection with Graphs." *Numerische Mathematic* 1:269-271, 1959.

Table 8.4 Dijkstra's Algorithm

1. Start building the tree by creating its root—the local system. The distance to this system is zero.

2. For whichever system was just added to the tree (initially it will be the local system), examine the link state database. For every neighbor of the system, compute the distance to that neighbor by adding the distance to the system just added and the distance from that system to its neighbor. If that distance is less than any other route to the neighbor, add the route to a temporary tree.

3. Search the temporary tree for the closest system. Add that system (and the route to it) to the final tree, and return to step 2. If there are no entries remaining in the temporary tree, the calculation is complete.

only find that system on the Dijkstra tree. Whichever path points to that system in the tree is the path to use to route to that system across the network.

With Figure 8.4 as an example, Kansas City would forward to Salt Lake City by way of Phoenix. Furthermore, Kansas City knows that Salt Lake City is 3,149 miles away.

Network Changes

The discussion so far has assumed a static network. Routers and links, once operational, remain operational indefinitely. Of course, real networks are not that stable. Routers restart and links fail, yet the network must continue to function. In fact, one of the greatest strengths of TCP/IP is it robustness in the face of unstable networks.

Fortunately, all the principles of the previous three subsections apply equally well to dynamic networks. The only difference is that all three phases happen in parallel, and they all take place continuously. Systems continuously introduce themselves to their neighbors, and they continue to receive hello packets from those neighbors. When a system hears of a new neighbor, it updates its link state advertisement and floods it again. The same thing happens

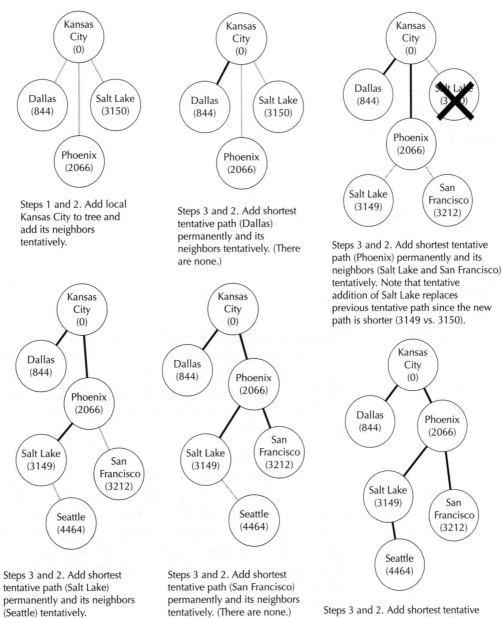

Steps 1 and 2. Add local Kansas City to tree and add its neighbors tentatively.

Steps 3 and 2. Add shortest tentative path (Dallas) permanently and its neighbors tentatively. (There are none.)

Steps 3 and 2. Add shortest tentative path (Phoenix) permanently and its neighbors (Salt Lake and San Francisco) tentatively. Note that tentative addition of Salt Lake replaces previous tentative path since the new path is shorter (3149 vs. 3150).

Steps 3 and 2. Add shortest tentative path (Salt Lake) permanently and its neighbors (Seattle) tentatively.

Steps 3 and 2. Add shortest tentative path (San Francisco) permanently and its neighbors tentatively. (There are none.)

Steps 3 and 2. Add shortest tentative path (Seattle) permanently and its neighbors tentatively. (There are none.) Since no more tentative paths exist, the calculation is complete.

Figure 8.4 Performing the Dijkstra calculation.

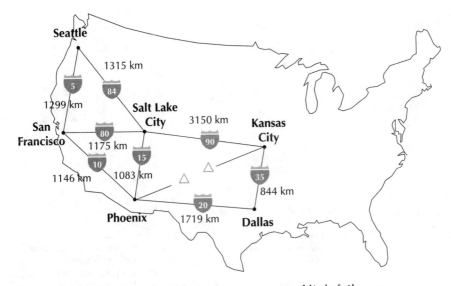

Figure 8.5 Link state routing in the presence of link failures.

if a system fails to hear from its neighbor. The flooding updates everyone's link state database. A new database requires a new Dijkstra calculation, so each router performs its computations again. As the network changes, OSPF tracks those changes, and routing continues to function successfully.

To reinforce this behavior, consider how the sample network responds to a link failure. Suppose, as Figure 8.5 illustrates, highway I-40 from Kansas City to Phoenix is closed. Eventually, both Kansas City and Phoenix recognize that the link is no longer available. If they fail to learn this directly, they will at least assume it when they cease to receive hello packets from the other. When the recognition dawns, both cities update their link state advertisements and flood them across the network. Of course, this flooding takes place without the benefit of highway I-40. Once the flooding is complete, every system will have an up-to-date link state database, as shown in Table 8.5.

With a new link state database, each system must perform the Dijkstra calculation again. As Figure 8.6 shows,

Table 8.5 Updated Link State Database

Kansas City	Dallas	Phoenix	Salt Lake	San Francisco	Seattle
Dallas 844	Kansas City 844	Dallas 1719	Kansas City 3150	Phoenix 1146	Salt Lake 1315
Salt Lake 3150	Phoenix 1719	Salt Lake 1083	Phoenix 1083	Salt Lake 1175	San Francisco 1299
		San Franciso 1146	San Franciso 1175	Seattle 1299	
			Seattle 1315		

that calculation changes how Kansas City routes to other destinations. Now, to reach Phoenix, it sends packets to Dallas. In fact, all routes that used to go through Phoenix now take other paths. Fortunately, the entire process—updating LSAs, flooding them across the network, and re-computing routes—typically happens in less than a second or two. Link state protocols react quickly to network changes, and the network continues to function.

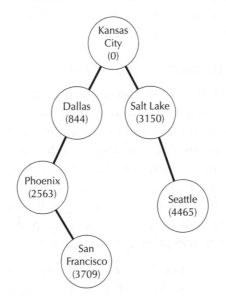

Figure 8.6 Recomputed routes.

OSPF and Network Organization

The Open Shortest Path First protocol employs all of the principles of a link state routing protocol. It meets neighbors, shares the information, and calculates routes. Of course, real networks introduce a few complications to these simple processes. One such complication is network organization.

In principle, OSPF could treat the entire Internet just like the U.S. highway example. Every router could exchange information with every other router. Unfortunately, that approach is not practical. There are just too many systems on the Internet. The required link state database would be enormous (far too large to store in any real system), and Dijkstra's calculation, even on high-performance supercomputers, would take hours. Even worse, the flooding of so many LSA packets would completely swamp the network, rendering it useless for actual user traffic.

To solve these problems of scale, OSPF establishes hierarchies within the network. Those hierarchies include autonomous systems, areas, backbones, stub areas, and not so stubby areas. This section looks at each of these divisions in turn.

Autonomous Systems

At the coarsest level, the Internet consists of many *autonomous systems*. Autonomous system is, perhaps, an unfortunate choice of name for this grouping. An autonomous system (AS) is actually a collection of many computer systems, routers, and other network devices. The equipment comprising an autonomous system shares a single administrative entity. That entity, which may be an educational institution, a corporation, a network provider, and so on, manages all equipment within the AS.

Figure 8.7 shows the organization of three autonomous systems. (In order to fit on the page, these ASs are considerably smaller than most real autonomous systems.) Each

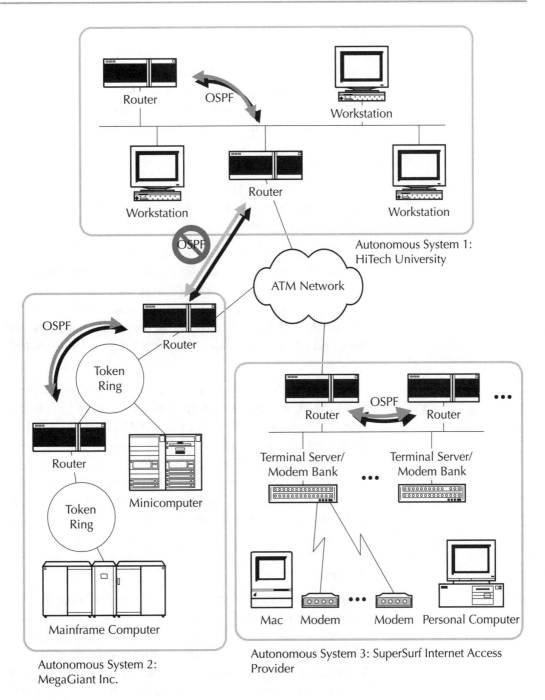

Figure 8.7 Autonomous systems.

AS forms a self-contained network, with its own administration and management. In most cases, though, networks provide more value when they connect more users. Increasing that connectivity means connecting autonomous systems. The figure shows such a connection through the ATM network in its center.

Autonomous systems define the limits of OSPF's interactions. Routers within an AS can exchange routing information with OSPF. They describe their links with LSA packets, and they can flood those packets throughout the autonomous system.

At the AS boundary, however, no OSPF traffic flows. The three routers in the center of Figure 8.7, for example, can use OSPF within their respective autonomous systems but they do not use OSPF to communicate with each other across the ATM network. Because they exist on the boundary of an AS, routers such as these three are *AS boundary routers*.

AS boundary routers can learn about the network beyond the autonomous system. They may learn information from routing protocols other than OSPF, or they may learn from manual configuration. In either case, AS boundary routers can use OSPF to distribute that information within the autonomous system. They do so by building special link state advertisements. These special LSAs are *external* LSAs, so called because they describe topology external to the AS.

Areas

Autonomous systems provide some relief to a routing protocol such as OSPF. They limit the scope of the protocol's influence, and reduce the memory, processor resources, and network bandwidth the protocol requires. Sometimes, however, even an autonomous system by itself is too big and unwieldy. When such problems arise, OSPF offers another mechanism that provides even more hierarchy to networks. That mechanism is the *area*.

Areas are arbitrary collections of networks, hosts, and routers. All systems within an area must be connected together, but otherwise there are no restrictions on what is allowed in an area. As an example of various areas, consider Figure 8.8, which shows a single autonomous system. The AS has three normal areas and a special area known as the backbone. The routers that connect different areas are known as *area border routers*.

Within each area, OSPF functions normally. Routers construct and flood link state advertisements listing all of their neighbors, and they distribute these LSAs to all other

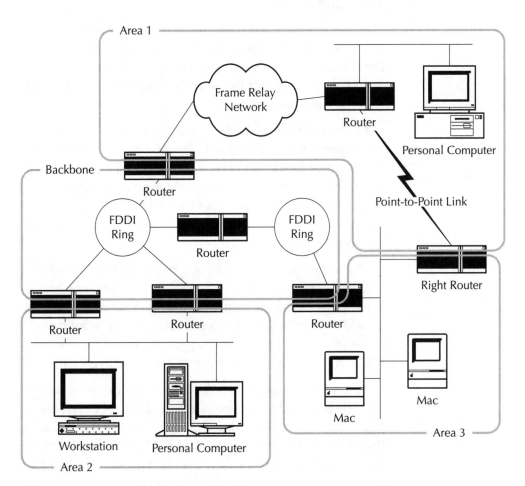

Figure 8.8 Areas within an autonomous system.

routers in the area. At the boundary between areas, however, the OSPF protocol does not exchange simple LSAs. Instead, area border routers construct special LSAs that summarize the information within their areas.

The router on the right side of the figure, for example, is an area border router connecting areas 1 and 3. It summarizes the topology of area 3 for area 1. To distribute that information, it floods summary LSAs into area 1. Similarly, the right router summarizes the topology of area 1 with LSAs that it floods into area 3.

The Backbone

The *backbone* is a special area within an autonomous system. It serves as the hub of the AS, and all other areas in the AS must connect to the backbone. As Figure 8.8 shows, areas can also connect to each other directly, without going through the backbone.

Routers within the backbone are known as *backbone routers*. Figure 8.8 includes five backbone routers. Four of them are also area border routers; they connect the backbone to another area. The exception is the router connecting the two FDDI ring networks. This router is still a backbone router, since it resides in the backbone area, but it is not an area border router.

OSPF considers the backbone a particularly important area, and it provides special features to account for a break in the backbone connectivity. Consider Figure 8.9, in which a backbone router is no longer operational. Without that router, the backbone is not completely connected. The two FDDI ring networks cannot communicate with each other.

This situation can be repaired by a network administrator. The administrator creates a virtual link between the two halves of the backbone. Figure 8.9 shows this virtual link winding through areas 1 and 3. Clearly, such a link is less efficient than the healthy backbone, particularly if the point-to-point link is not a high-speed link.

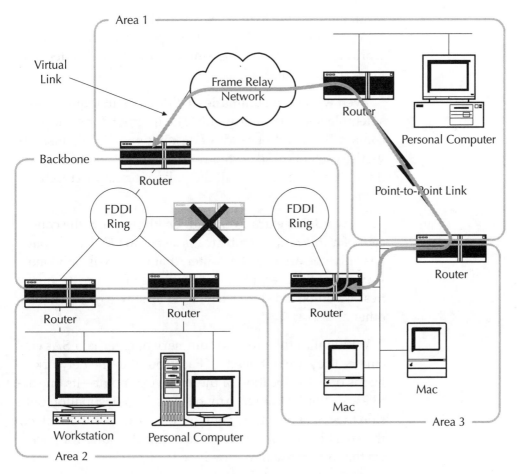

Figure 8.9 Repairing a broken backbone with a virtual link.

Nonetheless, virtual links do provide connectivity. By requiring manual configuration of virtual links, OSPF forces the network administrator to recognize the seriousness of a broken backbone and the resulting loss in efficiency.

Stub Areas

OSPF relies on both autonomous systems and areas to reduce its traffic requirements. Destinations beyond the autonomous system are summarized in external LSAs, and destinations outside the area are advertised in summary LSAs. In both cases, the detailed topology of the outside world is hidden. The LSAs simply indicate which destinations are available.

Even with such summaries, OSPF can still require considerable network bandwidth. The Internet, for example, contains tens of thousands of destinations. OSPF must advertise each of these destinations in an external LSA, even if it does not need to detail the links necessary to reach them.

To avoid this extra overhead, OSPF supports the concept of a *stub area*. A stub area is a special OSPF area that has only one area border router; that is, there is only one way out of the area. (None of the areas of Figure 8.9 qualifies as a stub area since each has at least two connections to other areas.)

Within the stub area, no summary or external LSAs circulate. They are not needed. Each router in the network learns only the location of the area's exit point—its one active area border router. Any packets for a destination outside the area are simply routed to that exit point. In effect, the area border router serves as a default router for packets that otherwise have nowhere to go.

Stub areas suffer from two restrictions. First, virtual links cannot pass through a stub area. A virtual link requires two separate places to connect to the area, but a stub area can only have one such connection point. As a second restriction, stub areas cannot have an AS boundary router within them. This restriction also makes perfect sense. If the AS boundary router were within a stub area, it would not be able to advertise external LSAs. Stub areas, after all, do not flood external LSAs. Note that a stub area's area border router can server as an AS boundary router as well. AS boundary routers are only prohibited inside a stub area.

Not So Stubby Areas

Stub areas are quite effective in reducing the burden on OSPF. Routers within a stub area learn about each other, and they learn how to get out of the area through the single area border router. In exchange, the routers forfeit the ability to exchange routes learned from any source other than OSPF. All such routes are classified as external routes, and OSPF does not propagate them within a stub area.

This restriction is sometimes too severe. It makes it difficult to coordinate additional routing protocols (such as the Routing Information Protocol detailed in Chapter 9) within an area. A *not so stubby area*, more commonly known as an NSSA, provides most of the benefits of stub areas, but with a little more flexibility. NSSAs allow routers to exchange some information about routes from other sources, without incurring the cost of becoming a full OSPF area. NSSA areas permit the distribution of special, NSSA link state advertisements. These NSSA LSAs are very similar to external LSAs; the only difference is how they are disseminated. External LSAs are not flooded in a not so stubby area, while NSSA LSAs are flooded only in a single NSSA.

Special Networks

Until now, the discussion of OSPF has focused on simple, point-to-point links. Real networks, of course, consist of a variety of network technologies. Many of those networks require, or at least benefit from, special treatment by a routing protocol. OSPF, in particular, makes special allowances for three special types of networks. The subsections that follow look at all three—broadcast networks, nonbroadcast networks, and demand networks.

Broadcast Networks

Broadcast networks provide an inherent broadcast or multicast capability, and they allow any system to communicate directly with any other system. By far, the most

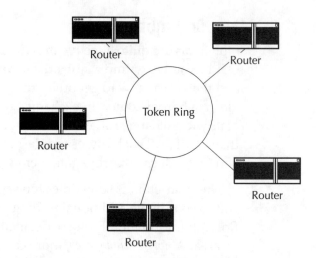

Figure 8.10 Routers on a broadcast network.

common type of broadcast network is a local area network such as Ethernet or Token Ring.

Broadcast networks deserve special treatment because of their any-to-any flexibility. Consider, for example, the Token Ring network in Figure 8.10. There are five routers attached to the ring. Since each router can communicate with the other four, each would normally consider that it had four neighbors. Five routers, each with four neighbors, creates a total of 20 entries in the link state database.

Twenty entries is not necessarily a great number of link state entries, but consider what happens as more routers attach to the network. As Figure 8.11 highlights, the number of entries grows as the square of the number of routers. (The top trace in the figure shows this behavior.) On large networks, this growth represents a serious problem.

To help keep the size of link state databases manageable, OSPF treats broadcast networks a special way. It elects a special router from among those present on the network. This router, known as the *designated router*, treats all routers on the network as neighbors, whereas the other routers consider only the designated router as their neigh-

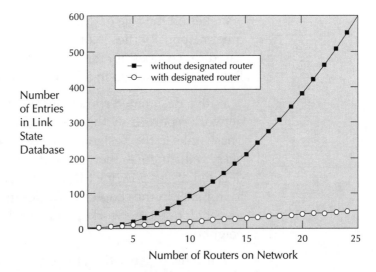

Figure 8.11 Growth of link state database.

bor. As far as routing calculations are concerned, traffic between two such routers must pass through the designated router.

Figure 8.12 shows the artificial topology that OSPF creates. This topology is artificial because the designated router does not really exist. Instead, one of the other rout-

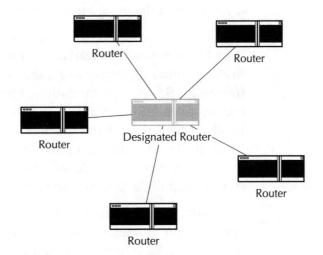

Figure 8.12 Designated router on broadcast networks.

ers takes on the role of designated router, in addition to its other responsibilities. Note from the figure that the designated router does not replace one of the normal routers. Rather, it is included in addition to those routers.

With a designated router elected, each true router on the network reports only the designated router as a neighbor. These links to the designated router are known as *network links*, to distinguish them from the normal *router links*. (A detailed discussion of OSPF's different link types can be found later in the chapter.) The designated router, acting on behalf of the network, reports each true router as a neighbor.

With this construction, there are only 10 entries in the link state database. Each of the five true routers lists one neighbor, and the designated router lists five. A glance at the bottom trace of Figure 8.11 shows how the savings continue to grow as the network size increases.

In order to force a correct route calculation, all neighbors advertised by the designated router are done so with a distance of zero. The distance between any two routers on the network is the sum of the distance to the designated router (which reflects the true cost of the network) and the distance from the designated router (defined to be zero).

OSPF takes advantage of broadcast networks when it floods LSA packets. Instead of sending a copy of the LSA to every router on the network, the designated router transmits LSA to a special multicast address. All OSPF routers listen for this address, and they all receive the flooded LSA packet. Since the designated router sends LSAs to all routers on the networks, regular routers do not worry about flooding LSA packets to all. Instead, they simply send LSAs to the designated router.

Clearly, the designated router plays a key role in OSPF's operation on a broadcast network. That importance could make networks vulnerable to failures of the designated routers. To reduce this vulnerability, OSPF elects a backup

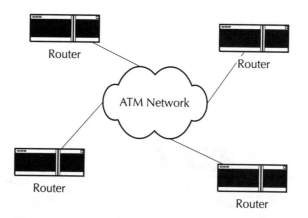

Figure 8.13 Nonbroadcast ATM network.

designated router when it elects a designated router. The backup keeps track of the same information as the designated router, but it normally remains silent. If the backup detects a failure of the designated router, however, it becomes active immediately.

Nonbroadcast Networks

OSPF originally developed the designated router concept for local area networks, all of which feature a broadcast or multicast capability. The same approach—electing a special router to reduce OSPF overhead—works effectively on other networks as well. How many entries in the link state database, for example, does the network in Figure 8.13 produce?

The figure shows an ATM network in which each of the four routers can communicate with all the others. Four routers, each with three neighbors, results in 12 entries in the link state database. The same formula applies here as it does with LANs, and OSPF handles the scaling problem in the same way—with a designated router.

Figure 8.14 presents a logical view of the same network after the election of a designated router. Now each router has only the designated router as a neighbor. The desig-

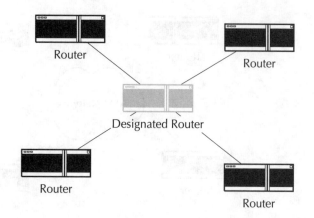

Figure 8.14 Designated router for a nonbroadcast network.

Point-to-Multipoint Networks

The designated router concept only applies to networks in which every router can communicate directly with every other router. With some networks, including Frame Relay and ATM, this level of communication is not required. Such networks can be configured (indeed, they often are) with virtual circuits only between some sites. OSPF terms such networks *point-to-multipoint networks*. As of this writing, OSPF support for such networks was still under development.

nated router reduces the total number of link state entries from 12 to 8, and, as with LANs, the savings are even more drastic as the network grows.

There are only two real differences between OSPF's broadcast and nonbroadcast networks. Most obviously, LSA flooding can only use broadcast services on a broadcast network. On nonbroadcast networks, the designated router must transmit copies of LSA packets to each router singly. Nonbroadcast networks also complicate the election of a designated router.

Demand Networks

Demand networks present another challenge to OSPF. These are networks whose expense is directly related to usage. Narrowband ISDN links, for example, often incur charges based on the length of time they remain active. Such networks earn the name *demand* because, ideally at least, they should only be active when actual application traffic demands their use.

OSPF, however, normally counts on links remaining active indefinitely. Routers continually exchange hello packets to reassure each other of their health. Link state

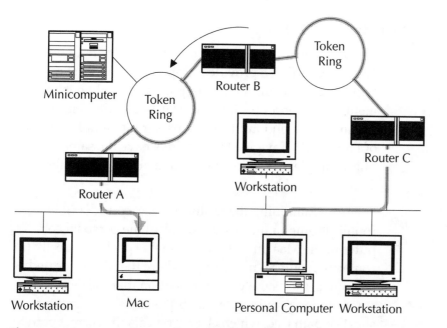

Figure 8.15 For unicast traffic from PC to Mac, router B forwards packets to router A.

advertisements are also periodically reflooded through a network. Even without user traffic, these packets will consume bandwidth—and incur cost—on a demand network.

OSPF copes with demand networks in two ways. First, it eliminates the periodic hello packets used for neighbor greeting. Once a router knows the identity of its peer, it leaves the link turned off. Second, OSPF refrains from sending periodic LSA packets across demand networks. Unless the LSA has changed, routers block its progress. To support this type of operation, OSPF relaxes a requirement of the LSA packets themselves. Normal LSA packets include an age limit. Once the packet has existed long enough to exceed this limit, routers discard it. The periodic reflooding of LSAs refreshes this age limit, and keeps routers from discarding packets that are still valid. If periodic reflooding is blocked, the LSA packets must indicate that they have no age limit.

Multicast Routing

So far, this text has considered routing for normal unicast packets. OSPF also provides support for multicast routing. Link state protocols, in fact, require only slight enhancements to support multicast. To clarify the differences between unicast and multicast, consider the sample network of Figure 8.15. Imagine that all links have the same cost. This example focuses on router B, which connects the two Token Ring LANs.

Before examining the multicast case, consider how router B routes a unicast packet from the personal computer to the Mac. In order to route this packet correctly (to router A), router B must know where the Mac is located. Of course, this is the very information that the Dijkstra computation provides. Figure 8.16 shows the resulting shortest path tree, which clearly reveals the correct path to the destination. The packet's next hop is router A.

Note two important (and related) facts about unicast routing. First, the root of the shortest path tree is router B itself, the system performing the calculation. Second, it does not matter where the packet being routed originated.

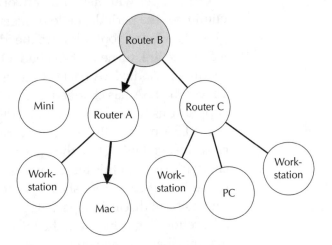

Figure 8.16 Router B's shortest path tree for unicast routing to Mac.

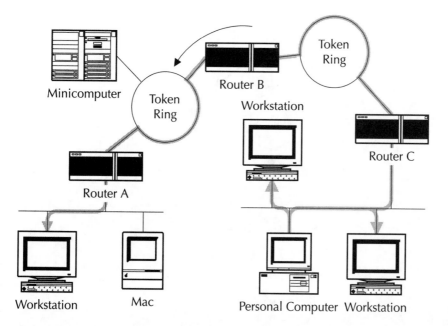

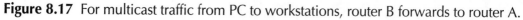

Figure 8.17 For multicast traffic from PC to workstations, router B forwards to router A.

In this example, the source is the PC, but that information does not affect the routing decision that router B makes.

Now consider that the same PC sends a single multicast packet to all workstations on the network, as Figure 8.17 illustrates. The packet travels throughout the network, eventually reaching every workstation. Imagine the packet arriving at router B. To decide how to route the packet, router B must know the location of all workstations. For a multicast packet, however, the router cannot rely on its standard shortest path tree. It must construct a different shortest path tree, one like Figure 8.18. When shown as a diagram, the tree's structure clearly indicates how to route the packet. Once again, the packet goes to router A next.

There is a major difference between the multicast tree and the unicast tree; the two trees have different roots. With the multicast tree, the root is the source of the packet, regardless of which system performs the calculation. Another difference is that there may be many destinations on

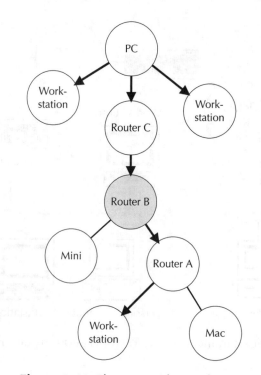

Figure 8.18 Shortest path tree from PC to workstations.

the multicast tree, one for each system in the multicast group.

To see why the source of the packet makes a difference, consider what happens when the minicomputer sends a multicast packet. Again assume it is destined for all workstations on the network. A quick glance at the network in Figure 8.19 reveals what router B should do with such a packet. It should send it to router C. This next hop differs from the last case, even though both use the same group destination.

Fortunately, a correct shortest path tree leads to the right routing decision. Figure 8.20 shows the tree for multicast packets from the minicomputer. It is clearly different from Figure 8.18, as the minicomputer now serves as the tree's root. The figure shows that the new tree correctly points to router C as the next hop.

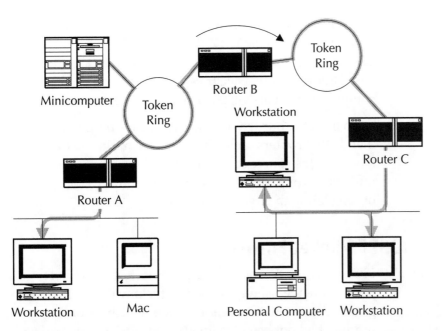

Figure 8.19 For traffic from minicomputer to workstations, router B forwards to router C.

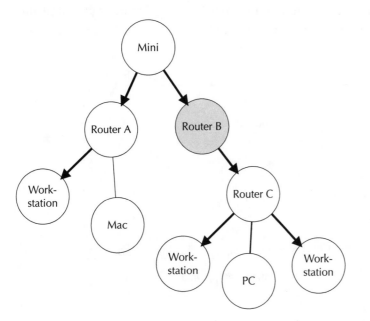

Figure 8.20 Shortest path tree from minicomputer to workstations.

As these examples prove, multicast routing can present a significant problem to OSPF routers. Those routers must calculate a different shortest path tree for each source system. Unfortunately, Dijkstra's calculation can be very computation-intensive, particularly with large networks.

To limit the burden on routers, OSPF strongly recommends that routers cache the results of multicast tree calculations. If the source sends additional packets to the multicast group, the routers can look at this cache instead of calculating the tree all over again.

OSPF Packet Format

A Caution on OSPF Packet Formats

As of this writing, engineers have barely sketched out the packet formats of OSPF for IPv6. The formats described in this text are likely to change before the protocol becomes a standard. Nonetheless, the principles that determine how OSPF builds its packets are unlikely to change drastically, and these packet formats serve to illustrate many important aspects of OSPF's operation.

Like ICMP, UDP, and TCP, Open Shortest Path First packets are themselves carried as the payload of IP datagrams. A specific next header value (which, as of this writing, had not been assigned) identifies the payload as OSPF. All OSPF packets begin with a common OSPF header. As Figure 8.21 shows, that header includes eight fields. The first byte indicates the OSPF version number; the current version number is 2. The second byte identifies the specific packet type. OSPF uses five different types of

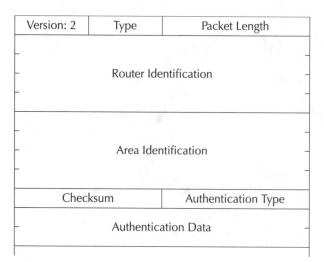

Figure 8.21 Common OSPF packet header.

Table 8.6 OSPF Packet Types

1	Hello Packet
2	Database Description Packet
3	Link State Request Packet
4	Link State Update Packet
5	Link State Acknowledgment Packet

Authenticating the Checksum

By neglecting the authentication field in its checksum calculation, OSPF allows that field to authenticate both the packet and its checksum. This approach provides an extra level of security. Although it might be possible to modify a packet so that the authentication field remains valid, such a modification would almost certainly invalidate the checksum. (If the checksum included the authentication field, then authentication would necessarily have to exclude the checksum, and a malicious party could alter the packet and then recompute the checksum.)

packets, listed in Table 8.6. Other than the common OSPF header, each packet type has its own unique format.

The packet length field, naturally, indicates the size of the packet in bytes, and includes the common header. The next field uniquely and unambiguously identifies the router that originated the packet. This value is one of the router's IP addresses.

The area ID is 16 bytes in size. It indicates the area to which the packet belongs. Most packets are restricted to a single area. A value of zero signifies the backbone area. It is used by packets traversing the backbone directly, or via a virtual link.

The checksum field contains the ones complement sum of the entire packet, excluding the authentication field. The next two bytes identify the type of authentication. Currently, the OSPF standards define only two types of authentication: none (type 0), and simple password (type 1). Work is in progress to standardize the much more secure message digest authentication algorithm. (See page 121.) The final eight bytes in the common header contain the authentication data itself.

Meeting Neighbors

OSPF uses hello packets to meet neighbors, the first step in link state routing. Routers exchange hello packets across point-to-point and demand networks, and they send them to multicast destinations on broadcast LANs. Notice from

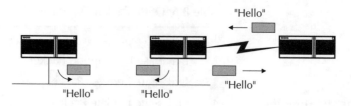

Figure 8.22 Routers exchange hello packets to greet each other.

the middle router in Figure 8.22 that routers generate hello packets on all their links and networks.

The hello packet itself (Figure 8.23) contains more than the sender's identity. The first field after the common header, the network mask, indicates the sender's idea of the prefix for the link or network. It specifies the number

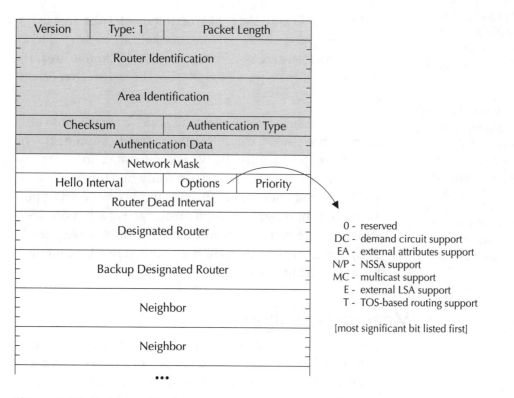

Figure 8.23 Hello packet format.

of bits in that prefix. The hello interval tells how frequently the sender retransmits its hello packets.

The options byte advertises the sender's OSPF capabilities. The priority byte defines the sender's willingness to become a designated router. Of all the routers on a network, the one with the highest priority gets the job. In the case of a tie, the router with the highest router ID wins.

The router dead interval tells how long it takes to declare a router unavailable. If the router has not been heard from in this number of seconds, it is considered dead, and all routes are calculated around it.

The next two fields indicate the current designated router for the network and its backup. The final field, which is repeated as many times as necessary, lists neighbors that the sender has already met. This list establishes two-way communications between routers. Two routers do not become neighbors just by hearing each other's hello packet. They must receive a hello packet that lists themselves as neighbors.

Without this requirement, OSPF could end up calculating useless routes. For example, router A in Figure 8.24 can transmit fine, but, due to a failure in its interface hardware, cannot receive frames from the Ethernet. Therefore, it will not hear router B's hello packets, and it will never list router B as a neighbor. If router B ignores this absence and considers A to be a neighbor, it, along with all other routers in the area, may calculate routes from B to A even when no such path actually exists.

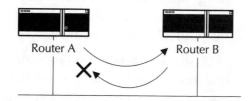

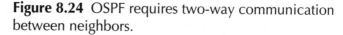

Figure 8.24 OSPF requires two-way communication between neighbors.

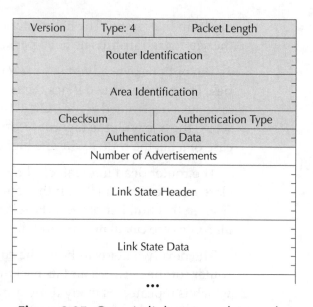

Figure 8.25 Generic link state update packet.

Advertising Link States

Once a router meets its neighbors by exchanging hello packets, it distributes that information to the rest of the network. To do this, it floods link state advertisements throughout the network. The link state advertisement takes the form of a link state update packet, shown in Figure 8.25. Note that its packet type is 4.

After the common OSPF header, the packet contains one 32-bit word with the number of individual advertisements in the packet. It is immediately followed by the advertisements themselves. Each advertisement has two parts. First is a generic link state header. All advertisements have a common header, which is sufficient to uniquely identify the particular advertisement.

Figure 8.26 details the link state header. It contains several interesting fields. The first 16 bits store the advertisement's age. This value starts at zero when the LSA is first issued, and it increments by one each second from that point forward. The age increases while the update packet

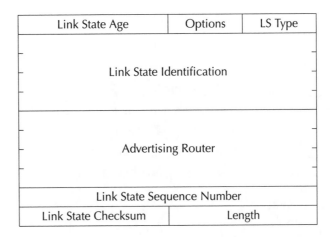

Link State Age	Options	LS Type
Link State Identification		
Advertising Router		
Link State Sequence Number		
Link State Checksum	Length	

Figure 8.26 Link state header.

traverses the network. Every router that keeps a copy in its link state database also increments the age of that copy. When an advertisement's age reaches 3,600 (one hour), it is always considered out of date.

When an advertisement in any router's link state database expires, that router immediately refloods the expired advertisement through the network. Of course, the LSA should automatically expire in every router at the same time, but in real life some routers have clocks that run faster or slower than others. Immediate reflooding makes sure that as soon as one router thinks an LSA has expired, all other routers will agree. This keeps the link state databases in all routers consistent, ensuring that they calculate consistent routes.

The options byte identifies the capabilities of the router that generated the LSA. It has the same format as the options field of the hello packet. (See Figure 8.23.) The LS type byte distinguishes the various types of link state advertisements. The header is the same for each LSA type, but the data varies considerably. Table 8.7 lists the different types of advertisements. "Router Links" (in the next subsection) begins a detailed description of the different IPv6 link types.

Fletcher's Checksum

Fletcher's checksum was originally used by many protocols of the International Standards Organization. It is generally viewed as a compromise between a simple ones complement checksum (easy to compute but not very robust) and the cyclic redundancy checks of many link levels (very robust, but expensive to compute in software). Because the checksum itself has become popular, several research papers have presented ways to implement it very efficiently. Anastase Nakassis provides perhaps the most comprehensive treatment in "Fletcher's Error Detection Algorithm: How to Implement it Efficiently and How to Avoid the Most Common Pitfalls" (*Computer Communications Review* 18.5 [October 1988], pp. 63-88). His paper includes references to the other major works on the subject.

Table 8.7 LSA Types

1	router link
2	network link
3	summary link to network
4	summary link to AS boundary router
5	external link
6	group membership
7	NSSA link
10	opaque link

The link state ID uniquely identifies each link, according to the advertising router. Usually, routers select the IP address (which they know is unique) of the link as its identification. The advertising router is, of course, the router ID of the system that originates the advertisement.

Since advertisements automatically expire after one hour, routers must reissue them more frequently than once an hour (assuming their data remains valid). The standard interval for reissuing LSAs is 30 minutes. To distinguish a reissued advertisement, routers use the link state sequence number. This field acts like a version number for the LSA. Each time the advertising router reissues an advertisement, it increments the sequence number.

The link state header concludes with a checksum and length field. The checksum is not TCP/IP's normal ones complement sum; it is a special error-detection code known as Fletcher's checksum. It covers the entire advertisement except the link state age field. The final length field indicates the size, in bytes, of the advertisement.

Router Links

The simplest link type is a router link. It represents a normal link between two routers. Figure 8.27 shows the structure of a router link advertisement, including both the link state header and its data.

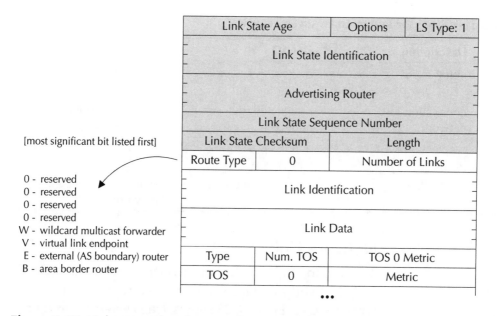

Link State Age		Options	LS Type: 1
Link State Identification			
Advertising Router			
Link State Sequence Number			
Link State Checksum		Length	
Route Type	0	Number of Links	
Link Identification			
Link Data			
Type	Num. TOS	TOS 0 Metric	
TOS	0	Metric	

[most significant bit listed first]

0 - reserved
0 - reserved
0 - reserved
0 - reserved
W - wildcard multicast forwarder
V - virtual link endpoint
E - external (AS boundary) router
B - area border router

•••

Figure 8.27 Link state advertisement for router links.

The *route type* defines the type of router. The figure lists its values. It is followed (after a reserved byte of zero) by a word that indicates how many links the LSA contains. Note that a single link state update packet may include many LSAs, and each router LSA may include many individual links.

The *link ID* field identifies what lies at the other end of the link from the router, while the *link data* field further defines that object. Both fields depend on the value of the link type field that follows. Table 8.8 lists the different link types, as well as the values for link ID and link data that they imply.

Each link entry concludes with a list of metrics, which are the costs to use the link, based on different measurement systems. The measurement systems are known as *types of service* (TOS), and every router is required to support at least the default (0) TOS. If the router supports other TOS values, it lists them here. Other values include such measurements as delay and reliability.

TOS Forwarding

If a network uses different types of service, then the routers calculate separate Dijkstra trees for each TOS, and they forward packets according to their marked service type. Unfortunately, computing multiple trees is a significant computational burden.

Table 8.8 Link Types for Router Links Advertisement

Type	Description	Link ID	Link Data
1	point-to-point connection to another router	neighbor's router ID	interface number
2	connection-to-transit network	designated router's address	router's IP address on network
3	connection-to-stub network	address prefix for subnetwork	length (in bits) of prefix
4	virtual link	neighbor's router ID	router's IP address on network

Network Links

The second kind of link state advertisement is the network LSA. Networks that have a designated router use the network LSA. As Figure 8.28 shows, true routers use router LSAs to advertise links to the designated router, while the designated router uses network LSAs for its links to the true routers. Figure 8.29 illustrates the network link state advertisement itself, header and data. As the figure shows, the LSA is quite simple. It includes the network prefix length (in bits) of the subnetwork, and a list of routers attached to the subnetwork.

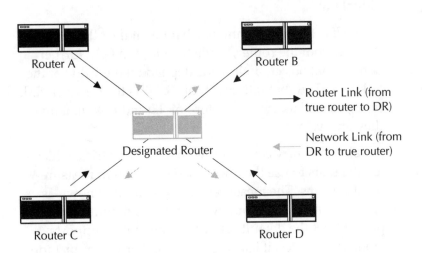

Figure 8.28 Router links and network links for a designated router.

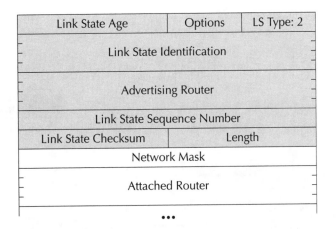

Link State Age	Options	LS Type: 2
Link State Identification		
Advertising Router		
Link State Sequence Number		
Link State Checksum	Length	
Network Mask		
Attached Router		

•••

Figure 8.29 Network link state advertisement.

Summary Links

The next two types of advertisements are summary LSAs. Area border routers distribute these within their areas to advertise destinations outside of the area. The different types indicate what those destinations represent. Type 3 LSAs identify other subnetworks within the autonomous system, yet outside of the area. Type 4 LSAs identify AS boundary routers.

Figure 8.30 shows an example network that requires both type 3 and type 4 LSAs. Router 0A is a good place to start a discussion. That router is attached to the backbone and to a frame relay network in area 1. That makes it an area border router. (In fact, because one of its areas is the backbone, this router is also a backbone router.)

As an area border router, Router 0A generates type 3 summary LSAs and floods them through each of its areas. The frame relay network lies in area 1, so the router floods LSAs describing that network into the backbone. In the same way, it generates LSAs describing the FDDI rings of the backbone, and floods those LSAs throughout area 1. Type 3 LSAs teach the backbone routers about the frame relay network and the area 1 routers about the FDDI rings.

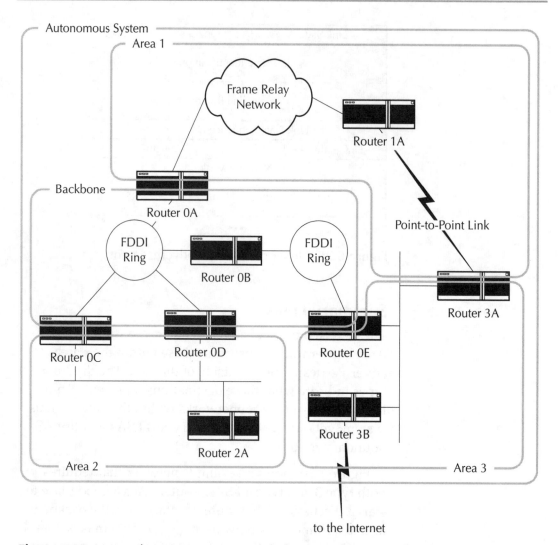

Figure 8.30 Network requiring summary link state advertisements.

Now consider Router 0C. It receives the summary LSAs from router 0A, and adds the frame relay network to the networks it knows about. As an area border router, it also builds summary LSAs. When it summarizes the backbone in the LSAs, it floods through area 2, and that summary includes the frame relay network as well as the FDDI rings. In fact, these LSAs also contain the Ethernet LAN in

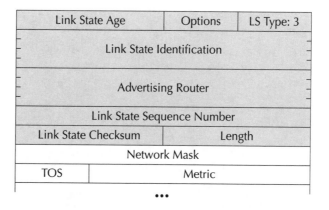

Figure 8.31 Type 3 summary link state advertisement.

area 3, as the router learns of that network from Router 0E's advertisements.

Router 2A, strictly in area 2, receives summary LSAs from both Router 0C and 0D. Through those advertisements, it learns of the world outside its area. It is able to calculate routes to the FDDI rings, the frame relay network, and the LAN in area 3.

Figure 8.31 shows the format of a type 3 LSA. The network mask field contains the number of bits in the network's address prefix. If the advertising router supports TOS routing, then it includes a metric for each TOS. All type 3 LSAs must include a metric for the default type of service. Routers can determine the number of TOS values present from the LSA length in the link state header. This structure implies that a type 3 LSA can only describe a single network, while link state update packets can include multiple type 3 LSAs.

Type 3 advertisements document what is outside of an area, but they only describe networks within a single autonomous system. To route beyond the autonomous system, routers need type 4 advertisements.

Figure 8.30's network has a single connection outside of the autonomous system. That connection is through

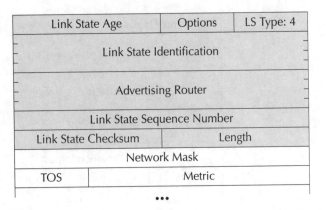

Link State Age		Options	LS Type: 4
Link State Identification			
Advertising Router			
Link State Sequence Number			
Link State Checksum		Length	
Network Mask			
TOS		Metric	

Figure 8.32 Type 4 summary link state advertisement.

Router 3B, so Router 3B is an AS boundary router. Router 3B tells other routers that it has a path to other ASs by issuing type 4 LSAs.

As Figure 8.32 shows, type 4 LSAs are identical to type 3 (except for the value of the LS type). The network mask, however, has no meaning for type 4 advertisements. Indeed, the main purpose of a type 4 LSA is simply to announce the presence of an AS boundary router.

External Links

When the rest of the autonomous system receives type 4 LSAs, they learn how to reach the AS boundary router. That information alone does not tell them what destinations are available beyond the AS. This is the job of an external (type 5) advertisement.

To see the structure of an external LSA, consider Figure 8.33. As the figure shows, the advertisement includes a network mask (the number of bits in the destination's address prefix), and five other fields. The advertisement repeats these five fields for each type of service available. The default TOS is always available.

The first bit following the mask indicates whether the metric is external. If this E bit is set, the metric is external,

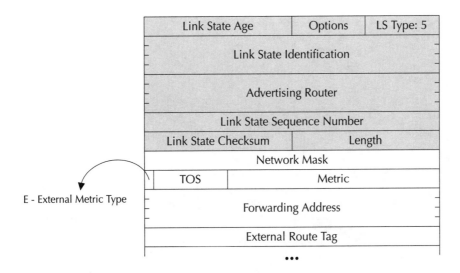

Link State Age		Options	LS Type: 5
Link State Identification			
Advertising Router			
Link State Sequence Number			
Link State Checksum		Length	
Network Mask			
TOS	Metric		
Forwarding Address			
External Route Tag			

E - External Metric Type

•••

Figure 8.33 External link state advertisement.

and it is not directly comparable to any metrics for the same TOS within the autonomous system. The next seven bits define the TOS value; they are followed by the metric value itself.

The forwarding address identifies the system to which packets should be forwarded. Often, this is the same as the advertising router. A value of zero for the forwarding address indicates this equivalence explicitly.

The final field for each TOS, the external route tag, is not relevant to OSPF itself. OSPF merely distributes this value in its link state updates. Other routing protocols can put whatever information they wish in this field, and they are free to use it in any manner whatsoever.

Figure 8.34 shows how the different advertisements combine to define a path to a remote destination. In the figure, Router 2A calculates a path to a destination on the Internet. That calculation requires three distinct stages. First, Router 2A searches the link state database for the desired destination. The search reveals that Router 3B, through its type 5 (external) advertisements, can reach the

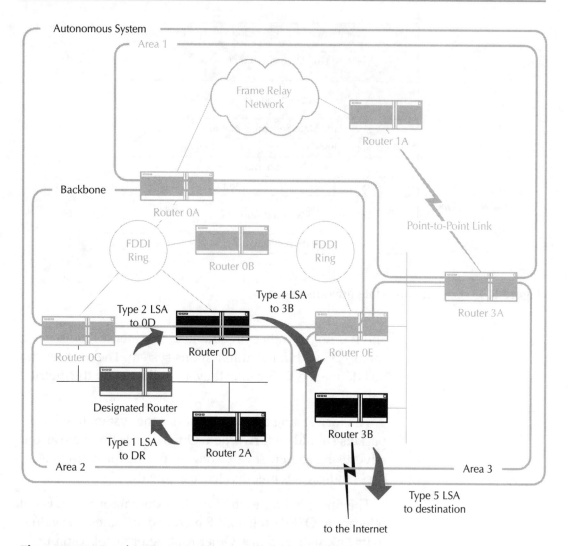

Figure 8.34 Combining LSA types to reach a destination.

desired network. Second, Router 2A must calculate the path to this AS boundary router. It finds type 4 summary advertisements from Router 0D that indicate such a path. Note that those summary LSAs do not specify the detailed path between Router 0D and Router 3B, so they do not identify the FDDI rings, or Routers 0B and 0E, or even area 3's Ethernet. Router 2A does find what it needs, though; Router 0D has a path to Router 3B.

The third stage is confined to area 2. Router 2A must find a path to Router 0D. Since the routers share a broadcast network, this path requires two separate steps. First, a router (type 1) LSA identifies the path to the network's designated router. Then a network (type 2) LSA completes the path from the designated router to the area border router 0D.

In summary, the path from Router 2A to the external destination takes four steps. First, there is the router link from 2A to the designated router. Second, the network link connects the designated router to 0D. Third, a summary link provides a path from 0D to 3B. The last link, an external link, connects 3B to the destination.

Group Membership Advertisements

Group addresses require their own advertisement type, and designated routers originate it. Designated routers keep track of group membership on their networks. For each group that has any members, they build a type 6 advertisement. That LSA, shown in Figure 8.35, uses the link ID field of the link state header to indicate the specific group address. It then lists one or more *vertices*; these are paths to members of the group.

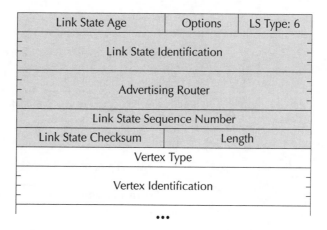

Figure 8.35 Group membership link state advertisement.

Vertices may be one of two types. In the simplest case (vertex type 1), either the router itself is a group member, or there are no other routers on the network. In this case, the router has complete information about group membership on the network and beyond. (Since there are no other routers, there is no "beyond.") The router inserts its own router ID as the vertex ID.

If other routers exist on the network along with group members, then more group members may be residing "on the other side" of those routers. In this case, the designated router marks the vertex as type 2, and it lists its own IP address on that network as the vertex ID.

NSSA Advertisements

As the "Not So Stubby Areas" section described, areas designated as NSSA differ from true stub areas in only one way—they permit the flooding of a special link state advertisement that carries the same information as an external advertisement.

The type 7 LSA, shown in Figure 8.36, is that special advertisement. Since it carries the same information as an

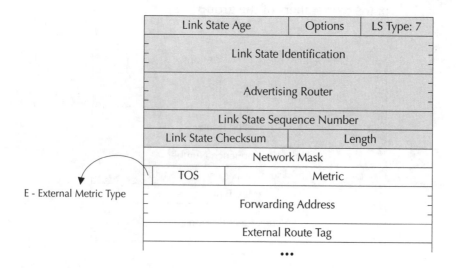

Figure 8.36 NSSA link state advertisement.

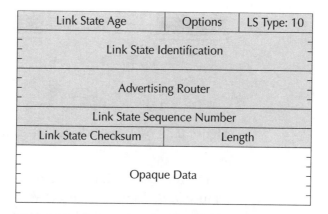

Figure 8.37 Opaque link state advertisement.

external LSA (page 286), it has the same format. Only the LS Type field has a different value.

Opaque Advertisements

The final type of link state advertisement is an opaque LSA. To date, no meaning has been attached to this type. It is intended for features that may be added to OSPF in the future. As Figure 8.37 illustrates, the link state data consists of nothing but a collection of bytes. OSPF routers built today, which cannot interpret this data, should simply flood the LSAs through the network. Once the details of the type 10 LSA are defined, the mechanisms will already be in place to disseminate them across a network.

Reliable Flooding

Together, the different types of link state advertisements define the complete topology of a network. In order to distribute that information to all of the network's routers, OSPF floods link state update packets throughout the network. OSPF takes the flooding procedure one step further, though. It requires routers to explicitly acknowledge when they receive an advertisement. Figure 8.38 shows the simple exchange on a point-to-point link.

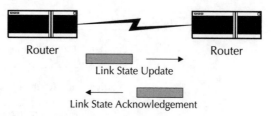

Figure 8.38 Acknowledging link state updates.

The link state acknowledgment packet itself is shown in Figure 8.39. As the figure shows, it contains a list of link state headers. Since the header is sufficient to identify an advertisement, there is no need to include the complete LSA. A single acknowledgment can acknowledge many link state updates.

Updating Neighbors

So far, this chapter has presented OSPF as if networks operated in a completely orderly manner. First routers learn their neighbors; they share that information, and then they compute routes. This approach almost gives the impression that there is a master switch for the network. Everything remains idle until someone turns that master switch on.

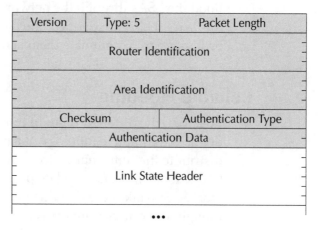

Figure 8.39 Link state acknowledgment.

Of course, real networks never function this neatly. In particular, routers are usually introduced to networks that are already functioning. A new router cannot simply tell the rest of the network to start over. Instead, it must rapidly catch up and learn the network's topology.

To catch up with the rest of the network, a newly introduced router relies on its neighbors. As soon as two routers greet each other (with hello packets), they exchange information about their link state database. They do so with database description packets.

Figure 8.40 shows a database description packet. After two bytes of zero, the packet contains the standard OSPF options field (see Figure 8.23). It then has five more bits equal to zero, and three flags. The first two flags, I and M, allow the neighbors to exchange multiple description packets. The first packet in the exchange will have the I bit set to one, and all but the final packet will set the M bit. For each exchange, one of the two routers plays the role of master, while the other acts as a slave. The MS bit identifies which is which.

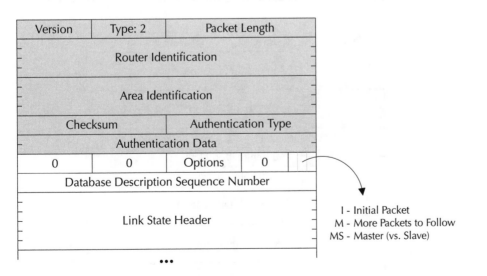

Figure 8.40 Database description packet.

Initial Sequence Number

Although it might seem simpler to always start a database exchange with sequence number 1, the OSPF standard specifies that it begin with an arbitrary value. (It suggests the time of day.) This helps to prevent confusion, should a router reset in the middle of an exchange. When it tries to start the exchange again, its neighbor will be able to distinguish its new packets from the earlier, aborted exchange.

The next 32 bits contain a database description sequence number. This number has an arbitrary value for the initial packet in an exchange, but it increments by one with each successive description packet. The packet concludes with a list of link state headers. These headers describe the contents of the sender's link state database. Note that the link state data itself is not part of the description packet.

Once a router receives a complete set of database description packets from its neighbor, it examines its own link state database. (If the router has just been turned on, its database will probably be empty.) Most likely, the router will find that its neighbor has information that it lacks. The neighbor may have entirely new LSAs, or it may have more up-to-date versions of existing LSAs. In either case, the router requests that updated information from its neighbor. It does so with a link state request packet, illustrated in Figure 8.41.

The link state request contains a list of LSAs that the sender wishes to receive. These LSAs are identified solely by their type, link state ID, and advertising router. When the neighbor receives a request, it finds the advertisements

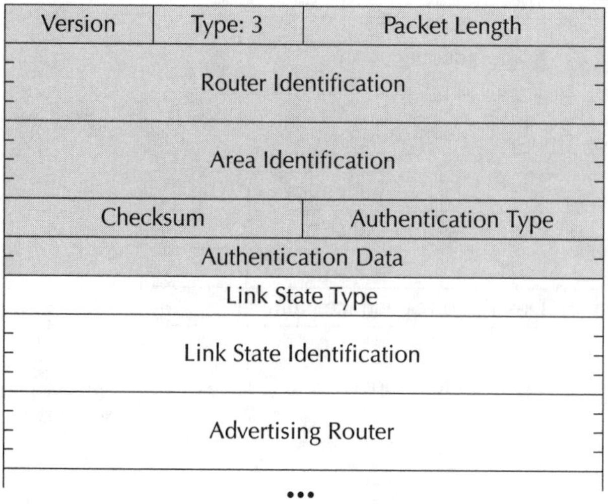

Version	Type: 3	Packet Length
Router Identification		
Area Identification		
Checksum		Authentication Type
Authentication Data		
Link State Type		
Link State Identification		
Advertising Router		
•••		

Figure 8.41 Link state request packet.

in its link state database and forwards them in link state update packets.

After exchanging database description packets, link state requests, and finally link state updates, two routers will have successfully synchronized their link state databases. At that point, both routers are up-to-date, and they can both participate in the network's routing.

Summary

Routers rely on routing protocols like OSPF to learn the map of a network, and from this map they see how to reach the network's destinations. OSPF is one of the family of link state routing protocols. Link state protocols proceed in three steps. First, each router learns the identity of its neighbors. Then it floods that information throughout the network. Finally, after collecting neighbor information from every other router, each router applies Dijkstra's algorithm to compute routes.

OSPF organizes networks into hierarchies. The highest level is an autonomous system. The AS boundary defines the limits of OSPF's influence. Within an AS, OSPF may divide the network into areas. Each router knows the full details of the network within its areas, but it only summarizes information outside of the area.

OSPF has the flexibility to function over a wide variety of links. In addition to point-to-point links, it supports broadcast networks like Ethernet, nonbroadcast networks such as Frame Relay, and demand networks including ISDN. In many cases, OSPF routers elect a designated router to reduce traffic demands on those networks.

OSPF also has support for multicast routing. For link state protocols, multicast routing is a simple extension of normal routing. It is computationally expensive, though. As the use of multicast increases, network engineers should gain greater understanding of OSPF's limitations.

9

RIP's Simpler Approach to Routing

OSPF, the subject of Chapter 8, provides fast and efficient routing. Its power carries a price, however, and that price is complexity. For smaller internetworks that do not require all of OSPF's power, TCP/IP offers an alternative routing protocol, the Routing Information Protocol (RIP).

Distance Vector Routing

RIP relies on a *distance vector* algorithm to compute routes, and for that reason, it is a *distance vector routing protocol*. Distance vector routing differs significantly from the link state routing of OSPF. With link state algorithms, routers share only the identity of their neighbors, but they flood this information through the entire network. (See page 246.) Distance vector algorithms adopt an opposite approach. Routers periodically share their knowledge of the entire network, but only with their neighbors.

At first, it might be hard to believe that such an approach actually works. After all, if routers only share information with their neighbors, how can they learn about distant destinations? Here is the trick: When a router learns something

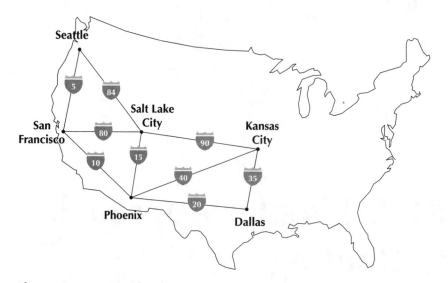

Figure 9.1 Routing for the U.S. interstate highway system.

The History of RIP

RIP actually began outside of the TCP/IP protocol suite. It was the original routing protocol of the Xerox Network Services (XNS) protocol suite. The University of California at Berkeley adapted RIP for TCP/IP, and Novell, Inc. adapted it for Netware. Both Novell and TCP/IP's designers recognized the limitations of RIP, and both developed more powerful, link state replacements. For TCP/IP, that replacement is OSPF, while Netware now incorporates the Novell Link Services Protocol (NLSP).

from one neighbor, it adds that to its store of knowledge, and then it passes that knowledge on to other neighbors. Slowly but surely, the information makes its way across the network from one router to another.

To see distance vector routing in action, Figure 9.1 turns once more to a (slightly distorted) part of the U.S. interstate highway system (once again, with apologies to those readers outside of the United States). Notice that this figure, unlike the link state example (Figure 8.1), does not list distances between each city. Despite the name, actual distances are generally irrelevant in distance vector routing.

Before any routing information is exchanged, each city will know some information about each of its neighbors. Because neighbors must, by definition, share a link, they share an IP address prefix. When Seattle, for example, is configured with the IP address prefix of interstate I-84, it will implicitly know one of the IP address prefixes of Salt Lake City. While link state routing uses neighbor greeting to learn the precise identity of each adjacent router, distance vector protocols are content knowing only the address prefix of their connected networks and links.

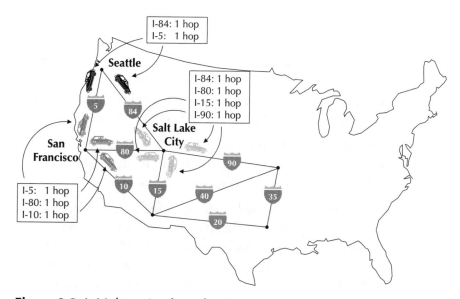

Figure 9.2 Initial routing broadcasts.

With this information as a starting point, Seattle broadcasts its routing knowledge to all links. That knowledge consists of the IP address prefix (in this example, the highway number) and the cost to reach that destination. Most distance vector protocols, including RIP, measure cost by counting hops. To Seattle, any city on I-84 or I-5 is a single hop away, so the cost it advertises is one. All cities broadcast this information simultaneously.

As Figure 9.2 shows, each city includes every destination it knows in its broadcasts. (For clarity, the figure only shows the actions of three cities.) As the figure implies, a city broadcasts the same information on all of its links.

Now consider what happens when Seattle receives the broadcasts from its neighbors. Assume that it hears from San Francisco first. As Seattle examines each route in the broadcast it says, in effect, "I can reach San Francisco in 1 hop, so anywhere San Francisco can reach in *n* hops, I can reach in *n*+1 hops by forwarding through San Francisco."

For example, from this first update Seattle learns that San Francisco can reach I-80 in one hop. Seattle, therefore, considers I-80 to be two hops away and reachable via San Francisco. It performs the same calculations for the other routes in San Francisco's broadcast: I-10 and I-5. Of course, the result of the I-5 calculation is not important. Seattle already knows how to reach I-5 in one hop. The fact that it is two hops away via San Francisco is of no value.

Seattle treats the broadcast from Salt Lake City the same way. Through that update, it can add routes to I-90 and I-15. Each is two hops away via Salt Lake City.

Sometime later, it will again be time for Seattle to broadcast its routing knowledge on all links. (Distance vector routing calls for periodic broadcasts.) At this stage, Seattle has more information, and its update includes these new routes. Figure 9.3 shows the second round of routing updates for the same three cities. Note once more that each city sends exactly the same information in all of its updates.

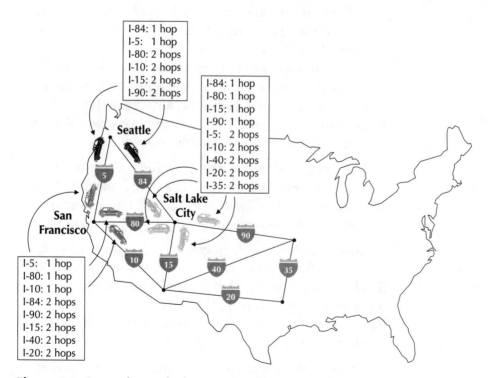

Figure 9.3 Second round of routing updates.

After this second round, Seattle will once again be able to add information to its routing table. This time, the new routes are to I-35, I-20, and I-40. Seattle learns of I-35, for example, in the update it receives from Salt Lake City. That update advertises a cost of two hops to reach I-35, so Seattle considers I-35 to be three hops away.

For the simple network of this example, three rounds are enough to disseminate complete routing information to all of the routers. After the third round, every router will have constructed a routing table that lists each destination on the network. For example, Seattle's complete routing table will look like Table 9.1.

Note that the table contains one additional piece of information for each destination—the next hop in the path to that destination. Routers determine this information by remembering where they learned of the route. For example, Seattle learns that I-15 is two hops away when it receives an update from Salt Lake City. Salt Lake City, therefore, is the next hop for that destination.

So far, this example has considered a stable, static network. Once the cities learn how to route to each other, they can, based on this example, stop exchanging RIP updates. After all, they have learned the complete topology of the

Table 9.1 Complete Routing Table for Seattle

Destination	Cost	Next Hop
I-5	1 hop	N/A
I-84	1 hop	N/A
I-10	2 hops	San Francisco
I-15	2 hops	Salt Lake City
I-80	2 hops	San Francisco
I-90	2 hops	Salt Lake City
I-20	3 hops	San Francisco
I-35	3 hops	Salt Lake City
I-40	3 hops	San Francisco

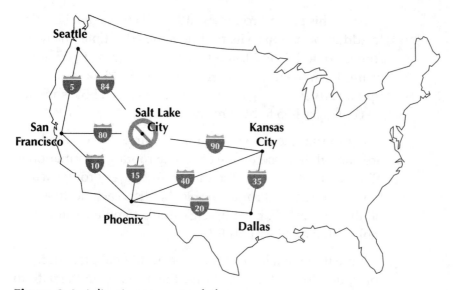

Figure 9.4 Adjusting to router failures.

network. Of course, this approach will not do for real networks. The real world is rarely stable and never static. So how does RIP deal with changes in the network's topology? What happens if, for example, Salt Lake City experiences a power failure and routes through it are no longer available (Figure 9.4.)?

Unlike OSPF, RIP does not have routers exchange hello packets to assure each other of their health. The routing updates themselves serve that purpose. When Seattle first gets an update from Salt Lake City, it does not accept the update's routing information permanently. Rather, Seattle accepts the information provisionally. Seattle only believes the information for a short period of time, and Salt Lake City must periodically reassure Seattle that the information remains valid. This periodic reassurance explains the need for RIP-based routers to periodically rebroadcast their routing updates.

To return to the example of Figure 9.4, once Salt Lake City loses power, it stops sending out its routing updates. After some period time (typically three minutes) the rout-

Table 9.2 Seattle's Routing Table after Salt Lake City Power Failure

Destination	Cost	Next Hop
I-5	1 hop	N/A
I-84	1 hop	N/A
I-10	2 hops	San Francisco
I-80	2 hops	San Francisco
I-15	3 hops	San Francisco
I-20	3 hops	San Francisco
I-40	3 hops	San Francisco
I-35	4 hops	San Francisco
I-90	4 hops	San Francisco

ers that had previously heard from Salt Lake City will time out that information. They will then recalculate routes based on the information they do have. Seattle, for example, will end up with a new routing table like that of Table 9.2.

Triggered Updates

In its simplest form, distance vector routing can be slow to disseminate complete routing information. Even in the simple network of Figure 9.1 it takes three full rounds of updates for routers to learn the network's routes. What does that mean for the network's routing? As one example, with the typical RIP update interval of 30 seconds, it could take Seattle as much as 90 seconds to learn that a bridge failure had closed I-35.

For computer networks, 90 seconds can be a very long time. As an extreme example, a single ATM link can transfer nearly 30 billion bytes of data in that time. Sending that much data along the wrong path is a substantial waste of network resources. Fortunately, distance vector protocols can use *triggered updates* to hasten the distribution of updated routing knowledge. The principle behind a triggered update is quite simple: As soon as a router learns of a

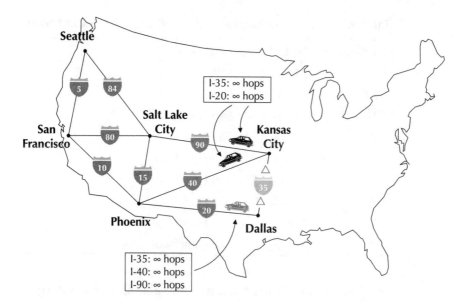

Figure 9.5 Initial triggered updates on failure of I-35.

change in the network topology, it immediately sends new routing updates. The router does not wait for its normal periodic update interval.

Figure 9.5 shows how Kansas City and Dallas respond to a failure of I-35. Each sends triggered updates to all their healthy links as soon as they detect the failure. The figure highlights three key features of triggered updates. First, routers indicate that a destination is unreachable by advertising it as an infinite number of hops away. Infinity is a special value discussed in the following section. Second, the triggered update includes all the routing information that has changed. Kansas City, for example, includes I-20 as well as I-35 in its list of unreachable destinations. It does so because, presumably, Kansas City was previously counting on reaching I-20 by routing along the failed I-35 to Dallas. For the same reason, Dallas lists changed routes to I-40 and I-90 in addition to I-35. It had been counting on Kansas City as the next hop to reach those destinations. As a third point, note that the triggered updates only contain the information that has changed. Kansas City does not

Shortcomings of Triggered Updates

Triggered updates can drastically improve the responsiveness of a distance vector protocol, but they are not effective in every situation. Consider the earlier example in this chapter, a power failure that shuts down Salt Lake City. In this case, the router itself has failed, and it clearly cannot generate a triggered update to tell everyone that fact. Instead, Salt Lake City's neighbors must patiently time out the routes they learned from Salt Lake City. After 180 seconds, when that timeout occurs, they can then issue triggered updates themselves, informing the rest of the network quickly. They cannot, however, avoid that initial 180 second delay.

include information for I-40 and I-90 in its triggered update. That routing information remains part of the normal, periodic update from Kansas City.

The figure shows only the initial triggered updates, but the process continues beyond Kansas City and Dallas. As soon as Salt Lake City receives the update from Kansas City, it realizes that the network has changed. It too, therefore, can send an immediate triggered update reflecting this information. The new information propagates rapidly through the entire network in this fashion, and soon all routers have correct routes.

Counting to Infinity

In some ways, distance vector protocols are naive protocols. Routers that implement them must place total trust in their neighbors. Of course, all protocols depend on mutual cooperation, and even link state protocols like OSPF function poorly when presented with a misbehaving peer. RIP, however, has a particular vulnerability that shows up even when neighbors are not malicious. That vulnerability results in a problem known as *counting to infinity*.

Figure 9.6 shows a sample network that can illustrate counting to infinity. This example concentrates on the interaction between the center and right routers, and the figure illustrates the RIP updates they exchange. Each

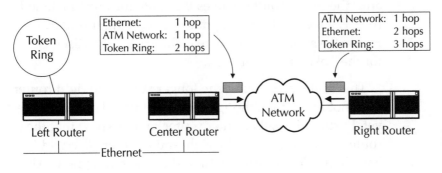

Figure 9.6 Stable network prior to count to infinity.

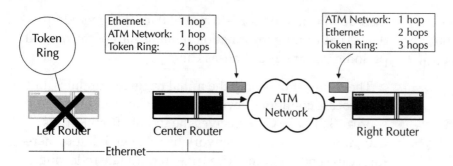

Figure 9.7 Network failure that triggers count to infinity.

advertises their routing tables, including the three networks of the figure.

Now suppose that the left router fails (Figure 9.7). With that failure, the Token Ring network is not reachable. No one realizes this right away, though, and the remaining routers continue exchanging updates. The two routers do not behave identically, though. The right router regularly receives updates from its peer, and it has no suspicion that anything is amiss. But the center router no longer hears from the failed router. It steadily counts down the time remaining for the route to the Token Ring network.

After 180 seconds, that route expires. The center router realizes that the Token Ring is no longer reachable via the left router. The right router's information, on the other hand, is not even close to expiration. After all, it has been receiving regular updates from the center router. Shortly after the center router deletes the route through the failed router, it receives a new update from the right router. As Figure 9.8 shows, this update includes an advertisement for the Token Ring network.

This route is, of course, no longer valid. The right router does not know that, though. It has not timed out the route yet. Furthermore, the center router cannot know that the route is invalid either. The right router, after all, could have had a "back door" path to the Token Ring network. With no other option, the center router believes that its

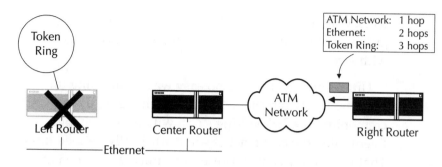

Figure 9.8 Routers begin counting to infinity.

peer does have a three-hop route to the Token Ring. And, if the right router is three hops from the Token Ring, the center router must be four hops away.

The center router installs this "new" route to the Token Ring and includes it in its own updates. Figure 9.9 shows the resulting advertisement. Attention now turns to the right router. Previously, it thought the Token Ring was three hops away. But that belief was based on the network being only two hops away from the center router. Now the center router claims that the network is four hops away. Figure 9.9 shows this update.

"Very well," one imagines the right router thinking, "my cost to reach the Token Ring has just grown from three (2+1) to five (4+1)." By now, the next step is obvious. The right router announces a route to the Token Ring net-

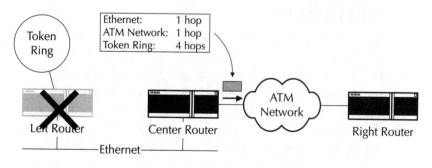

Figure 9.9 Counting to infinity.

work with a cost of five. The center router hears this, adjusts its own route accordingly, and announces a route with a cost of six.

Unfortunately, RIP has no easy way of stopping this process. The two routers continue exchanging updates, incrementing the Token Ring's cost with each exchange. Eventually, the cost reaches some artificially defined limit. That maximum value represents infinity, and, when the cost reaches that level, both routers finally agree that the Token Ring is unreachable.

Distance vector protocols face a difficult decision when choosing the value to represent infinity. As the example shows, it should not be too large. Otherwise, counting to infinity could take a long time and consume a lot of network resources. On the other hand, "infinity" should not be too small. Its value represents an upper limit on the true size of the network.

RIP uses a distance of 16 as infinity. With this value, no destination can be more than 15 hops away from any other. For larger internetworks, this limit may represent a severe constraint on the topology. On the other hand, 16 may seem excessive by some measures. Without triggered updates, it can still take eight minutes for two routers to count to infinity. Fortunately, most RIP implementations employ triggered updates. They hasten the count to infinity considerably.

Split Horizon

It is not possible for RIP to eliminate counting to infinity in all possible topologies, but most RIP implementations employ a technique known as *split horizon* to avoid the most common situations that require counting to infinity. With split horizon, routers are more selective in the routes they advertise. The rule they employ is rather simple. If a router learns of a route from updates received on a link, it does not advertise that route on updates that it transmits

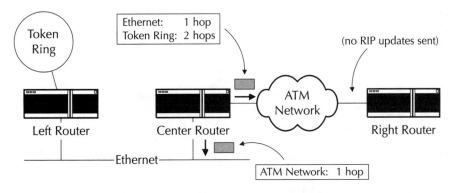

Figure 9.10 Split horizon limits contents of routing updates.

to the link. Consider Figure 9.10. The topology remains the same, but both routers now employ split horizon.

Notice the RIP updates sent by the center router. They no longer include the router's complete routing table. For example, the update it sends on the Ethernet omits any mention of the Ethernet or the Token Ring network. The center router learns about these destinations from the Ethernet, so it does not need to advertise them to that network. For the same reason, the router's updates on the ATM network do not mention that network, only the Ethernet and Token Ring.

Split horizon has an even more drastic effect on the right router. Since the only routes it knows are learned from the ATM network, they will all be omitted on updates sent to that network. The right router has no need to send RIP updates at all.

Given the updates of Figure 9.10, it is clear how split horizon avoids counting to infinity. When the left router fails, it will still take some time for routes to the Token Ring to expire in the center router. Once that happens, however, the center router no longer hears of an apparent alternate path from the right router. Immediately after the route's expiration, the center router knows that the Token Ring is no longer reachable.

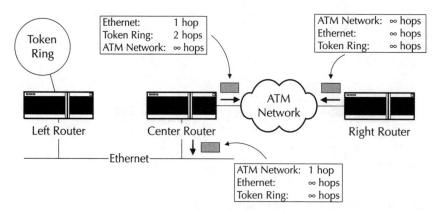

Figure 9.11 Split horizon with poison reverse.

Some RIP routers employ an even more drastic form of split horizon called *poison reverse*. With poison reverse, routers do not omit destinations they learn from an interface. They include those destinations, but advertise an infinite cost to reach them. Figure 9.11 shows poison reverse in action. Comparing it with Figure 9.10 highlights the difference between simple split horizon and split horizon with poison reverse.

Poison reverse obviously increases the size of routing updates. In return, it provides a positive indication that a particular destination is not reachable through a router. This positive indication is less ambiguous, and sometimes safer, than simply relying on the absence of any information about a route.

From these discussions, it may appear that split horizon eliminates the counting to infinity problem. Unfortunately, that is not the case. Some situations still require counting to recognize an unreachable destination. Figure 9.12 presents an example network in which split horizon is ineffective. In that network, suppose the bottom router's connection to the Ethernet fails. At that point, the Ethernet is no longer reachable from anywhere on the network.

Split horizon prevents the bottom router from being misled by any advertisements from the left or right rout-

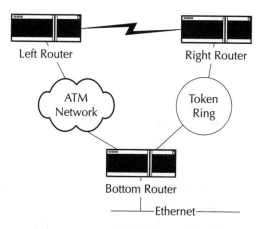

Figure 9.12 Split horizon fails to eliminate counting to infinity.

ers. It does not, however, protect those routers from misleading each other. They will each include a route to the Ethernet in updates on the point-to-point connection. Once the path through the bottom router goes away, they will begin the steady march to infinity in exchanges across this link.

RIP Message Format

With the necessary background on distance vector routing, RIP's message formats become almost trivial. RIP is carried in UDP datagrams (see Chapter 6). It has its own well-known port to distinguish it from other UDP applications. (As of this writing, no value had been assigned.) This port value is different from the one RIP uses for IPv4 routing. RIP for IPv4 is treated as a different protocol from RIP for IPv6.

All RIP messages share a common format, illustrated in Figure 9.13. The message begins with a 4-byte header. The first byte, labeled *command*, indicates whether the message is a request (when it contains a value of 1) or a response (value of 2). So far, all the update messages discussed in this text have been unsolicited. They are sent as responses.

The request command lets a router explicitly ask a neighbor for a route.

To request routing information for a specific destination, a router places that destination in a RIP request. The metric in the request is irrelevant. Any router that responds to a request fills in the metric in its response message.

A router can also use the request to ask for a neighbor's entire routing table. To do that, it sends the neighbor a RIP request with a single entry. That entry has a prefix address and length set to zero, and a metric of 16. Routers that respond to this request return their routing table, possibly in several response messages. Note that split horizon processing is not applied to responses sent in reply to RIP requests.

The next byte of the RIP header indicates the version of the RIP protocol in use. IPv6 currently relies on RIP version 1. Two reserved bytes follow the version number. These bytes always contain zero.

After the 4-byte header, RIP messages contain a list of route entries. Figure 9.13 shows two such entries. The entries are simply IP address prefixes with a length (in bits) and a cost metric. Consistent with the normal use of ad-

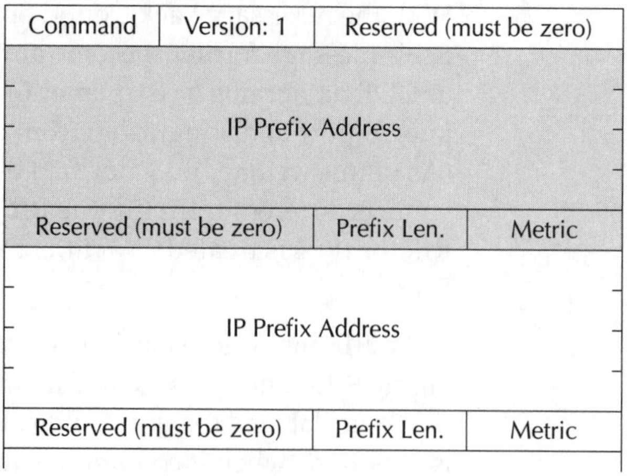

Command	Version: 1	Reserved (must be zero)	
IP Prefix Address			
Reserved (must be zero)		Prefix Len.	Metric
IP Prefix Address			
Reserved (must be zero)		Prefix Len.	Metric

Figure 9.13 RIP message format.

dress prefixes, a prefix length of zero indicates the *default route*. The default route defines the path to destinations for which no other information is available.

Addressing RIP Messages

When a router sends a RIP update, it must be careful to use the appropriate source IP address. In particular, the router must use its own IP address *on the network to which the update is sent*. This distinction is important because routers typically interface to multiple networks. They are likely, therefore, to have multiple IP addresses. When a router receives a RIP update, however, it relies on the source address to define the next hop for routes included in the update. To ensure consistency, this next hop must be an address on the network from which the update arrived.

When picking a destination IP address, RIP must consider whether it is sending across a point-to-point link or a broadcast network. For point-to-point links, the destination address should be the IP address of the router at the far end of the link. For broadcast networks such as Ethernet LANs, RIP's destination address is a multicast address confined to the local network. By multicasting RIP responses, a router sends its updates to all other routers on the network at once.

RIP Timers

RIP relies on three different timers to support its operation. The most obvious timer initiates periodic RIP updates. That timer has a nominal value of 30 seconds, but the RIP standard places extra restrictions on its value. In most cases, these restrictions require routers to randomize the update interval slightly. Randomization results in periodic RIP updates 25 to 35 seconds apart.

By randomizing its updates, a router avoids synchronizing with other routers on the network. Although researchers do not fully understand why routers synchronize with each other, the phenomenon definitely occurs[1]. Synchronization causes all routers to send their updates at the same time, stressing the network with a burst of traffic. Randomization reduces the probability of routers synchronizing, and it therefore spreads out their transmissions over time.

RIP requires an additional precaution to avoid synchronization. Triggered updates, regardless of when they are sent, do not reset the 30-second timer; otherwise, a major topology change could synchronize multiple routers. They would all restart their periodic timers simultaneously after sending the triggered updates. Instead, periodic updates take place as scheduled, even if their entire contents were just broadcast as a triggered update a few seconds earlier.

The second important timer on which RIP relies is the expiration timer. When a router hears a route to a particular destination, it initializes the expiration timer for that destination. The expiration timer is set for 180 seconds, but, in a stable network, it is always reinitialized about every 30 seconds. When the network is not stable, however, this timer may expire. Such an expiration indicates that the route is no longer valid.

RIP's final timer is the *garbage collection* timer. Should a route expire, routers do not immediately forget about that route. Instead, they mark the route as invalid (by setting its metric to infinity) and start the garbage collection timer. This timer runs for 120 seconds. During that time, the router continues to advertise the destination, though it does so with a metric cost of infinity. Advertising the route this way forces neighbors to purge the route rapidly from their routing tables.

---

[1] Sally Floyd and Van Jacobson. "The Synchronization of Periodic Routing Messages." *Computer Communications Review* 23.4 (October 1993): 33-44.

RIP versus OSPF

A quick comparison of this chapter and the previous one should convince most readers that RIP is far simpler than OSPF[2]. Of course, even simplicity has a cost, and RIP has several significant limitations when compared to OSPF. RIP cannot support large networks, it is slower to respond to network changes, and it has no support for multicast routing.

Limited Network Diameter

RIP defines infinity to be 16, and this definition places a strict limit on the size of any RIP-based internetwork. Since RIP's metric must be an integer, all networks must have a cost of at least one. With all paths limited to less than infinity, every system in a RIP-based internetwork must be no more than 15 networks away from any other system. This measure is the network's *diameter*, and, with RIP, it is limited to 15.

There is another significant consequence of this limitation. It restricts the flexibility that administrators might otherwise have in assigning costs. Consider the simple example of Figure 9.14. In the figure, the two primary routers are connected through ATM networks and by a narrowband ISDN network. The path through the ATM networks requires an intermediate stop at a secondary router. Because of the much greater throughput available (155 Mbit/s vs. 128 Kbit/s) the ATM path is much more desirable than the narrowband ISDN network.

If an administrator assigns metric costs in the most straightforward way, she will give each network a cost of one. With that assignment, however, RIP will choose the

---

[2] Indeed, such a comparison actually minimizes the differences between the two. Chapter 8 offers only a brief overview of the OSPF protocol. A careful study of all the associated RFCs is essential to a correct implementation. This chapter, on the other hand, presents a fairly complete picture of RIP.

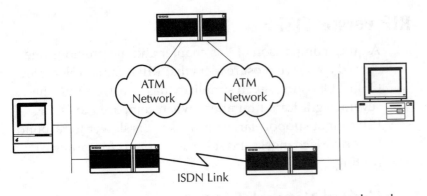

Figure 9.14 Increasing costs to force an optimum network path.

ISDN link as the lowest-cost path between the LANs. That path has only one hop, while the ATM networks require two hops.

To force a more appropriate decision, the administrator can artificially inflate the cost of the ISDN link. To make sure that the ATM networks become the preferred path, she can assign the ISDN link a cost of three. With this assignment, the ATM networks provide a lower-cost path, but the ISDN link remains available as a backup.

This flexibility comes at a cost. If links have typical costs of two or three, the maximum network diameter shrinks accordingly. Because of the counting to infinity problem, RIP is always stuck with a maximum cost of 15. OSPF, in contrast, places no practical limits on network diameter. OSPF metrics are 16-bit quantities, and there is no artificial limit to allow for counting to infinity.

Responsiveness to Network Changes

Another disadvantage of RIP is its responsiveness. Triggered updates help, but they can still require the exchange of more than a dozen packets to count to infinity. There are also scenarios that force RIP to wait 180 seconds before it recognizes routes that have become invalid. (See the sidebar on page 305.)

Distance Vector Protocols for Multicast Routing

Although link state protocols like OSPF are more naturally suited for distributing multicast routing information, it is possible to design a distance vector protocol for multicast routing. RFC 1075 documents just such a protocol for IPv4. That protocol is considered experimental; as of this writing, there were no efforts underway to adapt it for IPv6.

OSPF, on the other hand, suffers no such delays. With suitable tuning, it can recognize failed neighbors in a few seconds. Regardless of how OSPF learns of a network change, it can reconstruct the correct network topology as soon as it floods the appropriate advertisement. Instead of the 180 seconds (and more) that RIP sometimes requires, OSPF typically responds to changes in the network within a second or two.

Multicast Routing

A final shortcoming of RIP is its lack of support for multicast routing. RIP has no way to disseminate group membership information, and it offers no help in routing multicast packets. OSPF, on the other hand, includes explicit support for multicast routing. Indeed, link state protocols in general are well suited for distributing group membership. RIP can be used on a network that provides multicast services, but only for unicast routing. It must be augmented by another protocol that supports multicast routing.

Summary

The Routing Information Protocol offers a simpler alternative to OSPF. Like OSPF, RIP is designed for routing within an autonomous system, but RIP differs from OSPF in its basic technology. Instead of link state routing, RIP relies on distance vector algorithms. Distance vector algorithms are less complex than link state approaches, but they suffer significant limitations. In particular, RIP places limits on the size of its networks and on the speed with which they can respond to topology changes. Because of these limitations, RIP is better suited for small networks. Sophisticated networks require the complexity of OSPF.

10

Routing between Autonomous Systems Using IDRP

Both RIP and OSPF are interior gateway protocols, routing protocols that operate within an autonomous system. The Internet, of course, includes a lot of autonomous systems, and it needs a way to route between them. Protocols that provide this routing are *exterior gateway protocols*. (Gateway is an old name for a router.) The exterior gateway protocol that supports IPv6 is the Interdomain Routing Protocol, or IDRP.

As OSPF demonstrates, routing within an autonomous system can get complicated. Ultimately, though, it has a simple, unconstrained goal: figure out the best way to get from here to there. When paths cross AS borders, however, even the goals get complicated. An example that first appeared in Chapter 4 introduces some of the issues. Figure 10.1 repeats the network from that example.

Big Company's network has connections to both Giant Company and one of Giant's suppliers. It is not surprising that these connections exist, as Big needs to exchange in-

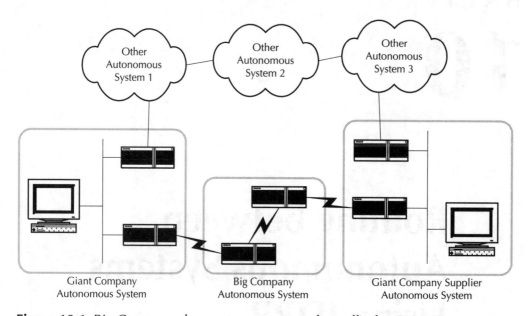

Figure 10.1 Big Company does not want to transfer traffic for Giant Company.

formation with both other firms. Big is adamant about one thing: it does not want to provide a service to Giant. That means that traffic between Giant and its supplier should not travel through Big's network. Such traffic must take the long way around, through the other autonomous systems at the top of the figure.

No longer is the routing goal simply to figure out the best way to get from here to there. Instead, the network now needs the best way to get from here to there without passing through a restricted area. Restricted areas define policies, and policies make routing between ASs especially complex.

In Chapter 4, the source system solves its policy problem by adding a routing header to all datagrams. In theory, this approach always works. In practice, it places much too great a burden on the host systems. In all but the simplest configurations, policy must be transparent to the hosts involved in the communication. Through its support of policy-based routing, IDRP provides just such a service.

Implementing Policy

Policies constrain communications. If every system were allowed to communicate with every other system without restrictions, then networks would not need policies. Policies can take many complex and sophisticated forms, but they all ultimately amount to a limitation on communication between systems.

Networks can implement policies in at least three different ways. Each approach corresponds to a different way to place limitations on communications. The simplest approach is based on bandwidth. If, for example, Big Company wants the make sure that Giant Company uses no more than 56 Kbit/s of bandwidth in its network, then Big Company can limit the connections between the two networks to 56 Kbit/s. Figure 10.2 illustrates this configuration. Clearly, with only 56 Kbit/s of bandwidth available,

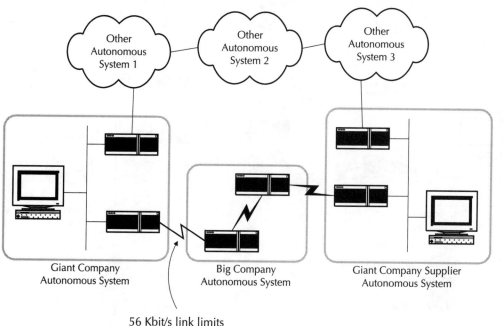

Figure 10.2 Implementing policy with bandwidth.

Giant must conform to Big's policy. In the extreme case, Big can simply refuse any connection to Giant, limiting the bandwidth to 0 bit/s.

Another place to implement policies is in the forwarding process. Every IP datagram that traverses Big's network travels through routers, and the IP layer in each router must make a forwarding decision. Routers can implement policies by constraining their forwarding decisions. Most commercial routers, in fact, support this form of policy through *packet filters*.

Packet filters, symbolized by the traffic lights of Figure 10.3, allow administrators to define exactly which datagrams routers will and will not forward. Unfortunately,

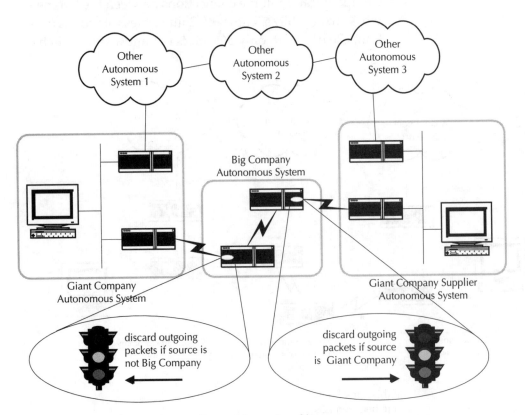

Figure 10.3 Implementing policy with packet filters.

these filters place a substantial computation burden on the routers. They must check every single datagram against the defined constraints. Administering packet filters is also quite a challenge. It usually requires in-depth knowledge of message formats and possible values for various fields within packets.

IDRP relies on the third way of implementing policy, *policy-based routing*. Policy-based routing places constraints on how routers distribute routing information. The idea is simple: If Giant's routers do not know that the supplier lies on the other side of Big's network, they do not forward traffic through it. In Figure 10.4 Big's routers consider that information "secret," refusing to advertise it to Giant's network.

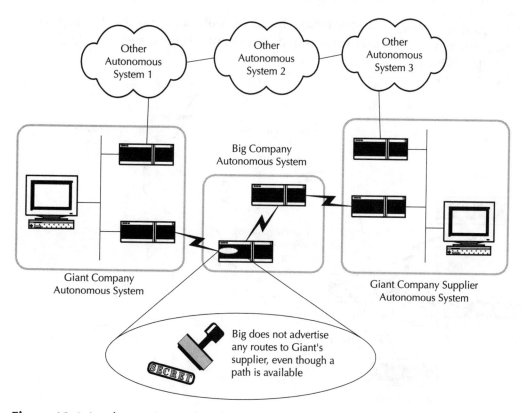

Figure 10.4 Implementing policy by restricting routing information.

Confusing Acronyms

Of all the TCP/IP protocols, IDRP has perhaps the most confusing acronym. The confusion arises because of a different protocol, the Inter Domain Policy Routing (IDPR) protocol. As its name hints, this protocol has the same scope (interdomain) and focus (policy routing) as IDRP. IDPR, however, is an experimental IPv4 protocol. As of this writing, there are no plans to adapt IDPR to the IPv6 environment.

This approach does not require special calculations for every IP datagram. Instead, routers simply implement their normal forwarding decision (although with less than complete information). Giant's routers find an alternate path to reach the supplier, and they forward traffic along that path.

Influencing Routing Information

Even though IDRP exists mainly to support policy-based routing, it is not concerned with the details of routing policies. IDRP itself has no understanding of the format, structure, administration, or any other aspect of policies. It merely acknowledges their existence, and it allows them to influence routing information. Figure 10.5 starts a discussion of this approach.

In the figure, the right router is connected to several other routers in different autonomous systems. IDRP al-

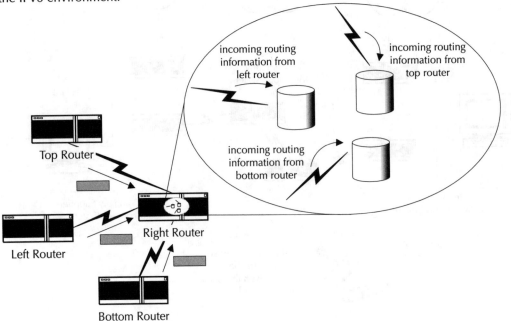

Figure 10.5 Receiving incoming routing information.

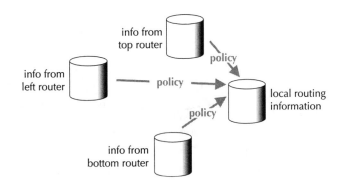

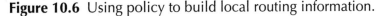

Figure 10.6 Using policy to build local routing information.

lows those routers to exchange routing information with each other. This routing information describes the topology of the network, as the sender understands it. Conceptually, the right router accepts routing information from each of its neighbors. IDRP is the protocol that conveys that information.

The right router then has to do something with the routing information it has gathered. It ultimately must decide how it will route data. As Figure 10.6 shows, the router applies policies to decide what information it keeps and what information it ignores. This process creates a database of local routing information. The incoming routing information describes how its neighbors view the network, while the local routing information defines how the router itself views the network.

This view is also what the router advertises as external routes in its OSPF link state advertisements (page 286) or RIP updates (page 312). Other routers within the autonomous system will reach a consistent view of the greater network beyond their AS.

IDRP supports an additional application of routing policy. It allows policies to determine what information a router shares with its neighbors. For these policy decisions, the router starts with its own local routing information. The router then decides what information it wishes to

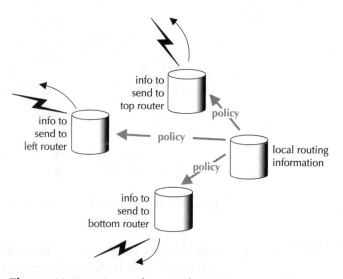

Figure 10.7 Using policy to determine outgoing routing information.

share with its neighbors. Logically, it constructs outgoing routing information for each neighbor. Again, this decision, depicted in Figure 10.7, is based on policy.

This step is where Big solves the problem of preventing Giant's routers from using its network. Big implements a policy in its routers that prohibits them from including routes to Giant's supplier in the information they send to Giant's routers.

Routing Confederations

When the Internet first introduced the concept of an autonomous system, ASs provided a useful way to combine many IP networks into one entity. Exterior gateway protocols could use the AS number as a convenient way to refer to an entire set of IP networks. The routing protocols could just worry about autonomous systems, without having to keep track of every network on the Internet. As internets continue to grow, however, the number of autonomous systems also increases. The Internet now has the same problem with autonomous systems that it used to have with IP networks—there are simply too many of them for the routing protocols to keep track of efficiently.

To help alleviate this problem, IDRP supports the concept of *routing confederations*. A routing confederation is a collection of autonomous systems. In IDRP, a single confederation can represent the entire set of autonomous systems that belong to it. IDRP only needs to keep track of the single confederation, and not all of its ASs. Of course, within a confederation, IDRP does distinguish different autonomous systems.

Figure 10.8 shows how a network can contain both autonomous systems and confederations. In the figure, every network is part of some autonomous system. The figure shows AS boundaries in gray. Some ASs, but not all, have chosen to combine into confederations. The figure shows confederation boundaries in black.

IDRP is quite flexible in its support for routing confederations. Confederations may be subsets of each other, and

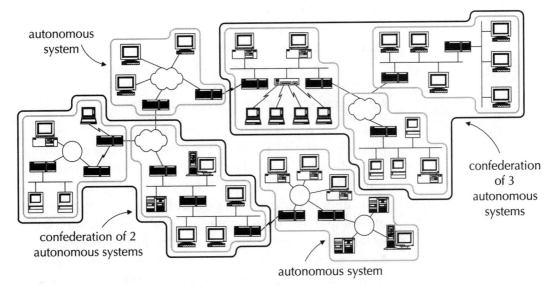

Figure 10.8 Autonomous systems combine to form confederations.

they can overlap each other. In this way, confederations have even more flexibility than autonomous systems. ASs cannot overlap each other, as that might create routing loops that OSPF or RIP could not resolve.

Path Vectors: A New Routing Approach

So far, routing between autonomous systems sounds a lot like routing within an autonomous system. The inter-AS approach has to support policy-based routing, but policies themselves are not part of the protocol. So why is a whole new protocol required? What is wrong with using OSPF or even RIP for exterior routing?

The answer to these questions lies in the goals of the protocol. Both OSPF and RIP assume that all routers have the same goal. As stated, that goal is to figure out how to get from here to there. IDRP routers also loosely share a goal: figure out how to get from here to there, subject to certain restrictions. The problem arises because the restrictions vary from router to router. Some organizations may have no concerns routing traffic through Big Company's network, while others (such as Giant Company) have different ideas. Giant's routers have a different restriction than other routers, and so Giant's routers and other routers do not share the same goal. Without a common goal, routers using OSPF or RIP cannot calculate paths consistently, and routing loops are almost certain to arise.

The root of this problem is the protocols' reliance on metrics. Both OSPF and RIP attach a metric, or cost, to possible paths. OSPF's link state advertisements include a metric for each link, and RIP assigns a metric to each route in its update packets. The protocols count on every router attaching the same meaning to each metric, allowing consistent, and therefore loop-free, calculation of routes. When routing policies are in place, routers value some metrics more than others, invalidating the assumptions on which OSPF and RIP rely.

Distance Vector Routing without Distances

IDRP solves this problem by eliminating (for the most part) metrics. Its approach is essentially that of a distance vector protocol, but without explicit distances. IDRP's routing algorithm is known as *path vector routing*. The essential difference between distance vector and path vector routing is the information exchanged in routing updates.

Distance vector protocols advertise a cost to reach each destination; path vector protocols explicitly list entire paths to each destination. Consider the example network of Figure 10.9. (In that network, autonomous systems are unrealistically small. Real ASs contain many subnetworks connected by many routers.)

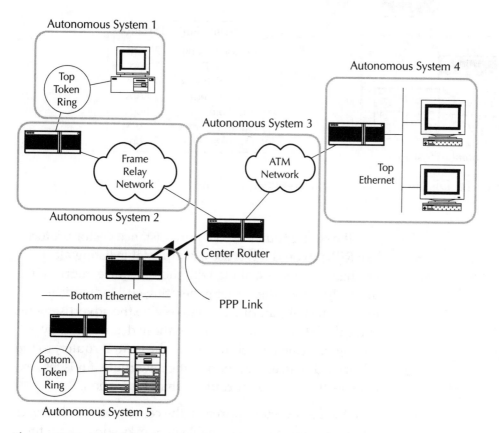

Figure 10.9 Network of autonomous systems.

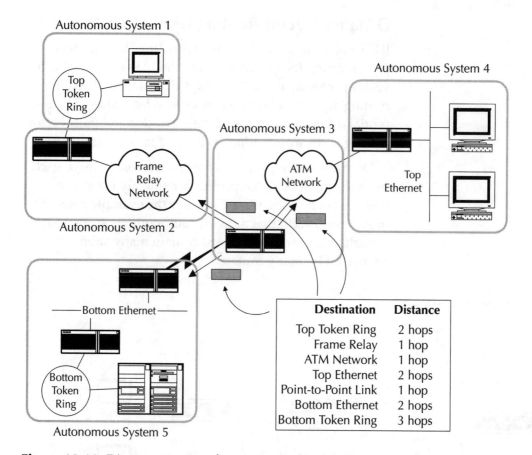

Destination	Distance
Top Token Ring	2 hops
Frame Relay	1 hop
ATM Network	1 hop
Top Ethernet	2 hops
Point-to-Point Link	1 hop
Bottom Ethernet	2 hops
Bottom Token Ring	3 hops

Figure 10.10 Distance vector advertisements list the distance to each destination.

If the center router used a pure distance vector protocol like RIP, it would advertise a routing table listing all reachable networks, along with their distance metric. Figure 10.10 shows the router generating such advertisements. The neighboring routers receive the advertisements and calculate their own routes to those destinations by adding one (the cost of the link to the central router) to the advertised cost, and accepting the new route if it is less expensive than any other route to that destination.

In the path vector approach, the center router advertises a routing table listing reachable networks, along with the

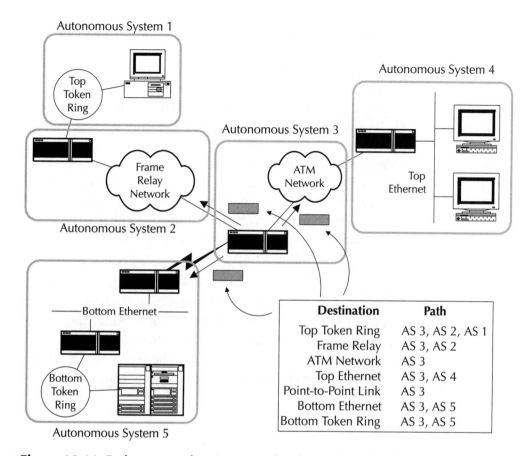

Destination	Path
Top Token Ring	AS 3, AS 2, AS 1
Frame Relay	AS 3, AS 2
ATM Network	AS 3
Top Ethernet	AS 3, AS 4
Point-to-Point Link	AS 3
Bottom Ethernet	AS 3, AS 5
Bottom Token Ring	AS 3, AS 5

Figure 10.11 Path vector advertisements list the paths to each destination.

router's path to those destinations. Figure 10.11 highlights the difference between this approach and distance vector advertisements. When a neighboring router receives this advertisement, it can compute its own paths to the destinations. These calculations define the incoming routing information from the central router. The neighbor router can then base its local route information on any appropriate policies. For example, the top right router, after hearing from the center router, knows a path to the Token Ring LAN. That path runs through ASs 3, 2, and 1. If the router's policy forbids it from using AS 2, then it will note that the Token Ring is unreachable.

Counting to Infinity

Path vectors also provide a neat solution to the counting to infinity problem. Recall that distance vector protocols sometimes must count to infinity to break a routing loop. Such loops can arise because, when one router receives an advertisement from another, it knows only the cost to the advertised destinations; it does not know the path to those destinations. In particular, the receiving router does not know if the advertising router is actually counting on the receiving router to reach the destination. With a path vector approach, receiving routers know the entire path. If they themselves are part of the path, then they can ignore the route, avoiding a routing loop.

Figure 10.12 gives a concrete example of path information breaking a potential routing loop. In the figure, the left router has lost its connection to the Token Ring, and can no longer reach that destination directly. It does, however, hear a routing advertisement from the center router. That advertisement claims that the Token Ring is reachable. The

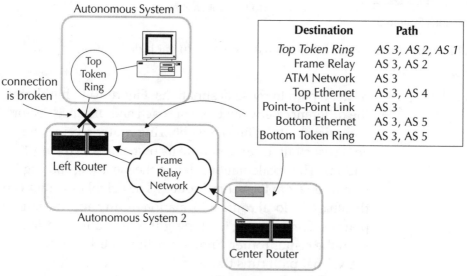

Destination	Path
Top Token Ring	*AS 3, AS 2, AS 1*
Frame Relay	AS 3, AS 2
ATM Network	AS 3
Top Ethernet	AS 3, AS 4
Point-to-Point Link	AS 3
Bottom Ethernet	AS 3, AS 5
Bottom Token Ring	AS 3, AS 5

Figure 10.12 Path information can avoid routing loops.

path, however, includes the right router's own autonomous system. The right router recognizes that it would do no good to send packets for the Token Ring to the center router. After all, that router would simply turn them right around and send them back through autonomous system number 2. The right router can detect this potential routing loop and avoid accepting that route.

Tracking Confederations

Confederations introduce some additional complexity in IDRP's path vectors. IDRP's goal is to represent all of the ASs that make up a confederation by a single identifier, but only in advertisements outside the confederation. Figure 10.13 shows an example. The left router sits on the edge of a confederation boundary. When it advertises a route outside of the confederation, that route simply lists the confederation in its path. The path does not include individual autonomous systems. But within the confederation, IDRP explicitly lists all ASs in its path. When sending traffic to a destination within the confederation,

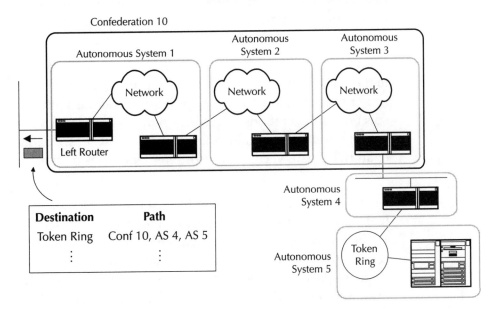

Destination	Path
Token Ring	Conf 10, AS 4, AS 5
⋮	⋮

Figure 10.13 Path specified as a confederation instead of individual ASs.

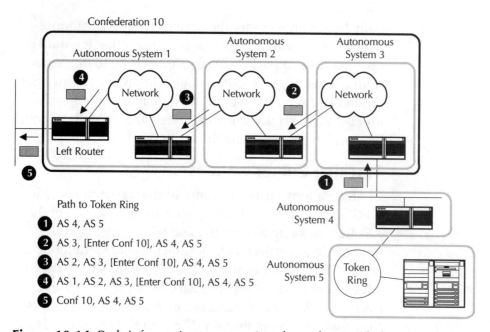

Figure 10.14 Path information propagating through a confederation.

outside routers know only to route toward the confederation. Once a datagram enters the confederation, routers must know through which autonomous systems it must travel to reach its destination.

To track this information, IDRP adds simple indicators to the paths it advertises. As the path propagates from router to router, those indications define its status with respect to confederations. Figure 10.14 traces the propagation of a route through the sample network. It shows parts of an IDRP path vector at five different locations on the network.

Propagation begins at the rightmost router. As soon as that router advertises the route into the confederation (step 1), the receiving router notes that the path has entered the confederation. The note appears explicitly in the advertisement packet. As the route propagates from right to left in subsequent IDRP packets, each router adds its own AS to the path. The confederation status remains unchanged.

Finally, the route reaches the leftmost router. Here, the router sees that the route is propagating beyond the confederation. As it generates its IDRP packet, the left router removes the explicit AS information in the path and replaces it with the confederation identifier. The intermediate steps removed from the path are those between the current location (the left router) and the point at which the path entered the confederation, which is marked in that path.

Route Aggregation

Confederations help reduce the size of IDRP's path vectors, but they do not decrease the number of reachable destinations. After all, confederations serve only to combine autonomous systems, while destinations are IP address prefixes. But the same scaling problem that affects ASs also affects destinations—their sheer number can overwhelm many routers. To alleviate this problem, IDRP supports *route aggregation*. Route aggregation lets an IDRP router combine multiple destinations and create a single advertisement for all of them. It reduces the number of individual destinations that other routers must remember, as well as shrinking the network overhead that route update packets require.

Route aggregation relies on the fact that destinations are just IP prefix addresses. Sometimes two different prefixes together specify all of a larger prefix. (In this sense, larger means to include more systems; the prefix itself actually contains fewer specified bits.) For example, suppose a router knows a path to the two different destinations of Table 10.1. If the router has a path to both of these 17-bit prefixes, then it must also have a path to the 16-bit prefix 4623::0/16. Any destination that matches the larger prefix (4623::/16) must, by definition, match one or the other of the smaller prefixes. The seventeenth bit of the destination must either be a one (in which case it matches 4623:8000::/17) or a zero (which matches 4623:0000::/17).

Table 10.1 Routes Subject to Aggregation

Prefix Bits	Prefix Value
17	4623:8000::0/17
17	4623:0000::0/17

Figure 10.15 shows how route aggregation can work in a real network. The left router knows paths to the two destinations in Table 10.1. When it creates an advertisement for the left network, though, it does not have to list each destination separately. Instead, it uses the larger prefix 4623::0/16.

The figure highlights a question facing IDRP. When a router combines routes, what path does it advertise for the aggregate? In the figure's example, the two destinations do not lie on the same path. The path to the top destination is AS 1, while the bottom network is in AS 2. Nonetheless, the left router must list a single path to the combined route in its update. The path it selects is the union of the paths to

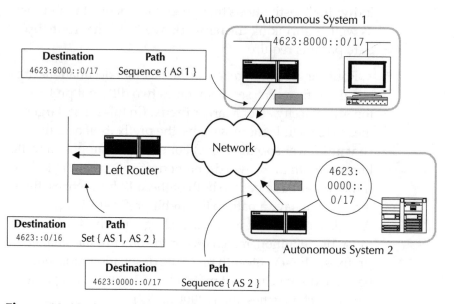

Figure 10.15 Aggregating routes.

each separate destination; in other words, both AS 1 and AS 2. To indicate that this path is a union, the left router marks it as a *set*. In contrast, regular paths that have not been aggregated are termed *sequences*.

IDRP Operation

Derived from ISO Standard

The IDRP protocol did not begin life as a TCP/IP protocol. It was originally part of the ISO protocol suite. The protocol is quite flexible, and easily adapted to IPv6. The TCP/IP developers found it much easier to make a few modifications to an existing protocol than to invent their own protocol. Because of its ISO background, the IDRP standard includes terminology that differs from many TCP/IP standards. This chapter uses the normal TCP/IP terms (to remain consistent with the rest of the text). Readers who refer to actual IDRP documents, however, may find a few translations helpful. In particular, the ISO term *routing domain* is equivalent to TCP/IP's autonomous system. Also, what ISO calls a *boundary intermediate system*, or BIS, is, according to TCP/IP, an AS boundary router.

To be as flexible as possible, IDRP requires the minimum amount of services from lower-layer protocols. It requires only IP support, not a transport level protocol such as UDP or TCP. To ensure the reliability of its communication, though, IDRP implements its own connection service. IDRP's flexibility extends to the details of its messages as well. It describes each destination with a series of attributes. Later protocol revisions can add more attributes without disturbing existing implementations.

IDRP Message Format

IDRP messages are carried as payloads of IP datagrams. Figure 10.16 shows the common format that all IDRP messages share. The IDRP header contains eight fields. The protocol identifier byte exists as a remnant of IDRP's ISO roots. (See sidebar.) It serves a purpose similar to IP's next header field. For IP networks, this protocol identifier is not important. It should always have a value of 133. The following two bytes specify the length (in bytes) of the IDRP message. This length includes the common IDRP header. The next byte identifies the type of IDRP message. IDRP uses six message types, listed in Table 10.2.

The next four fields—sequence number, acknowledgment number, credit offered, and credit available—support IDRP's connection service. The following subsection describes how IDRP uses them.

IDRP uses the last 16 bytes of the common header to ensure either data integrity or authentication. When two routers establish an IDRP connection, they agree on a validation technique to use on the connection. IDRP allows

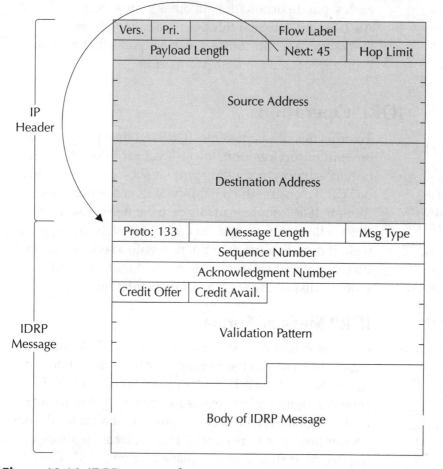

Figure 10.16 IDRP message format.

Table 10.2 IDRP Message Types

1	open message
2	update message
3	error message
4	keepalive message
5	cease message
6	route refresh message

several different validation techniques. The most basic approach has the sender perform a simple message digest algorithm on the message. The particular message digest function is MD4, a predecessor to the MD5 algorithm on which IP may base its authentication header. (See page 121.)

IDRP may also use a variation known as *keyed MD4* to provide both data integrity and authentication. MD4 is cryptographically weaker than MD5, but still suitable for assuring data integrity[1]. If these two options are not suitable, IDRP permits routers to use their own private validation functions. Two systems using such functions must, of course, agree on the exact algorithm they plan to use.

Connection-Oriented Service

Reinventing Connections

It may seem unusual that IDRP goes to the trouble of providing its own connection services. Instead, it could simply rely on TCP, much like its IPv4 predecessor, the Border Gateway Protocol. Avoiding TCP gives IDRP some independence from particular protocol suites. IDRP is designed to serve other suites, including ISO and, perhaps, IPX. Neither of those suites includes TCP.

IDRP operates directly over the IP layer, and so its messages receive only IP's standard best effort delivery service. Since IDRP cannot count on IP to provide a reliable service, it takes the steps to provide that service itself.

IDRP relies on the same mechanism as TCP to establish its connections—the three-way handshake. The handshake requires the exchange of three messages between the systems. One router begins the process by sending an *open* message, which has the format of Figure 10.17.

After the common header, the open message includes several additional fields plus options. The first extra field defines the IDRP version number, currently 1. The next two bytes specify a holding time, in seconds. Once the connection is established, the sender must hear something from its peer within this time, or it will consider that the connection has failed. A value of zero indicates an indefinite hold time. If it is not zero, IDRP requires that the hold time be at least three seconds so as not to burden the net-

---

[1] Charlie Kaufman, Radia Perlman, and Mike Speciner. *Network Security—Private Communication in a Public World.* PTR Prentice Hall: Englewood Cliffs, NJ, 1995. Page 106.

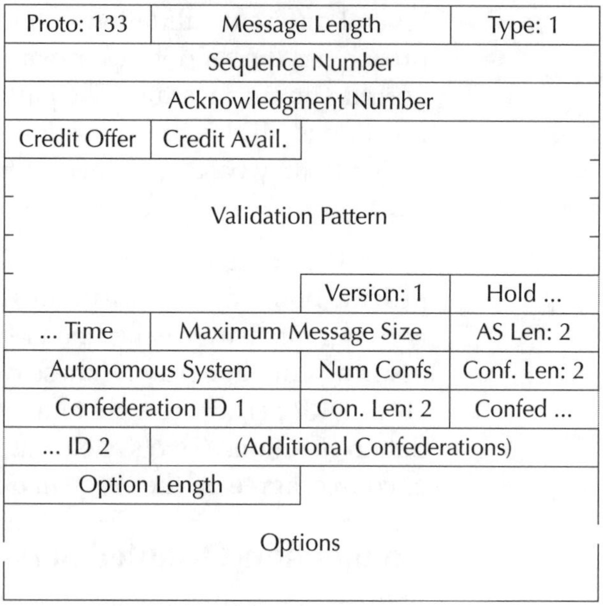

Proto: 133	Message Length		Type: 1
Sequence Number			
Acknowledgment Number			
Credit Offer	Credit Avail.		
Validation Pattern			
		Version: 1	Hold ...
... Time	Maximum Message Size		AS Len: 2
Autonomous System		Num Confs	Conf. Len: 2
Confederation ID 1		Con. Len: 2	Confed ...
... ID 2	(Additional Confederations)		
Option Length			
Options			

Figure 10.17 IDRP open message.

work with excessive IDRP traffic. The third field contains the maximum IDRP message size the sender can accept.

The next two fields list the autonomous system to which the sender belongs. The first byte contains the length of the autonomous system number, while the next field holds the number itself. Currently, all TCP/IP autonomous system numbers are 16 bits in size, but IDRP has the flexibility to allow those numbers to grow. Following the AS number is a list of confederations to which the sender belongs.

The options area includes optional data for the connection. So far, the only option defined is authentication information, which determines the authentication method the connection will employ. When the peer router receives this message, it responds with its own open packet. This message completes two-thirds of the three-way handshake. To complete the exchange, the system that began the process returns a *keepalive*, *update*, or *refresh* message. Keepalive messages normally acknowledge the receipt of

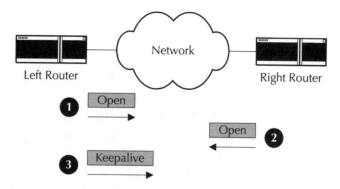

Figure 10.18 Opening an IDRP connection.

data, while updates or refreshes contain actual routing information. Figure 10.18 shows the complete three-way handshake process.

Once a connection is available, IDRP numbers the update and refresh messages exchanged on the connection. The sequence number field in the IDRP header contains these numbers. When the peer router receives a numbered message, it acknowledges that message by incrementing the acknowledgment number in the messages it returns. If a sender realizes that a message has been lost (because it does not get an acknowledgment), it resends the message.

Chapter 7 includes a complete discussion on windowing and retransmission, and the same principles apply to IDRP's connections. Note, though, that TCP numbers individual bytes of application data, while IDRP numbers entire packets.

Like TCP, IDRP incorporates a credit scheme for flow control. The *credits offered* field defines how many additional messages the sender is prepared to accept. IDRP includes the additional field *credits available*, which the sender uses to indicate how many more packets it believes it can send without exhausting its credit.

When a router wants to close an IDRP connection, it sends a *cease* message to its peer. The peer responds with its own cease message, and the connection no longer exists. (Cease messages have no extra fields beyond the 30-byte IDRP header.) An IDRP router also closes a connection when it receives an error message from its peer.

Transferring Routing Information

Once two routers establish a connection, they can use IDRP to exchange routing information. IDRP supports two methods of transferring this information. Routers can use update messages to transfer new or modified routes, or they can perform a refresh to transfer complete routing information.

Update Messages

Most commonly, routers exchange update messages, an example of which appears in Figure 10.19. These messages contain three separate parts. The first part of the message,

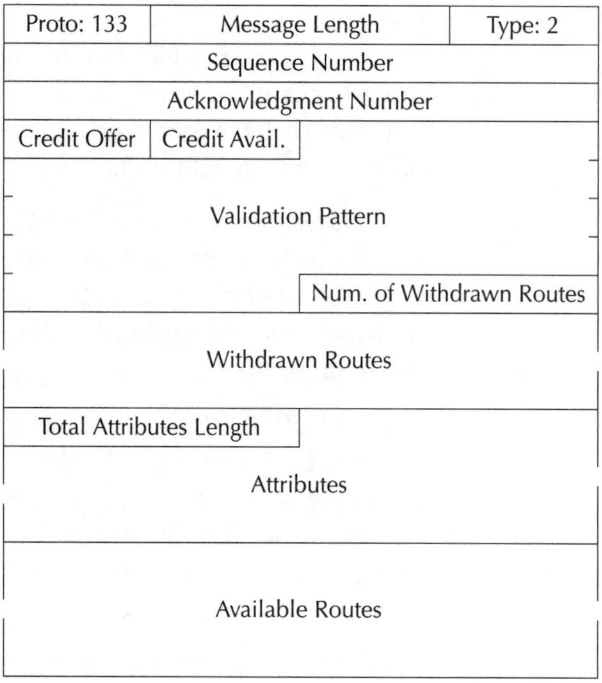

Figure 10.19 IDRP update message.

immediately after the common header, lists those destinations that are no longer reachable. This section allows a router to immediately tell its neighbors that a destination is no longer reachable without having to wait for those routes to time out.

IDRP routers must also use the withdrawn routes section when the path to a destination changes. Unlike simple distance vector protocols like RIP, IDRP cannot just announce the new path. It must explicitly withdraw the old route and then add a new route. Figure 10.20 illustrates the process on an example network. When that network gets a new link, the center router updates its path to the Token Ring in order to take advantage of the new link.

The figure also hints at the reason for this process. Suppose the center router neglected step 3 and just advertised the upper path. The left router, remembering the lower path from earlier advertisements, would then believe that two paths to the Token Ring existed. Since the upper path traverses Giant Company's network and the left router it-

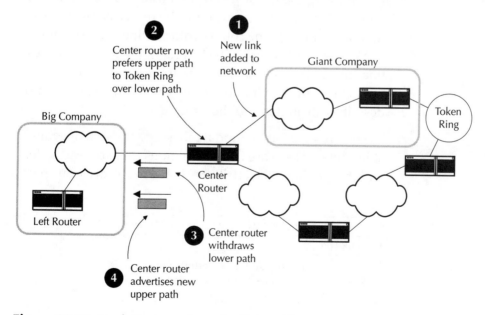

Figure 10.20 Updating a path to the Token Ring.

self belongs to Big Company, it might prefer the lower path. This decision is certainly valid policy, even though the upper path is shorter. Believing itself safe in that decision, the left router could forward traffic for the Token Ring to the center router. But, of course, as soon as that traffic reached the center router, it would take the path that the center router believes to be the best—right through Giant Company's network.

The format of the routes being withdrawn is shown in Figure 10.21. A route begins with an address family identifier and a length. The address family identifier lets IDRP support many different addressing architectures. For IPv6, the address family is 2. The route itself consists of an IP address prefix. The first byte specifies the number of bits in the prefix; it is followed by the prefix value. Unlike most other instances of IP prefixes (such as those of ICMP, RIP, or OSPF), IDRP only includes the minimum number of bytes necessary to hold the prefix. It does not force prefixes to be 16 bytes in length.

Following the list of withdrawn routes, an update message contains information about the routes being advertised as available. The route's information consists mostly of a series of attributes, which contain the path to the destination as well as other important information; they do not include the destination itself. The following subsection describes attributes and their formats.

The final part of the update message consists of available routes. These are the destinations that are reachable, and they all have the attributes listed in the previous part

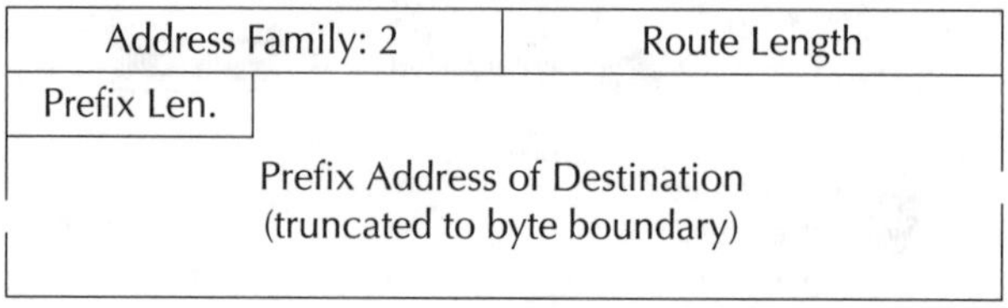

Address Family: 2	Route Length
Prefix Len.	
Prefix Address of Destination (truncated to byte boundary)	

Figure 10.21 Format of routes in an IDRP update.

of the message. Available routers follow the same format as withdrawn routes. (Figure 10.21.) Note that all routes advertised in a single update message must have identical attributes, which means, for example, that they must all share a common path.

Refreshing Routes

Normally, boundary routers only exchange update messages when paths change. This behavior minimizes the network bandwidth consumed by IDRP. Sometimes, however, it is necessary for a router to send its entire routing information to a neighbor. The neighbor may have just reset, for example, and must start from scratch. IDRP provides refresh messages for this purpose. They can be used to solicit a full routing table, or to send one unsolicited.

As Figure 10.22 shows, the refresh message adds little to the basic IDRP header. It includes a single code byte, as well as an area for options. So far, no options are defined. The code byte distinguishes the three different kinds of refresh messages. Table 10.3 lists all of them, along with their code values.

To see these messages in action, consider how the left router in Figure 10.23 continues after a reset. Because of the reset, the router has lost all of the information from its

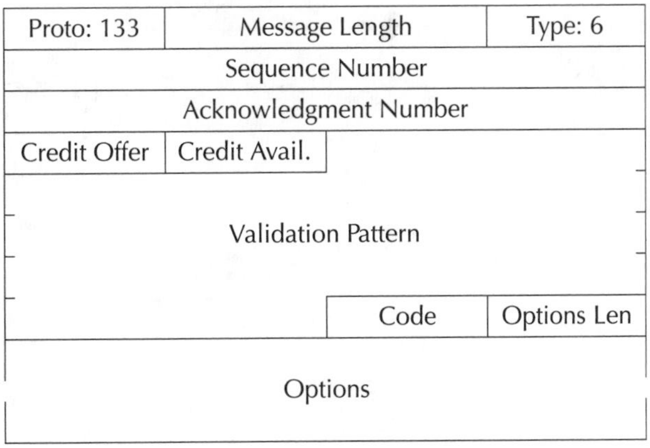

Proto: 133	Message Length	Type: 6
Sequence Number		
Acknowledgment Number		
Credit Offer	Credit Avail.	
Validation Pattern		
	Code	Options Len
Options		

Figure 10.22 IDRP refresh message.

Table 10.3 IDRP Refresh Codes

1	Refresh Request
2	Refresh Start
3	Refresh End

neighbor. To regain that information, it sends a *refresh request* to its peer. The neighbor's response acknowledges the request and returns a *refresh start* message. At that point, the routing refresh begins. The right router sends as many update messages as it takes to transfer its entire routing table. Keepalive messages acknowledge their receipt. Once the transfer is complete, the right router completes the exchange with a *refresh end* message.

This example shows a solicited refresh. IDRP also allows a router to refresh its neighbor without any solicitation. To do that, the router simply sends a refresh start message and begins the refresh. The process continues the same as in Figure 10.23, except that step 1 does not occur.

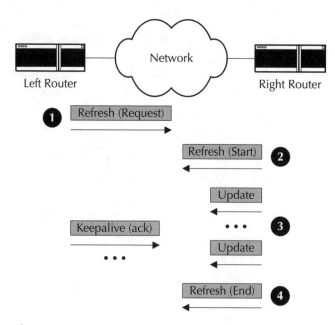

Figure 10.23 Requesting a routing refresh.

Attributes

Most of the information that update messages carry lies in the attributes section. Attributes include, for example, the element that gives path vector routing its name: the path to the destination. All attributes share the common format shown in Figure 10.24.

Each attribute begins with three flag bits. They indicate whether the particular attribute is optional, transitive, and partial. Optional attributes are just that—optional. Not all IDRP routers are required to understand them. If this bit is clear, though, the attribute is termed *well-known*. If a router receives a well-known attribute that it does not understand, the router generates an error message and closes the IDRP connection.

Well-known attributes can be one of two kinds, *mandatory* or *discretionary*. A mandatory attribute must be present in all updates, while a discretionary one can be omitted if it is not appropriate.

The second flag, known as the *transitive* flag applies only to optional attributes. It tells the router what to do if it receives an optional attribute that it does not recognize. If the flag is clear, then the router should not propagate the attribute any further, though it can continue to propagate the route. If the flag is set, the router should propagate the attribute along with the route. When a router propagates a

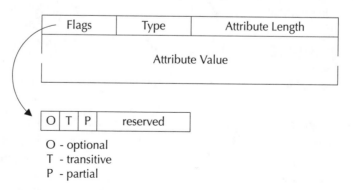

Figure 10.24 IDRP attribute format.

transitive attribute that it does not understand, it sets the partial flag, which tells subsequent routers that a previous router did not understand the attribute.

The type byte identifies the particular attribute. IDRP defines many different attributes. Table 10.4 lists them, along with a brief description of their use. In the table,

Table 10.4 IDRP Attribute Types

Type	Attribute	Must Recognize	Must Include	Transitive	Meaning
1	Route Separator	✓	✓		Ensures consistent routing decisions by routers within an AS.
2	External Information	✓			Information not learned via IDRP.
3	Path	✓	✓		Path to the destination.
4	Next Hop	✓			IP address of next hop to reach destination.
5	Distribution Allowed	✓			Explicit list of autonomous systems to which the route may be propagated.
6	Distribution Prohibited	✓			Explicit list of autonomous systems to which the route may not be propagated.
7	Multi-Exit Discriminator				Used to identify preferred connections to neighboring autonomous system.
12	Hierarchical	✓			Used to control routing within confederations.
13	Hop Count	✓	✓		Hops (in the form of autonomous systems) to reach destination.
15	Capacity	✓	✓		Relative bandwidth available for this path.
17	Aggregator			✓	Identity of router that aggregated the route.
18	Atomic Aggregate	✓			Using this route to advertise a more specific destination (more bits in the prefix) is prohibited.

Must Recognize indicates well-known attributes, and Must Include indicates mandatory attributes.

The most important attribute is the path attribute. This part of the message describes the path to the destination. This attribute also keeps track of when routes are propagated through confederations. The attribute data consists of a series of segments, each of which has the form shown in Figure 10.25.

Segments can describe either sequences or sets. As explained previously, sequences represent normal, ordered paths to a destination. Sets are unordered lists that result from route aggregation. The items that make up these lists are either autonomous systems or confederations. In general, it is not possible to tell the two apart. An exception to this rule occurs when a route is being propagated within a confederation. In such circumstances, that confederation is listed in a special segment that distinguishes confederations the route has entered. As they propagate the route, routers can determine when the route leaves the confederation. At that point, they can replace all the ASs that make up the confederation with that confederation alone. Refer to the "Tracking Confederations" section earlier in the chapter for a discussion that includes examples of this procedure.

To distinguish the different types of segments, IDRP uses the *segment type* field. Its values, listed in Table 10.5, indicate whether the segment describes a set, a sequence, a

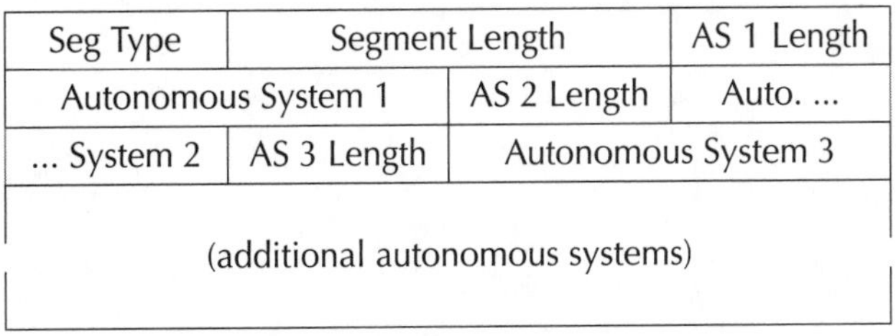

Seg Type	Segment Length		AS 1 Length
Autonomous System 1		AS 2 Length	Auto. ...
... System 2	AS 3 Length	Autonomous System 3	
(additional autonomous systems)			

Figure 10.25 Segment of a path attribute.

Table 10.5 Segment Type Values

1	Routing Domain Set
2	Routing Domain Sequence
3	Entered Sequence
4	Entered Set

set of confederations that the route has entered, or a sequence of confederations that have been entered.

Summary

This chapter introduced the Interdomain Routing Protocol. IDRP operates at a level above the more common routing protocols like RIP or OSPF. It disseminates routing information between autonomous systems. Unlike these other routing protocols, IDRP does not focus on finding the best path between systems. Instead, it tries to find a suitable path that adheres to the policy constraints of the systems involved. Policy constraints pose a challenge to routing protocols, as they may hide information that could be used in routing. IDRP accommodates policies by using a path vector algorithm. This algorithm resembles the distance vector approach of RIP, but it carries considerably more overhead to accomplish policy routing. IDRP can compact information in two ways. First, it allows autonomous systems to combine into routing confederations. Second, it aggregates routes to different destinations that share a common prefix.

11

RTP for Real Time Applications

As the history of TCP/IP demonstrates, network architectures evolve in many ways. Most obviously, the underlying technologies gain new power. The introduction of Fast Ethernet, Asynchronous Transfer Mode, and others offer proof of this development. Upgrades to existing network protocols also represent evolution. Some developments warrant even more radical change; they demand entirely new protocols. The Real Time Protocol (RTP) is just such a protocol. It is designed especially to support a new type of traffic—real time traffic.

This chapter begins by looking at real time traffic. It explains how that traffic differs from other traffic that networks can carry. The chapter then describes RTP's role in the TCP/IP architecture, and the key elements of RTP's operation. The chapter concludes with a description of RTP's message formats and those of its support protocol, the Real Time Control Protocol (RTCP).

Real Time Traffic

Because multimedia data often serves as an example of real time traffic, the two are frequently, though errone-

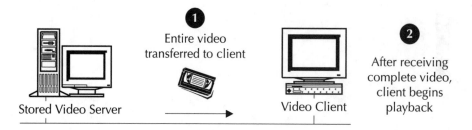

Figure 11.1 Video transfers that complete prior to playback are not real time.

ously, equated. Not all multimedia data is real time, and real time traffic includes much more than multimedia content. The following examples illustrate the difference.

First, Figure 11.1 considers a multimedia transfer that does *not* correspond to a real time traffic flow. It shows a client workstation receiving and then playing back a multimedia video. Note that the client retrieves the entire video before beginning playback. This is the approach of today's World Wide Web browsers; it is the electronic equivalent of renting a movie from a video store.

This traffic is not real time because the action (recorded in the video) does not take place while the transfer occurs. Consequently, there are no tight constraints on how fast the transfer has to happen. If the transfer takes a long time, the user may grow impatient, but once the transfer completes, the application still works. In the video rental analogy, a traffic jam may cause a 15 minute delay getting home from the store, but the video is still viewable despite the delay.

In contrast, consider the application shown in Figure 11.2. There, the network supports a live video conference. The client displays each video frame as soon as it arrives. In this application, there *are* tight constraints on how fast the data must traverse the network. If the network cannot deliver the frames fast enough, then the video conference application will fail.

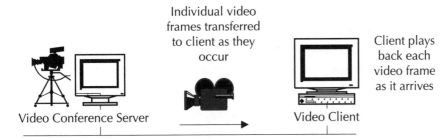

Figure 11.2 Data from a live video conference is real time traffic.

If the first example was equivalent to renting a video, this case is more like watching a broadcast television show. If viewers are 15 minutes late getting home, they may have missed a significant part of the show. Real time traffic, therefore, travels across the network while the action takes place. It requires delivery to its destination within a certain amount of time. If delivery is late, then the application fails.

The Benefits of Application Layer Framing

Application layer framing (ALF) offers better performance than a traditional architecture because of the way most networking software is organized. When such software uses distinct layers, the various protocols often have to interact with each other using inefficient methods such as interprocess communication. By relaxing the boundaries between protocols, ALF supports a more efficient interaction such as direct library function calls.

An Architecture for Real Time Traffic

RTP slightly revises the protocol architecture of Chapter 2. It adjusts the strict layering between protocols, adopting, instead, a more cooperative relationship. This approach, based on the research of Clark and Tennenhouse[1], better suits real time applications.

The architecture, known as *application layer framing*, replaces a sophisticated transport protocol like TCP with a simple framework that the applications themselves can use directly. Real time applications can easily forgo the complexity of TCP because they do not normally need its services. Most audio playback algorithms, for example, can tolerate missing data much better than they can lengthy delays. Instead of introducing delays with retransmissions,

---

[1] D.D.Clark and D.L.Tennenhouse. "Architectural Considerations for a New Generation of Protocols." *SIGCOMM Symposium on Communications Architectures and Protocols*. Philadelphia, PA: IEEE, September 1990. pp. 200-208.

these applications prefer the transport layer to simply forget about missing data. These same applications can also cope automatically with misordered data. They do not need a transport protocol to guarantee in-sequence delivery.

As a part of this architecture, the Real Time Protocol standard does not actually specify a complete protocol. Instead, it sketches a framework for a protocol, defining the basic roles, operations, and message formats. Specific applications start with this framework and add to it, the combination forming a complete protocol.

For example, Figure 11.3 shows that several different standards exist for encoding video data. Those standards include MPEG, JPEG, and H.261. RTP provides a suitable framework for any of those encoding methods. A complete protocol requires both: the framework of RTP and the payload format of, for example, H.261.

Timestamping Real Time Data

No matter the specific payload format, all real time traffic shares some important characteristics. Figure 11.4 shows a

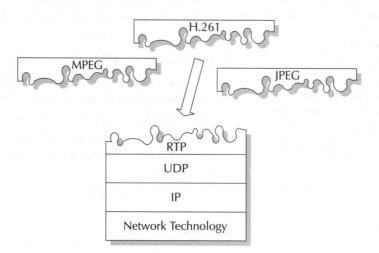

Figure 11.3 RTP combines with a payload format to form a full protocol.

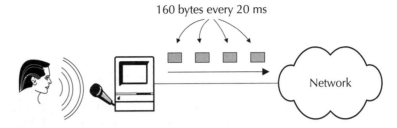

Figure 11.4 Real time traffic introduced at regular intervals.

sample audio application. The application, which happens to rely on the unsophisticated pulse code modulation (PCM) encoding, generates 160 bytes of data every 20 milliseconds. As the figure indicates, the Mac introduces the traffic into the network at the same regular rate.

TCP/IP-based networks do not preserve the time relationship between messages. Figure 11.5 shows what might happen when this audio data reaches a destination. The messages arrive at irregular intervals. They may also arrive out of order, and some may not even arrive at all.

Before the PC can play out the audio smoothly, it must reconstruct the timing of the original data. Since the network cannot do that, the job falls to the application. Real time applications rely on timestamps for this reconstruction. The data's source marks each message with a relative timestamp that indicates when the event occurred. The receiver can then play back the data in the same relative time. Since timestamps are common for nearly all real time applications, they are part of the RTP framework. If an

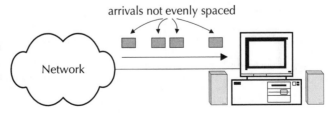

Figure 11.5 Data arrives at irregular intervals.

application needs more sophisticated timing information, that information must be part of its payload format.

Multicast Operation

Although the previous example includes only a single source and one destination, RTP focuses on audio and video conferences. Conferences usually include many participants, so RTP is designed for multicast operation. In fact, it relies on multicast not only for the real time traffic itself, but also for the control traffic associated with a session.

Figure 11.6 shows a video conference taking place on a network. For this example, consider the video data that the left workstation generates. Obviously, all the other workstations want to receive the data, so the left workstation's RTP application transmits the traffic to a multicast destination. All parties to the conference belong to that multicast group.

This use of multicast delivery should not seem surprising at all. What may be surprising, though, is that multicast datagrams also carry the feedback that the recipients report to the sender. Figure 11.7 illustrates this aspect of the conference, showing how the top workstation's feed-

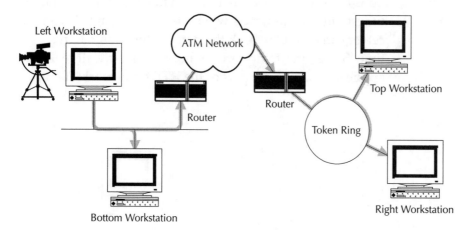

Figure 11.6 Video conference distributes data using multicast.

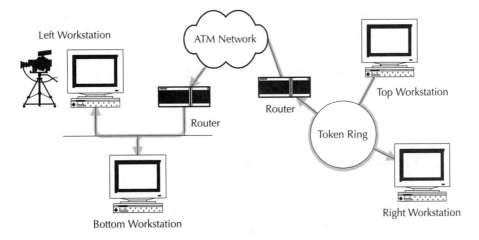

Figure 11.7 Feedback from receiver also travels via multicast.

back is actually delivered to all conference participants. Feedback is not delivered only to the sender.

This approach may seem like a waste of network bandwidth, but it actually has three significant advantages. First, it lets conferencing applications scale from a few to a great many participants. The key is that all systems hear each other's feedback. That means that they know how much total bandwidth the feedback is consuming, and they have some idea of the load that the total feedback presents to the sender. When the conference has many participants, that bandwidth and load could be considerable. Since all receivers know the load, however, they can slow down the rate at which they generate feedback, reducing the load to a manageable level.

Another advantage to multicasting feedback is that systems other than the sender can hear it. A network provider, for example, may decide to monitor the quality of a conference taking place on its network. Since the feedback information is multicast, the provider can listen to it simply by joining the multicast group.

A final reason for multicast feedback is human nature. With this approach, each participant knows how well every other participant is receiving the conference. When users experience poor reception, they have the information to readily answer the natural question "Is it just me, or is everyone else having problems too?" Experiments with real users have unequivocally demonstrated the value of this information.

Translators and Mixers

The obvious roles in a real time transmission are those of the sender and the recipient. All successful communication requires at least one of each. RTP defines two roles in addition to these; systems using RTP may also act as *translators* or *mixers*. Neither translators nor mixers are required in every case, but sometimes they are the only way a network can support a real time application.

Both translators and mixers reside "in the middle" of the network. They lie between senders and recipients and process the RTP packets as they pass through. Of the two, translators are the most straightforward. As the name implies, they simply translate from one payload format to another. Figure 11.8 shows a network that can use a translator. In that example, the PC wants to participate in a

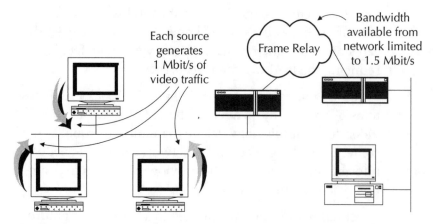

Each source generates 1 Mbit/s of video traffic

Frame Relay

Bandwidth available from network limited to 1.5 Mbit/s

Figure 11.8 Bandwidth requirements prohibit a PC from joining a video conference.

video conference with the workstations. Unfortunately, the workstations are using a high-quality video format that uses a lot of bandwidth, more bandwidth than the PC's frame relay connection has available.

To accommodate the PC, the workstations could revert to a different video format that required less bandwidth, but doing so would force the workstations' users to endure lower-quality video. Instead, the PC can rely on a translator. The translator accepts the video streams from each workstation and converts them to a different format. The new format provides lower-quality video, but it only needs 256 Kbit/s of bandwidth for each source. Now the conference can travel across the frame relay network, and the PC can participate. Figure 11.9 shows the translator's role in the conference.

Mixers perform a service similar to that of translators, but there is an important difference. Instead of translating individual source streams to a different format, mixers combine multiple source streams into one, preserving the original format. This approach can be particularly effective for audio data.

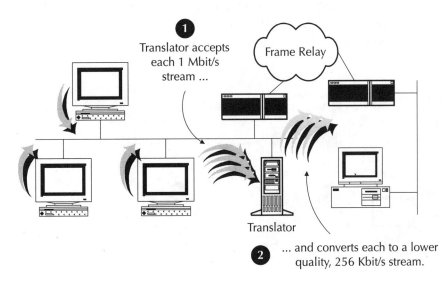

Figure 11.9 Translator lowers the bandwidth each source requires.

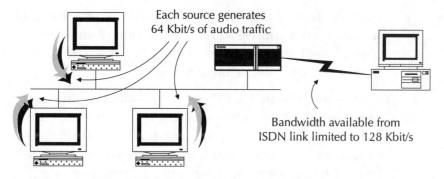

Figure 11.10 Bandwidth requirements prohibit a PC from joining an audio conference.

Figure 11.10 presents a scenario very much like Figure 11.8, but here, the application is an audio conference. Once again, the PC wants to join the conference, but the intervening link does not have enough bandwidth to carry each workstation's traffic. However, when the conference adds a mixer (as in Figure 11.11), the PC can participate. Instead of lowering the quality of each audio stream, the mixer combines all three of the workstation's streams into one. If the audio format is simple pulse code modulation (PCM) data, for example, the mixer can arithmetically sum the values from each source into a single data stream. In effect, the mixer replaces three microphones on three separate speakers with a single microphone in the same virtual

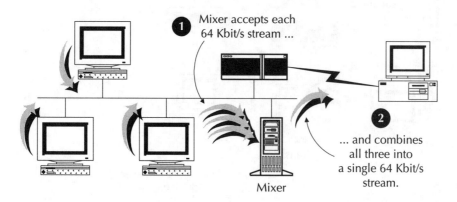

Figure 11.11 Mixer lowers bandwidth requirements of overall conference.

room as all three speakers. The resulting 64 Kbit/s stream has the same high quality as the original streams, but the traffic is now a single stream rather than three. Its bandwidth requirements are low enough to travel across the ISDN link to the PC.

Of course, not all applications can support the operation of a mixer. Multiple video sources, for example, cannot normally be combined into one. The approach does work quite well for audio conferences, particularly conferences with many participants.

RTP Message Format

RTP uses the same format for all of its messages. Because it supports application layer framing, this message format lends itself to various interpretations and for additions that particular applications may need. Figure 11.12 shows a basic RTP message, in this case contained in a UDP datagram. But note that RTP is not tied specifically to UDP; other transport protocols can carry RTP messages as well.

RTP traffic does not have a well-known UDP port. Since hosts are expected to use RTP for many different applications, a single well-known port is not sufficient. RTP has designated port 5004 as a default port, though, for use if an application has no other port available. Regardless of the particular port value, the RTP specification requires that it be even. The value one greater than RTP's (5005 by default) carries traffic for the Real Time Control Protocol described in the next section.

As Figure 11.12 shows, RTP uses a very compact header format. This prevents RTP from adding a lot of overhead to the application's data. Since real time applications tend to need a lot of bandwidth, and many rely on small message sizes to reduce delay, a small header helps RTP transport those applications efficiently.

The first two bytes in the header contain six separate fields. The first two bits define the RTP version. The cur-

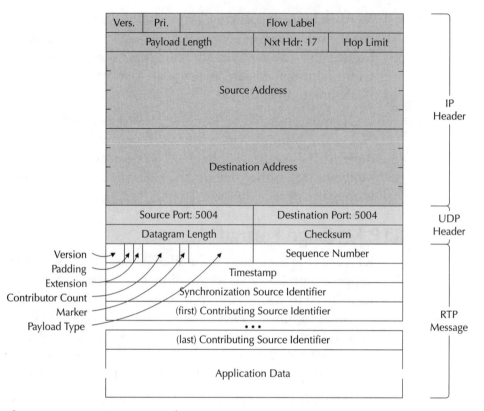

Figure 11.12 RTP message format.

rent version number is 1. The third bit indicates whether extra bytes have been added to pad the packet. If this bit has the value one, then the very last byte in the packet has a count of how many padding bytes have been added. Padding is most commonly needed for some encryption algorithms.

The *extension* bit is set if the message contains an extension header after the basic RTP header. So far, no extension headers have been defined. The next field, the *contributor count*, tells how many contributing source identifiers the message contains. Since this field is four bits in size, a message can have no more than 15 contributing sources. If a mixer must combine more sources, only 15 remain explicitly identified.

Table 11.1 RTP Payload Types

0	PCMU audio	16-22	unassigned audio
1	1016 audio	23	RGB8 video
2	G721 audio	24	HDCC video
3	GSM audio	25	CelB video
4	unassigned audio	26	JPEG video
5	DVI4 audio (8 KHz)	27	CUSM video
6	DVI4 audio (16 KHz)	28	nv video
7	LPC audio	29	PicW video
8	PCMA audio	30	CPV video
9	G722 audio	31	H261 video
10	L16 audio (stereo)	32	MPV video
11	L16 audio (mono)	33	MP2T video
12	TPS0 audio	34-71	unassigned video
13	VSC audio	72-76	reserved
14	MPA audio	77-95	unassigned
15	G728 audio	96-127	dynamic

The *marker* bit is available to the application. Typically, applications use it to mark boundaries in their data. The final seven bits of these first two bytes determine the *payload type* for the message. Table 11.1 lists the RTP payload types defined so far.

The *synchronization source identifier*, abbreviated SSRC, identifies the original sender of the message. This is the system that defines the sequence number and timestamp for the data. As Figure 11.13 shows, translators preserve this value in messages they translate. Mixers, on the other hand, resynchronize data from many sources. The mixer itself becomes the synchronizing source, and the original sources become *contributing sources* (CSRCs). Figure 11.14 illustrates the effects of a mixer.

When a source picks a source identifier, it picks a random value, and although the chance is not great, it is pos-

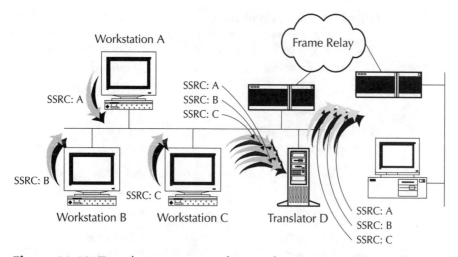

Figure 11.13 Translator preserves the synchronization source identifier.

sible that two different senders in the same conference could pick the same identifier. If that happens, the RTP protocol has the means to detect and resolve this conflict.

When a real application uses RTP, it associates its own meaning to the RTP header fields, and it may add its own application-specific header after the RTP header. As an example, Figure 11.15 shows how an H.261 video application builds its messages. The application also uses several fields in the basic RTP header. It sets the marker bit to one on the

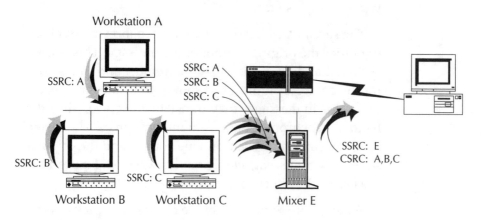

Figure 11.14 Mixer converts synchronization sources to contributing sources.

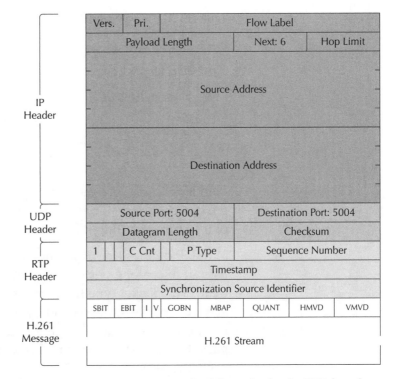

Vers.	Pri.				Flow Label		
Payload Length					Next: 6		Hop Limit
Source Address							
Destination Address							
Source Port: 5004				Destination Port: 5004			
Datagram Length				Checksum			
1			C Cnt	P Type	Sequence Number		
Timestamp							
Synchronization Source Identifier							
SBIT	EBIT	I	V	GOBN	MBAP	QUANT	HMVD	VMVD
H.261 Stream							

IP Header

UDP Header

RTP Header

H.261 Message

Figure 11.15 H.261 streams build on the basic RTP header.

last message of a video frame. In addition, H.261 specifies that the RTP timestamp is based on a 90 KHz clock.

Controlling Real Time Traffic

Sharp-eyed readers may have noticed that the RTP header does not have a field to distinguish different message types. Indeed, RTP supports only one type of message, those that carry application data. Although this may be adequate for primitive applications, many real time applications need feedback and other responses. RTP leaves those functions to a separate protocol, the real time control protocol (RTCP). In some ways, RTCP can be considered as an optional extension of RTP.

RTCP receives the technical designation as a separate protocol because its messages use a different UDP port

Table 11.2 RTCP Packet Types

200	Sender Report
201	Receiver Report
202	Source Description
203	Bye
204	Application Specific

than RTP traffic, but the two ports are as closely related as the protocols. The RTCP port value is one greater than that of the corresponding RTP traffic.

RTCP defines five different message types. Table 11.2 lists all five, along with the packet type values that identify them. The packet type field occurs in a consistent place in all RTCP packets (the second byte), but some of the surrounding fields take on different meanings with each packet type. For this reason, this section discusses each packet type separately.

Sender Reports

Figure 11.16 shows a sender report packet. Senders in a conference periodically transmit these packets to let the other participants know what they should have received. Like RTP packets, all RTCP packets begin with a 2-bit version field, which is set to 1. The padding bit follows. If this bit is set, then the packet contains extra padding added to its end. The very last byte in the message contains a count of the number of padding bytes.

The next five bits contain the receiver block count. This field indicates how many receiver blocks the packet contains. The second byte contains the packet type field. For sender reports, this field has the value 200.

The length field states the length of the packet in bytes. This length includes any added padding, as well as the message itself.

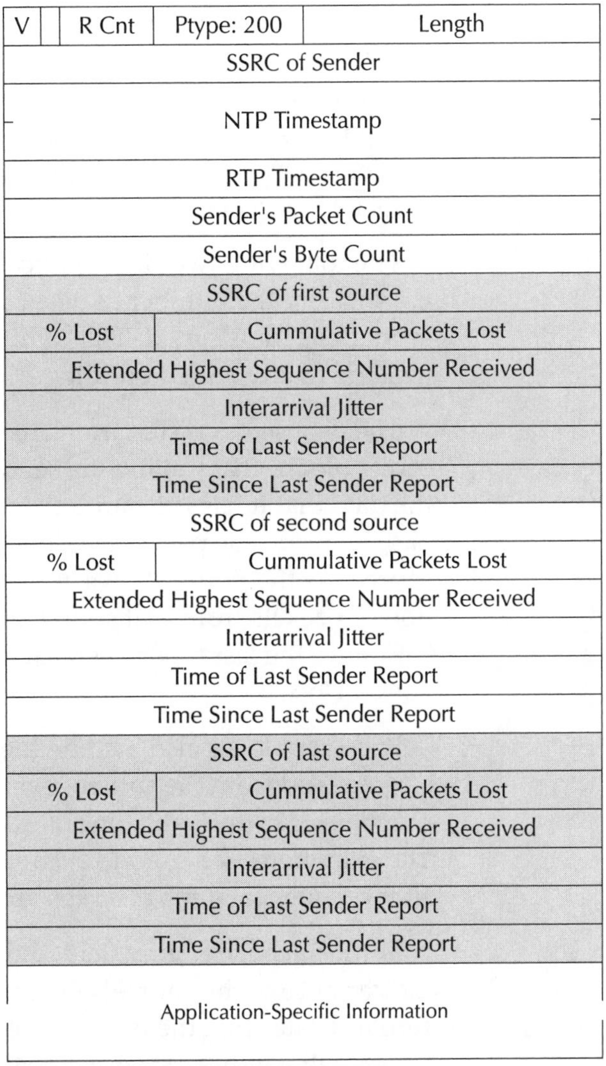

V		R Cnt	Ptype: 200	Length
SSRC of Sender			
NTP Timestamp			
RTP Timestamp			
Sender's Packet Count			
Sender's Byte Count			
SSRC of first source			
% Lost		Cummulative Packets Lost		
Extended Highest Sequence Number Received			
Interarrival Jitter			
Time of Last Sender Report			
Time Since Last Sender Report			
SSRC of second source			
% Lost		Cummulative Packets Lost		
Extended Highest Sequence Number Received			
Interarrival Jitter			
Time of Last Sender Report			
Time Since Last Sender Report			
SSRC of last source			
% Lost		Cummulative Packets Lost		
Extended Highest Sequence Number Received			
Interarrival Jitter			
Time of Last Sender Report			
Time Since Last Sender Report			
Application-Specific Information			

Figure 11.16 RTCP sender report.

The next four bytes contain the synchronization source identifier of the sender. This field ties the RTCP packet to any RTP data packets from the same source.

The next two fields contain timestamps. The first field defines the absolute time, using the same format as the Network Time Protocol (NTP). This format specifies the number of seconds since January 1, 1900, UTC. Unlike the RTP timestamp, this field specifies an actual time of day. The next field, an RTP timestamp, uses the same format as the sender's RTP data packets. It lets recipients place the sender report message in appropriate time order, relative to its RTP packets.

The following two fields indicate the number of RTP packets and the number of bytes of RTP data that the sender has transmitted. This byte count does not include headers or any added padding.

The next sections (Figure 11.16 includes three) are receiver blocks. They allow the sender to report not only on the data that it has transmitted, but also on the RTP data it has received. The packet uses one block for each remote source. As the figure shows, the block indicates the fraction of packets from that source that were lost (relative to 255) since the last report, as well as the total number of packets lost.

Receiver blocks also include the highest sequence number received from the source. Even though RTP sequence numbers are only 16 bits in size, this field is 32 bits long. The extra bytes are used to accumulate carries when the 16-bit sequence number wraps around from 0xFFFF to 0.

In the *interarrival jitter* field, the receiver block estimates the variance of the source's interarrival times. A jitter of zero indicates that the packets are arriving regularly, while a high value indicates a great deal of irregularity in those arrivals.

The last two fields tell when the last report from this source arrived. The first field gives the middle two bytes of the NTP timestamp in that report, and the second field indicates the delay, in units of 1/65536 seconds, between the reception of that report and the generation of this packet.

V		R Cnt	Ptype: 201	Length
SSRC of Sender				
SSRC of first source				
% Lost			Cummulative Packets Lost	
Extended Highest Sequence Number Received				
Interarrival Jitter				
Time of Last Sender Report				
Time Since Last Sender Report				
SSRC of second source				
% Lost			Cummulative Packets Lost	
Extended Highest Sequence Number Received				
Interarrival Jitter				
Time of Last Sender Report				
Time Since Last Sender Report				
SSRC of last source				
% Lost			Cummulative Packets Lost	
Extended Highest Sequence Number Received				
Interarrival Jitter				
Time of Last Sender Report				
Time Since Last Sender Report				
Application-Specific Information				

Figure 11.17 RTCP receiver report.

Receiver Reports

If a conference participant is not sending data itself, there is no need for it to generate sender report packets. Instead, RTCP allows it to transmit periodic receiver reports. As Figure 11.17 shows, receiver reports contain little more than a series of receiver blocks after the common RTCP header. These sections have the same format as the receiver blocks in sender reports, and they convey the same information.

Reporting Intervals

Sender and receiver reports provide important feedback to all participants in a real time conference. Without care, these messages can create a large bandwidth demand on the network. In the worst case, RTCP report packets load the network so heavily that it has trouble delivering the RTP data packets on time.

To prevent such a breakdown, RTCP has strict rules defining how often an application may send reports[2]. The rules contain two important principles. First, they keep the overall traffic requirements for RTCP packets roughly constant, regardless of how many systems participate in the conference. Since all RTCP is sent via multicast, every system can keep track of the number of other systems sending reports. As the total number of systems increases, the frequency of any particular system's reports decreases.

The second principle governing report generation is randomness. If all systems used the calculated interval to generate reports, they would likely synchronize with each other, and this synchronization places a heavy peak load on the network. To avoid it, RTCP requires that each sender randomize the calculated interval. Each sender ends up using an interval somewhere between half and one and a half times its nominal value.

Source Descriptions

The third type of RTCP packet is a source description (SDES). Sources use this packet to provide more information about themselves. Figure 11.18 shows its basic format, where the packet consists of a series of source identifiers (synchronization or contributing) and description items for each. The SDES items follow a common format. They begin with a single byte that identifies the particular item, followed by another byte that defines the length of the

---

[2] The latest draft specification actually includes complete C-language source code for calculating the interval between reports.

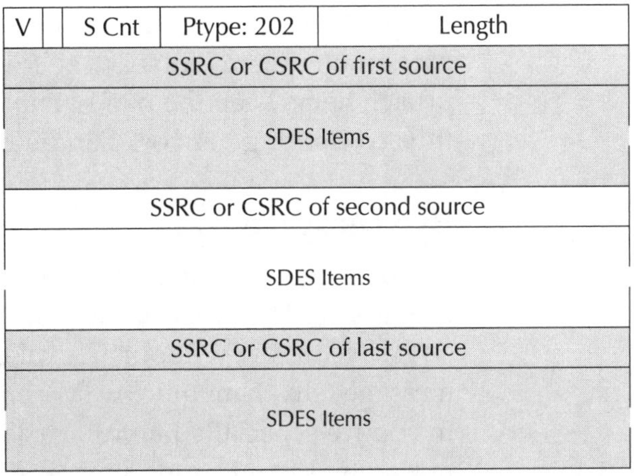

V		S Cnt	Ptype: 202	Length
			SSRC or CSRC of first source	
			SDES Items	
			SSRC or CSRC of second source	
			SDES Items	
			SSRC or CSRC of last source	
			SDES Items	

Figure 11.18 RTCP source description packet.

item. The information itself concludes the item. The length byte only counts the information. If a particular item ends up short of a 32-bit boundary in the packet, the sender inserts padding bytes before the next item.

Table 11.3 lists the items defined so far. Individual applications are free to use their own items as well. Sources generate SDES packets periodically, just as they do reports. Every SDES packet need not contain the same items, although some items—the canonical name for example—are crucial in establishing the identity of the source, and they should be included in every SDES message. (See Table

Table 11.3 Source Description Items

1	CNAME	unique and unambiguous name for the source
2	NAME	real user name of the source
3	EMAIL	email address
4	PHONE	telephone number
5	LOC	geographic location
6	TOOL	name of application generating the stream
7	NOTE	note about the source
8	PRIV	private extensions

11.3.) Other items are less critical, and sources can alternate among them with each successive SDES. This approach helps keep the packets no larger than necessary, thus conserving network bandwidth.

Bye Messages

Bye messages let a source announce that it is leaving the conference. The other participants would detect this absence eventually without an explicit message, but the bye message tells them quickly. Mixers, in particular, may find the notice especially helpful. As Figure 11.19 shows, the message format is quite simple. After the list of sources that are terminating, the packet includes space for an optional *reason for leaving*.

Application-Specific Messages

The final type of RTCP message is reserved for application-specific features. It is mainly intended as an easy way for applications to experiment with new kinds of messages. If a particular application-specific message proves to be useful, it may be converted into a full RTCP packet, with its own official packet type.

Combining RTCP Messages

Each RTCP message contains an explicit length indication, therefore, multiple RTCP messages may be packed to-

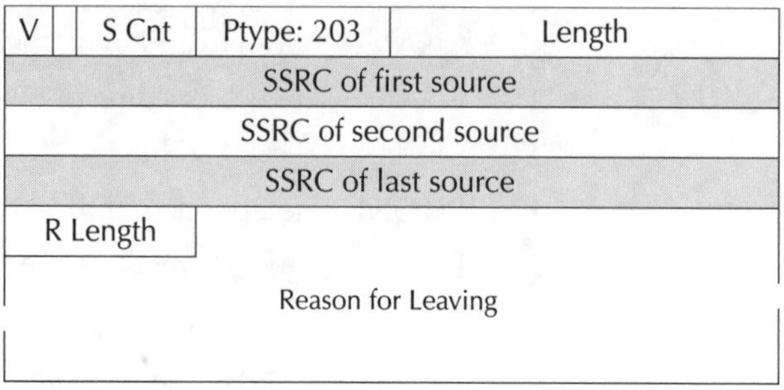

Figure 11.19 RTCP bye message.

Table 11.4 Creating Compound RTCP Packets

- All RTCP messages should be sent in a compound packet consisting of at least two separate messages.

- Statistics should be distributed as frequently as possible, therefore each compound packet should begin with a sender or receiver report.

- If there are more receiver blocks than will fit in a single report message, additional receiver reports should follow.

- Every compound packet should then include a source description containing, at a minimum, the canonical name; other items may be included as necessary.

- Bye messages should be the last message to reference a particular source identifier.

gether in a single UDP datagram. The RTP standard suggests using the guidelines listed in Table 11.4 for creating such a *compound packet*.

Summary

The real time protocol and its companion, the real time control protocol, give engineers a means to create real time, multiparticipant applications. Although designed primarily for audio and video conferences, these protocols may serve many uses, including distributed simulation modeling or real time control and measurement.

To achieve the best performance, RTP and RTCP rely on application layer framing. This approach relaxes the boundaries between protocol layers. The RTP and RTCP specifications combine with a specific payload format to define a complete protocol.

The real time protocols have a strong multicast orientation. This design reflects their primary environment, audio and video conferencing. In such an application, feedback and response messages rely on multicast delivery, as well as the data messages themselves.

RTP and RTCP define two special roles that systems may play in a conference. Translators convert between different payload formats, changing a high-quality stream into one that requires less bandwidth, for example. Mixers can achieve the same result, but they do so by combining several streams into one, without sacrificing quality.

CHAPTER

12

Reserving Resources for Real Time Traffic with RSVP

The Real Time Protocol of Chapter 11 can carry real time traffic across a TCP/IP network. Real time traffic usually has tight time constraints, and must reach its destination within a certain time period. On its own, RTP is at the mercy of the Internet Protocol's delivery service, and IP is an unreliable protocol, as it only makes a *best effort* to deliver data.

Some real time applications can accommodate unreliable delivery. They perform their own reordering and, if necessary, disregard or approximate any missing data. Other applications require more from the network. To ensure that networks serve their needs, these applications reserve network resources. Once reserved, these resources are dedicated to the application.

The Resource Reservation Protocol (RSVP) offers applications just such a reservation service. It defines how applications can place reservations, and how they can relinquish those resources once their need ends. This chapter examines RSVP, beginning with a closer look at resource reservation. It continues by discussing RSVP's operation, and it concludes with a description of the RSVP message format.

Resource Reservation

Even though IP offers only unreliable delivery, in many cases the underlying network technologies can provide suitable performance guarantees. And even when the guarantees cannot be absolute, such as with Ethernet LANs, they may be of high enough probability that applications can still function adequately.

If the networks themselves can provide suitable performance, success or failure of the application rests with IP. Consider the example of Figure 12.1, in which a real time video stream traverses a network. To keep the video acceptably smooth, the client must display 30 frames per second. That is the rate at which the server transmits the data. To prevent the client from falling behind, the network must deliver 30 frames per second to the destination. If each video frame contains about 1 million bits of data, then the application requires 31 Mbit/s of network bandwidth. (Fortunately, actual digital video traffic does not require nearly this much bandwidth.)

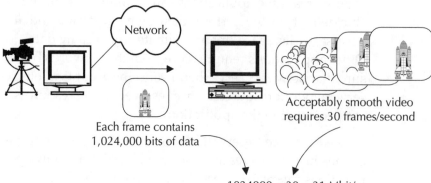

Figure 12.1 Bandwidth requirements of a real time video application.

Now consider the task facing a router inside the network. That router must support the real time video traffic flow, as well as other traffic on the network. Suppose, as Figure 12.2 illustrates, a separate file transfer is temporarily peaking at 30 Mbit/s. If the intervening network is a low-speed ATM network with an access rate of 51 Mbit/s, then the router cannot support both traffic flows at full speed. Their combined bandwidth requirement exceeds what the link can provide.

The router might try to share the limited resource (the ATM link) evenly between the two flows. The video flow might receive 26 Mbit/s of bandwidth, and the file transfer 25 Mbit/s. Of course, that allocation would be fine for the file transfer, but unacceptable to the real time video. It would be better if the router maintained the video transfer rate of 31 Mbit/s by limiting the file transfer to 20 Mbit/s. That allocation would satisfy both applications. The file transfer might take a little bit longer, but it would still succeed. More important, the real time video would continue to receive the bandwidth it requires.

Many routers are capable of making the "right" allocation of bandwidth, but they have to know what that allocation is. That is where resource reservation comes in.

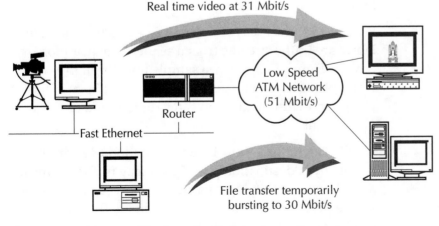

Figure 12.2 More traffic than the link can transfer.

With resource reservation, an application gives advance notice of the network resources that it requires. The video transfer, for example, could reserve 31 Mbit/s of network bandwidth. By granting the reservation, the affected hosts and routers commit to providing those resources. If, in the example, the router knows the video flow's requirements, it could limit the file transfer to 20 Mbit/s.

Resource reservation can also indicate when the necessary resources are not available. Suppose, for example, that the real time video required 62 Mbit/s of bandwidth. The network, with its 51 Mbit/s ATM link, clearly cannot support that requirement. When the video application attempted to reserve the resources it needs, the routers would have the chance to refuse the reservation. The application finds out right away that the network cannot support it; it does not have to resort to a costly trial and error approach.

RSVP Operation

RSVP is the protocol that allows applications to reserve network resources. It relies on two key concepts, flows and reservations. This section looks at how RSVP uses each.

Flows

When RSVP reserves resources, it reserves them for a *flow*. Flows are traffic streams from a sender to one or more receivers. Figure 12.3 shows a sample flow through a network. Datagrams belonging to the flow originate at the video server, travel through three routers, and arrive at the video client.

RSVP identifies a flow by its destination IP address and, optionally, a destination port. RSVP may further refine its definition by specifying a particular source IP address or source port, or by the *flow label* field in the IP basic header, together with the source address.

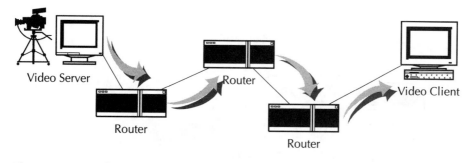

Figure 12.3 A flow traversing a network.

Along with the traffic that makes up a flow, RSVP identifies the particular quality of service that the flow requires. This quality of service determines the network resources the flow requires. RSVP itself does not actually understand this *flowspec*, as it is known; it simply passes it from the application to hosts and routers along the flow's path. Those systems can examine the flowspec to see if they can accept the reservation, and once accepted, they use the flowspec to actually reserve the required resources.

RSVP supports both unicast and multicast flows. A unicast flow has a single receiver, while a multicast flow may have many receivers. RSVP provides the same services to both flow types.

Reservations

Unlike other resource reservation protocols, RSVP expects traffic receivers to make the actual reservations. At first, this approach may seem backward. After all, the system that generates the traffic ought to know more about the resources its traffic requires; indeed, in the simplest cases, this is often true. RSVP, however, supports more than the simplest cases. Having receivers make the reservations gives the protocol greater flexibility for handling multicast flows, particularly those that are diverse or dynamic.

Figure 12.4 presents a situation that benefits from the flexibility of receiver-initiated reservations. In the figure,

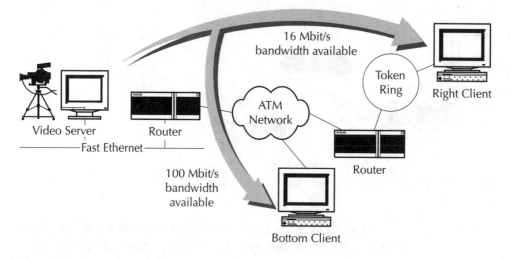

Figure 12.4 Multicast flow with different service for different destinations.

the server sends a flow to a multicast destination. Two clients belong to that multicast group, and they reside at different places in the network. The bottom client has a fast Ethernet and an ATM network between it and the server. The slowest link on that path is the Ethernet LAN, so throughput is limited to 100 Mbit/s. The right client, on the other hand, has a Token Ring LAN in its path. This link limits the throughput to 16 Mbit/s.

If the standard video stream requires 31 Mbit/s of bandwidth, then the right client is not on a fast enough path to receive the flow. Some video encoding methods can sacrifice quality for bandwidth. As a simple example, the right client might find that processing only 15 frames per second still provided adequate video quality, and that rate requires only 15 Mbit/s of bandwidth. It could achieve that by accepting only every other video frame.

This approach suggests that the two clients might need different resources reserved for the flow. The bottom client uses the full 31 Mbit/s, while the right client makes do with 15 Mbit/s. If the server were the system making the reservation, it would have to know the characteristics of all possible receivers, and structure its reservation accordingly. When the receivers reserve resources, things are much simpler. Each receiver need only understand its own capabilities and requirements.

Receiver-based registrations also easily support a dynamic environment. New receivers can join the flow, and existing ones can drop out, all without bothering the sender.

There are two complications with RSVP's receiver orientation. One question is how does a receiver know to make a reservation in the first place. In most cases, RSVP expects the application to handle this problem. Typically, applications announce the flow, either in advance, periodically during the flow's lifetime, or both. Even though they may go to the same destination, the announcements themselves should not require reserved resources. They are not time-critical, and can travel without RSVP's assistance.

Path Messages

A trickier problem is how the receiver knows which path the flow will take. Receivers must know this so they can reserve the appropriate resources. Suppose, for example, that the video clients know of an upcoming video broadcast for which they must reserve resources. They know the source of the broadcast, but they are not aware of the path that the broadcast will take.

At first glance, the dilemma may seem silly. After all, the path from the server to any client would seem to be just the reverse of the path from that client to the server. Figure 12.5 shows an example of why this reasoning can be wrong. There, a network has two parallel wide area network technologies. All of the network's routers are connected via satellite and frame relay. The satellite links suffer a long delay, and so they are not ideal for most traffic. In general, the routers prefer to use the frame relay network. But satellite transmission is inherently a broad-

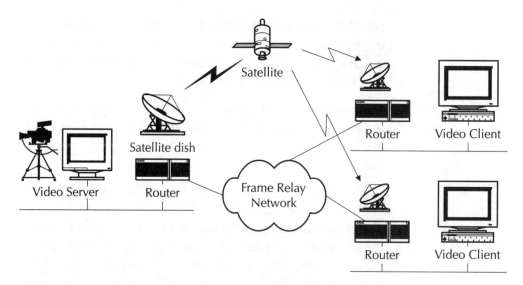

Figure 12.5 Multicast videos travel via satellite while return traffic uses frame relay.

cast medium, and the satellite is a very cost-effective way to distribute multicast traffic. For multicast video traffic, therefore, the routers will employ satellite instead of frame relay.

The problem with receiver reservations is evident from this example. If the clients simply send reservation messages to the server, those messages will travel across the frame relay network. In this case, however, there is no reason to reserve resources along that path.

To make sure that resources are reserved along the correct path, RSVP uses special *path* messages. Unlike reservation requests, path messages are generated by a flow's sender, and they travel in the same direction as the flow itself.

A path message primes the routers in the flow. It identifies the flow and tells the routers to expect reservation requests. To ensure that the path message follows the same path as the flow itself, it is sent to the same destination address as the flow. At each hop, the router inserts its own IP address as the message's last hop.

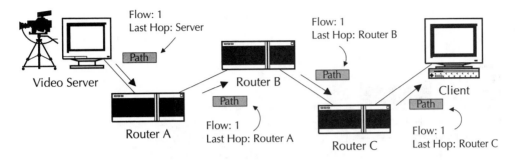

Figure 12.6 Path message travels through network.

As the message travels through the network, each router can look at the last hop field to learn where the flow came from. Should it later receive a reservation request for the flow, this last hop information tells it where to send the reservation request next. Figure 12.6 shows a path message as it winds its way through a network.

Since path messages start at the flow's source and precede reservation messages, they give the sender an opportunity to describe the flow to its receivers. If that is a complex undertaking, RSVP expects the sender to perform it separately. If, on the other hand, it takes only a few bytes to describe the flow, RSVP accommodates senders by providing room in the path messages. In the future, routers may also add their own information to path messages. Routers might give the receivers some idea of the resources available on the path, for example. This information could help the receivers construct reservation requests more appropriately.

Merging Reservation Requests

When a flow has a multicast destination, different destination systems may require different reserved resources. Refer back to Figure 12.4 for an example of this situation. When it arises, intermediate routers may be asked to merge multiple reservation requests for the same flow. Figure 12.7 shows this process.

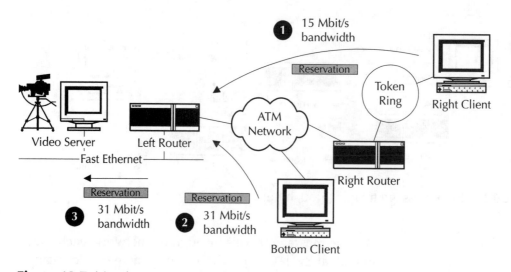

Figure 12.7 Merging two reservation requests.

In the figure, the left router receives two reservation requests for the flow. The first request requires only 15 Mbit/s of network bandwidth. (Recall that the right client has reduced its requirements because of the capabilities of the intervening Token Ring LAN.) The second request, from the bottom client, asks for 31 Mbit/s of network bandwidth. The router must combine these requests intelligently before forwarding a further request toward the video server. In this case, the intelligent way to combine the requests is to take the maximum of the two. The router does this in step 3 of the figure. Different resources may require different treatment. If the reservation specified a required delay, for example, the router would take the minimum of multiple requests. Other resources might require the summation of their values.

Reservation Styles

So far, this chapter has described an effective, though somewhat limited, style of reservation, which requires receivers to explicitly reserve resources for each flow they can accept. RSVP actually provides more flexibility than this limited approach, by defining different *reservation*

Table 12.1 RSVP Reservation Styles

FF	Fixed Filter	Reserve resources for one particular flow.
SE	Shared Explicit	Reserve resources for several specific flows at once, allowing those different flows to share the reserved resources.
WF	Wildcard Filter	Reserve resources for a general type of flow, without specifying the flows precisely; all flows of this type share the reserved resources.

styles. Table 12.1 lists the styles defined by the current protocol specifications. RSVP anticipates that its designers will add more styles in future revisions.

All the previous examples assumed the straightforward, fixed filter style where each flow needs its own reservation. Figure 12.8 shows an example that benefits from a different reservation style. In it, five personal computers are participating in an audio conference. All but one of the PCs resides on the same Ethernet LAN. That fifth PC re-

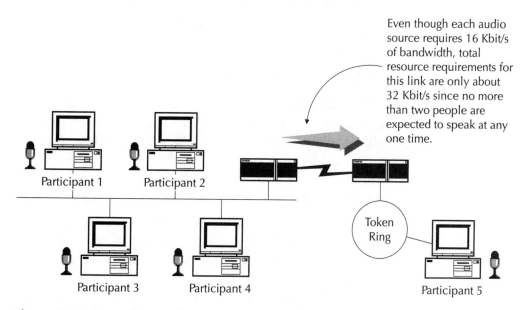

Even though each audio source requires 16 Kbit/s of bandwidth, total resource requirements for this link are only about 32 Kbit/s since no more than two people are expected to speak at any one time.

Participant 1   Participant 2   Participant 3   Participant 4   Participant 5   Token Ring

Figure 12.8 An audio conference can make use of various reservation styles.

quires two routers and a point-to-point link to connect it with the other participants. The example concentrates on the link between the two routers, and it focuses on traffic flowing from the Ethernet to the Token Ring.

Since there are four PCs on the Ethernet side of the link, there will be four separate flows that cross it. If fixed filter reservations were in use, separate reservations would be needed for each flow. Assuming that an audio transmission requires 16 Kbit/s of bandwidth, these reservations would consume 64 Kbit/s of the link's resources.

Audio conferences have a special property, however. Not everyone speaks at once (or, if they do, understanding is lost anyway, so it makes little sense for the network to function properly under that load). In the most polite conferences, all the application really needs is 16 Kbit/s of bandwidth. More realistically, it would be preferable to reserve about 32 Kbit/s of bandwidth so that some extra bandwidth is available to handle momentary outbursts.

To reserve this bandwidth, the application can have RSVP make either shared explicit or wildcard filter reservations. Each of these styles reserves a network resource (in this case, 32 Kbit/s of bandwidth), but shares that resource among multiple flows. The four flows sharing the bandwidth are the transmissions from the four PCs.

The difference between the two styles is how tightly the application must specify the flows that share the resource. With a shared explicit reservation, the application must explicitly identify every participating sender. In the example of Figure 12.8, the right PC would have to explicitly list the source addresses of participants 1 through 4.

The wildcard filter style lets an application share a resource without identifying every sender. Any flow that matches the reservations specification may use the resource, regardless of its sender. The right PC, for example, could reserve the resources for any traffic that has a destination port of 5004. Such a reservation assumes that no other traffic will use the same port, either accidentally or deliberately. Wildcard filters offer convenience in exchange for control and security.

RSVP and Dynamic Networks

In some ways, reserving network resources seems to conflict with the very nature of TCP/IP. The TCP/IP protocols—IP in particular—are designed for dynamic networks. What good is a reservation when one of its supporting routers fails? And how does RSVP adapt when a new, more efficient route suddenly becomes available?

RSVP copes with these events by relying on *soft state* in the network's routers. RSVP uses this term because both its paths and its reservations are always considered tentative. When a router accepts a reservation, it says, in effect, "I'll reserve these resources for you for now, but I won't hold them for you forever; if you intend to keep using them, you have to keep telling me."

Indeed, this is exactly how RSVP operates. A sender does not send a path message only when it starts a transmission. Instead, it continues to send path messages for the life of the flow. If the network experiences no changes, these subsequent path messages will merely refresh the existing path. If a new route appears, the path messages will introduce the flow to routers on that new path. Reservations work the same way. Receivers periodically send reservation requests. These requests may refresh existing reservations, or they may let a new router know what is required of it.

The next four figures show how a new client can join a video multicast already in progress. As they illustrate, such an operation requires the services of several different TCP/IP protocols. Figure 12.9 shows the situation before the new client appears. Two clients are receiving the video. As the figure points out, the sender periodically generates new path messages, and the receivers periodically refresh their reservations.

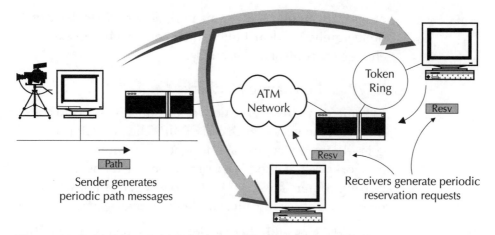

Figure 12.9 Multicast video before addition of new client.

In Figure 12.10 a new client wishes to receive the video. The client starts this process by joining the appropriate multicast group. To do this, it sends an ICMP Group Membership Report message on its local Ethernet (step 1). The router receives this message and updates its own record of what belongs to which group. To update the rest of

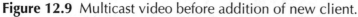

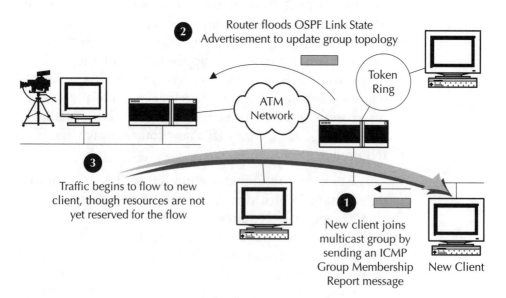

Figure 12.10 New client joins multicast group for video.

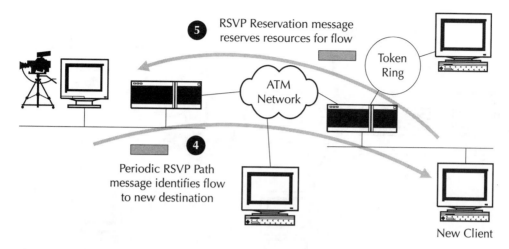

Figure 12.11 diagram labels:

⑤ RSVP Reservation message reserves resources for flow

Token Ring

ATM Network

④ Periodic RSVP Path message identifies flow to new destination

New Client

Figure 12.11 RSVP establishes resources for new client.

the network, the router builds an OSPF Link State Advertisement and floods it through the network (step 2). Once all the routers are updated, multicast traffic begins to flow to the new client (step 3). So far, no reservations have been placed. Without reserved resources, the traffic flow may not be suitable for the video transmission.

RSVP gets involved in Figure 12.11. Now that multicast traffic reaches the new client, path messages for the flow can reach it as well. In step 4, a periodic path message from the sender does reach the new client. With this path message in hand, the client can identify the flow and place its own reservations (step 5).

Figure 12.12 shows the results of this reservation. The video transmission continues with all three clients participating, each with the required resources reserved. The server continues its periodic path messages, and now all three clients periodically refresh their reservations.

RSVP Message Formats

As a control protocol like ICMP, RSVP places its messages in the payload of IP datagrams. The IP next header value

Figure 12.12 Flow continues to all three clients.

for RSVP is 46. RSVP messages may also be carried in UDP datagrams, but that option was designed to support older IPv4 systems that could not easily carry new protocols directly in IP datagrams; that limitation should not exist for IPv6 systems.

Each RSVP message begins with a common RSVP header. As Figure 12.13 shows, that header contains eight defined fields, plus two reserved areas. The RSVP message begins with a version number. The current version of RSVP is 2. The next four bits, labeled *flags*, are available for future extensions to the protocol; no values are currently defined.

The *RSVP type* byte identifies the particular type of RSVP message. This chapter has discussed two message types, path messages and reservation messages. In addition, RSVP defines error messages in response to these primary messages, and it defines messages to explicitly terminate a path or reservation. Table 12.2 lists the values that the type byte may take.

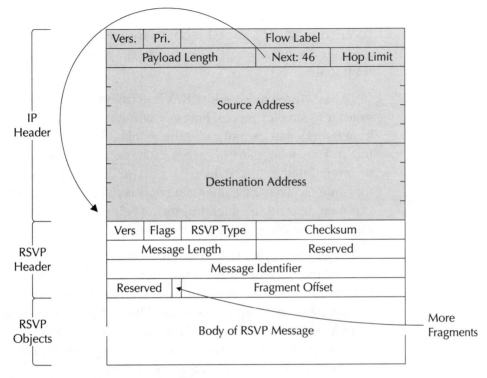

Figure 12.13 RSVP message format.

The next two fields in the RSVP header are fairly straightforward. The *checksum* contains the standard TCP/IP ones complement checksum of the entire message. It protects against the message being corrupted in transit.

Table 12.2 RSVP Message Types

1	path message
2	reservation message
3	error indication in response to path message
4	error indication in response to reservation message
5	path teardown message
6	reservation teardown message

The following two bytes contain the length of the whole RSVP message. If a packet is only a fragment of a complete message, then the length field counts only the size of the fragment.

The last three fields allow RSVP to fragment its messages into smaller pieces. Fragmentation may be necessary in networks that cannot carry the whole RSVP message intact. The *message identifier* tags each piece of the original, unfragmented message. Every fragment of a particular message receives the same value in this field. The recipient can then determine which fragments belong to which message, reassembling them appropriately.

The *fragment offset* field tells the receiver where in the original message the current fragment fits. It is measured in bytes. An offset of zero, for example, identifies the very beginning of the original message. The *more fragments* field completes the RSVP header. This bit is set to one on every fragment but the final one. The receiver uses this information to locate the end of a fragmented message.

The remainder of every RSVP message consists of a series of objects. These objects are Figure 12.13's message body. Each object has the same basic format, shown in Figure 12.14. The object length indicates the size of the object, while the class number and class type distinguish different object types. RSVP currently defines 15 different types of objects. Table 12.3 lists their class numbers and defined class types.

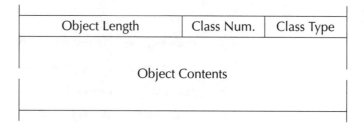

Object Length	Class Num.	Class Type
Object Contents		

Figure 12.14 Format of RSVP objects.

Table 12.3 RSVP Objects

Number	Object	Type	Description
0	NULL		ignored by recipient
1	SESSION	1	IPv4 session (destination of flow)
		2	IPv6 session (destination of flow)
3	RSVP_HOP	1	IPv4 previous or next hop address
		2	IPv6 previous or next hop address
4	INTEGRITY		keyed MD5 authentication data
5	TIME_VALUES	1	frequency of path or reservation refreshes
6	ERROR_SPEC	1	error information from an IPv4 system
		2	error information from an IPv6 system
7	SCOPE	1	list of IPv4 hosts to which wildcard style reservation refresh messages apply
		2	list of IPv6 hosts to which wildcard style reservation refresh messages apply
8	STYLE	1	style of reservation
9	FLOWSPEC	1	flow specification requiring controlled delay
		2	flow specification requiring predictive quality of service
		3	flow specification requiring guaranteed quality of service
		254	flow specification containing several, unmerged flows
10	FILTER_SPEC	1	IPv4-based filter to apply to flow
		2	IPv6-based filter using source port values
		3	IPv6-based filter using flow label values
11	SENDER_TEMPLATE	1	IPv4-based description of flow that sender is generating
		2	IPv6-based description of flow that sender is generating
12	SENDER_TSPEC	1	upper bound on traffic that sender will generate
13	ADSPEC		sender's advertised information for flow
14	POLICY_DATA	1	policy information for flow
		254	several unmerged policy data objects
20	TAG	1	collection of objects to be associated with a given name

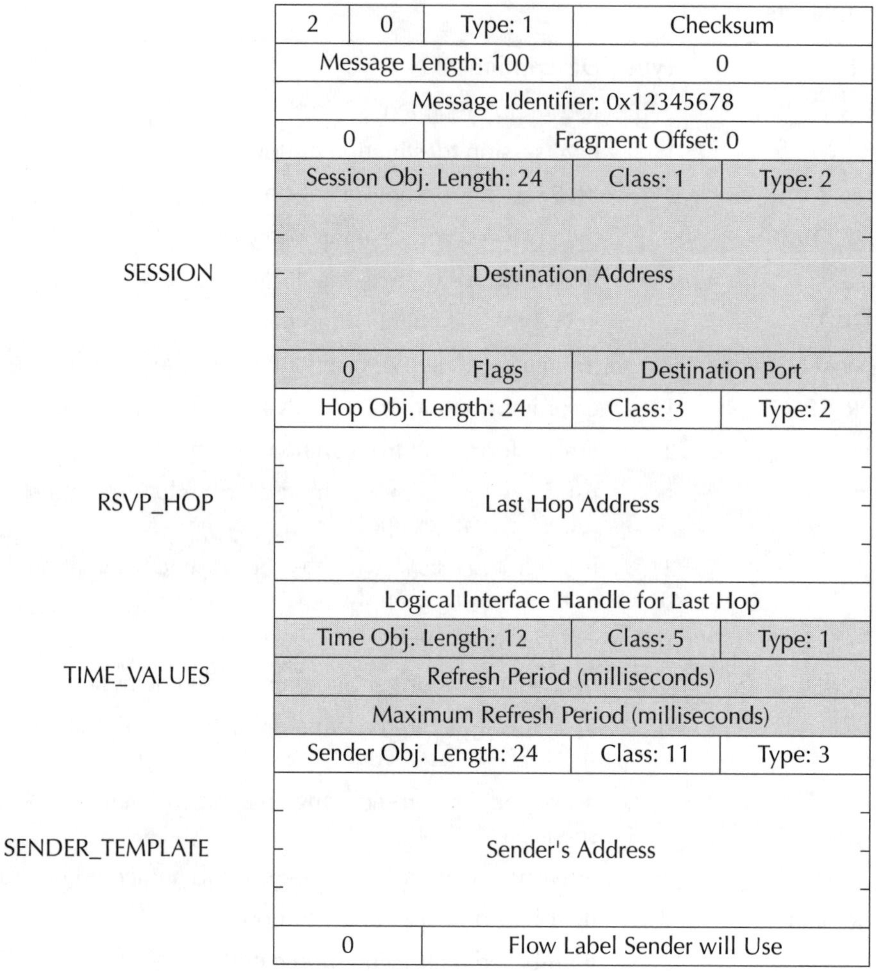

2	0	Type: 1	Checksum	
Message Length: 100			0	
Message Identifier: 0x12345678				
0		Fragment Offset: 0		
Session Obj. Length: 24		Class: 1	Type: 2	
Destination Address				
0	Flags	Destination Port		
Hop Obj. Length: 24		Class: 3	Type: 2	
Last Hop Address				
Logical Interface Handle for Last Hop				
Time Obj. Length: 12		Class: 5	Type: 1	
Refresh Period (milliseconds)				
Maximum Refresh Period (milliseconds)				
Sender Obj. Length: 24		Class: 11	Type: 3	
Sender's Address				
0		Flow Label Sender will Use		

Row labels at left: SESSION, RSVP_HOP, TIME_VALUES, SENDER_TEMPLATE

Figure 12.15 RSVP path message.

Path Messages

The RSVP specifications contain precise descriptions of path messages, including the objects that they may contain and the order in which those objects must appear in the message. This section considers a typical path message, shown in Figure 12.15.

Following the common RSVP header, the message contains four different objects, which identify the destination, the message's previous hop, the frequency at which it will be refreshed, and the flow itself. Most of the objects' values are straightforward and require no discussion. Some fields, on the other hand, are not as obvious. The SESSION object, for example, includes its own flags field. Currently, only the least significant bit of this field is defined. The source of a flow starts by setting this bit in its path messages. As the path message travels through the network, each system decides if it is capable of limiting the traffic for the flow. By limiting traffic, a router can make sure that the flow uses no more bandwidth than has been reserved for it. Exercising such a limit is known as *traffic policing*. The first system capable of traffic policing clears this bit, and the bit remains clear as the message travels to its destinations.

The RSVP_HOP object includes a *logical interface handle*. A router can set this field to help identify the flow. Any reservation requests from downstream systems will include this value.

The TIME_VALUES object announces the frequency at which the source will refresh path information. The first field tells how often the router will itself refresh the path. For example, if the refresh period is 100, then the router claims that it will send new path messages every 100 milliseconds. The second field allows subsequent systems to refresh less often, but it specifies an upper limit. A value of 500 would allow downstream systems to go as long as 500 milliseconds between new path messages.

Path messages are addressed to the same destination as the flow itself. Unlike the data flow, though, routers along the path must examine the contents of each message. Figure 12.16 illustrates this process by showing a path message traversing a network. As the figure shows, the RSVP message acts much like an IP hop-by-hop extension header. Every router examines the message, inserting its own address in the RSVP_HOP field.

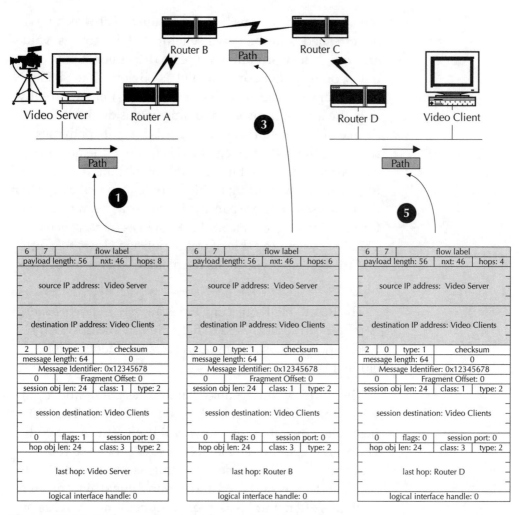

Figure 12.16 Path message travels across a network.

Path messages differ from IP extension headers in one important way. If the message travels through a router that does not understand RSVP, that router passes the message like any other traffic, oblivious to its contents. This behavior distinguishes path messages from true extension headers because routers must reject extension headers that they do not understand. When a router encounters an unknown hop-by-hop header, it must return an ICMP error message for the datagram.

RSVP achieves the same effect as an extension header—it provides information to routers along the path—without the extension header's inflexibility. Of course, a router that does not understand RSVP cannot reserve resources for the flow; neither will it block the flow, though. This approach makes it possible to introduce RSVP support into a network gracefully, without having to upgrade all routers at the same time.

Reservation Requests

Like path messages, reservation requests have a prescribed set of objects and order for those objects. They can get fairly complicated. Figure 12.17 presents a typical request with just a few important objects. The SESSION object describes the destination address and, optionally, the destination port of the flow being reserved. The RSVP_HOP object describes the last system to handle the reservation request. Since a reservation travels in the opposite direction of the flow itself, this object also identifies the system that will be the next hop for the flow.

The TIME_VALUES object serves the same purpose as in a path message. It tells how often the sender (of the reservation request) will refresh its reservation and how long other upstream systems may go before they refresh the reservation.

The next object, STYLE, as it name implies, indicates the reservation style. The three standard styles have their own style ID value (listed in Table 12.4), which is placed in the object's first byte. The *option vector* part of this object permits a more flexible style specification. The RSVP standard gives the rules for constructing it, but the standard styles of wildcard filter, fixed filter, and shared explicit filter, have option vectors of 17, 10, and 18, respectively.

The FLOWSPEC object carries the heart of the reservation request. It identifies the resources that the flow needs. RSVP itself does not interpret the object completely, but it

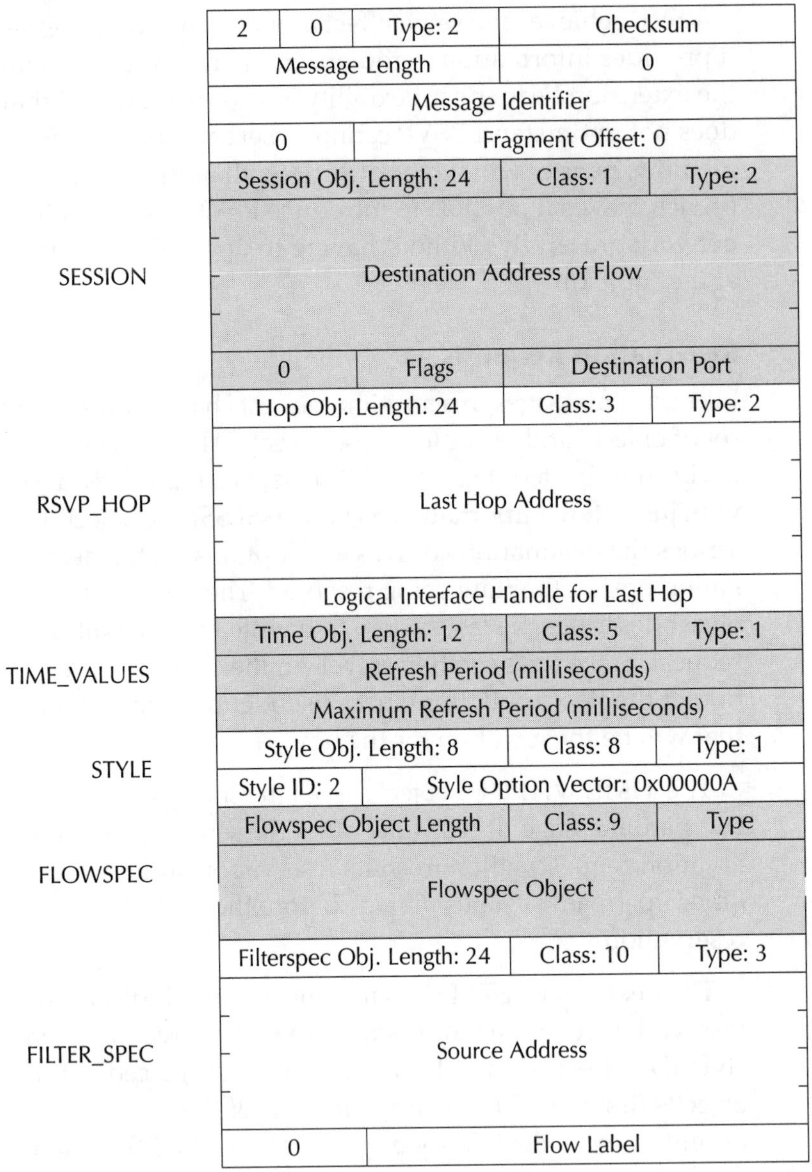

2	0	Type: 2	Checksum
Message Length		0	
Message Identifier			
0		Fragment Offset: 0	
Session Obj. Length: 24		Class: 1	Type: 2

SESSION

Destination Address of Flow

0	Flags	Destination Port
Hop Obj. Length: 24	Class: 3	Type: 2

RSVP_HOP

Last Hop Address

Logical Interface Handle for Last Hop

Time Obj. Length: 12	Class: 5	Type: 1

TIME_VALUES

Refresh Period (milliseconds)

Maximum Refresh Period (milliseconds)

STYLE

Style Obj. Length: 8	Class: 8	Type: 1
Style ID: 2	Style Option Vector: 0x00000A	
Flowspec Object Length	Class: 9	Type

FLOWSPEC

Flowspec Object

Filterspec Obj. Length: 24	Class: 10	Type: 3

FILTER_SPEC

Source Address

0	Flow Label

Figure 12.17 RSVP reservation request.

must understand it enough to merge reservations when appropriate; in general, it simply passes this value to that part of the router that actually reserves and assigns resources.

Table 12.4 Style ID Values

0	nonstandard style; use option vector
1	wildcard filter style
2	fixed filter style
3	shared explicit style

The final object, FILTER_SPEC, completes the description of the flow. In this example, it specifies a sending address and IP flow label.

Unlike path messages, reservation requests take a more conventional path through the network. At each stage, they use the destination address of the upstream system and the source address of the downstream system. Figure 12.18 shows the passage of a sample request through the network.

Error Messages

Both path messages and reservation requests may encounter errors. RSVP defines a separate error message for each. When an error is encountered, the error message usually follows the reverse path of the original message. This allows systems that previously accepted that message to release any resources they had reserved, assuming that the reservation would succeed.

In general, each error message includes enough objects to identify the message that caused the error. Path error messages contain SESSION and SENDER_TEMPLATE objects, while reservation error messages include SESSION, STYLE, FLOWSPEC, and FILTER_SPEC objects. Both types of messages also include an ERROR_SPEC object that indicates the error encountered. Figure 12.19 shows the format of this object.

The flags byte normally contains zero. The least significant bit can be set, however, in reservation error messages when the reservation in error has been merged, and it is

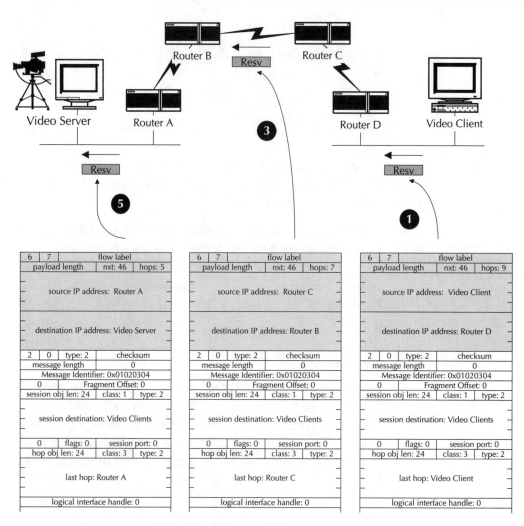

Figure 12.18 Reservation request traversing network.

Error Object Length: 24		Class: 6	Type: 2
Address of system that detected the error			
Flags	Error Code		Error Value

Figure 12.19 RSVP error object format.

not possible to determine which of the original reservations caused the error.

The error code and error value provide details of the problem encountered. The error code normally indicates a specific error, while the error value provides additional information. Table 12.5 lists the defined error codes. For those errors that indicate an unknown or missing object (code values 11 through 14), the error value contains the object class number and type that is unrecognized or missing.

The first two error codes, admission failure and administrative rejection, have a special format for the error value field, as shown in Figure 12.20. This format defines the severity of the error, and it provides more information on the error's cause. The most significant bit indicates the severity of the error. If it is set, the error is not fatal. The systems may continue to process the path message or reservation request that contained the error. Otherwise, the path or reservation is rejected.

Table 12.5 RSVP Error Codes

1	Admission failure, reservation could not be granted
2	Administrative rejection, reservation prohibited
3	No path information available for reservation
4	No sender for reservation
5	Ambiguous path
6	Ambiguous filter specification
7	Conflicting or unknown style
11	Missing required object
12	Unknown object class
13	Unknown object type
14	Object error
21	Traffic control error
22	RSVP system error

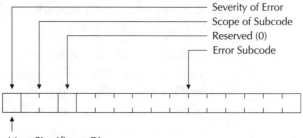

Figure 12.20 Error value format.

The next two most significant bits indicate the scope of the error value. If they are both zero, the error value contains a well-defined subcode. Otherwise, the error value subcode is local to the organization or the requested service. Tables 12.6 and 12.7 list the well-defined subcodes. The fourth most significant bit is currently reserved and always set to zero.

Teardown Messages

When a flow has concluded, the source and receivers can send RSVP messages to indicate that conclusion. A reservation teardown, sent by recipients of the flow, tells the network that the reserved resources are no longer needed. Like reservation messages, these packets are addressed hop by hop.

The path teardown, which the sender generates, allows systems to disregard any information they have been

Table 12.6 Error Subcodes for Admission Failure

1	delay bound cannot be met
2	requested bandwidth unavailable
11	service conflict
12	service unsupported
13	bad flow specification
14	maximum refresh period too small

Table 12.7 Error Subcodes for Administrative Rejection

1	required credentials not presented
2	request too large
3	insufficient quota or balance
4	administrative preemption

maintaining for the flow. These messages follow the same routing rules as path messages. They are directed to the destination address of the flow, and intervening routers must eavesdrop on the IP payload to detect and process them.

Summary

RSVP gives TCP/IP networks a feature they do not otherwise have—the ability to guarantee performance. Such a guarantee may be important to real time applications, as they must be assured that their traffic is delivered on time.

Real time traffic sources that require reserved resources periodically send path messages to all their recipients. Systems that receive path messages and wish to participate in the flow transmit reservation messages back toward the sender. These messages wind their way through the network, reserving resources as they go. RSVP also defines error messages that indicate failures, and teardown messages that systems use to relinquish resources.

13

Domain Name Service

To this point, this text has glossed over a major inconvenience of the TCP/IP protocols. All the protocols must identify systems, and TCP/IP identifies systems with IP addresses. The inconvenience of this identification is obvious: IP addresses are 16-byte, binary values. For humans, that often means 32 hexadecimal characters. Readers would doubtlessly pity any network user who had to deal with addresses like:

```
4E68:9F24:FFFF:1734:1592:0800:0219:7E14
```

all day. Even typing such an address is tedious and error-prone.

Fortunately, TCP/IP provides a solution to this problem. That solution is the Domain Name Service, or DNS. This service allows users to identify systems with simple, human-readable names. Protocols, which require IP addresses rather than names, use DNS to translate from one form to the other. But DNS provides more than a translation service. It also organizes names in a hierarchy. In fact, DNS probably uses hierarchies more than any other TCP/IP protocol. Not only are names hierarchical, but so are the servers that implement the protocol.

DNS itself is merely a communications protocol, one that happens to enforce a particular structure (a hierarchy) on the names it translates. Although this is a useful service, it alone does not account for the importance of DNS. What makes the Domain Name Service important is not really how it is used, but rather, what uses it. And for DNS, that "what" is the Internet.

A Hierarchy of Names

Figure 13.1 shows a small piece of the domain name hierarchy for the Internet. The figure highlights the tree-like structure of the hierarchy. At the top, it shows seven of the top-level domains of the Internet. Table 13.1 lists those domains and shows their organization. These domains serve to divide names into major functional categories.

In addition to the functional domains, the Internet supports, as top-level domain names, two-letter country codes. These divide names based on geographical location. For example, the Corporation for National Research Initiatives belongs to the hierarchy us (country: United States), va (state: Virginia), reston (city: Reston). The corporation's full name is nri.reston.va.us. This notation, separating individual levels with periods (.), is the customary way to write a full domain name.

Figure 13.1 shows how some of these top-level domains are further subdivided. The commercial domain includes traditional computer companies such as IBM, as well as companies like John Wiley & Sons, which serve other markets. The education domain contains the Georgia Institute of Technology, among others. Within the government do-

Table 13.1 Internet Functional Top-Level Domains

com	commercial organizations
edu	educational institutions
gov	U.S. government agencies
int	international entities
mil	U.S. military agencies
net	network providers
org	other organizations

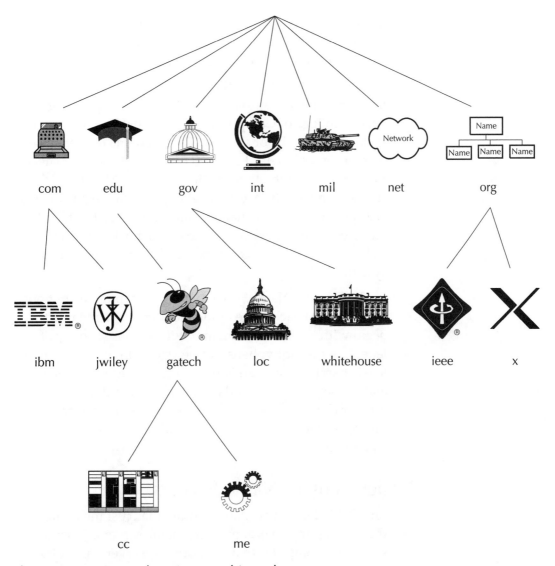

Figure 13.1 Internet domain name hierarchy.

main, the hierarchy recognizes the Library of Congress and the White House. Some of the organizations supported include the Institute of Electrical and Electronics Engineers and the X Consortium.

Each entity that uses its part of the Internet's name space can further subdivide as it feels appropriate. These divisions form their own subdomains. Georgia Tech, for example, may define separate subdomains for the College of Computing and the School of Mechanical Engineering.

This hierarchy allows the Internet to delegate authority for naming. For example, if an administrator at Georgia Tech's College of Computing wants to name a computer system burdell, he or she can. The full name of that system then becomes `burdell.cc.gatech.edu`. There is no need to coordinate with other entities such as IBM or the X Consortium. In fact, the Mechanical Engineering department at Georgia Tech can also name a machine burdell, safe in the knowledge that there will be no conflict between `burdell.me.gatech.edu` and the College of Computing's system.

The Domain Name Service does place some restrictions on names. At each stage of the hierarchy, a name must begin with an ASCII letter, and it must consist solely of letters, digits, or hyphens. Name size at any level is limited to 63 characters, and an entire name (including all levels and the separating periods) can be no more than 255 characters in length. Uppercase and lowercase names are indistinguishable, so `GATECH.EDU` and `gatech.edu` are equivalent.

A Hierarchy of Name Servers

The DNS hierarchy organizes more than just the names themselves. It also organizes the name servers. A name server is a computer that supports the server part of the DNS protocol. It translates names into IP addresses for its clients. Figure 13.2 shows how name servers form a hierarchy. At the top of the picture is the root server. In theory, it has responsibility for name translation for the entire Internet. As the figure shows, though, it has delegated some of that responsibility. It has two "child" servers, one each for the `edu` and `org` domains. This pattern continues further down the hierarchy, with servers for the `gatech.edu`, `cc.gatech.edu`, and other subdomains.

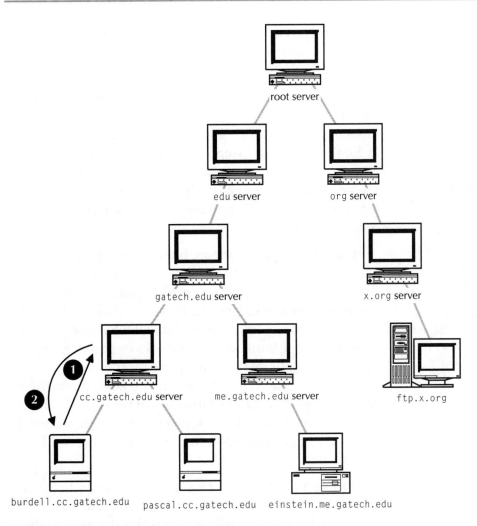

Figure 13.2 Single-level domain name query.

The area of responsibility given to a name server is known as its *zone*. Even though the figure shows a single zone for each level in the hierarchy, zones need not correspond directly to subdomains. Every subdomain is part of some zone, but zones can include multiple subdomains. Georgia Tech, for example, could use a single name server for the gatech.edu subdomain and all subdomains below it. That server would still have control over a single zone, but its zone would include many subdomains.

Finding a Name Server

Most name servers have names, but that is not how DNS clients identify them. The DNS protocol, like all TCP/IP protocols, requires IP addresses rather than names. A client has to know the IP address of a domain server before it can compose a domain query. Clearly, a client cannot ask the domain server for its IP address. DHCP (Chapter 14) is one protocol that can tell clients the IP address of their domain server.

It is also possible for a single system to serve multiple zones. The Internet, for example, could designate one server for both the `mil` and `gov` zones.

The action in Figure 13.2 takes place in the lower left corner. There, `burdell.cc.gatech.edu` needs the IP address of `pascal.cc.gatech.edu`. To start, `burdell` asks its local name server (step 1 in the figure). Since the target of the query (`pascal`) lies in the local server's zone, that server can answer immediately. It returns the corresponding IP address (step 2), and `burdell` can then establish communication.

Figure 13.3 presents a more interesting example. In it, `burdell` wants to talk to `einstein.me.gatech.edu`. As before, `burdell` composes a domain query and sends it to the local name server (step 1). This time, though, the target is not in the local server's zone. Since the server cannot answer directly, it turns around and asks its parent name server (step 2). In this case, the parent serves the `gatech.edu` zone. When the request makes it this far, the parent recognizes that the target lies in the `me.gatech.edu` zone, and that it has a child server supporting that zone. In step 3, the request travels down hierarchy to the child server.

At this point, the request has reached a server that can answer it. The `me.gatech.edu` server replies to the `gatech.edu` server (step 4), which relays the reply to the `cc.gatech.edu` server (step 5), which, in turn, relays the answer to `burdell` (step 6).

This example shows a *recursive query*. With such a query, the client makes a single request to its local name server, and that name server takes responsibility for finding the information. As this case shows, finding an answer may require the server to make additional inquiries on behalf of its client. Eventually, the local name server returns the answer to the client.

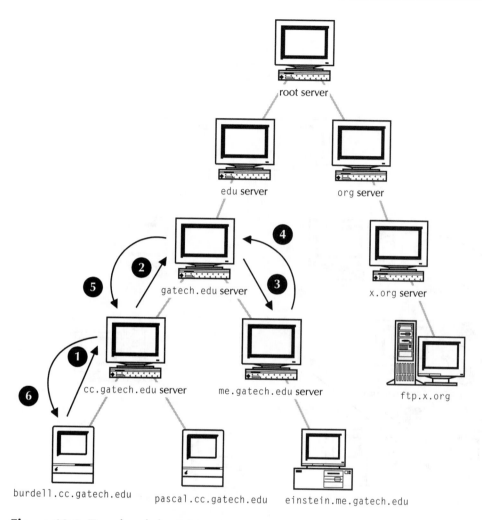

Figure 13.3 Two-level domain name query.

DNS can also operate in a nonrecursive manner. Figure 13.4 shows how `burdell` could find `einstein`'s IP address nonrecursively. As before, it starts with a query to its local name server (step 1). Then, instead of forwarding that query to the parent server, the local server replies immediately. That reply (step 2) does not contain an answer, but it does include a referral to the parent server.

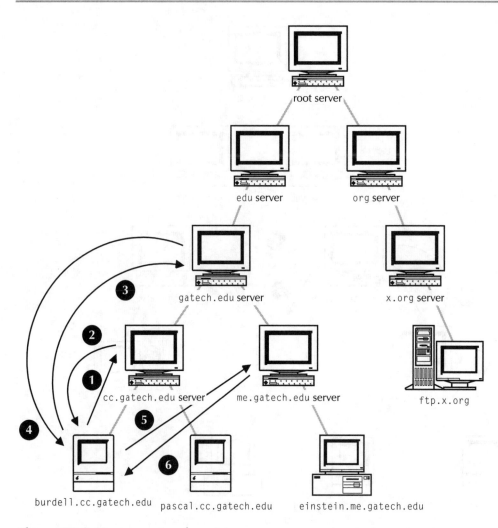

Figure 13.4 Nonrecursive domain name query.

When burdell receives this response, it reformulates its query and takes advantage of the referral, sending this query to the parent server (step 3). Once more, the answer is not available. The parent server replies with another referral (step 4). This referral indicates the server for the me.gatech.edu zone, and this time the query (step 5) is answered successfully (step 6); burdell can then send its first datagram to einstein.

The DNS Protocol

Domain Name Service relies on an extremely simple protocol. Clients send questions to servers, and servers respond with answers. The only aspect of DNS that can be confusing is the way it compresses names to save space in the packets.

Transport Services

DNS can use either UDP or TCP, and most servers support both services. As each query arrives, the server responds using the same transport service as the request. Often, clients that have a single query use the connectionless UDP because of its simplicity. Name servers that act as clients, on the other hand, often have a series of queries. They may want to update an entire table of information, for example. In such cases, TCP is normally the transport of choice.

Message Format

DNS uses the same format for both queries and responses. Figure 13.5 provides an illustration. The first two bytes in the message contain an identifier. The client picks a value

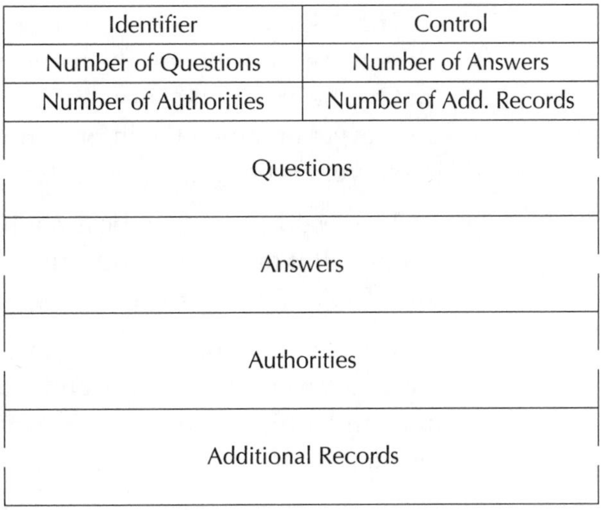

Identifier	Control
Number of Questions	Number of Answers
Number of Authorities	Number of Add. Records
Questions	
Answers	
Authorities	
Additional Records	

Figure 13.5 Domain Name Service message format.

Table 13.2 DNS Control Field Bits

Field	Bits	Purpose
QR	1	0 if message is a query; 1 if it is a response.
Opcode	4	0 if message is a standard query; 1 if it is an inverse query.
AA	1	1 if the answer is authoritative.
TC	1	1 if the message has been truncated because of size restrictions.
RD	1	1 if recursion is desired.
RA	1	1 if recursion is available.
Z	3	Reserved (must be zero).
Rcode	4	Response code.

for this field when it composes a query, and the server reflects the same value in its response. This field allows clients to have several queries outstanding with a server. When a reply arrives, they can use the identifier to match that reply with their original question.

The next two bytes contain the control bits. Table 13.2 summarizes their meaning. It lists the bits in order from most to least significant.

The AA bit is set when the response is from the server directly responsible for the name in question. This might not be the case if the answer is recursive or if the responding server obtained the information in some other server-to-server exchange.

The response code indicates whether the query succeeded. If it failed, this code gives the reason for the failure. Table 13.3 lists the DNS response codes.

The next four 16-bit words give the number of questions, answers, authorities, and additional records in the remainder of the message. That information follows the header.

Most queries include only a single question, with no other information, in which case, an entire DNS message

Table 13.3 DNS Response Codes

0	No error.
1	The query was formatted illegally.
2	The server failed.
3	The name in question does not exist.
4	The server does not support this kind of query.
5	The server refused to answer.

might look like Figure 13.6. Notice that the Questions section of the message includes three fields. The first field of this section is the name being queried. In this case, the sender asks for the IP address of `burdell.cc.gatech.edu`. As the figure shows, DNS does not use the familiar "dot" notation for names. Instead, it prefixes each label in the name with a length. The first label in the figure is `burdell`, and it starts with a length byte of 7. The name continues with a byte equal to 2, which gives the length of the `cc` label. A length of 0 indicates the end of the name.

The two bytes that follow the name specify the query type. DNS can support queries for many different kinds of data, and Table 13.4 lists some common query types relevant to TCP/IP. The final two bytes in the question indi-

Identifier: 0x1234		Control: 0x0100	
Num. Questions: 1		Num. Answers: 0	
Num. Authorities: 0		Num. Add. Records: 0	
7	'b'	'u'	'r'
'd'	'e'	'l'	'l'
2	'c'	'c'	6
'g'	'a'	't'	'e'
'c'	'h'	3	'e'
'd'	'u'	0	Qtype: 28
Qtype contd	Qclass: 1		

Figure 13.6 DNS query for `burdell.cc.gatech.edu`.

Table 13.4 Common DNS Query Types

Type	Value	Description
A	1	IPv4 address
NS	2	authoritative name server
CNAME	5	canonical name
SOA	6	start of a zone of authority
PTR	12	domain name pointer
MX	15	mail exchange
TXT	16	text strings
AAAA	28	IPv6 address
AXFR	252	transfer of an entire zone
*	255	request for all records

cate the query class. A value of 1 indicates Internet-related information.

For a query like Figure 13.6, the Questions section completes the packet. In contrast, responses generally contain answers, authorities, and additional records. Each of these is known as a *resource record*, and they follow the common format of Figure 13.7.

A resource record begins with a name, a type, and a class. All three fields have the same format as in the Questions section. The *Time to Live* field places a time limit on

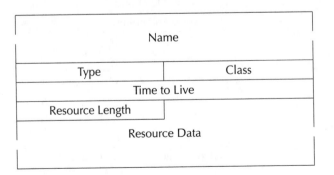

Figure 13.7 Resource record format.

the record's information. It specifies, in seconds, how long the receiver can consider the information valid.

The TTL field (to use its common abbreviation) lets a receiver cache DNS information. Much of the information that DNS maintains rarely changes. If a client needs the same information today that it needed yesterday, there is a very good chance that yesterday's information is still valid. If the client knows this and remembers yesterday's information, it can skip the DNS lookup altogether. Caching with the TTL formalizes this technique. Considering the number of transactions DNS may require, caching can save a significant amount of network traffic. (Imagine a nonrecursive lookup of ftp.x.org in Figure 13.4.)

Figure 13.8 shows how resource records might appear in a DNS response. This message is a possible reply to the earlier query. In the figure the message repeats the question and follows it with an answer and two authorities. Several names in this packet use a format different from the query's, beginning with the name in the answer's resource record. That format takes advantage of DNS's message compression.

Message compression avoids repeating the same name (or name suffix). Compression lets the sender include the entire name once, and then simply reference that name elsewhere in the message.

Figure 13.8 presents a clear example of compression at work. The second unshaded section contains the response's answer. Like all resource records, an answer begins with a domain name. In the example, that name is just 2 bytes, a 0xC0 followed by a 0x0C. The 0xC0 byte is in the place a name length normally would be. But 0xC0 (192 in decimal) clearly cannot be a label length, as DNS limits all labels to 63 bytes.

Anytime a label's length is 192 or greater, message compression is in use. (Lengths from 64 to 191 are illegal, but do not indicate compression.) The six least significant bits

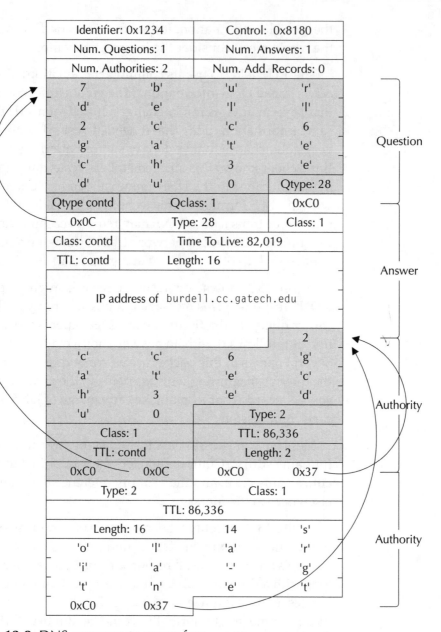

Figure 13.8 DNS response to query for `burdell.cc.gatech.edu`.

of the length byte, together with the next full byte, define
an offset to the real name. In this example, those 14 bits
have the value 12, and so the real name begins 12 bytes

into the message. The offset is always relative to the start of the DNS packet, so a zero offset would point to the first byte of the message's identifier.

The figure uses an arrow to show where the offset of 12 bytes points, in this case, to the domain name in the question, `burdell.cc.gatech.edu`. Of course, this makes complete sense. The original query asked for `burdell`'s IP address. That address is part of the answer record, but, like all records, the answer record has a name. And what name should be associated with `burdell`'s address other than `burdell`?

The last two sections in the message are authorities. These are the name servers that have authority over the name `burdell.cc.gatech.edu`. Both authorities list the name `cc.gatech.edu`. (The second uses compression.) This is the zone over which they have authority. The resource data for each authority is its own domain name. Note that the first authority uses message compression to indicate that its name is `burdell.cc.gatech.edu`. In fact, `burdell` is a name server for its zone! The second authority is the name server `solaria-gtnet.cc.gatech.edu`. Notice how its record mixes the normal name format with compression to specify the full domain name.

Table 13.5 explains how a receiver could interpret the DNS response of Figure 13.8. It looks at each of the five sections in the response.

Dynamic Updates

The Domain Name Service was originally designed for a very static environment. A host was assigned both an IP address and a name by a network administrator, and there was rarely a need to change either. TCP/IP has evolved, however, and the current network environment is much more dynamic. Laptops and other mobile systems move from network to network, changing their IP addresses as they move. (Each network has its own IP address prefix.)

Table 13.5 Interpreting the Message of Figure 13.8

1. This message is a response to query number 0x1234. Since that query requested recursion (RD=1), and recursion is available (RA=1) and this answer is not authoritative (AA=0), this reply was likely obtained recursively. The query encountered no error (Rcode=0).

2. The original question asked for the IPv6 address (Qtype=28) of `burdell.cc.gatech.edu`.

3. In answer to that question, `burdell.cc.gatech.edu` has the IPv6 address of [whatever value is in the packet]. That address should remain valid for at least another 22 hours (TTL=82,019).

4. One authority for that answer is a name server (Type=2) for the `cc.gatech.edu` zone. That name server is `burdell.cc.gatech.edu.` and it is expected to remain a name server for the zone for at least another 24 hours (TTL=86,336).

5. The second authority for the answer is also a name server for `cc.gatech.edu`. That second server is `solaria-gtnet.cc.gatech.edu`, and it should continue as an authority for 24 hours or more.

Home users dial in to a Internet access provider, sharing the limited pool of IP addresses assigned to that provider. And personal computers upgrade their LAN interface cards, obtaining new link addresses and, through address autoconfiguration, new IP addresses as well.

To accommodate this environment, DNS is now acquiring the ability to update itself dynamically. Instead of waiting for a network administrator to update name-to-address mapping for a system, DNS will allow that system to update the information itself.

Figure 13.9 shows how dynamic updates might work. As soon as the laptop connects to the Ethernet, it performs address autoconfiguration to learn its IP address. With that knowledge, the laptop then sends a DNS dynamic update request to its name server. The name server accepts the request and updates its information accordingly.

DNS supports four different dynamic update operations; Table 13.6 lists them. The operations are atomic, and they may be performed on records with different owners

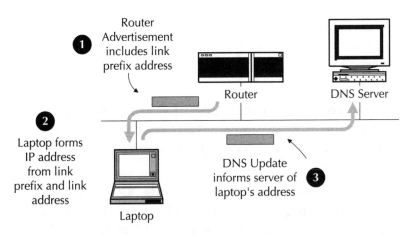

Figure 13.9 Laptop uses DNS update.

and record types, as long as all the names in the request belong to the same zone.

Once DNS supports dynamic updates, security becomes a critical concern. After all, if a system can easily change something as vital as its name-to-address mapping, then it is crucial to verify that the system really is what it says it is. DNS will provide this security through its own mechanisms (which are still under development) as well as through the security and authentication built into IPv6.

Summary

The Domain Name Service makes, perhaps, the biggest contribution to TCP/IP's ease of use—and ultimately to its popularity. DNS lets users and clients refer to systems

Table 13.6 DNS Dynamic Update Operations

ADDNAMENEW	Create a new name and assign it the included resource records.
ADDNAMEEXIST	Add new records to an existing name.
ADD	Add new records to a name, creating the name if it does not already exist.
DELETE	Remove the included records.

with names instead of complex IP addresses. Furthermore, DNS makes sure that those names are unique, so that each system need not worry about others claiming the same name.

DNS organizes names and name servers into hierarchies. The hierarchy of names ensures their uniqueness, and the hierarchy of servers keeps every server from having to know every name.

As it is defined today, DNS provides a static mapping from names to addresses, but work is underway to support a more dynamic environment. DNS dynamic updates allow systems to inform DNS servers when they move or otherwise change IP addresses. This service will rely heavily on DNS and IPv6 security features.

14

Configuring Hosts through DHCP

The Dynamic Host Configuration Protocol (DHCP) adds considerable convenience to TCP/IP networks. Hosts generally need configuration information before they can begin operating on a network. With DHCP, they can actually use the network to get this information.

In its present form, DHCP concentrates on providing network addresses to hosts. Although a host can always form a link-local address, such addresses confine traffic to the local link. If a host wants to communicate across an internet with other hosts not on its local link, the host needs additional network addresses.

Chapter 5's "Address Autoconfiguration" section describes one way for hosts to discover a network address, but that method has a few shortcomings. All networks that use autoconfiguration must have a router generating router advertisements, and administrators must make sure that all such routers have the correct prefix information.

Autoconfiguration also ties network addresses to particular hosts. An autoconfigured address is built from the host's link address. Two hosts with different link addresses cannot share a network address, even if they are never on the network together. Furthermore, this binding prevents an administrator from assigning network addresses based on a more natural identifier, such as the name of the person using the host.

DHCP resolves all of these issues with a more flexible and a more controllable method of autoconfiguring network addresses. The protocol also has the capability to relay other configuration information. So far, such optional features remain undefined, but, in the future, DHCP may be able to tell a host its file servers, printers, and domain name servers on the network.

Assigning Network Addresses

Network administrators use DHCP to assign network addresses to hosts on their networks. DHCP gives these administrators the flexibility to assign addresses in one of three ways. The approaches represent different allocation strategies.

Manual Allocation

The most rigid method is *manual allocation*. Through this method, the administrator explicitly assigns specific addresses to specific hosts. When those hosts use DHCP to discover their addresses, DHCP provides them with the manually allocated values.

Automatic Allocation

Automatic allocation provides the same service as ICMP's address autoconfiguration. It combines a link address with an address prefix to create a network address. DHCP uses a different approach to achieve that result, though. Instead of waiting for router advertisements, hosts actively request an address from a special computer acting as a DHCP server. The server puts the link address together with the network prefix, and it returns the resulting address to the host.

Administrators may choose to use DHCP's automatic allocation instead of address autoconfiguration for at least two reasons. First, DHCP does not require configuration and maintenance of routers on every network. Instead, address administration can be concentrated in a single host. Second, DHCP lets an administrator change allocation strategies easily. If the administrator changes some hosts from automatic allocation to another strategy, those hosts need never even know of the change.

Dynamic Allocation

Dynamic allocation represents the most adaptive allocation strategy. It lets a group of hosts share from a smaller pool of network addresses. This strategy is useful if addresses are in demand and only a limited number of the hosts need an address at any one time.

Figure 14.1 offers an example. A business allows six of its employees to dial in to its network from home, even though it has only two phone lines for data connections. Since no more than two users can be active at any time, there is no need to assign a network address to each of the six possible users. Instead, the administrator assigns just two addresses to the dialup data lines. DHCP allocates those addresses to the users active at any one time.

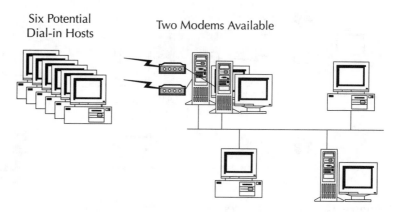

Figure 14.1 Sharing addresses among multiple hosts.

Client-Server Interactions

DHCP derives much of its power from making the allocation strategy transparent to the hosts it serves. A host that
needs a network address takes exactly the same steps, regardless of the allocation strategy the administrator has
selected.

DHCP interactions follow a simple client-server model.
A host that needs a network address becomes a client by
asking for that address. The system that answers the request acts a DHCP server. DHCP transactions conclude
when the client either accepts or rejects the response. Figure 14.2 shows how a home user can get a network address through DHCP. It identifies all three steps in the
transaction.

Since DHCP strives to support all the configuration
needs of its clients, it cannot presume that the clients have
any information about the network. In particular, clients
will not know the address of the DHCP server. Neverthe-
less, the client still has to send a message to the server, and
that message must have a destination address. To resolve
this impasse, DHCP relies on a well-known multicast address. The address FF02::1:0 refers to all DHCP servers.

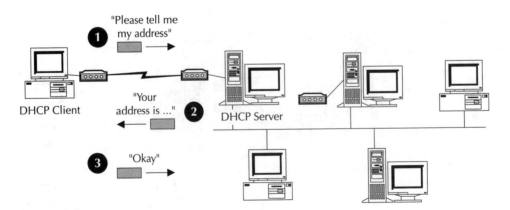

Figure 14.2 The three steps in a DHCP exchange.

When a client makes a request, it addresses it to
FF02::1:0. (If a host does know the address of a DHCP
server, however, it may send its requests directly to that
server.)

Relay Agents

In some cases, it may not be possible for the client and
server to communicate directly. The small office in these
examples may not want to have both dialup computers act
as DHCP servers. Instead, it might prefer a single computer acting as the DHCP server for both modem lines. In
such a topology, the server would not be on the same link
as the client, presenting a problem for the clients. The
DHCP server multicast address has a link-local scope.
Messages addressed to FF02::1:0 cannot travel beyond
the link on which they first appear.

DHCP solves this problem by defining a third role beyond that of server and client. The new role is a DHCP relay. A relay accepts a request from a client, but it does not
answer it directly. Instead, it relays the request to a true
DHCP server. The relay also forwards the server's response to the client. Figure 14.3 depicts this exchange.

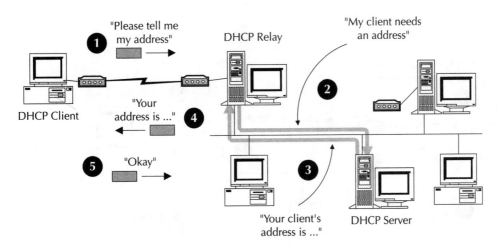

Figure 14.3 DHCP acts on behalf of a client.

DHCP and the Domain Name Service

DHCP servers also support their clients by interacting with the Domain Name Service. One thing that DHCP servers can do is autoregister their client's names. If a client knows its domain name, it can supply that name when it requests an address. The DHCP server queries DNS for the client's address. If DNS has no entry for the client, or if the server needs to assign the client a different address, it can update DNS through the DNS dynamic update mechanism. (See page 419.)

Figure 14.4 illustrates this coordination. In step 2, the DHCP server queries DNS on behalf of its client. When the domain name server replies that it has no address for the client, the DHCP server creates one using automatic or dynamic allocation. Then, in step 4, the DHCP server updates DNS with the address it has assigned. It also gives this address to the client.

A DHCP server can also provide a domain name to its client. If the client does not know its name beforehand, it may find it convenient to get a name the same way it finds

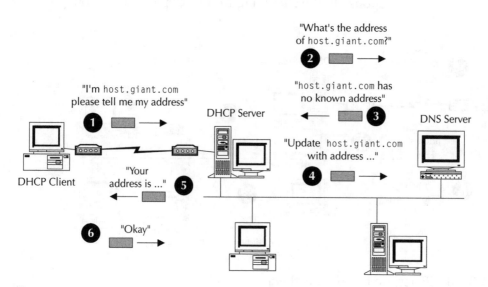

Figure 14.4 DHCP server coordinates with DNS.

its address. The DHCP server must coordinate with the domain name service in this case as well.

DHCP Message Formats

Figure 14.5 shows a DHCP message. These messages, normally carried in UDP datagrams[1], begin with a *message type* byte. This field distinguishes the different DHCP messages; it takes one of the values listed in Table 14.1.

The *message code* provides more details about a server's response. If it is has the value of one, then the server has detected an error. When the server generates this response, it declines to assign any address to the client. Both the client and the server should unassign any addresses they think belong to the client, and the client should start over by asking for a new address.

When the message code in a response has the value of two, the server indicates that it could not support a dynamic DNS update for the client.

The *name length* field gives the length of the domain name in the message. As Figure 14.5 shows, the domain name follows all other fields in the message, except any options. The *address count* and *interface token* fields help keep clients and servers synchronized. In general, a client may request (and receive) multiple addresses for the same interface. To make sure that the server knows that all such

Table 14.1 DHCP Message Types

1	Client request
2	Server response
3	Client's confirmation of a response
4	Client's rejection of a response

---

[1] DHCP can also use TCP as its transport protocol. TCP's reliable service is more suitable for negotiating configuration options rather than learning IP addresses. As of this writing, such negotiations remain undefined for IPng.

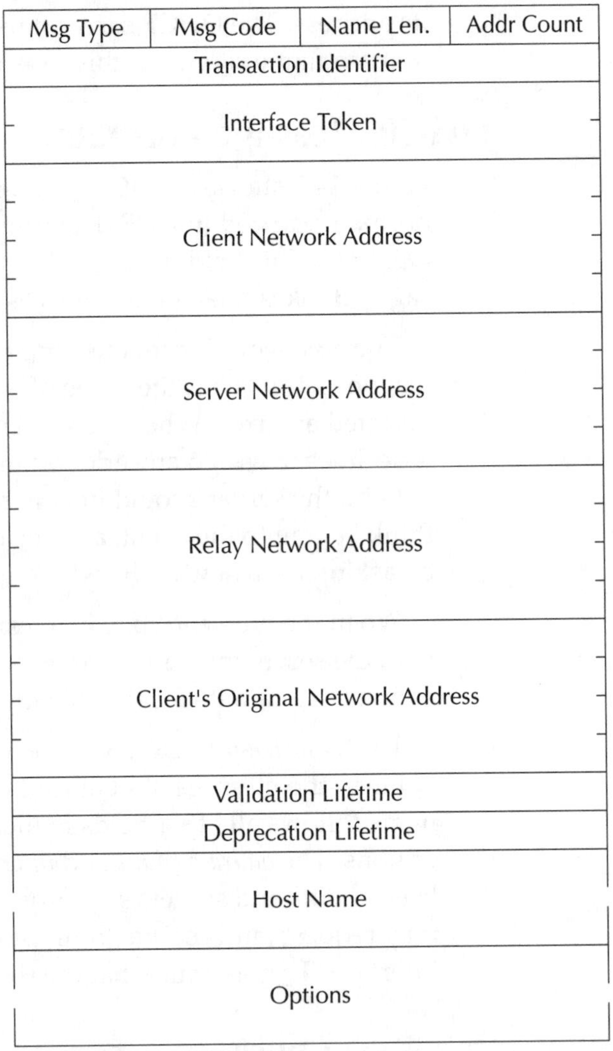

Msg Type	Msg Code	Name Len.	Addr Count
Transaction Identifier			
Interface Token			
Client Network Address			
Server Network Address			
Relay Network Address			
Client's Original Network Address			
Validation Lifetime			
Deprecation Lifetime			
Host Name			
Options			

Figure 14.5 DHCP message format.

addresses belong to the same interface, the client supplies a value for its interface token. This value must be unique among all other interfaces to the network. Typically, it is the link-level address of the interface.

When the client makes a request for an address, it includes the number of addresses it already has in the address count field.

The server also keeps track of this value, and it can detect when the two systems lose synchronization. The most common cause of this error would be a reboot of the client's computer. When the client restarts after the reboot, it will ask for a network address. Since it does not remember that it had an address before the reboot, it will set the address count to zero. When the server sees this address count, it returns an error to the client. At the same time, it removes any addresses previously assigned to the client, freeing them for reassignment elsewhere.

The *transaction identifier* associates requests and responses, as well as confirmation and rejection messages, with each other. Clients pick a value for this field, and servers reflect that value in their response.

The *client address* field contains the client's network address. When the client requests an address, it will not know what to put here, so it sets it to zero. (This is the unspecified address described on page 33.) If a client puts a real address in this field, then servers interpret the request as asking for a domain name, rather than a network address.

The *server address* provides the network address of the server that responds to a request. The field has no meaning in the requests themselves.

DHCP needs the *relay address* and *client's original address* fields when a transaction involves relays. When a relay accepts a request, it places its own address in the relay address field. It also fills in the *client's original address* with the source IP address of the request. Figure 14.6 shows this part of the exchange. As the figure also reveals, all other DHCP fields remain unchanged.

When the server accepts the request, it uses the relay address field to determine where to send its reply. The server also preserves the client's original address, so the relay will know where to send the response. Figure 14.7 shows how the response reaches the client.

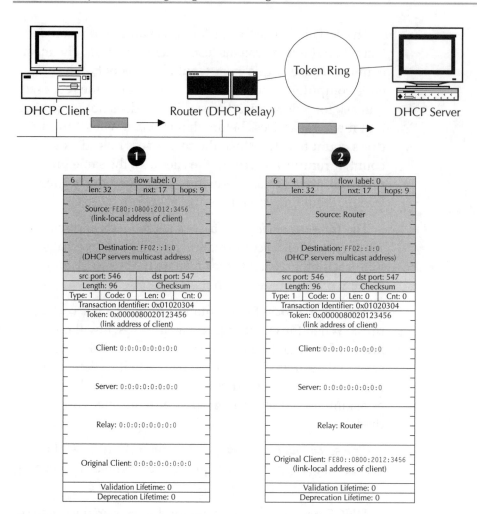

Figure 14.6 Relay updates fields in the request.

The last two required fields in a DHCP message are the validation and deprecation lifetimes. These values, both measured in seconds, determine how long the supplied address will remain valid. The validation lifetime places an absolute limit on the life of the address. Once this time has passed, the client must cease using the address.

The deprecation lifetime serves as an early warning on the address' expiration. When the deprecation lifetime concludes, the client should not use the address on any

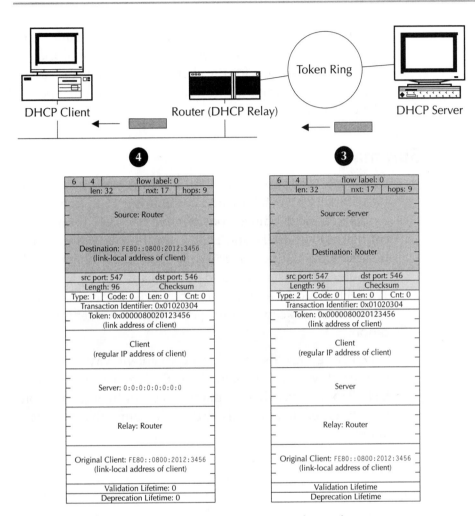

Figure 14.7 Server and relay return DHCP reply to client.

new conversations. It can continue using the address on *existing* conversations, however.

The *host name* field follows these two lifetime values. Clients use this field to request addresses for a particular domain name, and servers use this field to return requested domain names to clients.

After the host name, DHCP messages allow optional parameters. To date, the standard has not defined any particular options, but in the future, options may include configuration information such as file servers, printers, and domain name servers for the client. The options area can also carry configuration and tuning information for specific protocols.

Summary

DHCP exists because TCP/IP's designers have recognized the difficulty of installing and configuring TCP/IP networks. Classic IP gained considerable notoriety for its configuration pitfalls, and DHCP was first developed for IPv4 networks. IPng corrects some of IPv4's problems with its router advertisements and address autoconfiguration. The DHCP model is still useful, however, because it lets administrators keep all configuration data in a central location.

DHCP servers also provide a convenient way for hosts to interact with the Domain Name System. Hosts can use DHCP to discover their domain names, or they can rely on DHCP servers to autoregister domain names that they do know.

15

The Future of TCP/IP

Judging from the past, TCP/IP's future is bound inexorably to the future of the Internet. Researchers created the first TCP/IP protocols expressly for the original Internet, and they continue to expand and improve the protocols as the Internet evolves. The subject of this text represents, perhaps, the greatest testament to this support. Without IPng, it is doubtful that the Internet can continue to survive and grow.

The relationship is not one-sided, either. Just as developments on the Internet drive protocol designs, new TCP/IP protocols can have a profound effect on the Internet. In March 1989, scientists at the European Laboratory for Particle Physics proposed a new protocol for accessing various types of linked information. Their efforts spawned the World Wide Web, and its HTTP protocol is now the fastest-growing source of Internet traffic.

As TCP/IP and the Internet meet the twenty-first century, they will encounter both opportunities and challenges. By some estimates, the possibilities are tremendous—continued growth of the existing network, deployment of exciting new applications, and still more innovative uses of networking technology. Skeptics, however, pose several valid questions for TCP/IP and the Internet. Can IPng achieve successful deployment before time runs out on classic IP? Can the Internet adjust to a larger and more diverse set of users? Indeed, how will the Internet deal with its own effects on society as a whole?

Growth of the Existing Network

Many factors have contributed to the Internet's recent growth, and, in July 1995, few offer any hint of abating. Of the 100 largest U.S. corporations, only 60 have a presence on the Internet's World Wide Web. Several of the major on-line services began providing direct Internet access only recently. Microsoft's service, the Microsoft Network, is not even available yet. That service alone may add 500,000 to 1,000,000 new users by the end of the year.

The Internet is also reaching users in new places; in fact, it is rapidly approaching the point where it can reach users anywhere. Cellular phones, two-way pagers, and personal digital assistants offer communication without geographic limitations. The technology that will truly enable growth of these networks—personal communication services—is still under development, but that has not deterred deployment. Already, cellular digital packet data (CDPD) networks operate in six U.S. metropolitan areas; that number will triple by year's end. CDPD, which builds on existing mobile phone technology, uses TCP/IP to transport its users' data. Future networks, those built to carry data from their inception, will rely on TCP/IP as well.

New Applications

Just as new users are joining the Internet, TCP/IP's designers are busy developing new things for them to do. Electronic commerce represents a particularly interesting application. As a communication media, the Internet provides a direct connection between sellers and possible buyers. Today, the network does not provide enough security to exploit this connection. Except through a few limited programs, sellers and buyers cannot authenticate each other's identity, nor can they adequately protect any confidential information they exchange. In recognition of this problem, and of the enormous potential of the application, TCP/IP's designers have adopted the security framework of IPng to fit the architecture of classic IP. Security has become so important that it cannot wait for IPng.

From a less commercial perspective, audio and video conferencing represent exciting new applications for the Internet. Indeed, a subset of the network already has considerable experience in this area. Since 1992, some users have a limited ability to send and receive multicast traffic across the Internet. Those users form the Virtual Internet Backbone for Multicast IP, or MBONE for short. With this network subset, and with early versions of the RTP and RTCP protocols, more than 10,000 users in 30 countries[1] enjoy everything from TCP/IP engineering sessions to a rock concert by the Rolling Stones.

Still, the MBONE remains experimental and limited mostly to scholarly, scientific, and engineering conferences. In the future, three factors will push multimedia conferencing into the mainstream of the Internet. First, new network technologies will provide the bandwidth that multimedia craves. These technologies include ATM for the network infrastructure and data delivery to the home user via the cable television industry's plant. Second, the MBONE will grow to encompass most of the Internet. Multicast services were a late addition to classic IP, and retrofitting existing networks has been difficult. IPng, on the other hand, defines multicast delivery as a core function. As the Internet migrates to IPng, multicast support will become pervasive. The third factor driving multimedia conferencing is the progress of protocols that support

---

[1] Van Jacobson. "Multimedia Conferencing on the Internet." SIGCOMM 1994 Tutorial. University College London. London, England, August 30, 1994.

real time applications. RTP, RTCP, and RSVP will mature to the point that they become part of commercial products.

The convergence of fast network technology, multicast delivery, and commercial-quality applications poses some interesting questions. What happens when home and business users can buy shrink-wrapped software to run on their high-bandwidth networks with built-in support for multicast distribution? How well can schools supplement traditional classrooms with distance learning applications? How much do computer networks supplant television networks as the distribution method for multimedia entertainment? Answers to all these questions border on speculation, for now. Most assuredly, however, they will not remain unanswered much longer.

New Uses of the Technology

The implications of a pervasive network like the Internet extend beyond traditional computer communications, as engineers find new ways to exploit the technology. For example, all 14,000 residents of Glasgow, Kentucky rely on a network that may soon (probably by the time this text is printed) be a part of the Internet. Few of these residents, however, own a computer.

The electric power company in Glasgow has connected the whole town into a 2-Mbit/s network. Although the network can provide traditional communications services, its purpose is a lot more mundane—it reads electric power meters. This function may not seem particularly interesting, but the technology saves the city hundreds of thousands of dollars each year[2].

In fact, device control, like that promoted by the Glasgow Electric Plant Board, could represent a major market for TCP/IP networks. Potential gains in efficiency, econ-

---

[2] Todd Lappin. "Country Road Warrior." *Wired* 3.08 (August 1995), pp. 46-50.

omy, and functionality are available for many types of devices. Most modern automobiles now include a network that its components use to coordinate their operation. If those components could also communicate with a network that provided real time traffic and weather conditions, they may be able to further enhance the performance of the car and its driver. Airplanes, too, have succumbed to the lure of networking. The International Civil Aviation Organization has plans to integrate aircraft and ground control into a ubiquitous, global network.

Back on the ground, at least a dozen vending machines already own connections to the Internet. For now, this application remains confined to a few college experiments, although one vending service company plans to use wireless networks to continuously monitor all of its vending machines. It will instantly know which items need restocking and which machines need repair.

Challenges for the Future

To make even part of this vision reality, the Internet must overcome significant challenges. The most pressing technical problem is one of the factors that led to the development of IPng—routing table explosion. The network has already grown so large that some parts experience intermittent connectivity. The routers simply cannot keep pace with changes to so large and diverse a topology. IPng introduces a new address format that lets protocols like IDRP shrink routing tables. But even as TCP/IP's designers race to complete the IPng definition and begin deployment, some question whether the effort can be finished in time.

The Internet's growth has strained the network in other ways as well. Most noticeable is the change in the very culture of the network. Developed initially for research and engineering experimentation, the Internet originally served users with very similar interests and backgrounds.

This culture fostered cooperation to nurture and develop the network. The "tragedy of the commons" was not a cause for concern, as few users would even consider individual gain at the Internet's expense.

Since the early days, the network's appeal has broadened considerably. Now it is home to an incredibly diverse group of users, with a wide variety of talents and interests. Many new users are not experts in computer communications, and frequently misunderstand the ramifications of their actions. Some users may even act unscrupulously, and deliberately and knowingly attain personal profit at the network's expense. (At least some on the network consider such behavior unscrupulous.)

To continue its growth, the Internet must learn to accommodate these users. The network community must decide what limits to place on its users, and when and where those limits apply. It must devise ways to promote desirable behavior and discourage undesirable actions. In effect, the Internet needs to develop a government for the networked community.

Just as the Internet must adapt to all of society, its users, indeed most of the world, face several challenges arising from the power of computer networks. With the advent of digital cash, central banks in powerful countries risk the loss of much of their economic power. What currency will develop on the Internet? How will traditional governments manage and tax it?

Another important issue is privacy. Imagine a world of the not very distant future. Users shop from home, selecting catalogs and ordering items from thousands of suppliers. For entertainment, they request interactive movies or play multimedia games over the network. When they do leave their homes, mobile communication devices in their vehicles track their progress, automatically paying tolls as necessary, and alerting them to traffic and weather conditions ahead.

What some find frightening is the fact that computers can store information as easily as they can transfer it. At what cost to their privacy will citizens accept these new conveniences? Who will tolerate technology that can monitor every purchase, communication, leisure activity, and journey? Can network technology evolve to provide its benefits while ensuring its users that they have not lost more than they have gained?

An Outlook

Ultimately, TCP/IP and the Internet will solve these problems. Human nature and ingenuity cannot conspire otherwise. Computer communication is fundamentally just another form of communication, and society continues to demonstrate the value it places on all communications.

History contains many analogies to the Internet; perhaps none is more relevant than the telephone. With the first introduction of telephone services, each provider maintained its own, separate exchange. Joan could call her Uncle Bill only if they both shared the same exchange. If Joan and Bill relied on separate providers, communication was impossible. That situation would be unimaginable today. Indeed, it was barely tolerable at the time, and exchanges rapidly interconnected with each other as the technology to do so became available.

Computer networks now confront a similar situation. Society needs computers, and, more and more, it needs them to communicate. Given hints of the technology's possibilities, who will settle for scattered and isolated networks? The security system that automatically reports to its owner's home computer should also be able to notify that same owner at his office workstation or through the mobile phone in his car. Engineers working from home want the same access to video conferences as they have at work. The traveling executive, with a simple (wireless) connection to her client's LAN, needs access to the latest financial information from headquarters.

Achieving the same interconnectivity as the world's phone system requires a common framework. Computer networks throughout the world must share a common architecture, and they must employ compatible protocols. Today, the Internet offers the most promising architecture for this universal network. Its TCP/IP protocols already connect systems from supercomputers to household appliances. Its systems communicate using everything from dialup phone lines to fiber connections and satellite links. It can support applications as simple as electronic mail and as complex as large-scale video conferences. No other network technology has the breadth and depth of the TCP/IP Internet. With the introduction of IPng, none is better positioned for the future.

Migrating from IPv4

No matter how much power and how many features IPng can claim, all TCP/IP networks cannot switch from IPv4 overnight. The sheer number and immense variety of TCP/IP systems dictate a gradual migration. Fortunately, IPng accommodates a graceful, gradual, and nearly painless migration. It also offers total interoperability with IPv4 systems.

This appendix describes IPng's mechanisms for a simple transition from IPv4. After a quick review of classic IP, it documents how IPv6 can interoperate with IPv4. The appendix concludes with a discussion of actual deployment strategies.

IP Version 4

Version 4 of the Internet Protocol bears a strong family resemblance to IPv6. Figure A.1 shows the format of an IPv4 datagram. The figure uses IPng terms for IPv4 header fields; in some cases, these are not the customary IPv4 names.

Even though IPv4 appears different from IPv6, a quick comparison (page 94) shows only a few substantial differences, and they are listed in Table A.1. Other differences in the header formats appear mainly cosmetic, but they give

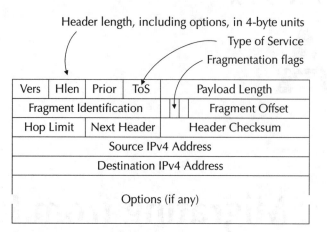

Figure A.1 IPv4 header format.

IPv6 a significant performance advantage over IPv4. IPv6, for example, does not contain a header length field. The basic IPv6 header is always fixed at 40 bytes in size, so IPv6-based systems can easily optimize their header processing software. IPv4 systems must contend with headers of arbitrary size.

Version 4 and Version 6 Interoperability

Because of the similarity between IPv4 and IPv6 headers, IPv4 and IPv6 systems speak essentially the same language. With the help of embedded IPv4 addresses, such systems can communicate with each other.

Embedded IPv4 Addresses

IPng defines two types of IPv6 addresses that can embed IPv4 addresses. As described on page 34, they are the

Table A.1 Major Differences between IPv4 and IPv6 Formats

	IPv4	IPv6
Address Size	32 bits	128 bits
Flow Labels	no	yes
Header Checksum	yes	no
Fragmentation Information	all datagrams	as an option

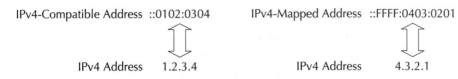

Figure A.2 Converting embedded IPv4 addresses.

Ones Complement Checksums

Embedded IPv4 addresses preserve checksum values, even when converted to pure IPv4 formats, because of a special property of the TCP/IP checksum algorithm. That algorithm specifies 16-bit, ones complement arithmetic, in which a negative number is represented by the binary complement of its positive value. (For example, –3 becomes 1100_2 in 4-bit ones complement.) The 96-bit IPv6 prefixes for embedded addresses merely add six words of 0 or –0 to the IPv4 checksum. Clearly, adding zero (positive or negative) has no effect on the final result.

IPv4-compatible and IPv4-mapped addresses. These embedded addresses have two special features. First, they can be converted easily from IPv6 to IPv4 and back. Figure A.2 shows that this conversion simply adds or deletes a 96-bit IPv6 prefix.

The second feature of embedded IPv4 addresses is their effect on checksums. Most TCP/IP transport protocols use a checksum to guarantee data integrity, and that checksum typically covers the packet's source and destination addresses as well as the transport header and payload. (See, for example, pages 129, 168, and 191.) The embedded address format lets transport implementations compute checksums consistently, whether the address is an IPv6 address or the 32-bit IPv4 address. If a sender computes a transport checksum using a pure IPv4 address, while the receiver uses the full IPv6 address, the results will still agree. As later sections of this appendix show, this property is essential for any migration strategy that relies on header translation.

IPv4-compatible addresses refer to systems that understand IPv6; such addresses simply provide a way to identify those systems in IPv4's architecture. IPv4-mapped addresses, on the other hand, identify systems that do not understand IPv6. The "Migration Strategies" section explains how each form may be used.

Header Equivalence

Embedded addresses translate between IPv4 and IPv6 addresses, but what about the rest of the header? Because of the similarity between the two protocols, such a translation

Table A.2 Converting between IPv4 and IPv6 Headers

- IPv4 header lengths are calculated based on the options present in the IPv6 datagram.
- IPv6 noncongestion-controlled priorities (those greater than 7) receive an IPv4 priority of 0.
- IPv4 type of service is ignored in the translation to IPv6; all IPv6 datagrams receive normal (zero-valued) IPv4 service.
- IPv4 fragmentation information derives from the IPv6 fragment header, if it is present, the IPv4 fragment identification is the 16 least significant bits of IPv6's fragment identification. A fragmented IPv4 datagram results in an IPv6 datagram with a fragment header.
- IPv4 header checksums must be calculated once the IPv4 header is formed.
- IPv6 flow labels are ignored when IPv6 datagrams are converted to IPv4; they are set to zero on IPv6 datagrams derived from IPv4.

is an easy matter. Most of the header fields map directly. The fields that do not directly translate can be simply converted. Table A.2 shows possible conversion steps.

Migration Strategies

IPng's migration strategy relies on three major components. Clearly, systems must add the capability to understand IPv6, with which they can use tunneling to reach other IPv6 systems, even across an IPv4 network. When IPv6's popularity causes some systems forget about IPv4 altogether, header translation offers a way for those systems to maintain contact with older IPv4 hosts.

Dual Stack

The first step in migrating to IPng is the deployment of systems that support IPv6. At least at first, those systems are not likely to have many other systems with which to communicate. Most other systems will still be using IPv4. These new IPv6 systems, therefore, will likely be *dual stack*

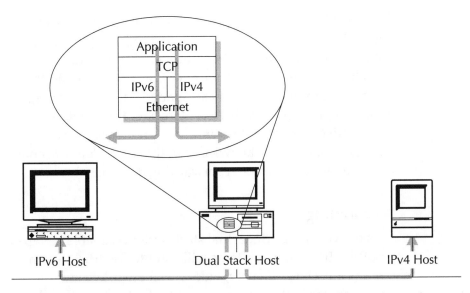

Figure A.3 Dualstack host communicates with both IPv4 and IPv6 hosts.

systems, able to use both IPv6 and IPv4. Figure A.3 shows that the layers above IP remain the same in either case. Dual stack systems can use IPv6 to communicate with IPv6 systems, and they can fall back to IPv4 to communicate with older systems.

To determine which IP protocol they can use, hosts can query the Domain Name System. If DNS returns an IPv6 address for the destination, the host can use IPv6; otherwise, it must fall back to IPv4. Note that adding IPv6 addresses to DNS does not require the DNS server to support IPv6-based communication. Indeed, the DNS client may use IPv4 to query the server, and the server can respond using IPv4, even though the information it returns is an IPv6 network address.

Once the host knows (from DNS) that the destination can understand IPv6, it still needs to decide how to deliver the datagram. The IP layer itself can make this decision automatically. If the destination is on the same link as the source, then the decision is easy: use IPv6. If the destination lies on a different link, however, the source must listen for IPv6 router advertisements. If any arrive, then the host should use IPv6 to send the datagram to the router. If the communication requires a tunnel, then the router can establish it. Only if no IPv6 router is available should the host perform the tunnel encapsulation itself. This strategy forces a preference for IPv6 routers over IPv4 routers. Since IPv6 routers understand both protocols, they are likely to have better knowledge of the network as a whole, and can thus make better forwarding decisions.

Tunneling

As networks introduce dual stack systems capable of supporting IPv6, more systems will want to use IPv6 to communicate. Unfortunately, older IPv4 networks may separate those IPv6 systems, and to reach each other, the IPv6 systems must tunnel through the IPv4 network.

The most straightforward approach to tunneling relies on IPv4-compatible addresses. When an IPv6 datagram reaches the boundary of the IPv4 network, the router encapsulates it in an IPv4 datagram. As an IPv4 datagram, the new message must have an IPv4 destination address. To derive that address, the router extracts the IPv4 address embedded in the IPv6 packet's destination. Figure A.4 shows that the encapsulated datagram travels all the way to its destination, where the receiving system recovers the original IPv6 message. The whole process requires no special configuration in any system; it goes by the name *automatic tunneling*.

The figure also reveals the next header value that appears in the IPv4 datagram. That value is 41, indicating that the IPv4 payload is an IPv6 datagram.

When IPv4-compatible addresses are unavailable, automatic tunneling is not possible. In these situations, *configured tunneling* lets IPv6 systems communicate. Configured tunneling requires explicit configuration at the entry point to the IPv4 network. That configuration must

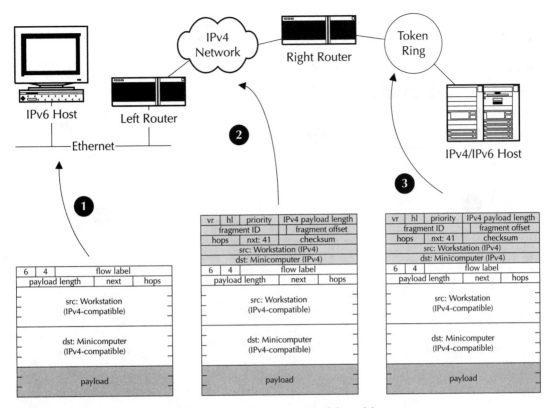

Figure A.4 Automatic tunneling with IPv4-compatible addresses.

specify the IPv4 destination to be used for the tunneled datagrams. Since the IPv6 destination is not an IPv4-compatible address, routers cannot automatically derive an IPv4 destination.

Unlike automatic tunneling, the IPv4's destination address is not the ultimate destination for the datagrams. When an encapsulated datagram reaches the tunnel endpoint, that router extracts the IPv6 datagram inside and forwards it to its real destination.

Figure A.5 shows a configured tunnel crossing an IPv4 network. Notice that the IPv4 datagram has the source and destination addresses of the two routers, not the workstation or minicomputer. Also note that the encapsulating IPv4 datagram does not travel all the way to the destina-

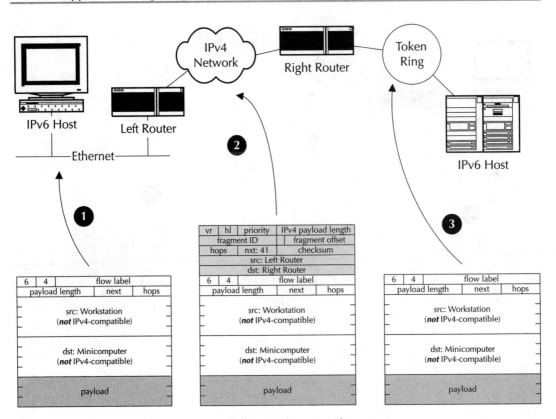

Figure A.5 Configured tunnel crosses an IPv4 network.

tion. The right router recovers the IPv6 message and sends that message to the minicomputer.

The routers require explicit configuration for this approach to succeed. In particular, the left router must know that an IPv6 destination of the minicomputer requires a tunnel to the IPv4 destination of the right router. Since the minicomputer will presumably respond to the workstation, the reverse direction requires similar configuration.

Header Translation

At some point during the migration, administrators may want to eliminate IPv4 from their network. That strategy

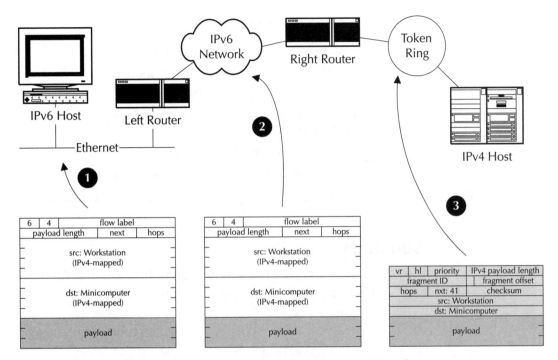

Figure A.6 Translating router converts IPv6 datagrams to IPv4 datagrams.

becomes practical after most of the systems have added support for IPv6. Even at such a stage, however, at least a few IPv4-only systems are likely to remain. Communicating with those systems requires header translation.

Figure A.6 illustrates header translation in action. The IPv6 message travels nearly all the way to the destination, but, since that destination does not understand IPv6, it cannot complete the journey. To deliver the minicomputer a message it can understand, the right router accepts the IPv6 datagram and converts it to IPv4 format. Header translation uses IPv4-mapped addresses. Notice that the right router completely strips the IPv6 header from the datagram and replaces it with an equivalent IPv4 header. When the minicomputer replies to this message, the right router has to perform the reverse of this translation, converting an IPv4 message to IPv6.

Table A.3 Migration Steps

1. Upgrade DNS server(s) to handle IPv6 addresses.
2. Introduce dual stack systems that support IPv4 and IPv6.
3. Add IPv6 addresses to the DNS records of those systems.
4. Rely on tunnels to connect IPv6 networks separated by IPv4 networks.
5. Remove support for IPv4 from systems.
6. Rely on header translation to reach remaining IPv4-only systems.

Summary

As a summary of what a migration to IPv6 entails, Table A.3 lists the steps in a typical migration.

B

Migrating Other Architectures to IPng

Despite the popularity of TCP/IP and the Internet, many computer networks rely on other protocol suites. In developing IPng, TCP/IP's designers created mechanisms that give administrators an option to migrate those other architectures to IP version 6. The IPng architecture includes explicit migration support for two popular architectures—Novell's Netware and the connectionless services designed by the International Standards Organization (ISO).

Connectionless Internetworking

Both of these protocol suites are good candidates for a migration to IPv6 because their architectures are very similar to TCP/IP's. In particular, both rely on an internetwork layer protocol to connect a variety of network technologies. Most important, in both cases, that internetwork protocol provides connectionless services.

Novell's Internetwork Packet Exchange

Novell's Netware has an architecture much like TCP/IP's. The internetwork layer provides a common set of services for the NCP and SPX transport protocols, which in turn service applications (though the division between NCP

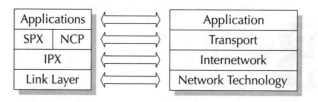

Figure B.1 Netware protocol architecture vs. TCP/IP.

and an application is less distinct). Figure B.1 shows how the various protocols fit in the Netware architecture, and how that architecture corresponds to TCP/IP's.

At Netware's internetwork layer lies the Internetwork Packet Exchange (IPX) protocol. IPX messages, illustrated in Figure B.2, look a lot like IP datagrams. The figure uses the same terminology as in the IP header rather than the traditional IPX field names. The only fields that have no direct analog in IP are the IPX source and destination sockets. These fields serve the same purpose as UDP port numbers, distinguishing different applications within a system.

As its header format reveals, IPX does not support many of the options available to IP. In particular, IPX does not perform fragmentation at all. Neither does IPX support source routing, or security.

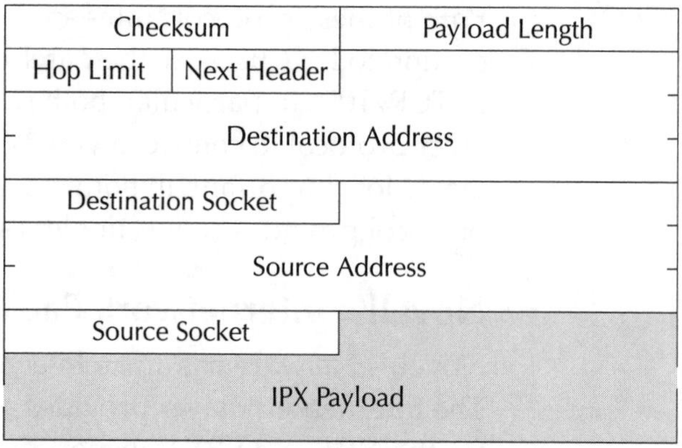

Checksum	Payload Length
Hop Limit | Next Header	
Destination Address	
Destination Socket	
Source Address	
Source Socket	
IPX Payload	

Figure B.2 IPX message format.

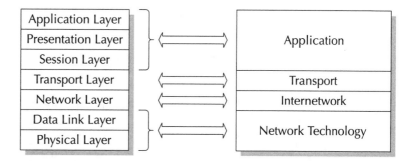

Figure B.3 ISO's layered protocol architecture vs. TCP/IP.

IPX network addresses are 10 bytes in size. They have a rigid, two-level hierarchy. The first four bytes, called a *network number*, act the same as a link prefix. The last six bytes identify a specific node on that network. These six bytes are traditionally the node's link address.

ISO's Connectionless Network Protocol

The International Standards Organization has organized its protocol architecture into seven different layers. Figure B.3 illustrates that architecture. Together, the data link and physical layers define a network technology. The session, presentation, and application layers correspond to a TCP/IP application.

At most of the protocol layers, ISO has defined both connectionless and connection-oriented protocols. The internetwork protocol of choice is the connectionless network protocol (CLNP), whose header format appears in Figure B.4; it has nearly the same functionality as IP.

CLNP's network addresses are known as NSAPs, short for network service access point[1]. NSAPs technically have an arbitrary length, though many ISO networks have settled on 20-byte NSAPs.

---

[1] These are the same structures used by ATM nodes to identify themselves. See page 85.

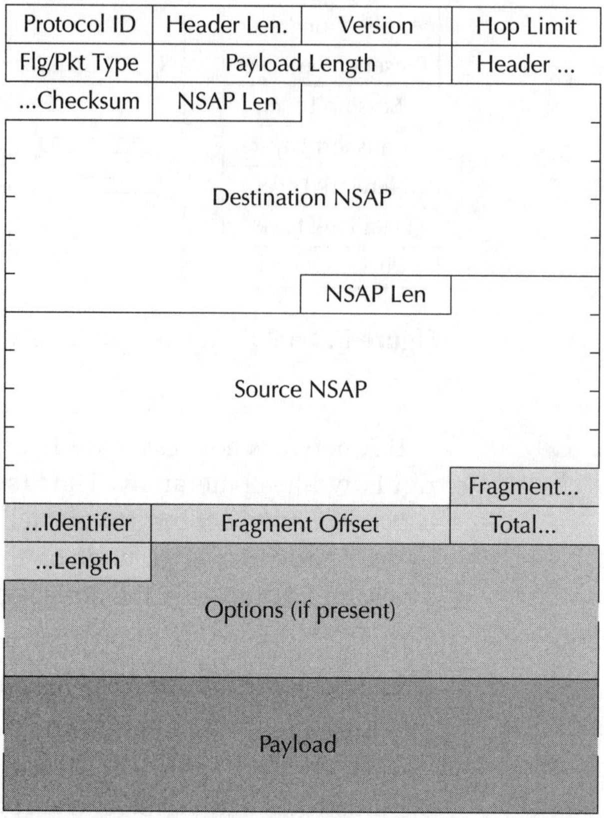

Protocol ID	Header Len.	Version	Hop Limit
Flg/Pkt Type	Payload Length		Header ...
...Checksum	NSAP Len		

Destination NSAP

| | | NSAP Len | |

Source NSAP

			Fragment...
...Identifier	Fragment Offset		Total...
...Length			

Options (if present)

Payload

Figure B.4 Highlights of CLNP header format.

NSAPs have a hierarchical structure similar to IPv6 addresses. Most systems use a format that reserves the first 13 bytes as an area prefix, and the next six bytes for a link address. The final byte of an NSAP is known as the NSAP selector. It serves the same role as IP's next header field, identifying the upper-level protocol that should receive the datagram's payload.

Compatible Addressing

The IPng addressing architecture leaves space for both IPX and CLNP network addresses. These addresses can provide the same functionality as that embedded IPv4 addresses do for the IPv4 migration.

The exact formats for embedding IPX addresses in IPv6 addresses are not yet defined. They all will begin with the prefix `400::/7`. Even with the 10-byte IPX address, plenty of room remains in the address to define IPX-compatible and IPX-mapped addresses, should they prove useful.

CLNP addresses cause a few more problems for IPng, mainly because CLNP addresses are actually larger than IPng's 16 bytes. An NSAP's size precludes IPv6 from embedding all of it in an IP address. The size mismatch is not great, however, and IPng has specified how to abbreviate the most common forms of ISO NSAPs into IPv6 addresses. It is also possible to embed an IPv6 address within a 20-byte NSAP.

Multiple Stack Systems

Just as IPv4 and IPv6 can coexist in a single system, so can IPX and CLNP. In fact, it is certainly possible for a single system to support all four protocols at once. In theory, such multiple stack systems could pick and chose from among several internetwork layer protocols, selecting whichever was necessary to communicate with the desired destination.

Tunneling IPv6

Both IPX and CLNP also provide the means to tunnel IPv6. This service allows IPv6 hosts to communicate across an IPX or CLNP network.

Both approaches rely on the subnetwork access protocol (SNAP) identifier used so often by lower-layer network technologies. (See, for example, Token Ring on page 58 or ATM on page 87.)

The IPX method, shown in Figure B.5, encapsulates a complete 802.2 frame, including the destination and source service access points and the control field. The figure shows their values when the frame carries an IPv6 data-

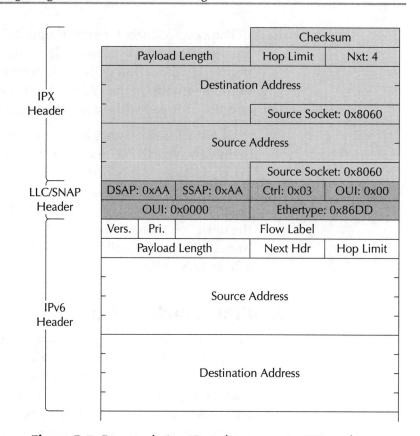

Figure B.5 Encapsulating IPv6 datagrams in IPX packets.

gram. CLNP, on the other hand, includes only the SNAP value itself, not the 802.2 header.

Figure B.6 illustrates CLNP's encapsulation format. The key is the NSAP selector of the destination NSAP. A value of zero indicates that the first byte of CLNP's payload contains a *subsequent protocol identifier* (SPI). An SPI value of 0x80 then indicates that a SNAP value follows. It is this SNAP value, through its inclusion of the *Ethertype* 0x86DD, that finally designates the remaining payload as IPv6.

Summary

Because Netware and ISO both provide connectionless internetworking services, they are candidates for a relatively

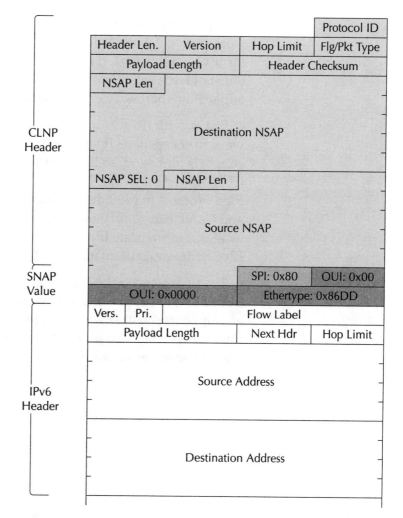

Figure B.6 Encapsulating IPv6 datagrams in CLNP packets.

smooth transition to IPng. Most of the mechanisms designed for the IPv4-to-IPv6 migration are also effective in moving from IPX or CLNP.

All four internetwork protocols (IPv6, IPv4, IPX, and CLNP) can coexist in the same host or router. During any transition period (indeed, indefinitely) systems can choose whichever protocol suite is appropriate for their communications. This approach assumes that the transport and upper-layer protocols do not require a particular internetwork protocol. Such independence is designed into IPv6 for IPv4 applications. It is less true of other architectures, but standards exist for carrying both Netware and ISO applications across TCP/IP networks.

Just as with IPv4, both IPX and CLNP have well-defined ways to encapsulate IPv6 datagrams. This encapsulation supports tunneling, so IPv6 traffic can traverse IPX- and CLNP-based networks. Encapsulation alone is sufficient for a protocol to provide configured tunnels, but both IPX and CLNP can go further. Since address mappings are available to translate IPX and common NSAP formats to IPv6 addresses, automatic tunneling is also feasible.

The final stage in the IPv4 migration—using header translation to support the few remaining IPv4 holdouts—also appears possible with IPX or CLNP. All are similar internetwork layer protocols. Should sufficient demand arise, header translating products will certainly follow.

C

TCP/IP Standards

The development of TCP/IP standards, including IPng, follows a process that is among the most open and accessible in the industry. Engineers creating TCP/IP standards routinely and frequently make their interim results publicly available, and literally anyone can join their efforts.

To explain this approach, this appendix first looks at the organizations that govern the Internet, their responsibilities, and their relationship to each other. It then examines the process by which protocols become standards. The appendix concludes with a review of the specifications that define the material in this text.

Governing the Internet

Since the Internet is merely a collection of many other networks, no single body has the authority to govern the whole internetwork. The Internet bases its operation much more on mutual cooperation than on regulation by a governing body. What regulation that does exist stems, ultimately, from the Internet Society (ISOC), which is a professional society dedicated to the growth of the Internet. Its concerns include technical, political, and social aspects of the worldwide network.

For technical matters, the Internet Society turns to the Internet Architecture Board (IAB). The IAB's charter in-

461

cludes the development of TCP/IP standards. To produce those standards, the IAB relies on the Internet Engineering Task Force (IETF), which is itself governed by the Internet Engineering Steering Group (IESG).

In addition to creating standards, the IAB has authority to publish TCP/IP documents, known as requests for comments (RFCs), and for coordinating values shared by multiple protocols. The IAB delegates these last two responsibilities to the RFC editor and to the Internet Assigned Numbers Authority (IANA), respectively.

Internet standards themselves generally arise from IETF working groups, which consist of the engineers and scientists who actually develop specifications. Each working group has a charter and a specific area of responsibility. Most working group activity takes place via electronic mail, and access to that activity is available to any interested party. In fact, since working groups have no formal membership lists, receiving a group's email is the simplest way to actually join the group.

The IETF organizes its working groups into areas. An area serves as an umbrella organization for related working groups. The current (September 1995) IETF areas can be found in Table C.1. Figure C.1 shows the relationships of all the organizations that control TCP/IP standards. All

Table C.1 IETF Areas

- Applications
- Internet
- IP: Next Generation
- Network Management
- Operational Requirements
- Routing
- Security
- Transport
- User Services

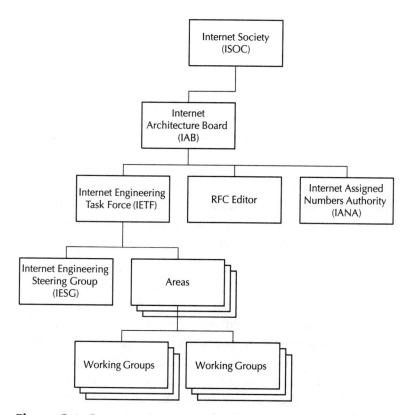

Figure C.1 Organizations contributing to Internet standards.

of the organizations in the figure can be reached by electronic mail over the Internet. Table C.2 lists several appropriate email addresses, as of September 1995.

TCP/IP Standards Documents

When an IETF working group develops an Internet standard, it publishes that standard as an Internet Request for Comments. RFCs are the official specification for TCP/IP protocols. But before becoming an RFC, most protocol specifications start out as an Internet draft. IETF working groups, as well as other interested groups and individuals, can publish Internet drafts for informal review and comment. The IETF makes these specifications publicly available by placing them in the /internet-drafts directory of

Table C.2 Contacts for Internet Organizations

rfc-editor@isi.edu	Request for Comments Editor
iana@isi.edu	Internet Assigned Numbers Authority
iesg@cnri.reston.va.us	Internet Engineering Steering Group
iab-contact@isi.edu	Internet Architecture Board
amr@isoc.org	Internet Society Executive Director

Internet Draft Directories

As of September 1995, /internet-drafts directories may be found throughout the world, including ftp.is.co.za (Africa), nic.nordu.net and ftp.nis.garr.it (both in Europe), munnari.oz.au (Pacific Rim), ftp.isi.edu (U.S. West Coast), and ds.internic.net (U.S. East Coast).

several hosts on the Internet. Internet drafts are not permanent documents; each has a life of no more than six months. When that life expires, the document is removed from the /internet-drafts directories.

Once a protocol specification is ready to advance beyond an Internet draft, it may be published as a Request for Comments. At that point, the specification enters the Internet *standards track*. Protocols on the standards track achieve three distinct maturity levels. For the first step, the protocol's specification receives the designation *proposed standard*. Proposed standards are considered technically complete and stable specifications, but sometimes they have little operational experience.

The next phase in the standards track, that of *draft standard*, does require operational experience. Only when multiple independent implementations of a protocol have demonstrated interoperability can a specification advance to draft standard status. The final step in the standards track results in an *Internet standard*. Internet standards are mature specifications with significant operational experience. These steps are diagrammed in Figure C.2.

Some RFCs document protocol specifications are not on the Internet's standards track. Such specifications may receive alternate designations in place of proposed standard, draft standard, and Internet standard. The alternate designations include *experimental*, *informational*, and *historic*.

Once an RFC is published, it is never revised. If the protocol it describes undergoes revision (such as an ad-

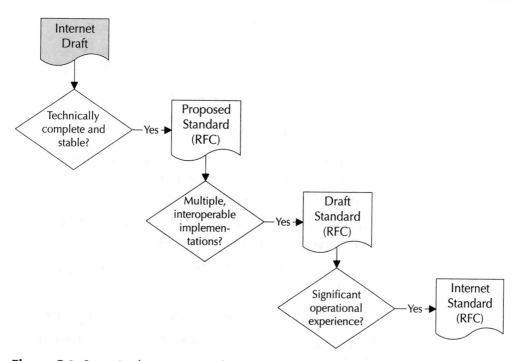

Figure C.2 Steps in the maturity of an Internet standard.

vance from proposed to draft standard), then the IETF issues a new RFC that supersedes the earlier one.

Protocols Described in the Text

The following subsections lists the protocol specifications on which this text relies. Some are full standards, while many are only works in progress. Some parts of the text, especially those based on Internet drafts, also depend on discussions of the various working groups and on private communication with working group members.

IPng Architecture

R. Hinden and S. Deering, ed. *IP Version 6 Addressing Architecture*. June 20, 1995. [draft-ietf-ipngwg-addr-arch-03.txt].

Network Technologies

T. Bradley, C. Brown, and A. Malis. *Multiprotocol Interconnect over Frame Relay*. July 1993, [RFC 1490].

Matt Crawford. *A Method for the Transmission of IPv6 Packets over Ethernet Networks*. October 10, 1995, [draft-ietf-ipngwg-ethernet-ntwrks-01.txt].

Matt Crawford. *A Method for the Transmission of IPv6 Packets over FDDI Networks*. August 15, 1995, [draft-ietf-ipngwg-fddi-ntwrks-00.txt].

Juha Heinanen. *Multiprotocol Encapsulation over ATM Adaptation Layer*. July 5, 1993, [RFC 1483].

B. Lloyd and W. Simpson. *PPP Authentication Protocols*. October 1992, [RFC 1334].

D. Rand. *PPP Reliable Transmission*. July 1994, [RFC 1663].

W. Simpson, ed. *The Point-to-Point Protocol*. July 1994, [RFC 1661]

W. Simpson, ed. *PPP in HDLC-like Framing*. July 1994, [RFC 1662].

W. Simpson. *PPP over ISDN*. May 1994, [RFC 1618].

W. Simpson, ed. *PPP LCP Extensions*. January 1994, [RFC 1570].

K. Sklower, B. Lloyd, G. McGregor, and D. Carr. *The PPP Multilink Protocol (MP)*. November 1994, [RFC 1717].

Stephen Thomas. *A Method for the Transmission of IPv6 Packets over Token Ring Networks*. September 6, 1995, [draft-ietf-ipngwg-token-ring-00.txt].

IPv6

R. Atkinson. *IP Authentication Header*. August 9, 1995, [RFC 1826].

R. Atkinson. *IP Encapsulating Security Payload (ESP)*. August 9, 1995, [RFC 1827].

R. Atkinson. *Security Architecture for the Internet Protocol.* August 9, 1995, [RFC 1825].

S. Deering and R. Hinden. *Internet Protocol, Version 6 (IPv6) Specification.* June 19, 1995, [draft-ietf-ipngwg-ipv6-spec-02.txt].

P. Metzger, P. Karn, and W. Simpson. *The ESP DES-CBC Transform.* August 9, 1995, [RFC 1829].

P. Metzger and W. Simpson. *IP Authentication Using Keyed MD5.* August 9, 1995, [RFC 1828].

C. Partridge. *Using the Flow Label Field in IPv6.* June 14, 1995, [RFC 1809].

ICMP

A. Conta and S. Deering. *Internet Control Message Protocol (ICMPv6) for the Internet Protocol Version 6 (IPv6 Specification.* June 1995, [draft-ietf-ipngwg-icmp-02.txt].

Thomas Narten, Erik Nordmark, and W. A. Simpson. *Neighbor Discovery for IP Version 6 (IPv6).* July 7, 1995, [draft-ietf-ipngwg-discovery-02.txt].

Susan Thomson. *IPv6 Stateless Address Autoconfiguration.* October 5, 1995, [draft-ietf-addrconf-ipv6-auto-04.txt].

UDP

J. Postel. *User Datagram Protocol.* August 28, 1980, [RFC 768].

TCP

V. Jacobson, R. Braden, and D. Borman. *TCP Extensions for High Performance.* May 1992, [RFC 1323].

Jon Postel, ed. *Transmission Control Protocol.* September 1981, [RFC 793].

OSPF

Fred Baker. *OSPF Extensions for IPv6*. December 1994, [draft-ietf-ospf-ipv6-ext-00.txt].

R. Coltun and V. Fuller. *The OSPF NSSA Option*. March 1994, [RFC 1587].

J. Moy. *Multicast Extensions to OSPF*. March 1994, [RFC 1584].

J. Moy. *OSPF Version 2*. March 1994, [RFC 1583].

RIP

G. Malkin. *RIPng for IPv6*. April 1995, [draft-ietf-rip-ripng-01.txt].

IDRP

Yakhov Rekhter and Paul Traina. *IDRP for IPv6*. January 1995, [draft-ietf-idr-idrp-v6-01.txt].

RTP

Schulzrinne, Casner, Frederick, and Jacobson. *RTP: A Transport Protocol for Real-Time Applications*. March 21, 1995, [draft-ietf-avt-rtp-07.ps].

RSVP

R. Braden, ed., and L. Zhang, D. Estrin, S. Herzog, and S. Jamin. *Resource Reservation Protocol (RSVP)—Version 1 Functional Specification*. July 7, 1995, [draft-ietf-rsvp-spec-07.ps].

DNS

P. Mockapetris. *Domain Names—Concepts and Facilities*. November 1987, [RFC 1034].

P. Mockapetris. *Domain Names—Implementation and Specification*. November 1987, [RFC 1035].

S. Thomson and C. Huitema. *DNS Extensions to Support IP version 6*. March 24, 1995, [draft-ietf-ipngwg-dns-00.txt].

Susan Thomson, Yakov Rekhter, and Jim Bound. *Dynamic Updates in the Domain Name System (DNS)*. August 1995, [draft-ietf-dnsind-dynDNS-03.txt.

DHCP

J. Bound. *Dynamic Host Configuration Protocol for IPv6*. July 1995, [draft-ietf-dhc-dhcpv6-02.txt].

Index